# GOLD NUGGETS
# AND
# OTHER GEMS
# FROM
# THE MINE
# OF
# SCRIPTURE

(With answers to questions you may never have
thought to ask)

# GOLD NUGGETS AND OTHER GEMS FROM THE MINE OF SCRIPTURE

(With answers to questions you may never have thought to ask)

## Dr. Robert J. Leland, D.Min.

**ARPress**
ILLUMINATING IDEAS.
EMPOWERING VOICES

**Author Reputation Press LLC**
45 Dan Road Suite 5
Canton MA 02021
*www.authorreputationpress.com*
Hotline: 1(888) 821-0229
Fax:      1(508) 545-7580

Ordering Information:
Quantity sales. Special discounts are available on quantity purchases by corporations, associations, and others. For details, contact the publisher at the address above.

Printed in the United States of America.

| ISBN-13: | Paperback | 979-8-89330-935-5 |
| | eBook | 979-8-89330-934-8 |

Library of Congress Control Number: 2024902486

# PREFACE

I don't know about you, but after years of reading my Bible and still having the same questions each time—and years of reading commentaries which usually skip over those same problem areas—I grew tired of not finding the answers I was seeking.

So…I decided to write my own "commentary" to deal with these issues as best I can. Some questions still have no answers, so I left the answer paragraph blank to be filled in later either by me or someone else. Some pages are blank altogether as I had no comment to make, but I included them anyway in case either you or I have something to add later on our own.

Some comments reflect what I hope is "sanctified" imagination; others are perhaps more assumption than fact; still others are a logical extension of what is there. What I hope is that whatever is written will stimulate your thinking either to expand on the answer given, or find a new and better one.

I have drawn upon my 31 years of teaching and experience in Papua, Indonesia, being "forced" almost daily to "find answers" for my students. What is written in the following pages represents a lot of effort in trying to find satisfying, Biblical answers to their questions and mine.

Generally, I have tried to stay away from material found in other commentaries since that would represent mere duplication of what others have already done.

I hope that you enjoy using this material as much as I have enjoyed "digging" it up, and that it will serve to whet your appetite to study the Word of God on an even deeper level.

## Bob Leland

77 Pine St.
Presque Isle, ME 04769
Email: baleland66@gmail.com

# TABLE OF CONTENTS

## OLD TESTAMENT

# NEW TESTAMENT

# ITEMS OF INTEREST
## CHARTS

## CHRONOLOGY OF SPECIFIC EVENTS

## COMMENTS ON SPECIFIC PASSAGES

# FAMILY TREES

# MAP / DIAGRAMS

# NARRATIVES

# PERSONAL HISTORIES

# POEMS

# OLD

# TESTAMENT

# GENESIS

**God of the Impossible:**

1. He brought forth everything out of nothing (creation) just by a word (1:1-2:3 with Heb.11:3).
2. He gave life to the inanimate (2:7).
3. He created a woman from the rib of a man (2:21,22).
4. He handed down various judgments because of sin, then seeing to it that each one was fulfilled (3:14-19).
5. He brought a flood on the entire earth (7:4).
6. He altered the earth's climates and seasons (8:22).
7. He put dread and fear in the heart of every beast toward human beings (9:2).
8. He mixed up mankind's language at Babel (11:7,8).
9. He protected Sarah from Pharaoh's desires (12:10,17-19).
10. He promised descendants to Abraham (12:1-3,7; 13:15-17) in spite of Sarah's barrenness (15:1-16:1). The promise repeated (17:1-21; 18:10). The key verse: "Is anything too hard for the LORD?" (18:14). Isaac was born (21:1-3).
11. He gave Abraham victory over the armies of five kings with only 318 trained servants in a night battle to deliver Lot and the Sodomites out of their hands (14:1-17).
12. He protected Sarah from Abimelech through a dream (20:3-7).
13. He provided Hagar and Ishmael with water in the wilderness and promised Ishmael a great nation (21:13-19).
14. If Abraham had sacrificed Isaac, God would have had to raise him from the dead, something never done before (22:5 with Heb. 11:17-19).
15. He immediately answered the prayer of Abraham's servant (24:12-15).
16. He enabled Rebekah, barren, to conceive (25:21-23).
17. He opened Leah's womb, closed Rachel's (29:31), then opened it (30:22).
18. He overruled any attempts of Laban's to do harm to Jacob (31:7,9-12,24,29,42).
19. He protected Jacob and family from revenge for the Shechem slaughter (35:5).
20. He made a ruler from a jailed slave (Joseph—39:20; 45:9).
21. He gave dream interpretations to Joseph (40:8; 41:25).

22. He governed the details of Jacob's life to accomplish his purpose (45:5-8; 50:20).

**\* \* \* \***

**1:1-28** Creation vs. Evolution:

| | |
|---|---|
| Day 1 (vs.2,3) earth and light | Day 4 (vs.14) sun, moon, stars |
| Day 2 (vs.8) the sky | Day 5 (vs.20) fish, birds |
| Day 3 (vs.11) vegetation | Day 6 (vs.24) animals, humans |

Observaton: Evolution puts the universe first before the earth.
Creation puts it <u>after</u> the earth was formed.

**Q. 1:3-5** What was this light?
**A.** (From my mother, Edith Leland) "Jesus is the light of the world … ."
  "Maybe the original light was God bringing his very presence into the creation he was making. This would be needed in exercising his design in all the wonderful things he had planned."

**1:3,8,13,19, etc.** "Evening and morning"—the first day, etc. Perhaps this is where the Jews got their concept of when the next day begins—at sunset—evening.

**Q. 3:1** Did the serpent speak because Satan had entered it and controlled it, or did animals speak before the Fall? Eve certainly didn't react as if it were something unusual that the snake should talk with her.
**A.** Apart from speculation as to the possibility, there really is no way for us to know for sure.

**Q.** By the way, who taught Adam how to talk? What language? Or did Adam and Eve invent a language?
**A.** Obviously God had given Adam a language since they readily communicated (1:28). Whatever that language was, it lasted until the Tower of Babel. I don't think that Adam and Eve invented a language, but they certainly invented words in that language as time went along, just like we do.

**3:3** "You must not touch it" (cf.2:16,17). I suspect that this phrase was added by Adam to further protect Eve from violating God's commands.

| **3:6a** Eve's temptation | Christ's temptation |
|---|---|
| She saw that the fruit was: | He: |
| a. good for food—lust of the flesh (1 Jn.2:16) | a. was hungry (Matt.4:3) |
| b. pleasing to the eye—lust of the eyes (1 Jn.2:16) | b. saw all the kingdoms of the world (Matt.4:8) |
| c. desirable for gaining wisdom—pride of life (1 Jn.2:16) | c. desired to be acknowledged as the Messiah (Matt.4:6) |

(Thus Christ was tempted in every way as we are, yet without sin — Heb.4:15.)

**3:6b** Eve was deceived. Adam was not. He disobeyed purposely. His dilemma was profound: if he obeyed, he would lose her, and there was no one else suitable for him. If he disobeyed, he would keep her, regardless of the consequences. Obviously he couldn't bear to part with her, so joined her in her disobedience, failing the test of love and faith. The consequences were far worse than he imagined.

**Q. 3:6** with **Ezek.28:12b-17** and **Isa.14:12-15,** how could perfect beings sin?

**A.** The fact that God created angels and human beings with free
will, the power to choose alternative actions and responses, the possibility of sin (acting contrary to God's will and character) was made possible.

In the process of time, Lucifer was confronted by the need to make a choice: to continue to live in obedient reverence to God, or, because of his great power and beauty, to lift himself up in rebellion against God. He chose the latter.

Because God doesn't want to be loved and served by automatons, he implanted within us the power to choose, so that our love for him would come from our heart, not from an outside force.

So when he created Lucifer, he created him with what would eventually force him to choose between love of God and love of self —his great power and beauty. Choosing love of self plunged him into the abyss of sin and rebellion against God.

Adam and Eve also had a choice to make. God allowed Satan to tempt Eve with direct disobedience to his command so that she and Adam would have to choose. Up to that time, their obedience was not actively confronted or challenged. Unfortunately, they didn't pass the test. Eve was deceived, but Adam wasn't. However, for whatever reason (as discussed above in **3:6b**), his attachment to Eve was so strong that he chose to share her fate in disobedience rather than face the consequences of whatever might come if he were to obey. At that point he loved her more than he loved God!

Lucifer's choice came because of his great power and beauty.

Eve's choice came through deception and a direct challenge to her obedience.

Adam's choice came because he didn't want to lose Eve (assumed).

But all of this gives rise to another question often asked:

**Q.** "If God knew (and he did) that it was going to turn out this way, why did he go ahead with creation?" Apart from, "I don't know," there are two partial answers to this question that at least get us along part way.

**A.** Giving someone freedom in love always carries the risk of rejection. However, God went ahead anyway because he wanted the fellowship and love of his created beings. When Satan entered the picture, tempting Adam and Eve to rebel against God, they did, and thus plunged human beings into the sinkhole of sin to the point where, as Paul describes in Romans 3:11, "There is no one who understands, no one who seeks God." So, apart from Divine intervention in giving us the will and ability to obey him (cf. Phil.2:13), we would continue in wholesale rebellion against him and go into a Christless eternity.

So God chose (elected) to rescue some and let the others go to the fate to which we all were headed. Why he chose some and not others, we cannot know but have to leave that in his hands. We cannot judge his ways by our standards.

Also, Romans 9:16-24 (esp. vs.23,24) implies that God allowed us the power of choice so that in whatever we chose the full spectrum of his character would be revealed: patience, power and wrath upon those who rejected him; mercy and glory upon those who accepted him.

Perhaps God will reveal other reasons later on, but whatever we cannot understand about this issue now, we can rest in the fact that he is just, loving and true in all his ways and will never act in any way that is unjust, capricious or false. So we need to believe him because of what we know of his character, and trust him in what we cannot understand, knowing that he does.

**3:7,8,12** Definitely <u>not</u> the results they expected!

**3:14** "You will eat dust all the days of your life." Snakes "taste" the dust particles of the air with their tongues for the scent of their prey.

**3:16** "He [your husband] will rule over you" (cf.1 Tim.2:12). When women try to take authority over men (assuming in the context of this statement that the husband is the physical and spiritual head of the family—which extends to the Church—see Eph.5:22-32), they are in rebellion against God's judgment because of Eve's sin. They have to live under that judgment just as men have to live under the judgment of making a living by the "sweat of [their] brow."

**Q. 3:22-24** What is the significance of this ban?
**A.** God said that if they disobeyed, they would die.

If they ate of the Tree of Life, they would <u>not</u> die, but seemingly live forever in a sinful state without the possibility, need or desire for cleansing. Thus evil would only increase without end forever. God's plan was to eradicate evil entirely in the eternal state. If Adam and Eve ate of the Tree of Life, the only way God could deal with the resulting "eternalness" of sin would be to completely destroy all human beings—which he could <u>not</u> do if they already possessed eternal life! An untenable situation to say the least! Thus the ban and expulsion from the Garden.

**3:14-19** When Adam and Eve sinned, they were punished, but not cursed. But the serpent was cursed and the ground was cursed. When Cain killed Abel, he also was cursed (4:11).

**4:12-17** Cain was punished by God to be a wanderer on the earth. He went out from the presence of God and built a city (vs. 17) so that he wouldn't have to wander! His life thus continued in rebellion against God, the results of which are seen in chapter 6.

**4:14** "Whoever"—others of Abel's family seeking revenge for Abel's death.

**4:16** The beginning of the need of missions.

**4:19** The beginning of polygamy.

**4:23,24** If Cain's murder would be avenged seven times, and he killed an innocent man, then Lamech claims that his murder would be avenged 77 times because he killed a man in self-defense. (The N.I.V. note on vs.23 seems to read a lot into what happened.)

**4:26** "Man began to call on [to proclaim] the name of the LORD" some 235 years after Adam was created (see 5:3-6). (The first "missionaries"?)

**5:3-32; 11:10-32** A genealogical picture from Adam to Terah (but see APPENDIX III, Adam to Benjamin).

**Q. 5:22** "After he became the father of Methuselah, Enoch walked with God 300 years." When he had lived 65 years, he begat Methuselah, then walked 300 years with God—and was not. What was it at Methuselah's birth that caused Enoch to walk with God?
**A.** Methuselah's name means, "When he is dead, it shall come." We know that he died the year of the flood. Thus we assume that somehow, Enoch knew that a judgment was coming because of sin, which motivated him to walk even closer to God.

**5:24** with **7:1** If Enoch represents the raptured Church, and Noah represents the sealed believers/Jews taken safely through the Tribulation, then this typology could furnish another possible proof for a Pre-Trib Rapture.

**Q. 6:1-5,11,12** with **2 Pet.2:4 & Jude 6.** What was so terrible about their sin that this group of angels was incarcerated to await final judgment?

**A.** Alternative views on Gen.6:1-5
1. *"Sons of God"* (*Seth's godly line*) *and* *"daughters of men"* (*Cain's wicked line*). The results of this union supersede what one would expect by

people marrying other people. Also "sons of God" is a term used almost exclusively in the Old Testament of angels, not of Seth's descendants.

2. *Angels lusted after women and married them.* This would explain the results of these marriages, but introduces a real problem since Christ specifically stated that angels, as spirit beings, cannot marry (Luke 20:34-36).

3. *Angels assumed human shape* (cf. Gen.18:1-8 where angels appeared as men and ate food). The assumption is that they could also perform other human functions while in the human body. There is no clear Biblical support for this view, however.

4. Yet the "gross sin" remains to be explained. One alternative view: In Genesis 6 it is clear that Satan was trying to get God to totally destroy all human beings so that Genesis 3:15 could not be fulfilled. How could this be done? How could Satan so corrupt the human race that God would have to destroy them all? I believe it might have happened this way:

A group of fallen angels, because of their sinful condition, began lusting after the beautiful women of earth. But they were totally frustrated in their lust because they couldn't fulfill it, not being physical beings. But because ungodly men and women were becoming more and more corrupt on their own, it is not unreasonable to assume that they became deeply involved in occult practices, thus becoming candidates for demon possession. These *demons then empowered men in great wickedness through whom they vicariously enjoyed the fulfillment of their lust.* The children born to these unions were also possessed by these demons and empowered to do great things (therefore the descriptions of "giants" and "heroes of old, men of renown").

This view seems to resolve the "angel" problem in this passage as well as explains the unusual results of the stated union between the "sons of God" and the "daughters of men" which prompted God to act in judgment, the flood, at which time these demons lost their host bodies and were themselves confined in everlasting chains until the final judgment.

Now, having said that, I still have an uneasy feeling that this alternative view still lacks something.

5. Another alternative view.

Let's return to explanation no.3 for a moment. As bizarre as it seems, this explanation has to be reconsidered. There are too many stories from Irian Jaya (now Papua) and Java, Indonesia, indicating "sex with demons" than can be ignored or off-handedly dismissed.

The typical scenario in Irian Jaya, among the Auyu (OW-you) and Asmat (AHS-maht) tribes, would be the following: Because of total lack of privacy in the home, the wife and husband agree to go out to their garden, or out into the jungle, to have sex. They go at separate times in order to avoid "appearances." So they meet, have sex, and the "husband," in this case, says he will return later; she should go on home. She leaves and meets her real husband coming out to have sex with her! Shocked is putting it mildly. "Who was this man, looking and acting exactly like my husband, with whom I just had sex?" In this culture, there is only one possible explanation: it was a demon impersonating her husband (or, in other cases, his wife).

The story from Java is similar. This time, the husband tells his wife that he is going out to the rice paddy, but will be in later for their "appointment." Sooner than expected, her "husband" returns and they have sex. Later in the afternoon, her real husband returns from the paddy, bathes, and wants to have sex. "But we just had sex." "No, I've been in the paddy all this time." Consternation! "Who, then, was this man, looking and acting exactly like my husband, with whom I just had sex?"

Sometimes the wife is so distraught that she commits suicide; other times the next baby born is considered the offspring of a demon and is either killed or left to die on its own. In many places they do not know that intercourse produces children. They look at the two events as totally separate one from the other. Often the husband will die three days later after having had sex with a demonic "woman."

It is at this point where any "proof" to help explain Genesis 6 fails since these events occur in more primitive, superstitious, demon-worshipping cultures where "clinical trials" are impossible to carry out (i.e., was the next baby born within the normal nine months' gestation period, or later?). Did the husband and wife have sex shortly after the "demon" experience or later on, etc.? So we are left with unanswerable questions. Does a demon, in human form, possess human abilities and functions?  As indicated above, the Bible is silent on this subject.

Yet, if this was indeed possible, if, in human form, the demons were able to satisfy their lust as well as bring about a hybrid of human/demon off-spring (which would satisfy the unusual descriptions of the children from these unions as mentioned above), God would <u>have</u> to totally destroy this gross aberration of his creation.  This would represent Satan's most masterful attempt to so corrupt the "seed of the woman" so as to make God's promise to her impossible to fulfill.  Corrupted seed, total destruction of all human beings, and *no seed to crush Satan's head*.  "*I win!*"

More than merely the gross moral corruption of human beings, such a horrendous and heinous sin as this would especially qualify these demons for the drastic punishment meted out to them: their incarceration in the deep, dark caves of Tartarus until the day of judgment (2 Pet.2:4).

Whichever explanation we accept as possible, the underlying purpose of Satan is clear: to so corrupt human beings that God would have to destroy them, and, as a result, the promised Seed could not come and Satan would be delivered from judgment.  The amazing thing is that in the midst of all this corruption, Noah walked with God in righteousness!

Another observation:  If human beings were so corrupt so as to have passed the line of repentance, thus falling under God's judicial sentence of condemnation, then it is not surprising that Noah had no converts; but if this total corruption was human/ demon in character, then his mission was utterly impossible since demons cannot be saved.

**6:4**  In order for this to happen, Noah had to have had some recessive "giant" genes in his DNA make-up, since "and also afterward" has to mean "after the flood" (see also Num.13:33).

**6:6** The Lord <u>knows</u> the grief and deep pain of a parent whose child is living in total rebellion.  He <u>understands</u> the urge to quit.

**6:16** "Make a window."  The commentary says that this "window" was an 18-inch high opening running the entire length of the ark to let in light and air.   Problem: (8:6) "After forty days Noah opened the window he had made." So much for light and air, unless he had something like bamboo blinds to keep out the rain and let in some light and air. But even then it would be somewhat dark and stuffy. Then "opening" the window would involve removing the blinds.

My guess is that he probably had an 18-inch high opening running the entire length of the ark for light and air, open galleries on the 2nd and 3rd levels to allow light and air into the 1st level, and a separate window somewhere through which they could throw out animal and food waste when cleaning the ark.

**6:17** "Flood waters on the earth." Some say it was a local flood only; others that it was worldwide. In light of the fact that the animal creation seems to be worldwide (Gen.1:20 would indicate fish and birds everywhere), their specific location is not indicated one way or another.

(1:24). Even if the land animals were originally created in one location, how far would they have naturally spread in the 1,642 years between creation and the flood? The fact that Noah had to take two of every kind of animal indicates that the flood would at least cover the entire inhabited world where any of these creatures could be found. Peter says (2 Pet.3:6) that the world that existed then was deluged and destroyed. The N.I.V. note supports a more local flood covering the world of people, saying nothing about the world of animals. If it was only the former, then why was Noah required to take animals with him into the ark, for they surely would have been much more prolific and wide-spread than human beings. Also, Genesis 7:4,11,12,19,23 does not sound like a local flood.

**6:21** "Take every kind of food that is to be eaten and store it away for you [people] and them [animals]." Obviously if the animals were eating, they were not in a Divine slumber for the entire trip as some have postulated. Noah and his family evidently were quite occupied with caring for their own needs and the animals' needs: feeding, watering, cleaning waste, making internal modifications, etc. They must have had a system rigged up for catching rain for their water supply. Storing enough water for over a year's use would have been quite a feat, not to mention how stale and slimy it would have become after a month or two! There was enough work to keep them from getting bored, and enough space to move around in to keep them from getting "cabin fever."

**Q. 7:2**    How would Noah have known the difference between "clean" and "unclean" animals since that distinction seems to have been made only when God gave the Law to Israel (cf. Lev.11).
**A.** Since Abel sacrificed to the Lord from his flocks, I suspect that God must have told Adam and Eve what animals were acceptable ("clean") for sacrifice and unacceptable ("unclean"). The godly line would have passed that practice on to their children.

**7:4,11,12**    For those who believe that the years of Adam and company were symbolic of long life, or counted differently than today, this account of literal days and a year would seem to discredit that view.    Moses would not speak of a figurative 600 years and a literal 17 days and 2 months (7:11) in the same context.

**Q. 7:9**  How long were Noah and his family in the ark?
**A.** At least 374 days!  (cp.7:10 with 8:14)

| Days | Month | Total Days | Event |
|---|---|---|---|
| 10-16 | 2 | 7 | Noah and family enter the ark. |
| 17-30 | 2 | 13 | |
| 1 –27 | 3 | 27 | 40 days and nights of rain and flood. |
| 28-30 | 3 | 3 | |
| 1 –30 | 4 | 30 | |
| 1 –30 | 5 | 30 | |
| 1 –30 | 6 | 30 | |
| 1 –17 | 7 | 17 | 110 days the waters flooded the earth. |
| ( 17 | 7 | -- | The ark rested on top of Mt. Ararat.) |
| 18-30 | 7 | 10 | |
| 1 –30 | 8 | 30 | |
| 1 –30 | 9 | 30 | |
| 1 | 10 | 1 | Mountain tops visible |
| 2 –30 | 10 | 29 | |
| 1 –10 | 11 | 10 | 40 days: Noah opened the window and sent out a raven and a dove. Dove  returned. |
| 11-17 | 11 | 7 | Dove sent out, returned with olive leaf. |
| 18-24 | 11 | 7 | Dove sent out, did not return. |
| 25-30 | 11 | 6 | |

| Days | Month | Total Days | Event |
|------|-------|-----------|-------|
| 1–30 | 12 | 30 | |
| 1 | 1 | 1 | Noah looked around and saw dry ground. |
| 2–30 | 1 | 29 | |
| 1–27 | 2 | 27 | Earth completely dry. Then God said, |
| | | 374 | "Leave the ark." |

So Noah and family were in the ark for 1 year and 2 weeks, or 374 days.

**Q. 8:13** What was this "covering" that Noah removed? (Most commentaries don't say.)

**A.** 1. According to Francis Schaeffer, it was the door of the ark (<u>Genesis</u>
<u>in Time and Space</u>, p.151). The problem is that describing a door as a "covering" is linguistically stretching the word's meaning.

2. The Septuagint uses the Greek word στέγην (**STE**gāin—"roof") in this verse. It wouldn't make sense for Noah to remove the entire roof (33,750 sq. feet) just to have a "look-see." He probably removed just enough to get himself up on top of the ark to look around at a full, unobstructed view of the surrounding terrain. He must have had quite a view!

**Q. 9:3,4** Why did God give animals to man for food after the flood?
**A.** Obviously there was a change in the relationship between human beings and animals. Where there first was mutual trust and coexistence, now there was fear and dread. <u>All</u> animals were given into man's hands (9:2), and were to become a source of food for him. Thus the "fear" of man was a protective device to ensure their survival. Also, animals began eating other animals (cf.1:29) where, before the flood, <u>all</u> living beings ate vegetation.

Evidently the flood destroyed most of the protein-giving vegetation for which meat now had to become a substitute. Humanity's sin and rebellion brought about all sorts of nasty results.

**9:13** The N.I.V. note claims that there were rain and rainbows before the flood. However, Genesis 2:5,6,10 say otherwise. In both the NKJV and ASV verse 6 reads that God sent a mist from the earth to water the ground <u>before</u> he caused it to rain on the earth (2:5). The N.I.V. says "streams" (alt. "mist") came up from the earth to water the whole surface of the ground. So I conclude that both rain and the rainbow were new things at the time of the flood.

**9:20-27** It's amazing how the sin of one man (Ham) affected the lives of nations to follow. Conversely, the righteousness of one man, Abraham, has affected the lives of all nations (Gen.12:3).

**10:5,11,20,25,31,32** A summary of what happened. Chapter 11:1,4,8 give us the reason why.

**Q.** How long after the flood did the Tower of Babel incident occur?
**A.** About 101 years.

$$
\begin{array}{ll}
\text{The Flood} + 2 \text{ years} - \text{Arphaxad} & (11:10) \\
35 \text{ years} - \text{Shelah} & (11:12) \\
30 \text{ years} - \text{Eber} & (11:13) \\
\underline{34 \text{ years}} - \text{Peleg} & (11:24 \text{ w}/ 10:25) \\
101 \text{ years} &
\end{array}
$$

**11:10-26** It is interesting to note that Abraham lived approximately 292 years after the flood. At that time Shem, Shelah and Eber were still living! Shem was about 450 years old when Abraham was born and died when Abraham was 150 years old. Shelah died when Abraham was 118 years old; and Eber outlived Abraham by about 4 years (11:17). Nothing is said about the spiritual lives of these men, but if Melchizedek is any indication (14:18-20), the witness of God was wider than just Abraham.

### Shem's Personal History

**11:11** Shem died about 25 years before Abraham, assuming that Abraham left Haran after the death of Terah (cf. Acts 7:4), which would have made Terah 130 years old when Abraham was born. So Shem was

- 100 when Arphaxad was born,
- 135 when Shelah was born,
- 165 when Eber was born,
- 199 when Peleg was born and the earth was linguistically divided,
- 229 when Reu was born,
- 261 when Serug was born,

291 when Nahor was born,
320 when Terah was born,
390 when Haran was born,
450 when Abraham was born,
600 when he died (Abraham was 150).

**Q. 11:26; 12:4** with **Acts 7:2-4**  How old was Terah when Abraham was born?

**A.** Genesis 11:26 doesn't say "when" he was 70, but "after" he was 70 years old he became the father of Abraham, Nahor and Haran. Abraham's name first does not necessarily mean that he was born first.  Ex: Noah's sons, Shem, Ham and Japheth (usually mentioned this way) are not listed in order of their ages.  Genesis 10:21 says that Japheth was Shem's <u>older</u> brother.   It seems they were listed according to the importance of their progeny in relation to Israel: Shem,  ancestor of Israel; Ham, ancestor of the Canaanites (in Israel's immediate vicinity); and Japheth, ancestor of other nations.  So the listing of Abraham, Nahor and Haran might not be chronological either but also listed by importance: Abraham being the prime character in relation to Israel, Nahor figuring a distant second, and Haran not at all since he died in Ur.  Haran or Nahor could have been the eldest, but I'm assuming it was Haran since it was Abraham, not Nahor, who assumed responsibility for Haran's children (Lot in this case—see comments on 12:1,4 below).  Stephen's comment in Acts 7:4 that Abraham left for Canaan <u>after</u> Terah died [at 205 years—Gen.11:32], and Genesis 12:4 stating that Abraham was 75 years old when he went, would have made Terah 130 years old when Abraham was born. [Interestingly, the  name "Terah" means "delay." Abraham delayed going to Canaan until his father had died.  "Haran" means "parched."  As long as Abraham stayed in Haran, God's plans for him were on hold—like the spiritual dryness we experience when out of God's will or delaying to do it.]

### Abraham's Personal History

Abraham was 75 years old when he left Haran for Canaan (12:4),
85 years old when Sarai gave him Hagar as wife (16:3),
86 when Ishmael was born (16:15,16),
99 when God again promised him a son by Sarai (17:1)
[Sarai was 90 at the time (17:17), nine years younger

than Abraham. Ishmael was 13 (17:25)],
100 when Isaac was born [Sarah 91; Ishmael 14],
102-3 when Isaac was weaned (21:8), [Sarah 93-94;
    Ishmael 16-17. At this time Abraham sent Hagar
    and Ishmael away.]
136 when Sarah died at 127 years (23:1) [Isaac 36],
140 when Isaac married Rebekah at 40 years (25:20),
160 when Esau and Jacob were born (25:26) [Isaac 60],
175 when he died (25:7) [Isaac 74; Ishmael 88].

**11:27-31** The family tree of Terah is interesting—more like a forest bramble than a tree!

### Terah's Family Tree

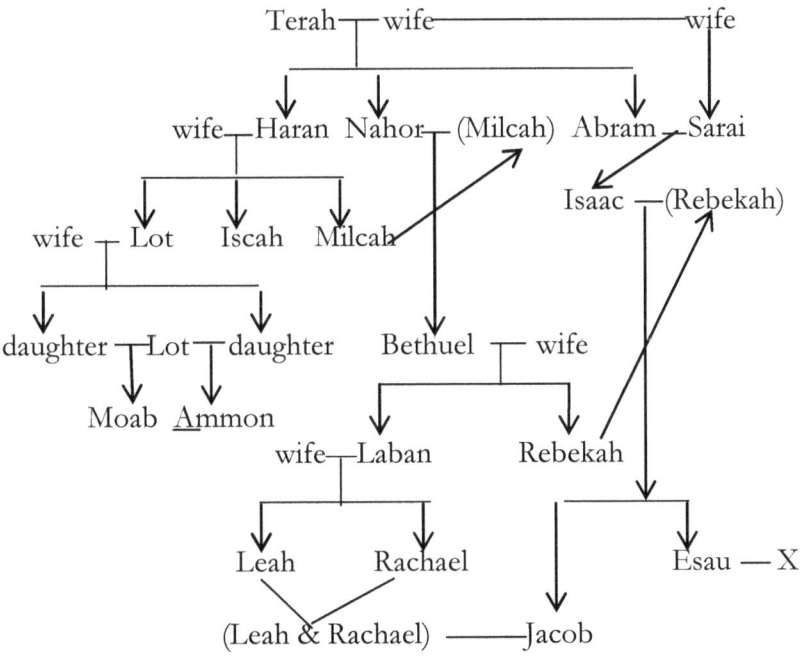

**12:1,4** It would seem that Abraham disobeyed God by taking Lot along with him to Canaan. Lot caused him nothing but grief (chs. 13,14). On the other hand, was Lot culturally considered a part of Abraham's family? Lot was the son of Haran, who died in Ur. It may have been Abraham's responsibility then, as the oldest surviving

son, to take Lot into his family as a son. In that case, he did not disobey God's command in verse one. On the other hand, by this time
Lot must have been old enough to make it on his own. Abraham
could have "set him up" in Haran, then left for Canaan, thus
avoiding future conflict. (See further discussion about his family
relationships under Genesis 11:26; 12:4 with Acts 7:2-4.)

**12:9-13** Living apart from God's will dulls our spiritual senses to the
point where we forget his promises and begin living as if everything
depended upon us and our wisdom. Abraham's fear that the
Egyptians would kill him (vs.12) totally disregarded God's earlier
promise to him (vs.1-3).

**12:16** Enter Hagar.

**13:1** I wonder how much Lot's Egypt experience influenced his
eventual choice to live in Sodom? There is a hint that it did (cf. 13:
10).

**13:14,15** Even the land Lot chose would eventually become Abraham's possession, but in God's time. Taking what God has promised
before its time is just as much living outside his will as is disobedience.

**16:2-5** Sarah had a problem: "The Lord has promised us descendants, but he has kept me from having children. Perhaps he will give
us children another way. Here, take Hagar. Perhaps I can have a
family through her." Sarah instigated this plan. Hagar became
pregnant and began to despise Sarah. Then Sarah turned on her
husband saying that all of this was his fault! What she did was
cultural, but not of faith.

**Q. 17:17; 18:12** What was the difference between Abraham's laughter
and Sarah's? [**NOTE**: Abraham laughed first, Sarah second, and
"Isaac" means "laughter." So in him the Lord "had the last laugh!"
(see Gen.21:6).] Sarah was rebuked for her laughter (18:13-15), but
Abraham wasn't. Yet he seemed to feel the same way as Sarah did
and twice offered God an alternative solution (Eliezer—15:2,3; then
Ishmael—17:18).
**A.** Possibly it was in their attitude of faith. Abraham doubted, but

was honest and open, giving God the options and leaving them with him. Sarah doubted, but tried to hide it. Instead of giving God the options, she instituted a plan of action to "help him out" (ch.16), which badly backfired. Although Abraham offered other alternatives to God, when God insisted, Abraham believed him and let it be (Gen.15:6; Rom.4:18-21).

**18:6,7** I wonder how long it took to get this meal ready? Twenty quarts of flour would have made quite a lot of bread. Perhaps Abraham was thinking of providing something for the rest of his guests' journey.

**18:19** With the Lord's call comes the Lord's enablement.

**18:23-26** Perhaps this is the reason (vs.25,26), that in spite of America's wickedness, God is still sparing our country.

**19:1** Mamre to Sodom was about a 70 mile trip. Lot sitting in the gateway of the city, a place of authority in administrative and judicial matters (see verse 9 where the men of Sodom use his position to mock him). Perhaps he was chosen because he could be trusted—his character was different from that of the Sodomites. In this position as judge, the details of Sodom's wickedness were graphically portrayed before him every day. In this light, Peter's statement in 2 Peter 2:8 takes on clearer meaning: "for that righteous man, living among them day after day, was tormented in his righteous soul by the lawless deeds he saw and heard."

**19:14** Truth in the midst of a compromised witness becomes a joke to the unbeliever.

**19:26** The slight hesitation of Lot's wife and her almost immediate encasement in salt show just how close the coming destruction was behind them and why they had to flee so quickly.

**19:29** "God remembered Abraham and brought Lot out."
**Q.** What did God "remember"?
**A.** Abraham's intercessory prayer (see 18:25).

**19:19,20,30** Lot was reluctant to leave the area; the mountains were too far to go. "I'll die if I have to go there!" Zoar was spared judgment so that Lot could flee there and live. Obviously it was not very far. From the first rays of dawn (vs.15) to the sun appearing on the horizon (vs.23) takes no more than an hour. So, with some delay (vs.16), Lot had maybe 45 minutes to run. Zoar must have been between 4 and 6 miles from Sodom. For some reason, Lot became afraid to stay in Zoar (vs.30). It could be that the wickedness of the town was as bad as, or worse than Sodom, making it very unsafe for him and his two daughters to stay there. Or perhaps the Zoarites didn't take kindly to strangers; or somehow blamed Lot for their present misfortunes. Whatever the cause, he and his daughters fled to the mountains and lived in a cave. Lot found out that God's command was best after all. But it did him little good.

**19:30** Lot's choice. By his wrong choice 23 years earlier (13:10,11), Lot lost everything: his great riches, his family, his wife, his security, his peace, his self-esteem, his honor, his way of life (the only reason he was saved at all was because of Abraham —19:29), and his spiritual perspective. He also sacrificed his relationship with God, loving what he had in this world and not wanting to give it up (19:16). And he sacrificed his relationship with Abraham (19:31,32). It could be that these two daughters were born to Lot in Sodom, and that they didn't even know Abraham. He also lost wisdom (19:32). His daughters only knew the wisdom of Sodom (cf.19:15). The implication seems to be that he had other daughters married to men of Sodom (19:14), unless these were his two daughters' fiancés.

**Q. 19:30,31** Why didn't Lot return to Abraham? He wasn't that far away (19:27). And it seemed like the angels were nudging him in that direction (19:17). Then his daughters wouldn't have had to resort to Sodom's wisdom for obtaining offspring.
**A.** 1. Perhaps he still entertained hopes for economic recovery in the plains area (noting his original reluctance to leave Sodom (19: 16,19,20).

2. Perhaps he was too proud to admit that he had been wrong, which coming to Abraham for help would mean. Abraham already bailed him out once (ch.14), now he had to prove that he could make it on his own.

3. Perhaps he was too ashamed to approach Abraham, feeling that his uncle was so godly and he so ungodly at this point, that he had no

right to come into Abraham's presence. Yet God obviously saw something in Lot, for he delivered him as being "righteous," in answer to Abraham's intercession (18:25,26), and also declared him to be a "righteous man" vexed daily with the sins and ungodliness of Sodom (2 Pet.2:7,8).

**21:12,13** God's promise to Abraham (12:3) extended also to Ishmael since he was also Abraham's son. This set in motion a whole new chapter of history.

**21:13-20** When we come to a total dead end, God will still be faithful to his promises, working miracles, if necessary, to accomplish them.

**21:14; 22:3** Abraham was quick to obey the Lord. This was evidence of his implicit faith in God.

**21:21** The Desert of Paran: about halfway down the eastern side of the Sinai Peninsula. Other people must have been around with connections to Egypt since Hagar took an Egyptian girl to be Ishmael's wife.

**22:5** Abraham was not lying to his servants. Isaac had to live, somehow, if God's promise to him was to be fulfilled (see Heb.11:17-19).

**Q. 23:10** What city was this of Ephron's?
**A.** Most likely Hebron.

**23:12-16** Abraham had to buy that which was already his by the promise of God (Gen.17:8). [Even though the earth has been promised to the meek (God's children—Matt.5:5), for now, we also must buy what we need. Now is not the time for us to enter and claim our "inheritance."]

**25:4** From Abraham's own family and relatives came the nations of Midian, Ammon, Moab, Edom, Amalek and descendants of Ishmael, all of whom became implacable enemies of Israel. This fact illustrates Matthew 10:36 that a person's enemies will arise from within his own house:
The Moabites and Ammonites descended from Lot's two

daughters (Gen.19:36-38; cf. Ps.83:2-8);

The <u>Amalekites</u> descended from Esau (Gen.36:12; Judg.6:3 with Ex. 17:8-13; Ps.83:7);

The <u>Edomites</u> descended from Esau (Gen.36:43; Ps.83:6);

The <u>Midianites</u> descended from Midian, Abraham's son by Ketura (Gen. 25:1,4 with Judg.6:3; Ps.83:9);

The <u>Ishmaelites</u> descended from Ishmael, Abraham's son by Hagar (Gen.25:12-18; 37:25; Ps.83:6).

**26:2,3** The blessing Abraham would have experienced had he stayed in Canaan rather than go down to Egypt.

**26:7,9-11** The sins of the father often become the sins of his children. Abraham lied with a half-truth, but Isaac lied totally. Isaac's fears were totally unjustified in light of 26:2-5.

### Isaac's Personal History

Isaac was born when Ishmael was 14 (17:25 w/ 18:10, implied),
 36 when Sarah died (23:1),
 40 when he married Rebekah (25:20),
 60 when Esau and Jacob were born (25:26),
 75 when Abraham died,
 95 when he lied about his wife to Abimelech (26:1,7),
 100 when Esau (40) married two Canaanite women (26:34),
 124 when Ishmael (137) died (25:17 with 35:28),
 137 when Jacob (77) stole the blessing (27:2),
 157 when Jacob (97) fled Padan Aram,
 167 when Joseph was sold into Egypt,
 180 when he died (35:28—Jacob and Esau (120) and Joseph
  (27, already 10 years in Egypt).

**Q.** 26:34 and 28:8,9 with 36:1. The names and origins of Esau's wives are all different. How can these two separate lists be reconciled?

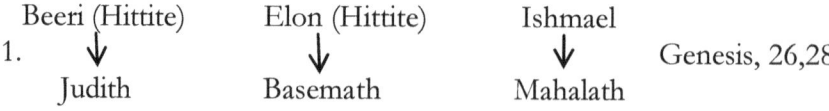

| Beeri (Hittite) | Elon (Hittite) | Ishmael | |
|---|---|---|---|
| 1. ↓ | ↓ | ↓ | Genesis, 26,28 |
| Judith | Basemath | Mahalath | |

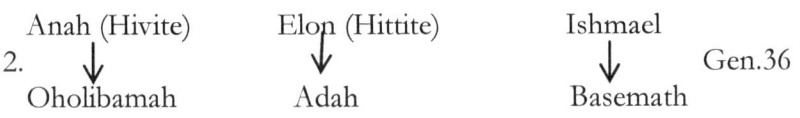

versus

Anah (Hivite)     Elon (Hittite)     Ishmael

2. ↓                 ↓                 ↓              Gen.36

Oholibamah        Adah              Basemath

**A.**

**Q.** 27:2  How old was Isaac when Jacob stole the blessing?

**A.** 137  (see Wood, <u>A Survey of Israel's History</u>, p.67).   Jacob was now 77 (since he was born when Isaac was 60).

### Jacob's Personal History

Born when Isaac was 60 years old,

64 when Ishmael died (Gen.26:1,34 with 25:27; 35:28;  cf. Isaac's Personal History),

77 when he fled to Padan Aram and met Rachael (I'm assuming that Rachael could have been about 10 at the time—young enough to watch the sheep and old enough to do strenuous work),

84 when he married Leah and Rachael (at 17).  All his children were born in the next 13 years; so at the time of his departure, Reuben would have been 12, Simeon 11, Levi 10, Judah 9, Joseph 7 (see discussion under Joseph's Personal History, p.28), Gad 6, and Asher 5 (the ages of the others would be pure conjecture),

106 when Rachael died in childbirth  (Since this event happened about 22 years after they were married, Rachael was probably around 39 years old when she died),

107 when Joseph was sold into slavery (Egypt),

120 when Isaac died,

130 when he went to Egypt (47:28),

147 when he died (47:28).

**27:16,23**  Esau must have been really hairy if Isaac could be deceived by goat skins tied to Jacob's neck and hands.

**27:29** The blessing <u>had</u> to go to Jacob (25:23; 27:37). He just went about getting it in the wrong way. How God would have worked it out we will never know. Obviously Esau had little care for his spiritual heritage which was wrapped up in both the birthright (25:34) and the blessing. He would have been interested in only the physical aspect (prosperity—27:28,37) of the blessing, not in its spiritual implications.

Isaac's blessing for whom he thought was Esau flies in the face of what God told him and Rebekah concerning their two sons (cp. vs.29a with 25: 23). He tried to undo what God said because he favored Esau, and Rebekah tried to make sure that what God said would happen because she favored Jacob. Both were wrong by not waiting for him, their actions colored by their favoritism (25:27, 28).

**27:30** Even though Esau accuses Jacob of deceiving him twice, there was only one deception—regarding the blessing. Esau knew what he was doing when he sold his birthright to Jacob (25:32-34).

**27:41** Sin begets more sin, and also begets separation (vs.43). Jacob fled about 440 miles from the face of Esau. Rebekah promised to call for Jacob once Esau's wrath subsided (vs.44,45), but she never did. Evidently she died before the opportunity came. Thus this was the last time Jacob would see her. How much better had they waited for the Lord to work things out!

**28:8,9** Esau tried to please his father but still married into the wrong line.

**28:10,11** Jacob had a long day, covering 50 miles (perhaps 12.5 hours of walking right along—assuming a pace of 4 mph).

**28:13-15** God's promise to Jacob was based upon his sovereign choice (25:23) and what Jacob was to become because of it—not upon what Jacob was like now. God's promised presence with him was a huge encouragement (vs.20,21), but he still schemed and deceived along the way. Some changes come very slowly.

**Q. 29:18-26** How could Jacob have lived in that culture for seven years and not been aware of this custom?

**A.** (Wood, <u>A Survey of Israel's History</u>, p.70, note.) It was <u>not</u> a custom of the country, but only local at best, if that. It was most likely a "family custom" made up by Laban to get Leah married off. By the time Jacob discovered the deceit, it was too late to do anything about it but complain, which prompted Laban's deceitful answer to "justify" his actions.

**30:27**  If Laban had to learn this by divination, he wasn't very observant!

**30:37-43**  Jacob's scheming according to superstition.
**Q.** What actually happened?
**A.** <u>God worked the changes</u>.   It could well have been recessive genes at work, however.  Jacob declares that each time Laban changed his mind regarding which sheep Jacob could claim as his own (31:7-9) that's the kind that was born.  Thus it was more than genetic, it was God's supernatural intervention to bless Jacob as he had promised (28:13-15; 31: 10-12).

**31:10,13**  In breeding season, Jacob had a dream in which God showed him what was really going on with the herds and also told him to leave this land at once.  But he was still there!  It took some nudging from the Lord (vs.1-3) before Jacob finally decided to get moving.

**31:13**  God said to Jacob, "Remember your vow.  I have kept My part of the bargain!" (cf.Gen.28:20-22)

**31:22,23**  Jacob had a 6-day head start on Laban (cf.30:36) which translates into 180 miles!  So Laban had to do some fancy footwork (about 56 miles/day!) to catch up with him just seven days later.  That means that Jacob had a 13-day trip of 30 miles per day before Laban arrived, time enough to arrive in the hill country of Gilead some 390 miles distant.  Laban was desperate to get back both his household gods and his lost wealth.  Even though God appeared to him in a dream, in his unbelief he must have considered him as one among many gods.

**31:26**  Jacob had good reason to fear Laban's response if he had announced his departure ahead of time (see vs.39-43).

**Q. 31:43** If Jacob received all he had as wages for his work, then how could Laban claim it all as his, including Jacob's family? Something cultural going on here (see Gen.48:5)?
**A.** All were "his" by right of being the patriarch of the family. The right of the firstborn was to "inherit" all this upon his father's death thus assuming the role of patriarch, and, positionally, the sole "owner" of everything. Since the family gods were significant for symbolizing inheritance rights (Wood, p.72), Rachael's action can be seen as trying to give Jacob the patriarchal position. It never worked out that way (35:2-4), but caused great consternation among Laban and his sons.

**32:9-11** Jacob now humble. No more bargaining with God.

**32:12** Prayer based upon God's promise, the only thing Jacob had to hold on to.

**32:20** Jacob tried to do what God had already done! (see 33:4,9)

**32:24-26** Jacob knew something else was going on here than just a wrestling match (vs.26b,30).

**32:28** "Israel" means, "He struggles with God." This is a very apt and prophetic name for the nation as they continually struggled with God throughout their history until now.

**33:12-14** Jacob, fearful, still scheming! Match this response to Esau with what Jacob had done in fleeing Laban (Gen.31:23) where he covered 30 miles a day—hardly a "slow" pace! And all his animals and people made it too!

**34:1,2** Dina could have been only 3 or 4 years old when Jacob fled Padan Aram; Simeon and Levi only 11 and 10. Thus the events of this chapter had to have happened at least 8 or 9 years later, making Dina's age between 11 and 13. Simeon and Levi would then be about 20 and 19, strong enough to avenge their sister's disgrace.
Meanwhile...back in Seir, Esau is wondering whatever became of Jacob (33:14)! [In the ninth year, because of the situation at Shechem, Jacob fled south, eventually arriving at Hebron. On the way, Rachael dies in childbirth.]

**34:8** Another Satanic attempt to corrupt the Messianic seed.

### Joseph's Personal History

Born when Jacob was 96 years old,
  7 when Jacob fled Padan Aram,
  15 or 16 when Rachel died,
  17 when he was sold into Egypt (37:2),
  27 when accosted by Potiphar's wife and jailed for over
    two years and when Isaac died (39:20; 40:1; 41:1),
  30 when he began to reign with Pharaoh (41:46),
  38 when the famine began,
  40 when his brothers came down to Egypt for food the
    second time (45:6) and when his father and family
    came down shortly afterwards (Jacob being 130 at
    the time—47:28),
110 when he died (50:22,26).

**NOTE:** From this information, and working backwards, we can deduce that Jacob was 90 when Joseph was born, which would have made Joseph seven years old when Jacob fled Padan Aram. That also would have made Rachael about 23 when Joseph was born.

Genesis 37:10 seems to indicate that, when Joseph had his dreams, Rachael was still living. Yet perhaps Jacob was speaking generally since internal evidence indicates Rachael's death occurred on the trip south to Hebron well before these dreams occurred (35:27; 37:14). Thus Benjamin was likely born when Joseph was about 16, before he had been sold into Egypt; otherwise Joseph would not have known about him.

**35:2** "Get rid of the foreign gods you have with you" included the household gods Rachael had stolen from her father as well as all the images taken from the plundering of Shechem. The women and children of Shechem must have been assimilated into Jacob's family or used as slaves, or both. (I wonder what Jacob must have thought if he recognized Laban's household gods among those gathered to be thrown away?)

**36:6-8** Interesting that Esau chose to move out of the land of Canaan, the Land of Promise. It meant nothing to him, but everything to Jacob.

**Q. 36:6-8** How is it that Esau chose to move to Edom (Seir) far
from his brother because of their great possessions when Jacob
wasn't even in the land? Esau was already in Seir <u>before</u> Jacob
returned from Padan Aram (32:3; 33:14).
**A.** Two facts perhaps help clarify this problem:
1. Jacob had been in Canaan for 13 years prior to Isaac's death but
after Esau had already moved to Seir.
2. Jacob also had the rights of the firstborn to his father's wealth;
therefore, in Esau's view, what was eventually going to become
Jacob's inheritance was too much for the land to support if added to
Esau's own livestock. In that sense, it would not be wrong to call
Isaac's possessions as "Jacob's," and hence for Esau to make the
decision to move. I suspect that Esau's move at first was temporary
until he saw what would become of Jacob. When Jacob returned
with such wealth himself, Esau lost heart of ever inheriting his
father's wealth, so perhaps decided at that point to remain in Seir
permanently.

**Q. 37:3** How can it be recorded that Joseph was Jacob's favorite son
because he had been born to him in his old age, when others were
born to him <u>after</u> Joseph, and <u>all</u> of them in Jacob's "old age"?
**A.** I suspect Joseph was his favorite son because he was the firstborn
of Rachael, the wife Jacob really loved. "Born to him in his old
age" could well be a euphemism for showing favoritism to one child
above the others.

**37:12** Hebron (37:14) to Shechem = 43 miles.
Shechem to Dothan (37:17) = <u>18</u> miles.
So Joseph was approximately 61 miles from home when he
was sold as a slave.

**37:33** Amazing that Joseph could have been torn in pieces but his
robe not, even though it was covered with blood. But in the emotion
of the moment, Jacob didn't stop to think of that. Had Joseph
indeed been torn to pieces, his bloodied robe would also have been
torn to shreds since the animal would have had to go through it to
get to Joseph. Had Joseph laid it aside first, then was attacked, the
robe wouldn't have been soaked with blood.

**37:28,36** How quickly people forget their lineage and ancestral links! These Midianites were related to Joseph since their ancestor was Midian, son of Abraham and Ketura, yet they weren't bothered in the least to go about their business in buying and selling slaves, even from among their "own" people.

**38:1** Judah, probably 19 and "feeling his oats," leaves home to strike out on his own; <u>or</u>, perhaps the guilt over selling Joseph as a slave, lying to his father, and enduring his father's extreme grief drove him to leave; it was a burden too heavy for him to live with every day. He marries a Canaanite woman who bears him three sons. Perhaps fourteen or fifteen years pass between verse 4 and verse 6. Obviously Shelah was born sometime later than Onan (vs.11). Er and Onan grew up with the wicked Canaanite influence of their mother and Judah's not-too-godly example either (cf. vs. 15). Their lives were so wicked that God judged them quickly.

**38:24** Talk about a double standard! Judah had no trouble sleeping with a prostitute, but was so incensed with the thought that Tamar had committed prostitution that he wanted her put to death for it!

### Judah's Personal History

[**NOTE:** Being fairly sure, in a general way, of Judah's age when he left Padan Aram with Jacob, and his age when he went to Egypt with his brothers, the following events in his life are an approximation only as to when they might have happened.]

> Born when Jacob was 88,
> 9 when he left Padan Aram with his father,
> 19 when Joseph was sold as a slave, and when he decided
>   to "leave home" and marry a Canaanite woman.

[**NOTE:** Perhaps, as said before (see comments on 38:1 above), he fled home because of the guilt he felt over the grief his actions had caused Jacob. His subsequent eloquent plea to Joseph and intercession on behalf of Benjamin (44:18-34) indicates that he could not endure this same situation again. He would rather become a slave himself and never see his father again than cause his father further grief over Benjamin.]

20 when Er was born,
22 when Onan was born,
25 when Shela was born,
36 when Er married Tamar, and died,
36 when Onan died for his sin,
40 when his wife died;
> Shela (15) not given to Tamar as promised (she had to be considerably older than he was which would have made for a very awkward marriage situation); Judah "visits" Tamar,

41 Tamar gives birth to twins whom Judah takes as his own (46:12; evidently Tamar becomes his wife or at least comes under his care),
42 when he returns home and goes with his brothers two times to Egypt for food. Perhaps the drought had something to do with his return.

[**NOTE:** Shela, Perez and Zerah then become the progenitors of the Tribe of Judah. Also, Judah <u>had</u> to come back to his brothers in order to fulfill his part in God's eternal plan, just as God had to reunite them all with Joseph in order to accomplish his purpose—and to fulfill Joseph's dreams.]

**39:11-15** The pattern of Potiphar's wife's attempted seduction and subsequent accusation of Joseph reflects Satan's attempts to make us sin, then accusing us to God when we do (cf. Rev.12:10)!

## GOD'S WITNESS IN EGYPT
Chs.39-43
1. to Potiphar—39:2-5
2. to the jail warden—39:21-23
3. to the cupbearer and baker—40:8
4. to Pharaoh—41:16
5. to Joseph's steward—43:23

**40:7** The prison where Joseph was confined was located at or under Potiphar's house since Joseph is referred to as being "in custody...in his master's house" (cf. Gen.39:1,20 where Potiphar is referred to as the captain of the guard in charge of the king's prison—see also 40:2-

4,15; 41:10,14).

**40:23**  Had the chief cupbearer remembered Joseph at that time, Joseph may have been freed and returned to Potiphar, or more likely, sold to someone else, and thereby entering obscurity.  God kept Joseph where he could easily be found.

**42:18-20**  I suspect that Joseph demanded that his brothers bring Benjamin before him as proof that they hadn't done any evil to him as they had done to Joseph.

**42:21,22**  Joseph's brothers lived with twenty-three years of guilt for what they did to him!  Even after 17 more years, they still were not "sure" of him.  They just didn't know his faith (45:7,8; 50:19, 20) or his love for them (45:9-11; 50:21), so turned to a ruse to try to elicit Joseph's forgiveness (50:16,17).  Their uncertainty stemmed from the fact that they had never asked Joseph to forgive them, so he never confirmed that to them even though he held no grudges.  Once forgiveness was sought for and received, the issue was finally put to rest.

**Q. 42:24**  Why was Simeon chosen to be imprisoned and the others let go?
**A.** My guess is that he was the ringleader in plotting against Joseph to kill him and Joseph was giving him a slight taste of what he himself had gone through.

**43:2**  Depending upon how much food they brought with them, they were gone for perhaps seven to nine months (see the next question below).  Certainly Simeon must have thought that they had left him to rot in prison.  He must have gotten a good dose of the loneliness and hopelessness that he had caused Joseph.

**Q.** How long was Simeon in the prison?
**A.** Consider:  the distance they had to travel could have been as far as 250 miles.  At 15 miles per day, they would have arrived at [Memphis?] in 17 days, stayed about three or four days, then 17 days back to Hebron, or about 38 days round trip.  They stayed at least two journey's worth of time after their food supply was used up.

So, adding one thing to another:
1. Simeon sat in prison for the 17 days' trip back to Hebron;
2. plus all the time necessary for the food supplies to be eaten;
3. plus 68 more days (time for two trips) because of their delay;
4. plus nine more days for their trip back to Egypt. Why nine instead of 17? Because, according to 43:15, "they hurried down to Egypt." That means they probably covered at least 30 miles per day as did Jacob when he was fleeing from Laban.
5. All this added together amounts to about 94 days of "travel time,"
6. plus 4-6 months' "eating time," which comes to between...
7. ...7.5 and 9.5 months, time enough for Simeon to do some serious soul-searching.

**45:20** Israel borrowed their essential belongings from the Egyptians when they entered the land and when they left the land (Ex.12:36)!

**48:10** Jacob began going blind (140's) at about the same age that Isaac was blind (137). The tendency must have been inherited.

**49:1** If the estimated ages of Jacob's sons are correct, then at the time of Jacob's blessing, Reuben would have been about 62, Simeon 61, Levi 60, Judah 59, Joseph 57, Gad 56, Ashur 55 and Benjamin about 41.

**Q. 49:13** Do these blessings actually look forward to the Millennial Kingdom rather than the "earthly kingdom"? (Ex. Zebulon was a landlocked tribe—so vs.13 couldn't have been true of it any time in the earthly kingdom of Israel.)
**A.** I believe the ultimate fulfillment lies in the Millennial Kingdom.
In Ezekiel 48 the land is divided for each tribe with boundaries going straight across from east to west from Dan to Beersheba, tribe by tribe. So at that time Zebulon's western boundary will be the Mediterranean Sea, thus fulfilling this blessing.

**Q. 49:3-27** How do these blessings tie in to the histories of the 12 tribes and what do the various symbols (like vs.21) mean?
**A.** (See Rose Book of Charts, Maps & Time Lines, pp.83-87, and also Jacob's Dozen, by William Varner for additional, helpful information.)

# EXODUS

## God of the Impossible (cont.):

23. He provided households for the midwives who feared him (1:21).
24. Contrary to the laws of Pharaoh, he caused Pharaoh's daughter to have compassion on Moses, allowing his mother to nurse him, then bringing him up in Pharaoh's own household. The irony of this situation is unbelievable! (2:1-10).
25. In his presence, the burning bush was not consumed (3:2,3).
26. He caused Aaron's rod to become a serpent (4:2,3), his hand to become leprous (4:6,7), and the poured water to become blood (4:9).
27. His promised plagues on Egypt and blessings on Israel (4:6,7) were carried out to the full (chs.7-12; 12:35,36).
28. He overrules any physical weakness or inability (4:11,12).
29. He freed a whole nation from bondage (6:1-8) when neither they nor their rulers wanted them to be (5:2; 6:12; 12:51)!
30. He made Moses like God to Pharaoh (6:30; 7:1), Israel "favorably disposed" to the Egyptians, and Moses highly regarded by Pharaoh's officials and the people (11:2,3; 12:36).
31. He kept the following plagues away from Israel (8:22,23; 9:4,6,26; 10:22,23; 11:7).
32. He promised the land of Canaan as Israel's possession (13:10,11).
33. He led Israel by a pillar of cloud by day and a pillar of fire by night (13:21,22). So Israel had its "night light" for the next 40 years.
34. He "set up" Pharaoh by putting Israel in an impossible situation (14:2-18).
35. He made an impenetrable darkness lie between Pharaoh's army and Israel, yet at the same time gave light to Israel (14:19,20).
36. He divided the waters of the Red Sea, causing dry land to appear (14:21,22).
37. He un-wheeled the Egyptian chariots, stalling the whole army, then brought back the water, drowning them (14:24-28).
38. Water impossible to drink (15:23,24). God showed Moses a tree that could make the water sweet (15:25).
39. He has control over disease to cause sickness or healing (15:26).
40. He provided manna for 40 years (16:35) for all Israel to eat 16:4)...

and quails at one time (16:13-16).

41. He made water come out of a rock—enough for all of Israel (perhaps over two million people!—17:6 with Num.20:11).
42. He helped Israel defeat Amalek (17:8-11).
43. He revealed his presence on Mt. Sinai with thunderings, lightnings, the sound of a trumpet blast, smoke and thick darkness (20:18,21).
44. He led Israel to the place prepared in spite of obstacles (23:20).
45. He caused greater and more numerous enemies to fear and flee (23:27-30).
46. He could have judged people with death and made of Moses a greater nation (32:9,10).
47. He promised protection when the land is defenseless (34:24).
48. He sustained Moses for 40 days & nights on the mountain without food or water (34:28).
49. He filled people with skill, wisdom, and understanding (35:30-36:1).

**\* \* \* \***

**Ch.1** Even before Israel was a nation they were persecuted!

**1:8** If this "new king" was Ahmos, founder of the 18<sup>th</sup> Dynasty, then Israel actually had about 300 years of peace and prosperity in Egypt followed by 130 years of bitter slavery (1580-1450 B.C.)—an exile of 430 years from their homeland (Ex.12:40,41).

**1:19** This may be true, but if the midwives lied, they were at least commended for refusing to kill the baby boys.

**2:7-9** Quite an unexpected turn of events—Moses' own mother hired to nurse him!

**2:10** God thwarting Pharaoh's plan (cf. Ex.1:16,22).

**Chs.3,4** Moses, the reluctant servant; but did a fine job once he got going (5:22; 6:12,30).

**Q. 3:11** Regarding Moses' reluctance to agree to God's call... How much did he understand about God before this? He may have been coming out of relative ignorance about who God really was.

**A.** Consider:

1. His mother had him until he was weaned (Ex.2:10)—two or three years of age. His knowledge of the "Hebrew God" would have been minimal at best.

2. He was trained for 40 years in the best Egyptian education, which included all the Egyptian gods. There is no reason to believe that he did not worship these gods (Acts 7:22).

3. Yet somehow, he realized that he was different (possibly from early childhood memories?), that he belonged to the Hebrews (Acts 7:23; Heb.11:24; Ex.2:11) and earnestly desired to free them from bondage.

4. He fled for his life after killing an Egyptian and stayed with Reuel (Jethro), priest of Midian (Ex.2:15-21).

5. Reuel is not said to be a priest of God Most High, like Melchizedek. In Exodus 18:11 he declares, "Now I know that the LORD is greater than all other gods." Assuming from this statement, that he did not know the LORD as such, Moses could not have learned of God through him, or at least may have learned about the "Hebrew god" as one among many, but inferior to the others as he had no name.

6. So Moses had 40 more years of idolatry until his life-changing experience at the burning bush where God introduced himself to him and commissioned him to go to Egypt (Ex.3:6). "What is your name?" All gods had names, so this was a logical question. "God of your father," etc. was too generic. But coming out of 80 years of idolatry, it's no wonder Moses had problems accepting this commission from God. This must have been a "world-shattering" experience for him.

**3:14** "I AM WHO I AM"—"I AM." This name of God explains several theological concepts, among which are God's eternalness, fulfilled prophecy, the security of the Believer and prayer. Consider:

God's eternalness. He dwells in the ever-present tense—I AM. With him there is no past tense, no future tense—all events are "in process" before him. So, in his present eternalness, for example, Adam and Eve are being created, Israel is leaving Egypt, David is reigning over Israel, the exiles are returning from Babylon, Christ is being crucified, the Rapture is occurring, the Millennium is in process, the eternal state is going on.

Prophecy. In terms of God's eternalness, living in the ever-present tense, all things past and future from our time perspective are going on in his present-tense perspective. So prophecy is nothing more than God telling us what is going on "right now" in his sight; for us it's future; for him it's present. That is why his prophets <u>had</u> to be 100% correct in their prophecies, for they were telling us what God was already seeing, just as he was seeing it as it was happening.

Security of the Believer. God chose us to be saved before the foundation of the world (Eph.1:4); and totally finished the process in which he planned, predestined, called, justified and glorified us (Rom.8:28-30—all these verbs are in the Greek aorist tense indicating that the whole process was, at one point in past time, enacted and finished). And we are <u>now</u> seated with Christ in the heavenly places (Eph.2:6). In God's eternal present tense, we are already seated before his throne, by his choice (based within himself alone) and by his grace (based upon his love for us), and there is nothing on earth or in heaven that can change that.

Prayer. Have you ever wondered about the effectiveness of prayers <u>after</u> the fact? Sometimes we have prayed for years for something, only to find out that it was answered shortly after we began praying for it! "What a waste of time!" we thought. In terms of time, <u>yes</u>, because we used a <u>lot</u> of time praying for the request after it was answered and didn't need praying for. But in terms of God's eternal present tense, <u>no</u>, because that situation we prayed for is happening "right now" in his sight, so our prayers apply to it "right now," even though, in terms of time, it was answered years ago.

**3:15** "I am the God of Abraham, the God of Isaac and the God of Jacob."
He is their God according to the character of each man:
    Abraham—the God of promise.
    Isaac    —the God of patience.
    Jacob    —the God of restoration.

**3:21,22** Israel received her "back wages" from the Egyptians at the time of their exodus from Egypt.

**4:10-16** Ironically, Moses became to Aaron what God wanted to become to Moses!

**Q. 4:24,25** Why was one son circumcised and the other not?
(According to Exodus 18:2, Moses sent Zipporah and his two sons, Gershom and Eliezer, back to her father, Jethro, after that incident.)
**A.**

**6:16**               **Personal History of Levi**

> Born when Jacob was 87,
> 10 when Jacob left Padan Aram,
> 18 or 19 when he and Simeon slew the Shechemites,
> 20 when Joseph was sold into slavery,
> 43 when he and his brothers went to Egypt the second time,
> 113 when Joseph died,
> 137 when he died (after 94 years in Egypt).

**6:16-20** (cf. Gen.15:16—the 4th generation).
[**NOTE:** If you like generational jigsaw puzzles, this one will give you a real challenge. I don't know if I'm even close to an answer, but I'm going to try anyway.]

Background: Jewish lineage is notorious for skipping generations to suit the purpose of the writer. So "the son of" could be as many generations removed from the "father" as the writer wants to skip for whatever reason. God told Abraham that his descendants would be in Egypt for 400 years (a rounded-off figure—Gen.15:13,16), and return in the 4th generation. According to Exodus 12:40,41, they were in Egypt until the 430th year from the day they entered the land.

One commentator said that the four generations were accounted for by calculating a generation as 100 years (Abraham's age when Isaac was born). Fine. But Israel was in Egypt 430 years, exceeding this calculation, and really stretching the idea of a generation, which, usually in the Bible, extends to about 40 years.

Perhaps there are two other ways of looking at this 4th generation that might answer the question.

**1.** Israel suffered about 130 years of slavery (see Ex.1:8 above). Divided by 4, that gives us roughly 3.5 generations. So Israel came out in the fourth generation of their slavery.

**2.** Considering skips in the lineage, it seems clear from Scripture that Kohath was born <u>before</u> Levi went to Egypt (Gen.46:11,15); so Levi and Kohath had to be father-son. Exodus 6:18 is expressed in such a way that a considerable gap could be introduced in the lineage. Making a time line of Israel's sojourn in Egypt does not allow for just four generations between Levi and Moses. Exodus 6:20 seems too clear that we have another father-son relationship here, rather than Amram and Jochebed being Moses' ancestors as the N.I.V. note tries to prove. The tenor of verses 21-25 would seem to bear this out. So we have four generations: two at the beginning of the Egyptian exile and two at the end. Thus, of the four generations considered in this passage, Israel came out in the 4th generation.

**6:18** with **Num.16:1** It seems that Korah was a cousin to Moses as he was the son of Izhar, Amram's brother. So there was possibly some family jealously in Korah's rebellion.

### Chronology of the Plagues on Egypt
### With their counterparts in Revelation

Day 1  Moses before Pharaoh (Ex.5:1)
  2,3  Straw for brick (Ex.5:6-9)
    4  Go in to Pharaoh
=====
    5  Rod becomes a serpent (Ex.7:10)
    6  Water becomes blood . . . . . .2nd Trumpet (Rev.8:8,9);
      (Ex.7:14-21)             2nd & 3rd Bowl (Rev.16:3-7)
  13  Frogs come up from the Nile . .6th Bowl (Rev.16:13)
    (Ex.8:1-6)
  14  Frogs dead everywhere
  15  Dust becomes lice (Ex.8:16,17)
  16  Swarms of flies (Egypt and
    Israel separated—Ex.8:20-24)
  18  Flies gone
  19,20  Anthrax (Ex.9:1-6)

21     Boils (Ex.9:8-11; . . . . . . 1$^{st}$ Bowl (Rev.16:2)
22,23 Hail (Ex.9:13-26; . . . . . . 1$^{st}$ Trumpet (Rev.8:7)
                                     7$^{th}$ Bowl (16:21)
24,25 Locusts (Ex.10:13-15. . . . 5$^{th}$ Trumpet (Rev.9:1-12)
26-28 Darkness [3 days] . . . . . 5$^{th}$ Bowl (Rev.16:10,11)
      (Ex.10:21-23)
29     Moses ordered out of Pharaoh's presence
43,44 All firstborn of Egypt die (Ex.11:4-6)
40 days of plagues (beginning with the rod turning into a snake)

[**NOTE:** These plagues were also directed upon the gods and goddesses of Egypt (Ex.12:12; Num.33:3,4). See The Bible Knowledge Commentary, p.120 for a chart and further details.]

**Ch.7** From Pharaoh's standpoint, it would have been more plausible had his magicians tried to reverse the effects of the plagues rather than add to them!

**7:3** "I will harden Pharaoh's heart." According to Romans 9:17, God raised Pharaoh up that his power might be displayed through him and that God's name might be proclaimed in all the earth. It was Pharaoh's choice as to how this would be done. It would seem that he hardened his heart six times (7:13,22; 8:15,19,32; 9:7); the seventh time (9:12—numerology coming into play here?) it is stated that the LORD hardened his heart. After the hail, Pharaoh sinned yet more and hardened his heart again. Both Pharaoh and God "worked together" on this one (9:34; 10:1): Pharaoh in sin and God in judgment. Then the LORD continued the process (10:20, 27; 14:4). So it appears that Pharaoh first hardened his own heart six times, then God continued the process five more times, thus completing what Pharaoh had started.

One reason Pharaoh "hardened" his heart was that, initially, there was no difference between what Moses and Aaron did and what his magicians did. Rods of both became snakes (7:11), they turned water into blood (7:22) and produced frogs (8:7). So in his sight, Moses and Aaron were no different than his magicians in occult power.

**7:9** Pharaoh asked/demanded from Moses and Aaron a miracle—I assume to authenticate their "supposed" authority. Had they not worked a miracle, he probably would have had them executed on the spot.

**Q. 7:10** Did this first miracle of the snake have any connection to the snake image on Pharaoh's headpiece?

**A.** Perhaps so. The word for "snake" in 4:3 (*nachash*) seems to indicate any kind of snake. The word for "snake" in 7:9-12 (*tanniym*) seems to indicate a much larger serpent (trans. "great dragon lying among your streams" in Ezekiel 29:3 in direct reference to Pharaoh of Egypt). Pharaoh could not have missed the similarity between the snake and the one on his headpiece. Nor could he have missed the significance of Aaron's snake swallowing up those of the magicians'. But for reasons of his own he chose to ignore the implications of this miracle, and hardened his heart instead.

**7:17** The N.I.V. note doesn't account for the broad scope of this plague, for the natural turning red of the Nile River wouldn't account for the redness in the canals, streams, ponds, reservoirs, wooden buckets and stone jars. However, if the Lord did use natural occurrences in connection with the plagues, that could help explain Pharaoh's hardened heart. "This has happened before, so what's the big deal?"

Also, the N.I.V. note here says that this plague occurred in late summer or early fall and the note on 8:16 saying late autumn ignores the brief sequence of the plagues. The turning of the water into blood occurred on the $6^{th}$ day (vs.19); the plague of the gnats (8:16) occurred on the $15^{th}$ day (see Chronology of the Plagues, p.38).

**Q. 8:22** According to this verse, the Israelites also suffered the first three plagues. Why?

**A.** (Cf. Ex.6:9) Possibly to redirect their attention to Moses and the Lord, then to establish Moses' authority before them, and to demonstrate God's grace in sparing them further suffering. They had crossed Moses' name off their list of deliverers. Also, they probably had sins of their own that had to be dealt with, and they had to know that God is the LORD (10:2). From this point on, it seems that they were free of the remaining plagues (8:22,23; 9:4,11,26; 10:12 [assumed separation by this description], 23; 11:7) and most willing to follow Moses (12:28).

**9:2** This verse answers the question as to how the Egyptians still had livestock (Ex.9:19) that could be destroyed by hail. The plague fell on all the livestock "in the field." The Egyptians had other livestock in pens and stalls where they were protected from the hail.

## 9:14,16    Reasons for the Plagues on Egypt

1. "So that you may know that there is none like me in all the earth."
"So that my name may be proclaimed in all the earth." [see Rom.9:17]
2. As a judgment on all the gods of Egypt (cf. Ex.12:12; 18:11).

**10:21** Darkness that could be felt. We have no concept of what that is like. But I can imagine that that kind of darkness would totally swallow up the light from any source so that it couldn't be seen (like the well-known phenomenon of the black hole).

**Q.** What must that have looked like from the land of Goshen where the Israelites had light?
**A.** The blackest, highest billowing bank of clouds man has ever seen with a curtain of deepest black falling to the ground, so black that it made them shudder to look at it.

**Q.** How can we know that the darkness swallowed up all the light?
**A.** (Ex.10:23) I'm assuming from this verse that the sedentary nature of the Egyptians during this plague was due to the fact that no torch or other form of light available to them worked in that darkness. If the darkness was gradual in coming, they no doubt lighted torches so that they could see. But the darkness enveloped that light, making it useless. If the Egyptians could have used torches, etc., to see, they would not have been sitting around twiddling their thumbs for three days! They'd have been up and around doing whatever they could under the circumstances.
If, on the other hand, the darkness was sudden, and caught them totally off guard, they would not have been in a position to find anything to light. But in the interior of various buildings there were usually lighted torches. So if they were still functional in the darkness, those who could see them would take light to the others. Such did not occur. So either way, I believe the darkness, divine in nature and source, literally swallowed up what light there was.

Can you imagine darkness that could be "felt"? A darkness that one could sense creeping over him, pressing him down and making it hard to move, sensing a threatening presence but unable to do anything to protect himself? Talk about terror! No thanks!

**11:2,3** "Back wages" owed to the Israelites (see also 12:35,36).

**12:38** A "mixed multitude" went up out of Egypt—understandable (people wanting to align themselves with a god more powerful than their gods) but the precursor of trouble. A very apt illustration of 2 Corinthians 6:14-18 (Num.11:4-6). This could be considered one more attempt by Satan to derail God's plans for Israel: to so corrupt them through the influence of the unbelieving Egyptians accompanying them that God would have to destroy them. Then, no Messiah! No defeat for Satan!

**12:43-49** The first Passover restrictions given to Moses put a definite division between the Israelites and the "hangers-on." Unless the "foreigner" was circumcised, indicating faith and a willingness to obey the God of Israel, he was to be excluded from this ordinance. So already there were categories created: "them" and "us," "believer" and "unbeliever."

**14:20** The Shekinah Glory Cloud was light to the Israelites but darkness to the Egyptians. Light could not penetrate that darkness, so the Egyptians stayed where they were. As soon as some of them tried to move off in the direction of the Israelite camp, they "felt" that same darkness that they had experienced two-and-one-half weeks ago. They quickly backtracked from that blackness to await the return of light on the coming day.

**14:21-28** That same night the Israelites went through the sea. From the context (vs.15-20) it would seem that this event began about evening of that day and continued on till the last watch of the night just before dawn (between 3:00 and 6:00 A.M.—or nearly ten hours later). Considering that the Israelites numbered 600,000 men, plus their families and livestock, plus all the hangers-on accompanying them, we're looking at a company of some two to three million people. It's a miracle in itself that they were all able to get across in less than 10 hours!

When the last ones were nearly over, the Egyptians suddenly sensed the absence of that deep darkness, began to see the pre-dawn stars, and, off in the distance was the light of the Shekinah Glory Cloud "showing up" the Israelites, making them an easy target. Within minutes the entire camp was aroused and in full pursuit of their hapless prey.

Nearly caught up to the last of the scrambling Israelites, and ready to strike, the head chariots suddenly lurched violently as their wheels unexpectedly came off, spilling their occupants in inglorious heaps left and right. "No time to fix wheels; AFTER THEM!" Charioteers still able, remounted their wheel-less vehicles and tried to drive the horses on in a hot pursuit that had just grown very, very cold and laborious. The ground began to soften and soon became a soggy mire that sucked at the horses' hooves, bringing the cavalry to a mucky standstill. All down the line, chariot after chariot lost its wheels. The might of Pharaoh's army was suddenly, totally and thoroughly immobilized. All they could do was sit there and watch the last of the Israelites reach the far shore and disappear forever.

Daylight was just breaking (vs.27). Suddenly the full realization of where they were and how they got there and what had just happened struck Pharaoh's men. A frantic "retreat" was sounded and a mad, muddy scramble for the Egyptian shore ensued. But too late. Without warning, the east wind stopped, and just as quickly the watery walls collapsed (vs.27,28) engulfing the whole of Pharaoh's army in a liquid grave, with Pharaoh, the god of Egypt, looking on helplessly, powerless to save his own army. End of chapter for Egypt...and the beginning of a new one for Israel.

**15:13-17; 23:20-31** If Israel had really believed what they sang (as well as believed God's promises), there would have been little grumbling and complaining, no trouble at Kadesh Barnea, and no 40 years of wandering in the desert.

If we really believed the songs we sing, two things could happen:

1. We would be spared a lot of trouble ("A Mighty Fortress Is Our God"), or...

2. We could be led into theological confusion ("A Charge to Keep I Have")!

But because they didn't believe what they sang, or at least it wasn't a part of them, or applicable to their everyday existence, they continually grumbled and complained. Consider what Moses had to put up with…

| <u>Complaints</u> | <u>Results</u> |
|---|---|

## BEFORE SINAI

<u>Excusable</u>:

1. Ex.14:10-12 Terrified because of Pharaoh's army, the people cried out in despair. They didn't understand God's intentions.

   Encouragement (vs.13,14). Don't be afraid. Stand still and see the salvation of the LORD.

2. Ex.15:24 Three days and no water. Water discovered, but bitter. "What are we to drink?!"

   Object lesson from God on healing that he will effect upon them <u>if</u> they obey him (vs.25,26).

<u>Lack of faith</u>: demonstrated by an unwillingness to obey—16:20,27,28. ("We don't want to be here; <u>you</u> brought us here; so <u>you</u> give us what we want!")

[NOTE: They grumbled against Moses and Aaron, but <u>he</u> said they were actually grumbling against the LORD (vs.8). This principle is demonstrated in Matthew 25:34-45 and Acts 9:4,5 where what we do or don't do to other Christians, Christ considers as done or not done to himself!]

3. Ex.16:1-3 "Starvation" rations. [One month out of Egypt—vs.1]

   a. God promised a daily provision of manna to meet their needs (vs.4,5).
   b. God sent quail that evening and manna the next morning; proof of his ability to provide for them (vs.13,14).

4. Ex.17:1-4,7 No water to drink. People very angry and quarrelsome. Ready to stone Moses.

   Moses told to strike the rock with his rod. Water came out. God "tested" by the Israelites (vs.5-7).

| Complaints | Results |
|---|---|

## AT SINAI

They arrived there three months to the day they left Egypt (Ex.19:1). No complaints recorded as long as they were at Sinai.

## AFTER SINAI

Inexcusable:

| Complaints | Results |
|---|---|
| 5. Num.11:1-3  Complaining in general. | God angry. Fire from God burned the outskirts of the camp.  Some died. |
| 6. Num.11:4-6  No meat to eat!  They despised the LORD (vs.20; Ps.78:22). | God angry (vs.10; Ps.78:21) Moses discouraged (vs.11-15).  Quail for a month (vs. 18-20,31,32).  Very great plague in which many die (vs.33). |
| 7. Num.12:1,2  Miriam & Aaron against Moses' marriage and authority (12:2). | God angry (vs.9).  Miriam leprous(vs.10) and shut out of the camp for seven days. |
| 8. Num.14:1-4  Rather die in Egypt than face the Canaanites in battle (vs.11). | Rejecting God, not believing him.  None but Caleb & Joshua would see the Promised Land (vs.22-24,28-30). God angry and rejected that generation—(vs.34,35). |
| 9. Num.16:1-14 Korah & Co. against Aaron.  They wanted a part in the priesthood. | Moses very angry (vs.15). God angry (vs.22).  Korah & Co. fell alive into the pit when the earth cracked open (vs.30-33).  Fire killed the rest (vs.35). |

| Complaints | Results |
|---|---|
| 10. Num.16:41 Accused Moses of killing the people of the LORD. | God angry (vs.45). Plague killing 14,700 people (vs.49). Aaron's rod that budded and bore fruit to rid God of Israel's murmuring against him and Moses (ch.17). |
| 11. Num.20:2-5 Contention because of no water. They refused to enter the place prepared for them by God, then complained that their present situation was so bad! It was all their doing, not Moses and Aaron's. This was rebellion against God's Spirit (Ps.106:33). | God told Moses to speak to the rock. Moses struck the rock [in frustration]. God angry (Deut.1:37; 3:26; Ps.106:32) because of this disobedience and lack of faith (vs.12,24). Therefore, Moses and Aaron were barred from leading Israel into the Promised Land. |
| 12. Num.21:4,5 Complained because of lack of food and water, and tired of manna (despised God's provision). | Fiery serpents (vs.6). Many people were bitten and died. |

* * * *

**16:23** Note: The Sabbath Day was instituted before the Law was given.

**17:8** Amalekites (descendants from Esau—Gen.36:12), a genealogical "dead end" (vs.14)

**17:10-13** An illustration regarding the importance of intercessory prayer.

**18:10,11** with **12:12** The judgments upon the gods of Egypt convinced Jethro of God's greatness (see also Num.33:3,4).

**19:4** "Carried you on eagle's wings" means miraculous and complete deliverance (cf. Rev.12:14).

**19:7-34:29** Moses made at least nine trips up and down Mount Sinai:
1. Up (19: 3) – down (19: 7)   6. Up (24: 9) – down (24:11,12)
2. Up (19: 8) – down (19:14)   7. Up (24:13) – down (32:15)
3. Up (19:20) – down (19:25)   8. Up (32:31) – down (33: 4)
4. Up (20:21) – down (between 23:33-24:1)
5. Up (24: 1) – down (24: 3)   9. Up (34: 4) – down (34:29)

**19:13** "Not a hand to be laid on him" because by touching that person or animal, the violation of God's holiness would be passed on to that person and he too would have to die (see vs.22,23).

**19:16,19** Sound of a very loud trumpet—supernatural (cf. 1 Thes. 4:16).

**20:1-17** Remember two nonsense words, and you'll never forget the Ten Commandments again! Ready? The words are GINASH and MASTEC.
1. No other **G**ods before me.
2. Make no **I**dols.
3. Don't misuse My **NA**me.
4. Keep the **S**abbath.
5. **H**onor your father and mother.
6. No **M**urder.
7. No **A**dultery.
8. No **S**tealing.
9. No false **TE**stimony.
10. No **C**oveting.

**20:20** "The fear of God will...keep you from sinning."

"Fear"—of doing anything that would displease him. Because of our love for him, we don't want to do anything that would grieve him.

"Fear"—of punishment if we did.

Fear can be a healthy deterrent from doing wrong (cf. Heb. 12:5-11).

**20:21** That same darkness that shut down Egypt (Ex.10:21) and kept the Egyptian army at bay (Ex.14:20), now covered the mountain. The same dread that the Israelites experienced in seeing that darkness from Goshen revisited them, but this time much closer, stronger and accompanied with much lighting, thunder, earth-shattering trumpet blasts, columns of billowing smoke and violent quaking of the earth (19:16-19). No way were they going to approach all that (20:18). Even Moses trembled with fear (Heb.12:21) though God had warned him ahead of time that this was how he was going to appear to him (19:9—in a dark cloud, but he didn't mention all the accompanying fireworks and sound effects!)

**20:25** N.I.V. note on "defile it [the altar] if you use a tool on it": "For reasons not now clear, but perhaps related to pagan practices." It is inconceivable that God would require Israel to do something based upon pagan practices. The issue here is the absence of human effort in achieving forgiveness of sin.

**21:23** "Eye for eye" justice was really a law of mercy since the human heart demands revenge, which often exceeds the original offense. "You hit me; I hit you harder!" None of this among God's people!

**24:9-11** The 70 elders, Aaron, Nadab and Abihu saw [a vision of] the Lord. This makes their sins more grievous since they purposely had to go against what they had just seen.

**Q. 24:13a** How far up the mountain did Joshua go with Moses?
He obviously set out with him (vs.13) and came down with him (32: 17).
**A.** Ex.24:13b,15,18; 32:7,15. It would seem from the sound of these verses that that Joshua only went part way up, then waited for Moses' return. That wait surely must have been a test of his faith and faithfulness!

**Q. 24:15,16** Why did God make Moses wait seven days before speaking to him?
**A.** One doesn't just rush into God's presence and expect him to "do his thing." We must be patient and await his timing.

**Q.** Did Moses sense the time passing, or was he so taken up with the glory of God that he didn't feel the time at all?

**A.** I suspect it was the latter.    Often in a church service, if the presence of God is there and the ministry of the Word really ministers to my heart, two hours could pass and they would seem like minutes. Moses probably felt the same way—totally unaware of the passing of time.

**25:8**   The pattern for the Tabernacle had to be exact because it prefigured Christ and his ministry. Consider...

### THE REFLECTION OF THE TABERNACLE IN JOHN'S GOSPEL

1. The brazen altar    = ch.1    "Behold the Lamb of God which takes away the sin of the world."

2. The laver    = ch.3    "Born of the water and the Spirit."

3. The table for the bread of the presence with its food and drink    = chs.4-6    "Living Water" discourse; "Living Bread" discourse.

4. The golden candlestick    = chs.8,9    "I am the light of the world"; the blind man given sight.

5. The altar of incense    = chs.14-17 Praying in the name of Jesus.

6. The ark and mercy seat    = chs.18-20 Christ's High Priestly ministry.

7. The Shekinah Cloud    = chs.20-21 Christ breathed on his disciples, giving them the Holy Spirit.

**Q. 25:17**   The Mercy Seat — exactly the same length and width of the ark with no height mentioned.   So it seems to have been a flat cover.  How did they keep it from slipping?  Was it heavy enough to sit there on its own, or did they put pegs on each inside corner, or a

lip around the inside to keep it in place? Verse 21 gives no hint.
**A.** Neither does anything else! From a Hollywood production of
"The Ten Commandments," they had an inner lip which fit snugly
into the box of the Ark (possibly). Or, it could have been made to fit
as a cover over the ark (more probable).

**28:2,3** If you are a tailor or seamstress, a craftsman, carpenter, metal-
lurgist, or apothecary (31:1-11), that's a God-given ability for you to
use for his glory (35:30-36:1).

**28:17-20** Comparing the stones on the priest's breastplate with those
in Ezek.28:13 and Rev.21:19-21 proves to be more confusing than
helpful since each could be something else in different contexts. For
instance, an emerald could be a carbuncle, which is a form of ruby,
which could be an agate, which could also be an onyx, or chalcedony,
which could be a sardonyx, or a form of chrysolite or chrysoprase,
which is a form of beryl! So we just need to be content with the utter
beauty described and leave the stones "unturned."

**31:12-18** The Sabbath Day—a <u>sign</u> between God and <u>Israel</u> (vs.
13,17). It was instituted <u>before</u> the 10 Commandments were given
(Ex.16:23-30). The emphasis was on <u>worship and rest</u>.
    **The Sabbath Day**     (see Ex.34:21; 35:2,3; Lev.23:3).
    **The Sabbath Year**    (every 7$^{th}$ year—see Lev.25:1-7).
    **The Sabbath Jubilee** (every 50$^{th}$ year—see Lev.25:8-12).
    **Sabbaths** (in general including any or all of the above—see
            Lev.26:2,34,35,43; Deut.5:12-15).

**32:1** After Moses went five times up and down the mountain, the
people expected him to return soon after his 6$^{th}$ ascent. When he was
not seen for over a month, they began to wonder what happened to
him. They seemed to equate him with the miracles in getting them
out of Egypt, and since he was presumably dead, what god did they
have left? They "believed" as long as they saw. But since idolatry
(Josh.24:14,23), not faith (Deut.29:4; Heb.4:2), was in their hearts,
they quickly turned out of the way. God had given additional
revelation to the elders of Israel (see comments on Ex. 24:9-11) to
show them that this was more than just Moses. Yet even they did
not believe, but probably interpreted this "revelation of God" as
another of Moses' "miracles." Aaron knew better, but was afraid to

go against the people (32:22-24). *So Moses was essentially leading a nation of unbelievers on a spiritual journey that demanded faith.* Talk about frustration!

**32:4,7,11** (A bit of tongue-in-cheek.) Everybody was saying that somebody else led the Israelites out of Egypt! Aaron said it was the calf (vs.4), God said that it was Moses (vs.7), and Moses said it was God (vs.11). It seems at this point nobody wanted to take the responsibility for them!

**32:5** The N.I.V. reference note with this verse says, "Apparently Aaron recognized the idolatrous consequences of his deed and acted quickly to keep the people from turning completely away from the Lord."

If this is so, it didn't work (vs.6-8). It was at best a compromise and an attempt at syncretism; at worst gross hypocrisy on Aaron's part since he was the one instrumental in making the calf! Either way, the people didn't care, but shamelessly carried on their sin. It did reveal the true nature of their hearts. The sacrifices they offered (vs.6) were not to the Lord, but to the calf. So the above note seems not only lame in character, but also not in harmony with the context. What's more, Moses accused Aaron of leading them into this great sin (vs.21), not trying to keep them from it.

**32:21-24** These verses are an interesting illustration of the avoidance and denial of guilt. Adam, Eve, Cain and King Saul all tried the same thing. In every case it didn't work. God holds us responsible for what we have done, not for what others do. For whatever reason, we choose to do what we do and cannot lay the blame on others.

**34:15,16** In a mixed marriage (or legal union of any other kind), the believer will always be the one who must compromise if the marriage (or union) is to be successful. And that often leads to a backslidden condition (cf. 2 Cor.6:14-18).

**34:28** The second time Moses received the 10 Commandments, he also stayed 40 days and nights on the mountain. This also was a "rerun," a test for Israel, to see what they would do in his absence. Lesson learned. They waited for him (vs.30-32) and didn't do anything foolish.

**Q. 34:35** Why did Moses veil his face?
**A.** 2 Corinthians 3:13 seems to imply the answer: so that the Israelites couldn't see the glory fading away.

**Q.** But why was this so important to Moses?
**A.** Perhaps he felt or feared that with the fading of that radiance, his authority would also decrease in the people's eyes. His radiant face became a symbol of his divine authority.

**Q. Chs.36-40** How long did it take the Israelites to prepare the materials, etc., for the Tabernacle?
**A.** Israel left Egypt on the 15$^{th}$ day of the 1$^{st}$ month (12:2,6).
   Arrived at Sinai on the 15$^{th}$ day of the 3$^{rd}$ month (19:1), a two-month journey.
   Moses up and down the mountain five times: about 5 days.
   Moses up the mountain for 40 days.
   Moses caring for the "calf" problem: 1 day.
   Several days (chs.33-34:3).
   Moses up the mountain for 40 days (34:28).
   Moses gives instructions for the Tabernacle: 1 day.
   People gather materials: about 7 days. (Now about 100 days after arriving at Sinai.)
   185 days* (6 mo.) to prepare/make the items for the Tabernacle.
   Tabernacle set up on the 1$^{st}$ day of the 1$^{st}$ month, or 9.5 months (285 days) after arriving at Sinai.

   *285 minus 100 days = 185 days @ 30 days per month = <u>about 6 months</u>.

**Q. 38:1-4** with **Lev.6:8-13.** Was the open space below the grate to allow the ashes to be removed while the fire was still burning above?
**A.** Yes, since it would be impossible to remove the ashes otherwise.

**Q. 38:24-29** What is the value, in today's money, of the gold, silver and bronze used in constructing the Tabernacle?
**A.** Figuring the amount used is easier than the value since the value changes many times a year. So the following will be an approximation based on figures as of June 2011 off the Internet. But regardless how the values change, what we come out with is that the

Israelites had a very valuable and expensive place in which to meet God, fitting for the glory he wanted to show them at that time.

Basic weights:
  One talent    = 75 lbs.
  3,000 shekels = 1 talent, or 75 lbs.
  730 shekels   = 18 lbs. 4 oz.

So...            Tal. Lbs.  Lbs.
Gold weight:    29 x 75 + 18.25 = 2,193 lbs. 4 oz. (short of a long ton)

Silver weight:  100 x 75 + 44.4  = 7,544 lbs. 6 oz. (just short of 4 tons)

Bronze weight:  70 x 75 + 60.0  = 5,310 lbs.    (just over 2.5 tons)

Gold value: $1,520/oz. (as of 6/2011—Internet) = $53,339,840.00
Silver value: $34.34/oz. (as of 6/2011—Internet) = $   259,061.50
Bronze value: $4.00/oz. (as of 6/2011—Internet) = $   339,840.00
                                        $53,938,741.50

And this was only a fraction of the wealth the Israelites received from the Egyptians upon their exiting the land!

**God of the Impossible (cont.):**

50. He sent fire from heaven to consume the burnt offering (9:24).
51. He sent fire from heaven as judgment on Nadab and Abihu (10:1,2).
52. He promised to provide three years' worth of food in one year (25:21).
53. He has power to bless and power to curse (ch.26).
54. He broke the yoke of Egyptian bondage (26:13).

**\* \* \* \***

Leviticus is *holiness legislated.*
Our salvation in Christ is *holiness imputed*
    (Lev.11:44 with Heb.10:14).
Leviticus: holiness is **determined** by what we do;
In Christ: holiness is **demonstrated** by what we do.

**Q. 4:3**  How does the sin of the high priest bring guilt upon the people?

**A.** 1. In the same way Adam's sin brought guilt and sin upon all mankind (Rom.5:12)—as he (the high priest) represented the people before God.  If he sins, the people are with him in his transgression and will suffer the consequences.  It is the same as with a king or president of a country.  He represents the people before other nations.  If he insults another king, that king is likely to declare war on his country, and all the people become guilty in the enemy's sight, and suffer the consequences.  "If the king thinks that way, his people must too, for he has influenced them against me."

2. This statement leads to a second way the people become guilty, that is, if they follow the influence of the sinning priest and sin themselves.  His example could cause them to take a lighter attitude toward sin, hence decreasing God's glory and holiness in their sight (cf. Malachi 2; esp. vs.8).  Thus they too are guilty.

**Q. 4:7**  With all the blood being poured out at the base of the altar, wouldn't the ground become a soggy, blood-soaked mire? (Lev.4:7, 18,25,30; 8:15; 9:9)

**A.** (?) They must have had some sort of drainage system in which the blood could be washed away with water or rain.

(?) But then blood could soak into the ground and coagulate, thus tending to become a solid mass.

(?) Any other ideas?

**4:13** Unintentional sin is still sin in God's sight, and the sinner has to be held accountable for it, <u>even</u> if he is unaware of it. David obviously wrestled with this problem which gave rise to Psalm 139:23,24.

**Q. 6:12,13** What did they do when it rained?
**A.**

**Q. 7:22-25** Why the prohibition against eating fat?
**A.** Perhaps it was the Lord's way of keeping their cholesterol down, thus averting its various associated diseases.

**Q. 8:30,33** with **10:7** Aaron and his sons had to remain at the entrance of the Tabernacle for seven days. How then could they "relieve" themselves without incurring God's wrath? If they "relieved" themselves at the Tabernacle entrance, that would violate the holiness of the Tabernacle, and they would die. If they left the Tabernacle to "relieve" themselves outside the grounds, they also would die since the anointing oil was upon them (10:7). So they were in a no-win situation!
**A.** I believe that for that time the Lord suspended their bodily functions (as no doubt he did for Moses during the 40 days he was in God's presence without eating or drinking), so they didn't have to "relieve" themselves.

**Q. Ch.11** Why the difference between animals that may be eaten and those that may not?
**A.** According to **11:44,45**, the primary object lesson is on holiness. A secondary reason could be for health reasons. Some animals, improperly cooked, can bring disease and death: trichinosis and tape

worm from pork, for instance. However, this cannot be the primary reason because 1 Timothy 4:3-5 states that all animals may be eaten —none are forbidden. Considering the primary object lesson on holiness, what is there about these forbidden animals that makes them "unclean"? Several thoughts:

1. The pig returns to its wallowing in the mud (2 Pet.2:22) and is by nature a very destructive animal (ask any gardener).
2. The dog returns to its vomit (2 Pet.2:22) and also eats the waste from other dogs—very unclean habits!
3. Various birds of prey feed on carcasses, the touching of which brings defilement (Lev.11:24,25). Therefore, to eat them is to touch that which is unclean.
4. Various kinds of insects (flies, blue bottles, ants, etc.) also feed on carcasses, garbage and other trash, qualifying them as "unclean" (Lev.11:24,25).
5. Bats, part of the rodent family forbidden to eat, love darkness and shun light—the perfect description of the condition of a person's sinful heart (Jn.3:19,20).
6. The snake (11:42) symbolizes Satan and all that is evil (Rev.12:9).

From these facts, I assume then, that if we had additional information, the other animals listed would also have "unclean" characteristics or habits that would disqualify them from the Israelite menu which, indeed, is the case. I want to quote extensively from the book, Is God a Moral Monster?, by Paul Copan, pp.80,81). Here he writes:

"Genesis 1 divides animals into three spheres: animals that walk on the land, animals that swim in the water, animals that fly in the air. Leviticus 11 lists as unclean certain animals that are connected to land (vv.2-8), water (vv.9-12), and air (vv.13-25). As we've seen, these animals symbolize a mixing or blurring of categories. In contrast, the clean animal has all the defining features of its class given at creation. So animals that 'transgressed' boundaries or overlapped spheres were to be avoided as unclean.

"Water: To be clean, aquatic animals must have scales *and* fins (Lev.11: 10; Deut.14:10); so eels or shellfish, which don't fit this category, are unclean and thus prohibited.

"Land: Clean animals are four-footed ones that hop, walk, or jump. A clear indication of a land animal's operating according to its sphere is that is *both* (1) has split hoofs and (2) is a cud-chewer. These two features make obvious that an animal belongs to the land sphere (e.g., sheep and goat). Camels, hares, conies (which chew the cud but don't have divided hoofs), and pigs (which have divided hoofs but don't chew the cud) are borderline cases; so they're excluded as appropriate land animals to eat.

"Air: Birds have two wings for flying. Birds like pelicans and gulls inhabit both water and sky, which makes them unclean. Insects that fly but have *many* legs are unclean; they operate in two spheres—land and air. However, insects with four feet—two of which are jointed for hopping on the ground—are considered clean (Deut.11:21-23). These insects—the locust, katydid, cricket, and grasshopper—are like birds of the air, which hop on the ground with two legs. Therefore they're clean.

"Unclean animals symbolized what Israel was to avoid—mixing in with the unclean beliefs and practices of the surrounding nations. Israel was to be like the clean animals—distinct, in their own category, and not having mixed features. After all, the Israelites were God's set-apart people who were to reject the religion and practices of surrounding nations.

"…As the people of God, the Israelites were reminded that holiness requires persons to conform to their class as God's set-apart people. So what the Israelites did in their everyday lives— even down to their eating habits—was to signal that they were God's chosen people who were to live lives distinct from the surrounding nations.

"…So no religious overlap, blurring distinctions, or compromise could exist between Israel and its neighbors. Israel was called to integrity and purity of life, to avoid what would restrict or inhibit drawing near to God. …God's holy people were to belong to their distinct sphere; they weren't to mix their religion with surrounding pagan nations or intermarry with those who rejected the God of Israel (cf. Ezra 9:1-4; Neh.13:23-30)."

Thus animals with unclean habits as well as blurred sphere distinctions both qualify as "unclean" animals that could not be eaten. The Israelites had to separate themselves from everything that would bring defilement or uncleanness to them in any way, and, by extension, to separate themselves from sin, thus living holy lives and able to approach their holy God.

**Q. 12:1-5** Why the difference in purification between giving birth to a boy (40 days) and to a girl (80 days)?

**A.** Again I quote at length from the book, <u>Is God a Moral Monster?</u>, by Paul Copan, p.106, where he writes: "In general, a Jewish mother's lengthier separation from the tabernacle (or temple) after giving birth to a girl made a theological and ethical statement. In ancient Near Eastern polytheism, the strong emphasis was on fertility rites, cult prostitution, and the dramatization of the births of gods and goddesses. The distance between the birth event and temple worship—especially with baby girls—was carefully maintained.

"Another plausible explanation focuses on a natural source of uncleanness—namely, the flow of blood. Verse 5 refers to the reason: it's because of 'the blood of her purification.' The mother experiences vaginal bleeding at birth. Yet such vaginal bleeding is common in newborn girls as well, due to the withdrawal of the mother's estrogen when the infant girl exits the mother's womb. So we have *two* sources of ritual uncleanness with a girl's birth but *only one* with a boy's."

**Chs.13-15** The ceremonial cleanness that the Israelites had to maintain by the rituals of washings and sacrifices, etc., was accomplished for us by Christ on the cross (Heb.10:14) thus enabling us to boldly approach the Throne of Grace at any time, at any place without fear of rejection as being unclean (Heb.4:14-16).

**General thought:** Trying to get rid of our sins by doing good works is like trying to cleanse our dirty hands by helping others. No matter how many good works we do, our hands are still dirty. Only by applying soap and water will they become clean. No matter how many good works we do, our hearts are still soiled with sin. Only when the blood of Christ is applied will they become clean.

**14:14,17** Oil covers the blood showing us that the Holy Spirit, symbolized by the oil, is the seal that covers the blood of our redemption.

**15:31** The "physical" presence of a holy God among his people put an awesome burden upon them. They <u>had</u> to be holy (clean) or die. For a people in a condition of unbelief (see Heb.4:2), this was a terrible situation to be in.

But lest one blame God for "forcing" the issue, remember two things: 1. He was bound to fulfill his covenant with Abraham (Heb. 6:16-18) to make of him a great nation and bring blessing to the world. 2. The Israelites themselves promised to obey whatever the

LORD said (Ex.19: 8), so their disobedience (Heb.3:16-19; 4:6,11; 8:9) was a violation of their own promise to God. God promised (Ex. 15:26; 19:5,6), they agreed (Ex.19:8) and thus bound themselves to his plan, his presence and all the associated requirements.

In principle, I see a parallel attitude between the Israelites then and many Christians now who accept Christ as Savior but refuse to submit to him as Lord, wanting his promises but not his presence, desiring Divine intervention but not Divine directive. Were we also living under the Law, our situation would not be much different than Israel's!

In this light, the letter to the Galatians becomes our spiritual Emancipation Proclamation. We would do well not to carelessly regard our freedom in Christ!

**17:3-5** Principle: Going into the field to "worship" is not the same as going to God's house to worship. God takes a dim view of "field worship" (cf. Heb.10:24,25).

**19:17** If we see a person doing wrong and say nothing to him to correct the situation, we share in his guilt (cf. Heb.3:12,13)! But confronting him must be done in the context of the same love we have for ourselves (vs.18). This means correcting him in the same spirit we would accept if we were being corrected for the same thing ("Who likes to be corrected?"). Having this attitude would really change the way we approach people needing correcting (cf. Matt.18:15-20 and Gal.6:1,2).

**Q. 20:17** What is the difference between the prohibition in this verse and Abraham's marriage to Sarah, his half-sister (Gen.20: 12)?
**A. Rom.5:13** says that "before the law was given, sin was in the world.

But sin is not taken into account when there is no law." God did not reveal himself to Abraham as he did to Moses and Israel, so Abraham was not responsible for what God had not revealed to him. He fully followed what he did know, and that was all that God required from him.

**22:4-6** The Pharisees carried this command out to an unintended degree shunning physical contact with anyone defiled (in their opinion) or deemed "less spiritual" than they were, lest they be defiled. The original intent was good, but it led to a sterile ministry (cf. Lk.10:31,32) equally defiled by their hypocrisy (Matt.23:27,28).

**23:17** "With yeast"—Anticipates the formation of the Church on the day of Pentecost. The Body of Christ is composed of sinners ("yeast").

**Q. 25:15** This verse seems to be saying two opposing things:

"You are to buy land on the basis of the number of years <u>since</u> the Jubilee."

"You are to sell the land on the basis of the number of years <u>left</u> for harvesting crops [<u>before</u> the next Jubilee]." So, which is it?

**A.** It's actually saying the same thing but from two perspectives.

From the last Jubilee, the buyer counts 46 years; 4 years remain.

To the next Jubilee, the seller counts 4 years, and sells the land at the price of 4 years' crops (vs.16).

So there is really no conflict.

Also, the two ways of calculating the right year is arrived at in two different ways, thus guaranteeing that the right year is determined (see the same principle at work in the buying and redeeming of slaves—Lev.25:50-52).

**26:3-13** O.T. version of Matthew 6:33.

**Q. 27:28,29** How would a person be "devoted" to the LORD [the ir-revocable giving over of a person to the LORD]; "put under the ban" which may doom him to destruction?

**A.** The same word ("devoted") in Joshua 7:1 is translated "accursed."

The word "herrem" (Hebrew) in Joshua 6:17 is translated "utterly destroy" in verse 21. It also means "to ban, destroy, devote" in the sense of belonging to God.

There seems to be two senses in which this word is used:

1. The involvement of total destruction of people as in enemies (Deut.7:2), animals (1 Sam.15:3) or material goods (Josh.6:17-19).
2. The turning over of persons, animals or goods to the priests for whatever use the priests would have for them (Num.18:14).

## God of the Impossible (cont.)

55. He judged the people with fire because they complained (11:1,2).
56. He provided quail for Israel for a whole month until they loathed it (11:18-20,31-33).
57. He sent a plague on those who had yielded to their cravings (11:33).
58. He struck Miriam with leprosy for speaking against Moses (12:1,10).
59. He could give Israel victory over impossible odds (13:28-30; 14:6-9).
60. He made the entire nation wander for 40 years in the wilderness (14:32-35 with 26:64,65).
61. He judged the ten spies with a deadly plague (14:37).
62. He caused the ground to split open to swallow up Korah, Dathan, Abiram and On, and fire fell and consumed the 250 men with them (16:31-35), then plagued Israel for their murmuring (16:45-50).
63. He made Aaron's rod bud, blossom and bear fruit overnight (17:7-9).
64. He brought about the defeat of the Canaanites (21:1-3).
65. He provided healing for the people from snakebites if they looked on the brazen serpent (21:9).
66. He delivered Sihon and Og into Israel's hands (21:34,35).
67. He overruled Balaam's attempts to curse Israel (chs.22-24).

**＊＊＊＊**

## Census of Israel

| Num.1 – Just out of Egypt | | Num.26 – Just before entering Canaan | | |
|---|---|---|---|---|
| Tribe | Total | Total | | Difference |
| Reuben | 46,500 | 43,730 | - | 2,770 |
| Simeon | 59,300 | 22,200 | - | 37,100 |
| Gad | 45,650 | 40,500 | - | 5,150 |

(Continued next page)

| Num.1 – Just out of Egypt | | Num.26 – Just before entering Canaan | | |
|---|---|---|---|---|
| Tribe | Total | Total | | Difference |
| Judah | 74,600 | 76,500 | + | 1,900 |
| Issachar | 54,400 | 64,300 | + | 9,900 |
| Zebulun | 57,400 | 60,500 | + | 3,100 |
| Ephraim | 40,500 | 32,500 | - | 8,000 |
| Manasseh | 32,200 | 52,700 | + | 20,500 |
| Benjamin | 35,400 | 45,600 | + | 10,200 |
| Dan | 62,700 | 64,400 | + | 1,700 |
| Asher | 41,500 | 53,400 | + | 11,900 |
| Naphtali | 53,400 | 45,500 | - | 7,900 |
| | 603,550 | 601,730 | - | 1,820 |
| + Levi | 22,273 | 23,000 | + | 727 |
| | 625,823 | 624,730 | - | 1,093 |

Altogether, Israel lost 61,020 people and gained back 59,927—a net loss of 1,093 people.

**Chs.2,10**  Location of the tribes around the Tabernacle (ch.2) and order of march (**ch.10**: #1-7 on the diagram below):
1. Priests with the Ark,
2. Judah's camp,
3. Gershom and Merari with the Tabernacle,
4. Reuben's camp,
5. Kohath with the Tabernacle furnishings/articles,
6. Ephraim's camp, and
7. Dan's camp as the rear guard.
   (See diagram on page 63.)

**Q. Ch.2** What was the actual camp arrangement of the Israelites?
**A.** From the description here and in Revelation 21:12,13 (general
   mention), it's very difficult to tell for sure.   Three possible
explanations:
   1. A clockwise listing? [Would make the smoothest procession]
   2. Or N/S, E/W listing (per N.I.V. note)?
      [*East*, n/s: JUDAH, Issachar, Zebulun;
      *South*, e/w: REUBEN, Simeon, Gad;
      *West*, s/n: EPHRAIM, Manasseh, Benjamin;
      *North*, e/w: Naphtali, Asher, DAN.]

3. Or the Leading Tribe in the middle with the others flanking them (per E.S.V. note)?

[*East*, n/s: Issachar JUDAH Zebulun; *South*, e/w: Gad RUBEN Simeon; *West*, n/s: Benjamin EPHRAIM Manasseh; *North*, e/w: Asher, DAN, Naphtali.] But that would make far too broad a procession to go through wilderness conditions.

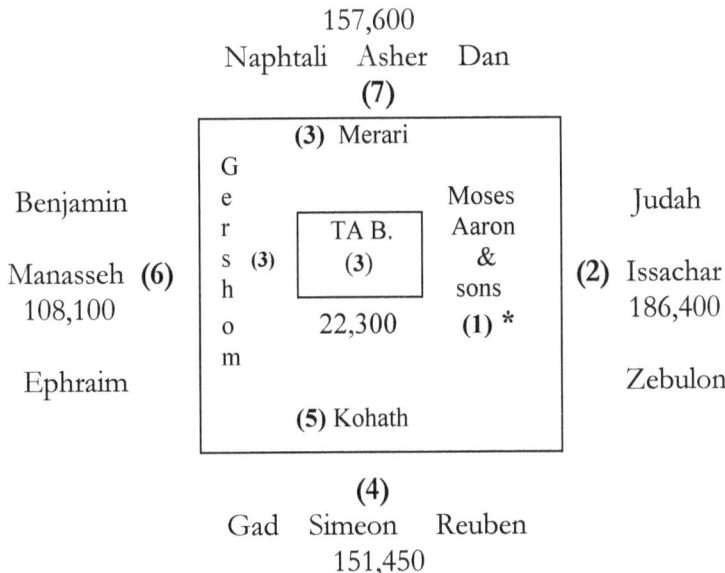

157,600

Naphtali   Asher   Dan

(7)

**(3)** Merari

G
e      Moses
r   TA B.   Aaron
s **(3)**  **(3)**   &
h      sons
o   22,300   **(1)** *
m

Benjamin      Judah

Manasseh **(6)**      **(2)** Issachar
108,100      186,400

Ephraim      Zebulon

**(5)** Kohath

**(4)**

Gad   Simeon   Reuben

151,450

*The number indicates listed order of march when breaking camp.

It would be logical and make for the smoothest departure and arrival (as above) for Reuben and Dan to be on the east of their encampment since they would set out first before the others. As for the east and west encampments, Judah and Ephraim could be in any position with the other two tribes following in their listed order. But in the end... (?)

**2:9** The N.I.V. note shows each group of three tribes marching out three abreast, however, knowing the terrain through which they traveled , that would be impossible. At best they had to march "single file," each tribe moving ahead of the following one, and all pretty well strung out.

**Q. 3:22,28,34** The number of Levites totals 22,300, not 22,000. So the additional 273 firstborn of Israel should have been covered with an excess of 27 left over. Yet the calculations used considered the 273 in excess of the number of Levites. (?)

**A.** Some MSS on 3:28 read 8,300 rather than 8,600. Thus a copyist error could be allowed. 8,300 is supported by the rest of the context.

**Q. 4:3** Why was the age for Levites beginning their service at the Tabernacle set at 30 here, but in Numbers 8:24 set at 25.

**A.** Perhaps, per N.I.V. note, the first five years were something of an apprenticeship

...or...

According to a <u>U.S. News & World Report</u> article on the development of the teenage brain ("Inside the Teen Brain," August 9, 1999, pp.44-54), the decision-making functions of the teenage brain are not yet fully developed. Hence the often erratic behavior of teens, conflicting decisions and unnecessary risk-taking. So the Lord perhaps set their age of service to begin at the point where they could begin making more mature decisions.

**Q. 4:5-14** Is there any significance in the coverings for the Tabernacle furniture?

| Furniture | Coverings |
|---|---|
| Ark of the Covenant | the Veil, badger skins, blue cloth |
| Table of Showbread | blue cloth, scarlet cloth, badger skins |
| Lampstand | blue cloth, badger skins |
| Golden Altar | blue cloth, badger skins |
| Utensils of service | blue cloth, badger skins |
| Altar of Sacrifice | purple cloth, badger skins |

**A.**

1. <u>Functional purposes</u>:
   Blue cloth covering the Ark easily distinguished from everything else.
   Badger skins protected the furniture from the elements (sun, rain?).

2. <u>Symbolic meaning</u> [educated guesses at this point]:

Blue   =  Heaven (these items were a pattern of what is in Heaven—cf. Heb.8:5), so all covered with blue cloth.

Purple =  royalty [but how is this color associated with the Altar of Sacrifice? Possibly reminding us that the King of kings died in our place?]

Scarlet = blood [but what connection does this have with the bread? The bread symbolized life — Christ said that he was the Bread of Life (Jn.6:35)—and blood *is* the life of living creatures (Gen.9:4); so perhaps the two come together in this case as symbolizing life].

Brown/Black (badger skins) = perhaps nothing more than a covering [or, symbolizing God's protection—?].

**4:4,15,20** See 2 Samuel 6:3-7 where Uzzah died touching the Ark. If the Levites would die for just going in to look at it, how much more Uzzah for grabbing hold of it! The Tabernacle was "off limits" even for the Levites. They could not look at nor touch its articles of furniture lest they die. Only the priests could do that.

This illustrated how totally separated Israel was from God—that only those who were holy could enter his presence.

Thus only Christ, our High Priest, could enter the presence of God to minister on our behalf. If we were to look on or touch heavenly things, we would die because those things are holy. God told Moses that anyone seeing his face would die.

Holiness consumes what is not holy (cf. Heb.12:10,14,29). So we cannot presume to enter God's presence—but must be separated from him. However, Christ, at his death, tore down the curtain separating us from God (Matt.27:51), thus opening the way for us to approach God directly. Through him we have been made a kingdom of priests to God (Rev.5:10). So now we can look upon and touch what is holy without fear of death. It is now our privilege to come directly into God's presence and minister on the behalf of others through prayer and meeting their needs.

**5:1-4** The unclean have to be expelled from the camp so as not to defile it. Another object lesson in the need for holiness among God's people in his presence; without blemish.

**5:6**  When we wrong others, we are unfaithful to the Lord! (cf. Matt.25:40 with Acts 9:1-4).

**5:5-9**  Restitution for wrongs done.  If restitution cannot be made to that person or any of his relatives, it must be made to the Lord, for the conscience still needs to be cleared from past wrongs.

**6:24-26**  I can see, whether intended or not, how the priestly blessing could reflect the Trinity:

"The LORD ...
|  |  |
|---|---|
| bless you and keep you | = the Father (Jn.17:11) |
| make his face to shine upon you and be gracious to you | = the Son (Jn.1:14) |
| turn his face toward you and give you peace" | = the Holy Spirit (Rom.8:6) |

**8:14**  The Levites were not counted among the 12 tribes of Israel (see 1:49,50), but were separated from them as God's special possession. Likewise the Church is not of Israel, but has been made a special possession of God, and, like the Levites, a kingdom of priests to serve him (1 Pet.2:9; see also Num.18:20 with Jn.17:14; 15:19).

**Q.** Is the statement above on 8:14 a valid comparison?
**A.** I believe that it is.

**10:31** (cf.9:15-23)  Moses asked his brother-in-law, Hobab, to go with Israel and be their eyes in the desert, telling them where they should camp.

**Q.** But what about the Cloud?  Why did they need Hobab when the LORD was so obviously directing them?
**A.** I've always assumed that when the Cloud lifted, it always went before  the Israelites to lead them.  If this were so, then Moses' request to Hobab makes no sense whatever, and indicates a lack of faith in God to lead them.  That cannot be said of Moses!

However, if the Cloud merely lifted, indicating the time to move on (9:21,22), then overspreading the Israelites for shade on the journey (10:34), where were they to go?  Enter Hobab who knew the area.

**Q.** But, 9:17 indicates a more directive role for the Cloud than just lifting up and overspreading the Israelites for shade. When the Cloud descended, that indicated where they were to camp.

**A.** The KJV (10:31) may help here where it says not "<u>Where</u> we should camp" but "<u>how</u> we are to camp in that place." This would indicate Hobab's role as more of a camping facilitator than a guide, (i.e., "When the Cloud descends) <u>how</u> is the best way to camp in that place?" That would be a very practical consideration for Moses in enlisting Hobab's desert expertise, thus perhaps resolving the question of the "guidance" issue.

**Q. 11:4,34** Was this the Lord's way of cleansing the Israelite community from the non-Israelites since they would only be a continual source of sin and stumbling to Israel?

**A.** I believe so. Israel had enough problems of its own in relation to God without being compounded by Egyptian idol-worshippers and hangers-on who had no faith and no interest in the God of Abraham, Isaac and Jacob. They had no place nor part in what God was doing with Israel.

**Q. 11:21,22** Why didn't the Israelites occasionally slaughter an animal to eat meat and so bring some variety into their diet? The LORD didn't tell them they had to eat manna only.

**A.** Perhaps they did, but that would only give them meat on rare occasions, given the lengthy life-cycle of most animals, the number of people in the desert (2 to 3 million) and the "rabble" who wanted it daily (indicated by vs.19,20).

**11:28** Joshua was probably a teenager when Israel came out of Egypt.

**12:1** "Talk" is in the feminine singular indicating that Miriam led in this criticism, and thus was judged (vs.10).

**Q. 13:4-15** Why wasn't anyone chosen from the tribe of Levi as a spy?
**A.** Because the Levites weren't going to inherit any of the land. The LORD was their inheritance.

**13:31-14:4** An exaggerated, bad report led the people to the exaggerated and bad conclusion that the Lord had only brought them to this land to destroy them. This response is what we'd expect from hearts of unbelief (cf. Heb.4:2).

**14:11**  Proof that miracles will not produce faith in hearts of unbelief (cf. Rom.10:17).

**14:13-19**  Moses was far more concerned for the LORD's name than for his own (see also Ex.32:9-13).  This is a strong argument against Replacement Theology which substitutes the Church for Israel saying that the Jews failed, so God replaced them with the Church.  God didn't choose Israel based upon what they did or did not do; he chose them because *he wanted to*, keeps them because *he purposed to*, and will bring them through to their appointed destiny because *he promised to* (cf. Rom.11:29).  Otherwise, some would say, "He wasn't able to bring them through because of their unbelief and disobedience, so chose the Church instead."  In that case, everything depends upon us rather than him, and that flies in the face of Romans 9:11,16; Ephesians 1:11 and other such verses.  What's more, if God substituted the Church for Israel because of their unbelief and disobedience, what will keep him from substituting something else for the Church if we are unfaithful?

**14:39-45**  How like little children the Israelites were: when caught in their sin and their punishment declared, they suddenly had a "change of heart" and decided to obey, but by then it was too late.  Now obeying the first command meant disobeying the second, which got them into even more trouble!

**16:1 with 1 Chr.6:2**  Korah was Moses' cousin.  Perhaps this close association plus his special responsibilities regarding the Tabernacle furniture gave rise to jealousy of Moses' position (vs.8-10).  A very similar response to that found in Isaiah 14:12-15 regarding Lucifer, jealous of God's position and rebelling in order to obtain it for himself.  He likewise failed (cf. Num.16:31-33).  As Lucifer took others with him, so did Korah.

**16:1-17:12**  Israel didn't want Moses, didn't want Aaron and didn't want the Lord.  They would rather return to slavery in Egypt than yield to God's standard of holiness.  Their unbelief and spirit of rebellion is flagrant.  No wonder God sought to destroy them completely four times already (see Ex.32:9,10; Num.14:11,12; 16:20,21, 41-45).

**16:22**  The Lord knew the sin was far more wide-spread than this (see vs.41-49).

**16:49** Rather than digging individual or even mass graves for burying these 14,700 dead, the Israelites probably located a gully or ravine large enough to hold them all, then covered them with rocks. It could well be that they cremated the bodies first before covering them over with rocks (cf. Josh.7:25,26), thus greatly decreasing the area needing to be covered.

**17:12** The Israelites' statement reveals the spirit of rebellion against the consistency and inflexibility of God's holiness; frustration with the standard of holiness he demands.

**20:1-11** With grief over Miriam's death and 40 years of the people's incessant complaining, we can understand Moses' response at Kadesh when, in anger, he struck the rock. He was at a real emotional low point. Satan hits us when we're weak, and Moses was no exception. However, God still held him accountable for what he did (Deut.32:50-51). When we're "down," we need to be extra alert and wary of temptation, lest we also fall.

## 21:5   GOD "FORCING" ISRAEL OUT OF EGYPT

**Q.** Why did God "force" Israel out of Egypt, into the desert and into his ways of holiness when they were basically a nation of unbelievers? This is a sure recipe for failure (as evidenced above) and he knew that. Wasn't this grossly unfair to them? (See also the notes on Lev.15:31 in regard to this question.)
**A.** No, not in terms of what God wanted to do for them and through them   (see Rom.11:15,25-29; Heb.8:10-12). Also, he was dealing with Israel in faithfulness to his promises to Abraham (Gen.12:1-3; 15:13-16; Deut.7: 7,8 where Moses confirms this). But when the time came for their deliverance, only a remnant still remembered him (Rom.9:27-29) and worshipped him; the rest had gone off into idolatry, worshipping the gods of Egypt (Josh.24:14). So God <u>had</u> to deal with Israel in terms of his promises to Abraham. These were his chosen people through whom the Messiah was to come, so he <u>had</u> to prepare them for this role, and that meant delivering them from Egypt whether or not they wanted to be, making them into a nation regardless of their desire to return to slavery, and making them holy even though they earnestly desired the old life of sin.

Thought:

Moses resisted God's call, but finally yielded and was greatly used.

Pharaoh resisted God's call and was destroyed in his rebellion.

Israel resisted God's call and has greatly suffered for it—even until today. Where miracles (Num.14:11) and discipline (Num.16: 41) did not work, the outpouring of his Spirit will (Joel 2:28-32). Israel will be sovereignly changed to become a blessing to the nations as God has intended them to be all along (Rom.11:15).

Since it is God's choice as to when and how he works with mankind, we have to leave the timing and methods to his discretion. With Moses, it was a matter of a day; with Pharaoh, weeks; with us, years; with Israel, several millennia. In the end, we will see his wisdom in it all.

**21:8,9** The bronze serpent had typological significance (see Jn.3: 14,15), yet the Israelites worshipped it until the reign of Hezekiah (see 2 Kings 18:4)!

**21:10ff** The list of places where they camped. Nothing to write about—no more complaining—until the war with Sihon and Og and the situation with the Moabites and Balaam. The issue of idolatry was still of vital concern (25:1-18).

**Q. 22:5** He "sent...to Balaam...at Pethor, which is near the River in the land of his kindred." Whose kindred? Balaam's or Balak's?
**A.** The context would seem to indicate Balak. His kindred probably originated from the Pethor area. That connection would account for his knowledge of Balaam.

**26:12-14,62** Perhaps because of Jacob's "curse" on Simeon and Levi when he "blessed" them (Gen.49:5-7), they not only were scattered among the tribes of Israel but also became the smallest of the tribes: Simeon—22,200 (Num.26:14); and Levi—23,000 (Num.26:62). Yet it is also interesting to see how God used the scattering of Levi among the tribes to insure the presence of his ministers everywhere to teach Israel the Law of God, etc. If the Levites had been centered in one place, then God's witness among the Israelites would have been severely restricted.

**31:49** Probably the only time in Israel's history that this happened.

**33:5-49** I suspect that were we to know the Hebrew meanings of these names, they might throw some light on other unknown details of Israel's experiences in the desert.

### Personal History of Miriam, Aaron and Moses
### (Num.33:38 with Ex.7:7)

Miriam probably 7 or 8 (Aaron 3) when Moses was born (old enough to watch the baby and talk intelligently to Pharaoh's daughter).

Aaron  43 when Moses (40) fled Egypt (Miriam~48).
83 when he and Moses (80) appeared before Pharaoh (Miriam ~ 88).
123 (Moses 120) when Miriam (~128) died (1$^{st}$ mo. of the 40$^{th}$ yr.—Num.20:1).
123 when Moses (120) struck the rock at Kadesh, and where Miriam died (Num.20:2-11).
123 when he died 4 mo. later (5$^{th}$ mo. of the 40$^{th}$ yr.— Num.33:38,39).

Moses 120 when he died (Deut.34:7), probably in the 11$^{th}$ month of the 40$^{th}$ year (Deut.1:3).

[**NOTE:** All three died in the 40$^{th}$ year. ]

**Q. 35:4,5** There seems to be two different measurements for the Levites' pasturelands outside their towns. (?)
**A.** Possibly: verse 4 deals with the land given to the Levites; verse 5 to the town. If there were others from the local tribe also living in the towns where the Levites were appointed, then their pasture areas would extend 1500 feet beyond the Levites' areas. This would be pictured as the town in the inner circle, the Levites' pastureland as the middle circle, and the town's pastureland as the outer circle. If these towns were given solely to the Levites, then these verses make absolutely no sense.

That others also lived in the cities given to the Levites is clear from Scripture. Consider Caleb, from Judah who conquered and lived in Hebron (Josh.14:6,14; 15:13-19), a city of refuge (Josh.20:7) and given to the Levites (Josh.21:10-13). According to the N.I.V. notes on

Joshua 21:11, "The priests and Levites were to be given space in their assigned cities along with other inhabitants."

**Q. 35:25** Why must the slayer stay in the city of refuge until the death of the High Priest?

**A.** Perhaps to allow time for the avenger to cool off and have his grief settled. Yet, technically, if the slayer ran to a city of refuge and was judged innocent, if that very day the High Priest died, he would be free to return to his own property. So something more than just a cooling off period is involved here. The death of the High Priest becomes, for whatever reason, a general amnesty.

**Q.** But what does the death of the High Priest symbolize to make this general amnesty possible?

**A.** Verse 33 gives us a clue. Bloodshed pollutes the land and demands the blood of the one who shed it. Even if a person is not guilty of murder, the land is still polluted and must be cleansed. The High Priest represents all the people before God, thus also represents the innocent slayer. God graciously commuted the slayer's death sentence to the High Priest, so that when he died, he died as the slayer's substitute, thus cleansing the land and freeing the slayer from all consequences of his situation.

This "substitution" reflects what Christ, our High Priest, did for us on the cross, but with one exception: we were guilty!

**36:6** "They may marry anyone they please" (cf. 1 Cor.7:39) with certain restrictions: here only within their tribe (in 1 Corinthians, only in the Lord). So the idea that God has "that special one" chosen just for us may not be that "provable" from Scripture. We have the freedom to choose whomever we want to marry within the restrictions stated.

## God of the Impossible (cont.):

68. He provided completely for Israel 40 years in the wilderness so that they lacked nothing (2.5-3 million people!—2:7).
69. He took away the power of giants so that they were beaten by normal-sized men (2:20-23).
70. He hardens or softens men's hearts as he wills (2:30).
71. He kept Israel's clothing from wearing out (in 40 years—8:4)!
72. He gave Israel rest from her enemies (12:10).

**\* \* \* \***

**Q. 1:22** Why did the people ask for spies when they had the Cloud of God's presence right there to guide them, as well as the priests with the Ark? (Why do <u>we</u> so often resort to worldly methods when we have the Word of God to direct our efforts?)
**A.** It was a lack of faith, an unwillingness to step out into the "unknown" (i.e., that which departs from human wisdom—Deut.1:26-28).

**Principle:** If we <u>knew</u> what was ahead, we'd often take steps to avoid it. Moving ahead by faith, without knowing the future, gives God space and opportunity to work in ways that will both amaze us and strengthen our faith in him (cf. Deut.2:25). So it's a good thing we can't send "spies" into our future!

**1:29-32** Even miracles will not convince people of God's sovereignty where there is no faith. Miracles will not inspire faith where there is no heart nor will to believe.

**2:25** How Israel <u>would</u> have won had they believed God 40 years earlier (cf.1:26-28)!

**3:11** If Og's bed was 13 feet long and six feet wide, he was a <u>big</u> <u>man</u>, perhaps 11 or 12 feet tall! No wonder the spies "felt like grasshoppers" before the Canaanites (Num.13:32,33). Yet if people without faith could beat them (2:20-23), God's people <u>in</u> <u>faith</u> would surely win—and did (3:5,6).

**4:6** Following God's laws and demonstrating his wisdom would draw all nations to him, just as a lamp shining in a dark place will draw myriad of night insects. His plan was not for them to go forth and evangelize, but to be a beacon in the darkness. As a nation, this could be done effectively. But in this age of Grace, there is no nation to do this. So scattered believers across the world are commanded to "go into all the world and preach the Gospel to everyone" (Mk.16:15).

**4:9** In light of Judges 2:10, Israel failed to do this.

**5:22** "These are the commandments the LORD proclaimed in a loud voice to your whole assembly there on the mountain." But what the people heard was thunder and a loud trumpet (Ex.20:18; see also Ex.19:19 and Acts 22:9).

**7:6,7** with **1 Cor.1:26-29** God generally and consistently wants to use the weak and non-influential to accomplish his purposes so that it is clear that the work was accomplished by his power, not theirs.

**7:25,26** A stern warning about bringing idols or even parts of idols [including fetishes] into one's house. Don't do it! Why? Because they are detestable to God and you will inevitably suffer the consequences.

I know of a missionary who took some fetishes from a fetish-burning to show his supporting churches what the people use in the worship of their gods and the performing of black magic. Almost immediately, his family began suffering such sickness and dysfunctional problems that they had to leave the field. Their situation continued on in the States until, sometime later under counseling, he recalled the beginning of these problems: the day he brought the fetishes into his home. He immediately destroyed them, and his family life returned to normal.

I once read an energetic and lengthy article by a missions-related leader who claimed that the idols are only objects with no latent power within them to do good or bad. The power lies in the demon <u>behind</u> them and the <u>belief</u> of the worshipper in that power. Thus those who <u>don't</u> <u>believe</u> in that power won't be affected. So far so good. But according to these verses, I believe he missed the final point. It's not the power of these inanimate objects that bring on problems, but the fact that they are detestable to our holy God. It's sort of like dumping your garbage on the Communion Table to show the congregation the refuse from the things you eat. Everyone's revulsion would be evident. God feels that revulsion even more strongly toward idols and fetishes used in grossly wicked ways in worshipping other gods and/or Satan himself. And if we bring them into our homes, God <u>has</u> to turn away from them in disgust, and in his turning, we are opened to the powers of darkness to do whatever they want with us—still, of course, limited by God's sovereignty and love for us. The resulting troubles are his way of disciplining us to get rid of what is defiling our relationship with him. He can no longer bless us as long as these detestable items are in our possession.

**8:2** Sometimes God takes us through hard experiences in order to reveal to us what is actually in our hearts (as he did with Abraham and Isaac—Gen.22). When things are going well, we usually think we're pretty good and that God is blessing us because it's what we deserve. Drop shoe #2 and that kind of theology drops with it. Habakkuk had his theology straight (Hab.3:17,18); so did Shadrach, Meshach and Abednego (Dan.3:17,18). God also said that his blessings to Israel were <u>not</u> based upon their goodness or being deserving of them, but to accomplish his purposes only (cf. Deut.8: 17,18; 9:4-6).

**11:18-20** One gross failing of the majority of Christian parents is not paying attention to the principles found in these verses:
1. making God's Word personal and practical in their lives (being an example);
2. freely talking about God and his Word to their children, anytime, anywhere (teaching);
3. framing God's Word here and there throughout the house for all to see (reinforcement).

The Church would be in for some fantastic changes if its families would follow these verses.

**12:13,14** The Lord takes a dim view of neglecting his house to worship in the field." Hebrews 10:25 is the N.T. counterpart to this passage.

**13:1-4** There was absolutely no reason for the Israelites to be deceived—ever, as long as they heeded and obeyed God's Word. Note in verses 2 and 3 that the fulfilling of the miraculous sign or wonder was <u>God's</u> doing, not the false prophet's.

**13:10,11** Initial swift judgment (suitable to the crime) <u>does</u> have a deterring effect in spite of what the criminologists and politicians say. If it didn't, God wouldn't have said this.

> **Deut.17:19,20** the king,       ⎤ were promised blessing and
> **Josh.1:8** the army commander, ⎬ success *if* they meditated on
> **Psalm 1:1** and everyone else     ⎦ God's Word.

**18:14-19** Key passage authenticating who Christ was (is—see Jn.8:28, 38).

**18:20** The Scriptural basis for the Pharisees' accusation against Christ. However, they knew better, but did not want to admit it (see Matt. 27:18 and Jn.11:45-53).

**19:21** This is a merciful and just provision considering the revenge mentality of the culture. Revenge often, if not always, exceeds the offense.

**Q. 22:16-21** What is this proof offered by the parents to prove their
daughter's virginity? Whatever was done had to have been done <u>before</u> the wedding night since the "proof" of her virginity was still in her parents' hands. They had to have been present whenever this particular rite/ ceremony was performed.

A girl who "lost her virginity" through promiscuity/prostitution "lost the proof" of her virginity in the process, thus her parents would have nothing to show on her behalf.

The question then is: "Just what <u>is</u> this that the girl loses in promiscuity that she retains if she waits for the 'rite' [assumed] in her parents' home?"

**A.** Was it perhaps a ritual cutting or removal of the hymen membrane
(which causes minor bleeding—hence blood on the cloth) in preparation for her wedding night? Would the removed membrane also be kept in the cloth as proof against any charges? This would seem reasonable, since a promiscuous girl would lose her virginity outside the home, and thus the necessary "proof" of her virginity would not be available.

**22:30** This command seems ludicrous to us today, but in that time it was not unusual for a much older man to take a young wife in addition to, or to replace his first wife. Meanwhile, the husband dies, leaving his young wife free to remarry. If he was still living, the term "marry" would not be used here (cf. 1 Cor.5:1 where obviously the father was still living). The man's son by another wife sees this "young thing," falls in love with her and wants to marry her. However, marrying her "dishonors his father's bed" since marriage within the family was strictly forbidden (Lev.18:8). [See also Amos 2:7 re: father and son going in to the same woman to have sexual relations.]

**23:18** The LORD refuses to profit from money gained through sinful practices. Before a holy God, that money is defiled, therefore of no use to him; he detests it!

**23:24,25** Local "restaurant" but no "doggie bags"!

**Q. 25:2,3** What is the significance of the number 40?
**A.** Some say that it indicates a special "testing" which can be under-
stood in most examples of "40" that we see in Scripture. But these verses use the number 40 as an indication of <u>completion</u> of a punishment. The whipping was <u>complete</u> at 40 lashes; Israel's wandering in the wilderness was <u>complete</u> at the end of 40 years; the spies' mission was <u>complete</u> at the end of 40 days, as were also Moses' two major trips up Sinai; the flood rains <u>completed</u> their purpose at the end of 40 days and 40 nights. So I see the idea of *completion* as a simpler explanation of 40 than the idea of *testing* which demands one, two or three meanings in order to apply each occurrence. I don't think this is an overly critical issue, but worthy of some thought anyway.

**Q. 29:4** God had not given Israel the ability to believe, yet ran them through the whole covenant process anyway (cf. vs.9-15). Why?
**A.** Here he is dealing with them (and their descendants—vs.14,15) as a nation with the whole span of future historical time before him. So their present state of unbelief did not alter God's future purposes for Israel.

**29:4** Really an unresolvable dilemma. In spite of signs, wonders, miracles and massive provisions over 40 years, Israel *still* did not, could not believe because God had not given them faith! Yet they still were held accountable for what God did among them.

Only God, in his eternal counsel, knows how this all works together with his holiness, justice and love. Here we must rest upon who we know God is, trust him that he will always do what is just and right, and leave the imponderables with him (cf. Deut.32:4).

Verse 29 hints at this problem where Moses says that the secret things belong to God. There will come a time when the Lord will open the hearts of his people so that they can respond to him in faith (Deut.30:6; Rom.11: 25-27).

**29:4; 30:6; Eph.2:8** God wouldn't give us the gift of faith unless he intended to save us! This forms another solid basis for our assurance of salvation. He's not going to back out on what he intends to do (cf. Rom.11: 29).

**32:28,29** cp. with **Deut.29:4** They would be understanding and discerning if God gave them a mind to understand, eyes to see and ears to hear; but he didn't, so they couldn't. Man, left to himself without God's divine intervention, would never seek God (cf. Rom. 3:10-12). Faith is a gift from God to enable us to believe (Eph.2:8, 9).

**Q.** If he so yearns for them to understand and follow him, then why doesn't he give them the faith to do it?

**A.** Part of the answer:

**Rom.9:22-24** God must reveal his full character to mankind. Since all people have sinned and alienated themselves from him (Rom.3:23), only his wrath and power in judgment would be shown upon them. Yet he wanted also to demonstrate his glory and mercy to them. So, for reasons known only to him, from among condemned mankind, he chose those whom he would save, giving them the gift of faith and the ability to follow and obey him.

From creation, he wanted fellowship with mankind. But that fellowship was with risk. He gave them the right to choose to obey him or reject him. They chose to reject him and go their own way.

So the whole business of salvation and election is God bringing back to himself that portion of mankind he has chosen to save so that all of them, in total, would not be condemned to an eternity in Hell.

**32:47** We live by eating but a person's life is prolonged by obeying the Word of God (cf. Matt.4:4).

**Ch.33** Moses' blessings on Israel compared with Jacob's in Gen.49.

## Comparison of Jacob's and Moses' Blessings

| Genesis 49 | | Deuteronomy 33 | |
|---|---|---|---|
| vs.3,4 | Reuben | vs.6 | Reuben |
| | Unstable as water | | Let him live and not die |
| | He no longer will excel | | Let his men be few |
| | | | |
| vs.5 | Simeon and Levi | vs.8 | Levi |
| | Cursed be their anger and violence | | His the Thummim and Urim and care of the Tabernacle; teachers of the Law; offer sacrifices |
| | I will scatter them in Israel | | |
| | | | |
| vs.8-12 | Judah | vs.7 | Judah |
| | Praise from his brothers | | He defends his cause |
| | Victory | | He defends his cause |
| | Lion-like ruler; Settled and prosperous | | Help against his foes |
| | | | |
| vs.13 | Zebulon | vs.18,19 | Zebulon |
| | Live by the seashore | | Rejoice in your going out [sea trade?] |
| | Become a haven for ships | | |
| | Border toward Sidon | | |

**Q.** [Yet maps show Zebulun's border at least 10 miles from the sea! Something is wrong here. Or is this possibly looking forward to the Millennium?]

**A.** In the Millennium, every tribe's territory will border on the Mediterranean Sea. So evidently this blessing looks forward to that time (cf. Ezek.48:26).

| | | | |
|---|---|---|---|
| vs.14,15 | Issachar | vs.18,19 | Issachar |
| | Donkey lying down between saddle bags | | Tent-dweller |
| | Bend his shoulder to the burden | | Offering sacrifices of righteousness on the mountain |
| | Submit to forced labor | | Feast on fish and treasures of the sand |

| Genesis 49 | Deuteronomy 33 |
|---|---|
| vs.16 <u>Dan</u><br>Provide justice for his people<br>Roadside serpent—treacherous | vs.22 <u>Dan</u><br>Like a lion's cub springing<br>out of Bashan |
| vs.19 <u>Gad</u><br>Attacked by raiders<br>He counter-attacks | vs.20,21 <u>Gad</u><br>Lives like a lion;<br>Best land (for livestock);<br>Carried out the LORD'S<br>righteous will and his<br>judgments re: Israel. |
| vs.20 <u>Asher</u><br>Rich food<br>Provide delicacies fit<br>for a king | vs.24,25 <u>Asher</u><br>Favored by his brothers<br>Most beloved<br>Bathe his feet in oil<br>Gate bolts of iron and<br>bronze<br>Your strength will equal<br>your days |
| vs.21 <u>Naphtali</u><br>A doe set free that bears<br>beautiful fawns | vs.23 <u>Naphtali</u><br>Abounding with the favor<br>of the LORD<br>Full of the LORD'S bless-<br>ing<br>Inherit southward to the<br>lake |
| vs.22-26 <u>Joseph</u><br>Fruitful<br>Helped by God<br>Universal blessing<br>Prince among his brothers | vs.13-17 <u>Joseph</u><br>Fruitful<br>God's favor<br>Universal blessing<br>Prince among his brothers<br>Majestic like a firstborn<br>bull [with 2 horns:<br>Ephraim and Manasseh] |
| vs.27 <u>Benjamin</u><br>Ravenous wolf | vs.12 <u>Benjamin</u><br>Beloved of the LORD |

| Genesis 49 | Deuteronomy 33 |
|---|---|
| vs.27 Benjamin | vs.12 Benjamin (cont.) |
| Morning devours prey | --- |
| Evening divides plunder | |

**Q.** Why is Simeon not mentioned in Moses' blessings?

**A.** Possibly because Simeon was incorporated into Judah and thus partook of Judah's blessings (?). Or did he forfeit his blessing because of his cruelty (in the Dinah affair) and possibly masterminding the murder of Joseph (which never took place). Simeon was the one Joseph jailed while his brothers went back to Jacob—so there had to be a reason for that action.

**34:1-3** A counter-clockwise panorama. Either Mt. Nebo is a very high mountain (elevation around 3,000 feet) or else God gave Moses unusual visual acuity in order to see the length and breadth of the entire land.

## God of the Impossible (cont.):

73. He brought terror to the hearts of Israel's enemies (2:9-11,24).
74. He dried up the Jordan River (3:13-4:1,18).
75. He gave Jericho into Israel's hands (6:12-16,20,21).
76. He spared Rahab's house (built on the wall—so evidently that part of the wall didn't fall—6:22,23).
77. He caused the lot to fall on Achan who sinned (7:18-21).
78. He promised victory beforehand (10:8).
79. He cast down large hail stones upon the Amorite army killing more than Israel did (10:10,11).
80. He caused the sun and moon to stop—increasing daylight hours so that Israel could continue fighting the Amorites (10:12,13).
81. He promised victory and fulfilled it (11:6-8).
82. He hardened the hearts of those he intended to destroy (11:20).
83. He gave Caleb the same strength at 85 as he had at 40 (14:10,11).
84. He fulfilled his promise to Israel, giving them the land, rest (peace), and victory (when they chose to fight—see 21:43-45; 23:14).

**\* \* \* \***

**1:3** "The Law of Appropriation": God gives, but we must take. If we "mark time," we won't get a thing. We must march forward.

**1:9** "Do not be terrified [by those who oppose you]; do not be discouraged [by the problems you will face], for the LORD your God will be with you wherever you go." This boils down to a matter of <u>faith</u>. Which is bigger, God or our circumstances? If God is bigger, then we will be strong and courageous; if our circumstances are bigger, we will be terrified and discouraged.

**2:9-11** Even after 40 years, the fear of Israel's God was still active in the hearts of the Canaanites! This was 40 years of grace for them before judgment fell. Forty years to seek the God of Israel and repent of their sins. But it seems that only Rahab had a heart to seek him and believe in him. Everyone else feared, but kept to their own gods.

**Q. 2:21** Why did Rahab immediately tie the scarlet cord in the window? It would still be over two weeks before the Israelite army approached Jericho:

| | | |
|---|---|---|
| Spies hid in the hills | 3 days | (2:22,23) |
| Officers prepare the camp | 3 days | (3:2) |
| Israel crosses the Jordan | 1 day | (4:19) |
| Israel circumcised | 3 days | (5:7,8) |
| Israel celebrates Passover | 1 day | (5:10) |
| Feast of Unleavened Bread | 7 days | (5:11 with Lev.23:4-8) |
| | 18 days | |

**A.** Rahab evidently tied the rope to be sure that it would <u>still</u> be there when she needed it. Otherwise someone from her family might see the cord and take it to use for something else, and it would be <u>gone</u> when it was wanted.

**Q. 5:9** What was this "reproach of Egypt" that the Lord refers to?
**A.** (From <u>The Bible Knowledge Commentary</u>) "Since the Israelites were slaves in Egypt, they did not practice circumcision until they were about to leave. No doubt the Egyptians prohibited the practice since it was reserved for their own priests and upper class citizens."

Since God's comment is in the context of circumcision, it must have more to do with that rather than other unrelated reasons found in other commentaries. Uncircumcision would be a denial of the Covenant between God and Israel, and for Israel to live in this condition would be a reproach indeed (cf. Ex.4:24,25).

**5:13-15** That this is a Theophany and not an angel (N.I.V. note) is clear from the context. Receiving worship and declaring holy ground is *not* angelic.

**5:13,14** The oft-spoken phrase, "God is on our side" is presumption, most inaccurate and trivializes God's role among mankind. It puts us a notch above him, making him our "Divine Genie" as it were. No, God is on *his own side* (Deut.9:3-6) and it is up to us to choose to be on *his side* or not (cf. Josh.7:1,10-12). Whether we win or lose is not a sign of his favor or disfavor. He is working in both situations for his own purposes and for our ultimate good (cf. Rom.8:28,29). Like Joshua, our attitude also must be to "fall facedown to the ground in reverence" (humble ourselves) and ask him, "What message does my Lord have for his servant?"

**6:2,10** The Lord told Joshua that Jericho actually belonged to the Israelites already, for he had <u>given</u> it to them. They only had to obey certain commands before they could <u>possess</u> it. Verse 10—such discipline and obedience!

## 6:12-17 THE FALL OF JERICHO

Picture the scene:

**Day 1** With alarm trumpets sounding before the approaching Israelite army, all the men of Jericho mounted the walled defenses, prepared to fight, but scared to death of the Israelite god. Suddenly, still out of bowshot range, the priests turned and the silent army took a wide detour around the city and returned to their camp. Stunned and puzzled, the Jerichoites tried to make sense of what had happened. "Maybe our gods are stronger than the Israelite god after all! Why didn't they attack? I bet they were afraid when they saw how strong our walls are."

**Day 2** A replica of Day 1. Not a sound came from the Israelite army except the blowing of the seven trumpets and the pounding of marching feet. The Jerichoites on the wall began to call and mock at the Israelites, taunting them to come and fight like men.

**Day 3** More of the same. The Jerichoites began to relax and "have fun" at Israel's expense. "This is getting bor---ing."

**Day 4** Women and children joined the men on the wall to see the spectacle and add their laughter and taunts. Some of them even waved swords and spears as the army approached...and turned aside. "They're even afraid of women and children!"

**Day 5** A party spirit develops. The "latest outing" is to mount the wall and laugh at the impotent Israeli army while eating and drinking and generally having a good time.

**Day 6** "This is getting tiresome." Most people have returned to their daily lives, wishing that that nuisance outside the walls would go away.

No harm done, but they sure are a bother!

**Day 7** "Here we go again!" ... "Huh? What's going on here?? They're coming around a second time! Hey, everybody, get up here! Something different is happening!" All the men come to enjoy the spectacle as before, but wonder why the frightened Israelis aren't returning to camp as usual. Three times around, four, five. The Jerichoites begin to have an uneasy feeling about this—something is wrong, eerily wrong! "Get your weapons!" Six and counting; seven, and the silent Israeli army stops and faces Jericho. "O.K. men, this is it. Be ready to let them have it as soon as they get into range! Our gods have beaten them; we are sure to win!"

The unearthly quiet is suddenly shattered by a new trumpet alarm; then every Israeli voice broke their six-day silence with a deafening shout, but they didn't move. Puzzled, the Jerichoites tensely wait. Suddenly, ever so slightly, the ground begins to tremble, then quickly gains motion. The men of Jericho had trouble maintaining their footing. "W-w-what's going on?!" Parts of the walls began to crumble and fall outward carrying terrified defenders to their deaths. Others scrambled to more secure areas only to find themselves being hurled down as those sections began to fall. When the dust settled, not a defender was left alive, and the Israeli army entered straight into the city to finish the work. Jericho had fallen.

**7:1,4,5,10-12** It is sobering to realize how the sin of one person can affect the whole (cf. 1 Cor.5:6 and Gal.5:9).

**7:15** Achan was a dead man if he came forward to confess his sin. So his only hope was to keep silent in case the lot-casting didn't work. But it did, and he was soon found out and judged.

**8:2** Had Achan only waited, he could have had even greater wealth than that which he had taken from Jericho—and lived to enjoy it!

**9:9-13** The Gibeonites wisely didn't mention Jericho and Ai in their litany of Israel's victories, otherwise they would have "blown their cover."

**10:11** This hail storm was a miracle in effect that the stones hit and killed only the enemy!

**Q.** Joshua, chapters 13-16,24 with Judges, chapters 1,2 are chronologically confusing.    Joshua is apparently 20 years younger than
Caleb, and his death is recorded three times (Josh. ch.24; Judg. chs.1,2)
with certain events preceding and following it in both books.  What is
going on?
**A.** Background: Putting various pieces of this puzzle together helps
give us an answer, but perhaps not the answer as more information
than that which is given in these passages is needed to put our question
to rest.

Joshua was referred to as a "young man" in Exodus 33:11, two
years before the spy episode.  Since the army service began at 20
(Num.14:29), the age Joshua would have had to be in order to go out
with the spies, he would have perhaps been 18 while at Sinai.  So the
personal histories of Joshua and Caleb might look like the following:

### Personal History of Joshua and Caleb

| Situation | Joshua | Caleb |
|---|---|---|
| At Sinai: | 18 | 38 |
| Spying out the land: | 20 | 40 (Josh.14:7) |
| Entering Canaan: | 60 | 80 |
| Caleb requests Hebron | 65 | 85 which Joshua |
| grants (14:13-15) | | |
| Joshua dies | 110 | 130 |
| Caleb takes Hebron | --- | |
| with Othniel's help | --- | 130-131 (Judg.1:1,11-15) |
| Caleb dies | --- | ??? |

This 45 year lapse from when Caleb asked for Hebron until he
finally got it doesn't make sense considering Caleb's faith, strength and
eagerness to possess his inheritance.  But Judges 1:1-15 seems clear
enough that he didn't get possession of Hebron until after Joshua's
death.

**Q.** So what is the answer to this chronological enigma?
**A.** Perhaps…
    1. In Joshua 14:13-15 Joshua gives Hebron to Caleb.  For some
reason, Caleb was unable to take possession of it at that time.  Forty-
five or 46 years later, when he was too old to fight, he enlisted the help
of Othniel to do the job.

2. It would seem, though not conclusively, that Judges 2:1-5 takes place around Joshua 9, since the Angel went up from Gilgal where Joshua had just made a covenant with the Gibeonites; and Judges 2:6-9 takes place at Josh.24:28-31 (because of the strong similarity of wording). [Yet Israel's general disobedience, in spite of renewing the Covenant (Josh.24:1-27), resulted in their inability to drive out the remaining Canaanite tribes (Josh. 15:13-19,63; 16:10; 17:12; Judg.1:19-21,27-36).]

3. Also, it seems that at least parts of Joshua were written after his death (see refs. in #2 above), if not the whole book, probably taken from Joshua's personal accounts and added to by another author. This overlapping of authorship may help account for some of the chronological ambiguities encountered in these two books. If Judges 2:1-9 is a flashback to events in Joshua 9 and 24, and also an explanation of why Israel couldn't dislodge the remaining Canaanites (Judg.1), then we can understand Judges 1 as setting the tone of the book, Judges 2 telling us why that happened, and Judges 3-21 showing us Israel's utter failure for the next 339 years from Othniel (1382 B.C.) to Saul (1043 B.C.).

**Chs.13,18  NOTE** on the inheritance of the Levites:
> **13:14** with **Deut.18:1** The offerings made by fire to the LORD are the Levites' inheritance.
> **13:33** The LORD, the God of Israel, is their inheritance.
> **18:7** The priestly service of the LORD is their inheritance.

**15:19** What good is land without water? What good is our ministry without the life-giving "water" of the Holy Spirit?

**16:10; 17:12,13 w/ Judg.1:27-35** Incomplete obedience paves the way for future defeat (Judg.2:1-3).

**20:7** Hebron, Caleb's city, was designated as a city of refuge (cf. Josh.15: 13), and given to the Levites (21:11). We read in 20:7 that "they set apart... Hebron." Obviously, Caleb offered his choice city to the Lord (totally consistent with his love for God), but still retained his "land rights" in the surrounding area (21:12 and see notes on Num. 35:4,5).

**21:4-7** It is interesting to note the location of the various clans of Levi throughout Israel:

Kohathites
 SOUTH and CENTRAL (Judah, Simeon, Benjamin, Ephraim, Dan
  and Manasseh);
 Gershom
 NORTH (Issachar, Asher, Naphtali) and NORTHEAST (Manasseh
  [Bashan]);
 Merari
 NORTH (Reuben) and SOUTHEAST (Gad and Zebulun)

**Q. 21:43-45** If God's promises to Israel were fulfilled, then why were
 so many of the Canaanites left alive to live in the land?
**A.** The Lord's promise was fulfilled on his part. Israel didn't fully appropriate it, probably for economic reasons among others.

**24:2,14,23** with **Judg.2:11,19**  Abraham came out of idolatry; Israel worshipped the gods of Egypt while there; Israel still held to their idols in spite of the first and second Commandments; then returned wholeheartedly to idol worship once in Canaan. The total ignorance of the next generation (Judg.2:10) regarding the LORD and his works shows that their parents' "obedience" to the LORD was all form and no substance. Had it really mattered to them, they would have lived it and passed it on to their children (cf. Deut.6:4-9).

**24:1-13** Summary of God's mighty working on behalf of Israel.

**Q. 24:31** Perhaps one reason that Israel so quickly went astray (Judges) is that Joshua had no designated leader to take his place. Israel
was led by a coalition of elders with no central leader to look to. Why did Joshua not disciple a leader as Moses had done with him?
**A.** With the land basically taken, the High Priest as their mediator be-
 tween them and God, and God as their King, Joshua probably
thought that everything was in order for a successful national existence. It should and would have been except for the failure of that generation to pass on to the next what God had done, etc.

## God of the Impossible (cont.):

85. He alternately strengthened Israel and her enemies in the accomplishing of his purposes (3:8-10,12-15,31; 4:2,3,6,7,14,15,23,24; 6:1).
86. He uses the weak to overcome the mighty (6:14-16; 7:7,22). Gideon was a "mighty man of valor" (6:12) not because he was one but because <u>God said he was</u> and empowered him accordingly (6:14-16, 34).
87. He sent a spirit of ill will between Abimelech and the men of Shechem (9:23,24).
88. He promised Manoah's wife, barren, a son (13:3).
89. He gave Samson great physical strength (14:6,19; 15:14; 16:3,9,12,14,28-30).
90. He provided Samson water where there was none (15:18,19).
91. He brought about the defeat of Benjamin by the other tribes after they suffered 40,000 casualties (20:28,35).

**\* \* \* \***

**1:8,21** No conflict between these verses. One half of Jerusalem was on Mt. Zion (which Judah took and destroyed); one half on Mt. Moriah (which Benjamin "took" but could not conquer). However, possession of the city was only temporary (see Judg.19:10-12).

**Q. 2:1,2** "You have not obeyed my voice" with Joshua 23:8, "Hold fast to the LORD your God, as you have done to this day." Yet why does the rest of the chapter indicate an ambivalent attitude?
**A.** Outward conformity with no inward reality.

**2:21-23** A person's (nation's) true character and faith are revealed in adversity.

### Oppressors and Judges of Israel

| Oppressor | Judge | Tribe | Years Involved |
|---|---|---|---|
| Cushan-Rishathaim, king of Aram | | | 8 years of oppression |
| | Othniel | Judah | **40 years of peace** |
| Eglon, king of Moab | | | 18 years of oppression |

## Oppressors and Judges of Israel, cont.

| Oppressor | Judge | Tribe | Years Involved |
|---|---|---|---|
| | Ehud | Benjamin | **80 years of peace** |
| Jabin, king of Canaan | | | 20 years of oppression |
| | Deborah | Ephraim | **40 years of peace** |
| Midian | | | 7 years of oppression |
| | Gideon | Manasseh | **40 years of peace** |
| | (Abimelech | Manasseh | 3 years) |
| | Tola | Issachar | **23 years of peace** |
| | Jair | Gad | **22 years of peace** |
| Philistines & Ammonites | | | 18 years of oppression |
| | Jephthah | E. Manasseh | **6 years of peace** |
| | Ibzan | Judah | **7 years of peace** |
| | Elon | Zebulun | **10 years of peace** |
| | Abdon | Ephraim | **8 years of peace** |
| Philistines | | | 40 years of oppression |
| | Samson | Dan | 20 years of struggle |
| | Samuel | Ephraim | *42 years of struggle |

[***NOTE:** Some of the years of successive judges seem to overlap (since they judged in different areas of Israel), so a strict chronology cannot be drawn up. Samuel's judgeship, for instance, began when Samson was still judging, and ended just a few years before King Saul's death. Samuel's 42 years is also an approximation. Born in 1069 B.C., received God's call at 12 (1057 B.C.—Josephus), and died a few years (?) before Saul—1015 B.C., which would have given him about a 42-year judgeship.]

**6:8** First mention of a prophet's ministry apart from Moses.

**6:14** Our strength for the task is insignificant if God is enabling us to do the job. With his call comes his enablement (vs.16,34).

**6:22** Gideon obviously didn't realize with whom he was talking until the very end.

**Q.** If this was a Theophany, why wasn't Gideon commanded to take off his shoes because of standing on holy ground (cf. Ex.3:5; Josh.5:15)?

**A.** No need as he was probably barefoot while doing his work.

**7:7** When facing a task, our number, whether many or few, is insignificant if God is enabling us to do the job (cf. 2 Chr.14:11). If we trust him, his power will accomplish what our power cannot.

**Q. 7:13,14** How would that particular individual know all this about Gideon?

**A.** Perhaps word came down from the gathering of Israel's army across from the Midianite army (7:1) as to who the Israelite general was and how he thought he would overcome the Midianites. The tone of voice is not indicated in vs.14—if the speaker was scared, matter-of-fact, or mocking to reassure his friend that his dream meant nothing. Nevertheless, the message to Gideon was clear enough.

## GIDEON'S 300

**7:19-22** The middle watch began about 9:00 P.M. Picture the situation: Just as those of the first watch were returning to their tents, suddenly the edges of the camp erupted with war cries, the deafening blast of 300 trumpets from all sides, echoing and reechoing from hill to hill, and 300 torches showing the enemy that they were totally surrounded.

Since only a few men in each army carried trumpets, the Midianites assumed that they were being attacked by a far greater force than theirs of 135,000. Awakened so suddenly out of their sleep, and seeing people running in the camp, in their panic they assumed these to be the enemy attacking. The darkness compounded their confusion (being untrained for night warfare) and they began striking out at whoever was close at hand.

Many began looking for an area of darkness where there were no torches and hopefully no enemy forces, and fled pell-mell out of the valley. With the self-slaughter in the valley, and the cutting down of fleeing soldiers, Midian lost 120,000 men. Fifteen thousand survivors fled across the Jordan with Gideon and his 300 in hot pursuit.

Thinking they were finally safely out of reach, the Midianite army let down their guard and collapsed in exhaustion (8:11). Suddenly Gideon and company fell upon the unsuspecting army and routed the entire force by the Pass of Heres (vs.12), later executing the two remaining Midianite kings.

## JEPHTHAH'S DAUGHTER

**Q. 11:30,31,39,40** What actually happened to Jephthah's daughter?
**A.** Jephthah promised the Lord a burnt offering of whatever came out
of the door of his house to meet him after his victory. In verses
36,37 his daughter said that he should do to her just as he had
promised, only let her weep with her friends for two months because
she will never marry, being dead (not remaining celibate, as many
claim, because that violates the context and the resulting custom
among the women of Israel [vs.39,40]).

The "inconceivable" problem here is that of human sacrifice
offered to God, which he does not require nor is pleased with, and
which we find equally repulsive. But we of the West have little
appreciation for the importance and binding character of the vow that
is characteristic of Middle Eastern society. That is why Jephthah
laments, "Oh! My daughter! You have made me miserable and
wretched, because I have made a vow to the LORD that I cannot
break." To do other with his daughter than what he had vowed would
be to break his vow, which was inconceivable to him. (Other examples
of the absolute binding nature of even rash vows and the distress they
caused because they had to be fulfilled are found in Judges 21:1,2; 1
Samuel 14:24 and Matthew 14: 6-10.)

Perhaps Solomon had Jephthah in mind when he wrote Proverbs
20:25, "It is a trap for a man to dedicate something rashly and only
later to consider his vows." Ecclesiastes 5:4,5 says, "When you make a
vow to God, do not delay in fulfilling it. He has no pleasure in fools;
fulfill your vow. It is better not to vow than to make a vow and not
fulfill it." Deuteronomy 23:21 enjoins the Israelites to promptly fulfill
their vows to the Lord, "for the LORD your God will certainly demand
it of you and you will be guilty of sin" (the "sin" here being not the act
of the vow but the breaking of one's promise to the Lord).

So I believe, as repulsive as it is, that Jephthah did to his daughter as
he had vowed, and offered her as a burnt offering to God.

**12:5,6** "Shibboleth"—the shortest pass-fail linguistic test ever given
where failure meant death!

**16:3** From Gaza to the top of the hill that faces Hebron is 38 miles
uphill!

**16:6-24** One would think that Samson would have caught on to what was happening. His love for Delilah or whatever it was he felt for her, blinded him to her treachery and held him tightly in spite of her nagging. Samson's life-style eventually gave the Philistines opportunity to praise their god, Dagon, rather than acknowledge the God of Israel. If we play around with our commitment to the Lord, in the end, we also will fall and give cause for others to mock the Faith.

**Q. Chs.17-19** The idolatry of Micah and the Danites center on a Levite. The Benjamite War centers on a Levite. Is the Lord trying to make a statement by selecting these two tales from among many?
**A.** Possibly he was showing that the ones who should have been guarding the holiness of God's name in Israel and diligently teaching Israel to follow him, were the very ones leading Israel into continued idolatry, immorality, and treating women like so much baggage (definitely not the intention God had for a husband-wife relationship in Genesis 2:24 and Ephesians 5:22-33).

**18:30** Moses' grandson evidently was having problems at home, for when still young (17:7), he left home to seek some other place to stay. His ambition, perhaps vanity and materialism, are revealed by his attitude toward the Danites' offer to make him their tribal priest.

**18:30,31** Satan thumbing his nose at God through Moses' descendants.

**20:27** This situation with the Levite and his concubine happened early in the period of the Judges, as did also the situation with Jonathan, grandson of Moses (cf. ch.19; 1:34 with 18:1 where Dan had not yet settled in his inheritance and Phinehas was still High Priest—20:28).

**Q. 20:8-25** Why did the Lord allow the Benjamites to kill 40,000 or 1/10 of the Israelite army when it was Benjamin who was in the wrong?
**A. 20:26-28** Because they were trying to right a wrong in their own strength without cleansing sin from their plate first. When they finally humbled themselves and made the appropriate offerings to care for their sin, then the Lord gave them victory.

**21:1,2,5,7,10,11,15,18,20-22** Israel totally boxed itself in and brought much grief on everybody because of all their oath-taking. Had they sought the Lord first, they would have saved themselves a <u>lot</u> of trouble.

# RUTH

**God of the Impossible (cont.):**

92. He caused Ruth to work in the field of Boaz, a close relative (2:3).

* * * *

**Historical Note**

Ruth probably lived during Gideon's stint as judge. She was David's great grandmother. Figuring a generation at 40 years, and David's reign beginning when he was 30 (1011 B.C.), puts his birth at about 1041 B.C. Add 120 years = 1161 when Ruth may have lived. Gideon judged Israel from 1177 to 1137 B.C.

**\* \* \* \***

**2:8,9** What a difference between Boaz's attitude toward women and that of the Levite in Judges 19!

**Chapters 1-4** Ruth's character is exemplary:

| | | | |
|---|---|---|---|
| Faithful | 1:16,17 | Humble | 2:13 |
| Responsible | 2:2 | Obedient | 3:5 |
| Industrious | 2:7 | Noble character | 3:11 |
| Woman of faith | 2:12 | Loving, selfless devotion | 4:15 |

## God of the Impossible (cont.):

93. He caused Hannah to have a child (she was barren—1:5,19, 20).
94. He caused Dagon to fall on his face before the Ark of the Covenant and finally breaking off his head and hands (5:3,4).
95. He struck the Philistines with tumors (5:6,9,11,12) and a plague of rats (6:4,5).
96. He thundered against the Philistines and threw them into confusion (7:10).
97. He empowers the weak to do great things (9:21; 10:6,7; 11:6,7).
98. He enabled David to kill the lion, the bear, and Goliath(17:36, 37,49-51).
99. He protected David by making Saul's messengers and Saul prophesy (19:20-24).
100. He protected David so that Saul could not find him no matter how hard he tried (23:14). Yet Jonathan had no trouble locating him (23:16)!
101. He caused other circumstances to arise that protected David after Saul did find him (23:26,27).
102. He kept Saul and his army in a deep sleep so that David and Abishai could enter and leave his camp unnoticed (26:12).
103. He kept David and his men from fighting against Israel (29:3-11) thus enabling them to rescue their families. Had they gone to battle, their families would have been long gone and lost to them. Even so it was 3 days or more before the rescue took place.
104. He allowed Samuel to appear to announce judgment upon Saul (28:11-19).

**\* \* \* \***

**Q. 1:9** How does Eli figure in genealogically since Chronicles does not mention him?
**A. 1 Chr.6:1-8,** et. al.

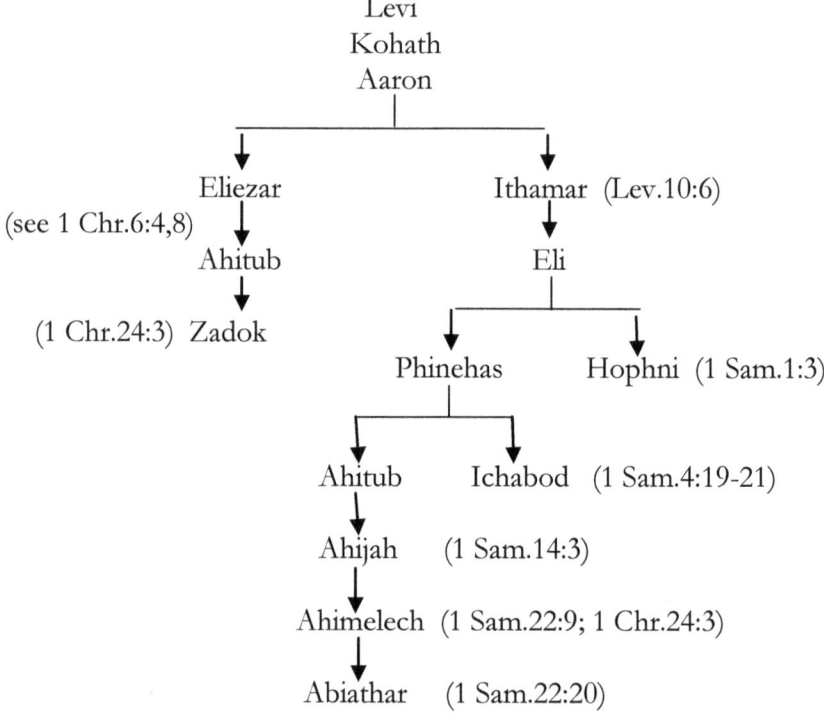

Levi
Kohath
Aaron

Eliezar          Ithamar  (Lev.10:6)

(see 1 Chr.6:4,8)

Ahitub                  Eli

(1 Chr.24:3) Zadok

Phinehas          Hophni  (1 Sam.1:3)

Ahitub          Ichabod  (1 Sam.4:19-21)

Ahijah     (1 Sam.14:3)

Ahimelech  (1 Sam.22:9; 1 Chr.24:3)

Abiathar   (1 Sam.22:20)

**2:27-36; 3:11-14,18** Since Eli refused to repent or correct his sons, the LORD finally declared no forgiveness! Eli merely shrugged and resigned himself to his fate—"Whatever!"

**3:5-9** The N.I.V. note says that Eli's failure to recognize at once that the Lord had called Samuel, and that that may be indicative of his own unfamiliarity with the Lord, I believe misses the point. No matter how spiritual you are, when your child wakes you up from a sound sleep saying you called him, anyone's first thought would be, "He was dreaming." Dreams are often repeated. So the second time is also explained. However, the third time would be most unusual, and then we, like Eli, would begin to suspect something else was going on, hence his answer to Samuel in verse nine.

**3:14** There comes a point when sin can no longer be forgiven. Even Eli had passed the point of repentance (see vs.18)!

**4:3** Israel used the Ark as a fetish. Misplaced faith!

**4:4** The defiled carrying the holy. Repulsive to the LORD.

**4:8** God's power still being talked about over 300 years later!

**6:6** In that same light the lessons from Israel's history were not lost on the Philistines, only misinterpreted.

**Q. 9:16** If the scepter belonged to Judah, then why did God appoint Saul from the tribe of Benjamin as king?

**A.** Perhaps because this was not God's time for them to have a king (the king from Judah that <u>God</u> wanted wasn't ready yet). But since they were rejecting him as their King and wanted to be like the other nations around them (8:19,20), he selected a king for them according to the worldly standards they would use (tall, handsome, wealthy— 9:1,2; 10:23,24). The tribe was insignificant at this point. Had Samuel done a better job with his sons, this situation might have been averted (8:1-5).

**9:6,7,18** I find it amazing that Saul didn't know Samuel, though all the elders of Israel did (8:4), and his servant knew something of him (9:6,7), but only in a general way. Since Samuel's circuit was only in the tribe of Benjamin (Bethel, Mizpah and Ramah) and the southern arm of Manasseh (Gilgal), many people would probably <u>not</u> know him unless they had some specific dealings with him requiring his assistance.

**9:21** As with Gideon (Judg.6:15) so with Saul: "The last shall be first." God uses the weak things to shame the strong (1 Cor.1:26-29).

**10:26** Saul was from Gibeah, the same town in the tribe of Benjamin that gave the Levite so much trouble (Judg.19:14) and resulted in the near extermination of that tribe.

**Q. 13:1,2** If Saul was 30 when he began to reign, and had committed 1,000 troops to Jonathan, Jonathan had to be old enough to fight and lead a command. How can these verses be reconciled in terms of their respective ages?

**A.** 1. (Hypothesis) If Saul was married at 15 and had Jonathan at 16, and the normal age for a fighting man was 20 years of age (Num. 1:3), then there has to be a gap of at least 6 years between verses 1 and

2, making Saul about 36 at the time he offered the sacrifice. At best, this is but a wild guess.

2. Since the Hebrew text doesn't mention years (30 and 42 are only found in later Septuagint versions), Saul could have been somewhat older than 30 years when he began ruling, thus minimizing this age problem between him and Jonathan.

**13:8,9** Even though God changed Saul's heart (10:9) and he became a different man (10:6), he still had to exercise personal faith and obedience to God. In this he failed when the crucial test was given. Jonathan, on the other hand, had the faith his father should have had (14: 6,10). This is one reason he and David got along so well—"kindred spirits."

**13:22** The Israelite army had no spears or swords. The Philistines had probably confiscated all those weapons by then. What was left were bows and arrows, slingshots and farm tools (mattocks, forks, axes and goads), and now just 600 men (vs.15)! Saul had a real problem!

**14:18,19** Saul sacrifices dependence upon God's direction for expediency. He let the pressure of the situation dictate his response rather than God: more evidence of his lack of faith. Expediency, not faith, dictates Saul's actions.

**14:20,21** The historical basis for the Philistine generals wanting to exclude David from their battle against Israel (29:4,9).

**14:24** Saul's oath was also an indication of his lack of faith. In his own wisdom, he tried to do what <u>he</u> thought would insure a total victory. He did not want anyone "wasting good fighting time" by sitting down to eat. "Keep at 'em, boys, till they're wiped out!" Jonathan calls his father's actions foolish. For had Israel been able to eat, and be refreshed, the slaughter would have been greater (vs.29,30). Saul's oath also caused the famished Israelite army to consume greedily all the food they found (after evidently a whole day of hard fighting without any food (vs.31) and in total physical exhaustion, without properly cleaning it (vs.32,33), eating blood and all.

**14:36,37** When Saul felt he "had time," <u>then</u> he was willing to inquire of God. But God remains silent. Saul rightly judges that some sin had been committed, but overreacts to the possibility by sentencing the offender <u>before</u> the offense is known!  But the people were not in agreement with him (vs.39,45).

**14:38-46**  In the end, Saul's oath produced just the opposite of its intended effect: unnecessary delay in carrying on the battle while the enemy was in flight, which allowed many of them to escape.  This whole chapter illustrates the futility of human wisdom apart from God's direction.

**Q. 15:2,3** Judgment over 400 years later?!  Is this an example of Deuteronomy 5:9?   But then what about Ezekiel 18:20 where the son is
not held guilty for the father's sin?    Since Deuteronomy 5:9 and
Ezekiel 18:20 are in the context of God's covenant to Israel, do these
statements, then, apply <u>only</u> to Israel?  If so, then the Gentile nations
remain continually under a cloud of guilt, not only for present sins, but
for past sins as well, and thus liable for judgment at any time.
**A.** There seems to be two levels of God's dealing with mankind: on an
   individual level (for the lifetime of that person) and on a national
level (for the "life-time" of that nation).  Thus as a person can have
unresolved sin in his life from many years back, so can a nation.  And
God can call both into judgment at any time he wishes.

**15:12-26**  Saul had problems:  pride (vs.12),  hypocrisy (vs.13),  ration-
alization (vs.15), greed (vs.19), self-justification (vs.20), abdication of
responsibility (vs.21), rebellion and arrogance (vs.23), admission of
guilt when he couldn't do otherwise (vs.24)!  These are not the
characteristics God wanted for the king of Israel (vs.28).

**15:15**  The whole Amalekite nation was to be the "sacrifice"!

**15:24**  Amazing. Saul was king.  His word was law.  Yet he listened to
the people more than God and gave in to them.  Is this perhaps
another fallout from when the army stood up to him in the issue with
Jonathan concerning Saul's rash oath (14:45; see also 22:7,8)?

**15:25,30**  Saul had a real fear of rejection by the people, and especially
if Samuel outwardly rejected him.  Building a monument to oneself
(vs.12) and pleading for public honor (vs.30) are not characteristics of
a secure person.  Saul's life basically demonstrates the plight of those

who reject faith and obedience to God and opt for proceeding on their own. They inevitably become "crowd pleasers" and "hungry for public honor" to "assure" themselves of their position, tenuous though it be. Add to this Saul's knowledge that God had already rejected him and his kingdom, and you have the recipe for all the troubles that follow, including his paranoia over David (cf. 1 Sam.18:6-9 and 22:6-19 below).

**16:18** God beginning to work David into position.

**17:25** Saul had another problem. He was head and shoulders taller than anyone else in Israel, therefore qualified as #1 to fight Goliath. Fearful of sure defeat, he offers great wealth, his daughter in marriage and freedom from taxes to whoever kills Goliath; but if Saul had no chance against Goliath, who else could possibly hope for victory? His offer was essentially meaningless, for no one would take him up on it, and he knew it...*except* ...David (vs.32).

**17:34-37** Seeing the Lord work in one impossible situation gives faith for other impossible situations.

**17:38-40** Man's attempt to equip himself for spiritual battle becomes very awkward at best. He needs liberating faith in order to operate unhindered.

**Q. 17:40** Why did David choose five smooth stones instead of one?
**A.** Goliath had four brothers (2 Sam.21:15-22)! However, I suspect that David wanted a "full arsenal" when facing Goliath. If one stone missed, he'd have others to use.

## Chs.18-23    STORY OF A RELATIONSHIP GONE SOUR

| | |
|---|---|
| **18:1-4** | Faith responds to faith—Jonathan loved David as himself. |
| 5-7 | David's success everywhere. |
| 8,9 | Saul's pride hurt by this public declaration (vs.7). Anger and jealousy toward David. |
| 10,11 | Saul's behavior no doubt interpreted as temporary insanity. |
| 12 | Fear and desperation to hold on to what he has. |

| | |
|---|---|
| 13-16 | David demoted but still successful. |
| 17-19 | Attempted murder by proxy (cf. 2 Sam.11:15). |
| | Saul fails to keep his promise (cf. 1 Sam.17:25). |
| 20,21 | Saul uses his daughter Michal to get at David. |
| 22 | An outright lie! |
| 24,25 | Price?  What about his promise in 17:25? |
| | Again, attempted murder by proxy. |
| 26,27,30 | David's further success. |
| 28,29 | Saul more afraid, becomes David's enemy. |
| **19:**1,2,10-13 | Saul tries to kill David. |
| 14,16,17 | Michal lies to protect David.  That's the last he sees of her for years and Saul gives her to Paltial (25:44). |

## SAUL'S PARANOIA

| | |
|---|---|
| **22:**6-19 | Saul totally paranoid. |
| 7 | Political speech to boost his standing. |
| 8-15 | Sure of a conspiracy against him by everybody. |
| 8 | Unpitied, "woe is me" attitude. |
| 8 | Even his own son has "incited" David to kill him. |
| 16 | Assuming the conspiracy is more widespread, including the priests! |
| 17 | Blind to truth; won't consider reason. |
| 17-19 | Kills all the priests and their families. |
| **23:**7-9 | Continues to plot against David and spends most of his remaining strength and effort in hunting him down. |

**19:17** Michal's lie saved her skin, but only added fuel to Saul's fire, increasing his desire to kill David, and eventually give Michal to Paltial.

**20:30-33** Saul's ambition was for Jonathan to become king and he had to kill David to guarantee it.  It was but a feeble human attempt to thwart the edict of God already given (13:13,14; 15:27-29), but he tried time and again anyway, just in case the next time might work (see also 23:17; 24:20).  This attitude reflects that of Satan.  God has announced his defeat, yet he keeps accusing, keeps opposing, keeps disrupting, thinking that there just might be one time yet that will change his fate and bring him victory.  Both Saul and Satan had no understanding of God's sovereignty or else chose to ignore it, hoping that it would just "go away."

**21:1-8**  David's lies to Abimelech were partly true, but still lies.
  2   Two outright lies.
  5   "Women have been kept from [me] about three days since I
        came out [because I was hiding from Saul that long]. And
        [my] vessel is holy."
  8   "I have brought neither my sword nor my weapons with me,
        because the king's business [of killing me] required [my] haste
        [to get away]."

**21:10,11**  The Philistines already considered David as king of Israel
based upon the purely cultural expression of a song which revealed the
true inner feelings of the Israelite people.

**21:13**  He feigned madness before Achish in order to escape from him.

**22:6-19**  An example of Saul's paranoia:
  7         Political speech debunking the opposition.
  8         "Conspiracy theory."
            Self-pity—"No one is concerned about me!"
            False assumption—"David is lying in wait for me," when
              in fact, David was fleeing from Saul!
  9,10    Conspiracy "confirmed" through incomplete information.
  13       False accusation based on incomplete information and
              assumptions.
  14-17  Saul blind to the truth because of his paranoia.
  16,17  Assuming the conspiracy to be more widely spread.
  18,19  Again, the judgment far exceeds the "crime."

**22:7,8**  The implication here is that general public sympathy still rests
with David, even though Saul is king. Part of this may be because of
Saul's fits of insanity and the recognition that his desire to kill David
was totally unjust; so also was his order to kill the priests (vs.17).

**22:8,13**  In his consuming desire to kill David, Saul begins to believe
that David also wants to kill him! Our sins are often projected upon
others whether or not they are guilty. 1 Samuel 24:10-13 and 26:9-
13,22-24 prove to Saul that killing him is _not_ David's goal.

**22:13,17**  Once Saul suspected something, nothing would change his
mind. He was judge, jury and executioner and judged others by his

feelings and suspicions. His judgments far exceeded the supposed crimes, and he ended up killing a lot of innocent people just to satisfy his own rage (vs.18,19).

**23:7** Saul falsely assumes that God has given David into his hands.
**23:9** David warned: perhaps a message sent from Jonathan? (vs.16)

**23:14** Saul knew the truth but fought it (see vs.17; 24:20).

**23:17** Jonathan envisioned a "coalition government." Understandable, but it would never work, and God knew it.

**25:44** Saul gave Michal, David's wife, to another man (Paltial), thus committing her from 8 to10 years of adultery (see 2 Sam.3:13,14 below). Saul probably did this on the grounds that David didn't love Michal but "deserted" her when the going got rough, regardless of the fact that it was Saul who forced him to leave. So he gave her to someone he thought would care for her.

**26:21** Saul lied and David knew it (27:1).

**Q. 27:2** How is it that David could now go to Achish and be accepted whereas he was rejected the first time (21:10-11)?
**A.** The first time he was alone and was still regarded as a "palace in-insider," hence a "spy." This time, however, it was obvious that he was Saul's enemy, so he was accepted without question.

**28:11,12** The reaction of the woman, the revelation of truth, and the reiteration of Saul's doom (vs.16-19) all point to an actual appearance of Samuel's spirit (vs.15). Other explanations just don't fit what happened.

**29:4,5** Yet when it came to battle, the old song wouldn't go away, and David was sent "packing" once more. Good thing. He had troubles awaiting him in the ruins of Ziklag (30:1,2).

## God of the Impossible, (cont.)

105. He gave David victory after victory over the Philistines (5:17-25).
106. He gave David a kingdom and riches, etc. (12:7,8).
107. He raised up adversity to him from his own house because of his sin (12:11).
108. He overruled Absalom's insurrection (17:14; 18:28).
109. He delivered David form enemies much stronger than he (22:17,18).

**\* \* \* \***

**1:6-10** The man who "killed" Saul had two things going against him:
    1. He "willfully killed" the Lord's anointed (whether true or not).
    2. He was an Amalekite, whose people had just destroyed Ziklag, etc. He didn't have a prayer (1:14,15)!

**Q. 1:10** Did the Amalekite actually kill Saul? (First mention of "assisted suicide" or "mercy killing" in the Bible.)
**A.** Somehow I doubt it, though it can't really be proved one way or the other. Consider the evidence:

| Military Account | Amalekite's Account |
|---|---|
| 1 Sam.31:3 Saul critically wounded | |
| 31:4 Saul fell on his own sword (with the enemy closing in) | 1:6 Saul leaning on his spear (with the enemy closing in) |
| 31:5 His armor bearer, seeing he was dead, killed himself. | 1:9,10 "I killed him at his request." |

Judgment: Obviously a soldier would know how to kill himself. Having tried and failed, and being critically wounded, he would be in no condition to stand up to lean against his spear. And laying down, he could not lean on his spear unless he stuck it in the ground to sit against it. But in any case, being that conscious, he would have used his sword again to finish the job.
    His armor bearer saw him lose consciousness, hence "die."
    Whoever reported his death (so this account of it could be recorded) assumed him to be dead as well.

He could have later regained consciousness and asked the Amalekite to finish the job. But considering the extent of his wounds, and his self-inflicted sword wound, intending to kill himself, regaining consciousness is highly unlikely.

Therefore, I conclude that the Amalekite was lying, even though David seemed to take him at his word and executed him accordingly. So much for trying to get in the good graces of the new king!

## HEBRON IN ISRAEL'S HISTORY

**2:1** It seems that Hebron plays a significant role in Israel's history. Consider that it was:

1. home and burial place of Abraham, Isaac and Jacob (Gen.13:18; 23:2,19; 35:27).

2. occupied by descendants of Anak it while Israel was in Egypt (Num.13:22).

3. repossessed by Caleb (Josh.14:12-14).

4. given to the Levites as a city of refuge (Josh.20:7).

5. the place where Samson carried Gaza's city gates (Judg.16:3).

6. where David was crowned king of Judah (2 Sam.2:4).

7. where David was crowned king of Israel (2 Sam.5:1-3).

8. where Abner was killed by Joab and buried (2 Sam.3:27-32).

9. the capitol of Judah for 7.5 years (2 Sam.5:5).

10. where Absalom was crowned king of Israel (2 Sam.15:7-10).

11. fortified by Rehoboam (2 Chr.11:10) and then

12. faded into Biblical obscurity as it is no more mentioned.

**Q. 3:13,14** How long was Michal "married" to Paltiel before David reclaimed her?

**A.** Possibly 8 to 10 years. David was 30 when crowned king of Judah.

Ish-Bosheth reigned over Israel for two years until the problem with Abner arose when Abner agreed to turn the kingdom over to David—but David demanded that he return Michal to him first. So he was 32 when Abner brought her back. Figuring backwards:

### David's Personal History

32  when Michal returns (2 Sam.3:13-16)

30  when crowned king of Judah (2 Sam.2:4; 5:4)

26  at Ziklag (1 yr. 4 mo. with the Philistines; 1 Sam.27:7)

(23-24?) Flees Saul (1 Sam.19:12)
  (22?)  Marries Michal (1 Sam.18:20,21,27)
   20    when he killed Goliath (since he is immediately given a
         military commission—so he had to be at least 20; 1 Sam.17)
(17-19?)  Harp player and armor bearer for Saul (1 Sam.16:17,18,21).

### 3:27 Joab had a problem:

1. Death in war cannot be avenged, but he sought revenge anyway for the death of his brother, Asahel.

2. The manslayer is safe in the city of refuge, but Joab murdered Abner in Hebron on false charges of spying for Israel (to cover for his revenge).

### David had a problem:

1. Joab was worthy of death at that point, but all David did was curse his actions and his posterity (vs.28, 29).

2. Somehow, Joab and Abishai had gained such widespread influence in Israel that David was afraid to act against them (vs.38,39). Joab was a great military leader, but also was a continual thorn in David's side until the day of his death.  David left it to Solomon to deal with him (1 Ki.2:5,6).

### David's inability to act is seen in other situations as well:

1. He did nothing when Amnon raped Tamar (13:21) because of his own adultery with Bathsheba.

2. He did nothing when Absalom murdered Amnon (14:23) because of his own murdering of Uriah the Hittite.

3. He did nothing to investigate Ziba's false charges against Mephibosheth (16:3,4), probably because he was so preoccupied with other things.  His rebuff of Mephibosheth (19:26-29) was totally unwarranted.

**6:3-15**  Doing the right thing in the wrong way (vs.3) always brings trouble.  No one could touch the ark and live, priests included, so Uzzah had to die (the unholy touching the holy—vs.6,7).  David's reactions were logical: anger, then fear and frustration (vs.8,9), then relief (vs.12).  Then he did the right thing in the right way (v.13) and the Lord blessed him (7:1-16).

**6:20 with 1 Sam.19:13**  Michal's reaction may have been influenced by her innate idolatry, hence her offense at David's public show for God. Obviously her heart was not in accord with David's as far as God was concerned. Her love for him turned to hate (6:16), probably simmering over her forced return to him ("I'm just so much baggage!"), his alleged unfaithfulness to her, and his "undignified" (for a king) dancing before the Ark.

**6:20,23** The fact that Michal went childless till the day of her death may have been that from that day on, David had no more relations with her, but secluded her in his harem. Or, the Lord closed her womb because of her disrespect to David.

**10:12** Joab's faith was similar to Eli's—fatalistic; though the basis of their faith was different. Eli's was passive fatalism because he didn't want to deal with the sin issue; Joab's was active fatalism because he went to battle anyway having no idea what God would do. Actually, his many victories were because of God's blessing on David. Joab was an ungodly scoundrel. This again demonstrates how the blessings of God to his own people can extend even to those who don't deserve them.

**11:16,17** David's plan to kill Uriah "by proxy" also resulted in the deaths of several other soldiers.

**11:1-12:29** It took some time for Joab to take Rabbah. Bathsheba gave birth twice before the city was taken, making the siege at least 18-20 months in duration.

**12:24,25** You can't second-guess God's grace. It is revealed at the most unexpected times and in the most unexpected ways.

**13:12-14** Reason and constructive suggestions fail in the face of passionate lust—or any other strong emotion for that matter.

**13:15** Lust gratified usually turns to hate.

**13:21** David was furious over the rape of Tamar, but was powerless to act because of his own adultery. The fact that God spared him from the death penalty made it impossible for him to demand death for Amnon. Moreover, Amnon would have thrown Bathsheba back in his face had he tried. So he did nothing, which set him up for further disaster. Thus a servant of God, having committed adultery, even if he is forgiven and restored to ministry, will have a much more difficult, if not impossible, time confronting sin in the lives of others. Like David, he has lost his moral authority to act: a sobering thought.

**13:38,39** Rather than extend to Absalom the forgiveness and mercy that he himself received from God, David let Absalom stay in exile. He finally gave him the kiss of pardon, but not of forgiveness (14:33).

**14:23,24** David's refusal to forgive Absalom carried a heavy price: rebellion and civil war in the kingdom (20,000 lives lost!—18:7), the loss of his best friend, Ahithophel, and the death of Absalom (chs.15-18). Everything David wanted to avoid came crashing down upon him.

**15:7** A bit long to fulfill a vow—over 4 years later! David should have guessed something wasn't quite right.

**15:7,8** The practice of "strategic lying" came back upon David via Absalom. The sins of the fathers become the sins of their children (cf. Abraham's deceit regarding Sarah; Isaac's regarding Rebekah; Jacob's life of deceit; Jacob's sons' deceit regarding Joseph's fate. We reap what we sow!).

**Q. 18:18** Absalom had built a pillar as a monument to himself because he "had no sons" to carry on the memory of his name. Yet, according to 14:27, he had three sons! How is this?
**A.** Evidently they had died very young since they're not even named. Obviously they were not living at this time.

**17:2-4** Ahithophel, David's closest friend and advisor, and Absalom, his son, conspired to murder David for the kingdom. No fear to strike down the Lord's anointed!

**18:33** If David really felt this way, he should never have left Jerusalem(!), though he was thinking more of the city than himself at that point (cf.15: 14).

**19:5-7** David was very human. He had his weaknesses and made his share of mistakes, even as king of Israel. Yet his heart was turned toward the Lord, which pleased God (1 Sam.13:14).

**Q. 19:18-23** Did David have a problem with forgiveness? (cf. 1 Ki. 2:8,9).

**A.** I don't think so, generally. Shimei's confession was probably more opportunistic than true repentance. He only "changed his tune" when it was obvious that David had won after all, so his guilt remained.

## Q. 21:1

1. Why did God wait all this time before judging Saul's sin?

2. How does the law stating that the children would not be put to death for the sins of their father come into play here? (see Deut.24:16)

**A.** 1. <u>Perhaps</u>: David knew of Saul's violation of the peace accord with the Gibeonites and did nothing to settle it. He may have thought: "It was Saul's problem, not mine. He died under God's judgment, and that situation probably died with him as well." But being a "national treaty," it had to be resolved on a national level—which it never was. David forgot about it, but God didn't. And after so long a time during which God waited for David to do something, he finally had to get David's attention concerning it.

2. Since the Gibeonites were not Jews—unknown if they had assimilated into Israel by this time—they were not under the Law. It was their right to make demands since it was Saul who broke the covenant. We don't know how many people Saul killed, but the Gibeonites' demand for just seven of his descendants had to be extraordinary, because they could have demanded much more.

3. According to Deuteronomy 5:9, God <u>could</u> have waited longer before judging this situation, making Solomon or Rehoboam deal with it.

**Q. 22:21-25** with **chs.11,12** How could David say these things in light of his sin with Bathsheba?

**A.** In the larger picture of his life, this was true. Where he departed from God's Law, he confessed it and was forgiven—thus had "clean hands." The bent of his heart was always toward the Lord (see also 1 Ki.15:4,5).

**22:1-51** "Lord, without you, I couldn't have done a thing!"

**Q. 23:8-39** with **1 Chr.11:10-47** Why the differences between these two lists of David's mighty men?

**A.** See <u>The Bible Knowledge Commentary</u> for a complete comparative list and a good explanation. Some men were known by two different names and others probably replaced those who were killed.

**Q. 23:11,33** Is Shammah the Hararite in verse 11 the same as Shammah the Hararite in vs.33?
**A.** Possibly, but there is no way to know for sure.

**23:34** Eliam, son of Ahithophel the Gilonite. According to 2 Samuel 11:3, Eliam was Bathsheba's father, which would make Ahithophel, David's counselor, Bathsheba's grandfather. Uriah the Hittite, Bathsheba's husband, was also among David's mighty men (vs.39). I wonder what effect David's adultery with Bathsheba might have had on Ahithophel's ultimate decision to side with Absalom in his rebellion against his father? I'm assuming that Ahithophel's long-simmering hurt over resulting family disruption and many unhealed wounds finally found its outlet in Absalom's rebellion, so he joined forces with him.

**24:3** I suspect Joab opposed the king's wishes because he wasn't looking forward to the work it would involve (see verse 8 and 1 Chr. 21:6).

# 1 KINGS

**God of the Impossible (cont.):**

110. He gave 10 tribes to Jeroboam (11:11,34-37; 12:8,15,24; 2 Chr.10:15; 11:4).
111. He raised up adversaries to Solomon (11:14,23,26).
112. He restored Jeroboam's withered hand and split the altar (13:3-6).
113. He revealed Jeroboam's wife to blind Ahijah (14:5).
114. He fulfilled the prophecy of 14:10-13 (15:27-29).
115. He gave Baasha strength to become king (16:2), but Baasha misused that strength.
116. He fulfilled the prophecy of 1 Ki.16:3,4 (16:10,21).
117. He fulfilled the prophecy regarding the rebuilding of Jericho (Josh.6:26; 1 Ki.16:34).
118. He provided for Elijah through ravens (17:2-6).
119. He multiplied the contents of the flour bin and jar of oil (17:14-16).
120. He brought a child back to life (17:17-22).
121. He sent fire that consumed both the sacrifice and the altar (18:38).
122. He gave Elijah strength to run faster than Ahab's chariot (18:46).
123. He provided for Elijah's long journey (19:5-8).
124. He fulfilled prophecy (21:19 with 22:35,38).

**\* \* \* \***

**2:9** Already Solomon was demonstrating unusual wisdom.

**2:28-30** I had always thought that Adonijah and Joab took hold of the Altar of Sacrifice, but this passage seems to indicate that it was the Alter of Incense. Benaiah went <u>inside</u> (N.I.V.) the tent to order Joab out, and there was only one altar inside the tent, the Altar of Incense.
**Q.** But how could these two men enter a place restricted <u>only</u> to the priests? They both would have had to be executed for such trespassing (Num.18:7).
**A.** Exodus 21:14 refers to someone going to the altar for protection and being taken away from it if he was guilty. According to <u>The</u>

Bible Knowledge Commentary, "Now Joab, like Adonijah, sought the protection of the horns of the brazen altar in the courtyard of the tent (tabernacle) in Jerusalem (cf. 1 Ki.1:50). This was a place of refuge for those whose lives were in danger. The Mosaic Law provided refuge there for all but murderers (Ex.21: 13-14)."

To understand the N.I.V. translation, "So Benaiah entered the tent of the LORD" as to his literally entering the tent seems to be generalization. In light of the strict "priests only" regulation, "entered the tent" must refer to entering the courtyard of the tent where the bronze altar was located.

**Q. 2:30b** Why did Joab insist on dying at the Bronze Altar?
**A.** During his life, Joab was a very ungodly, ruthless and ambitious
   man. He knew the altar was the place of refuge, a place of sacrifice for sin, and perhaps, in some way, dying there, in the presence of God, might expiate his past sins and "guarantee his acceptance by God." This action might be construed as a "death bed conversion," but in the end, only God knows.

**3:1-3b** Seeds for future trouble: taking foreign wives and sacrificing in locations other than the place of the Ark of the Covenant (Jerusalem—3:15).

**Q. 4:8-19** From what tribes came these district governors? Six are
   not mentioned (in CAPS).
**A.**

| | | | |
|---|---|---|---|
| 1. Ben-Hur | – Ephraim | 7. Ahinidab | – GAD |
| 2. Ben-Deker | – JUDAH | 8. Ahimaaz | – Naphtali |
| 3. Ben-Hesed | – W.MANASSEH | 9. Baana | – Asher |
| 4. Ben-Abinidab | – ASHER | 10. Jehoshaphat | – Issachar |
| 5. Baana | – W.MANASSEH | 11. Shimei | – Benjamin |
| 6. Ben-Geb | – W.Manasseh | 12. Geber | – E.MANASSEH |

**4:31** Outstanding wise men of Israel:
   Ethan the Ezrahite – author of Psalm 89.
   Heman, Calcol and Darda, sons of Zerah (Mahol), descendant
   of Judah (1 Chr.2:6).
   Solomon, wiser than them all.

**6:5-7** The Temple was a totally prefabricated building! All that the workers had to do on site was put it together. Quite an engineering feat for that day considering the tools they had to work with.

**6:20-35** The amount of gold needed for this job is staggering, and its value nearly incalculable. "Magnificent" wouldn't even begin to describe the appearance of the Temple.

4.5 tons of gold = 9,000 lbs.= 144,000 oz. @ $1,520/oz =
$218,880,000.

(9:28) 16 tons of gold = 32,000 lbs. = 512,000 oz. @1,520 oz. =
$778,240,000.

**8:41-43** A contrast between O.T. and N.T. missions:

## O.T. Missions
FOCUS      = Israel and the Temple
DYNAMIC = Godly living, answered prayer and national prosperity, so strikingly different from that of other nations
that the world's attention would be drawn to Israel
and their God (vs.59-61; see also Ps.67:1,2).
TARGET   = all peoples of the earth (vs.60).
PATTERN = hear, come, see and confess (cf. Queen of Sheba's
visit to Solomon – 10:1 [hear, come], 10:4,5 [see],
10:9 [confess].

## N.T. Missions
FOCUS      = the Cross of Christ and his teachings (Matt.28:20)
DYNAMIC = the changed life (Matt.5:16)
TARGET   = all peoples of the earth (Mk.16:15)
PATTERN = go, disciple, baptize and teach (Matt.28:18-20)

**8:46-51** Manasseh is an illustration of the answer to Solomon's prayer (cf. 2 Chr.33:13).

**10:14-17** Solomon's wealth in gold alone:
vs.14   Yearly received 666 talents = 800,000 oz. @ $1,520/oz.
= $1,216,000,000.00
(vs.10) gift from Queen of Sheba = 144,000 oz.
= $  218,880,000.00
vs.16 200 15-lb. gold shields     = 240 oz. ea. X 200 X $1,520
= $    72,960,000.00

vs.17 300 5-lb. gold shields    = 80 oz. ea. X 300 X $1,520
           = $  36,480,000.00

*So in one year alone, he had a total gold income of* $1,544,320,000.00!

Add to this his yearly income of $1,544,320,000.00 (vs.14) of gold alone for 40 years and he had quite an allowance—$61.7 trillion! He obviously had <u>big</u> expenses, too, which ate up a sizable amount of that income! If we added in all other sources of yearly income, including heavy taxes, that would put Solomon's total income for 40 years "out of sight" for all the zeros that would follow the 61.7!

**10:21,28; 11:1** Solomon broke three cardinal principles God laid down for the king to follow, and they were the cause of his and the kingdom's ultimate ruin (11:2-13; see comments on 1 Ki.15:4,5 below).

**Chs.11,14** Beginning with Ahijah who prophesied to Jeroboam, the Lord began to send prophets to Israel and Judah to urge the people to return to him. It was generally a lost cause.

| King | Prophets serving the Northern Kingdom |
|---|---|
| Jeroboam | — Ahijah (Ephraim)    (1 Ki.11:29) |
| | Unnamed man of God (1 Ki.13:1) |
| Baasha | — Jehu  (1 Ki.16:1) |
| Elah | — " |
| Ahab | — Elijah (1 Ki.17:1) |
| | Unnamed prophet    (1 Ki.20:13) |
| | Another unnamed prophet (1 Ki.20:28) |
| | Micaiah  (1 Ki.22:8) |
| Ahaziah | — Elijah    (2 Ki.1:3) |
| Joram | "      (2 Ki.1:17) |
| | Elisha  (2 Ki.3:11) |
| Jehu | — "  + a man of the prophets (2 Ki.9:1) |
| Jehoahaz | — "  [Assumed since he was still prophesying under Jehoash] |
| Jehoash | — "  (2 Ki.13:14) |
| Jeroboam II | Jonah  (2 Ki.14:25) |
| Pekah | —Oded  (2 Chr.28:9) |

## Earlier prophets in Judah serving as advisors to David and Solomon

```
David        — Gad    (2 Sam.24:11)
               Nathan (2 Sam.12:1)
Solomon      —  "     (1 Ki.1:10)
               Unnamed (poss. Ahijah of Shiloh—2 Chr.9:29)
               Iddo    (2 Chr.9:29)
```

## Other prophets serving the Judean kings

```
Rehoboam     — Iddo         (2 Chr.12:15)
               Shemiah      (2 Chr.11:2)
Asa          — Azariah      (2 Chr.15:1)
               Hanani       (2 Chr.16:7)
Jehoshaphat  — Micaiah      (2 Chr.18:7)
               Jehu         (2 Chr.19:2)
               Jahaziel     (2 Chr.20:14)
               Eliezer      (2 Chr.20:37)
Jehoram      — Elijah       (2 Chr.21:12)
Ahaziah      — Elisha       (2 Ki.9:1)
Joash        — Unnamed prophets (2 Chr.24:19)
               Zechariah    (2 Chr.24:20)
Amaziah      — Man of God (2 Chr.25:7)
               A prophet    (2 Chr.25:15)
Uzziah       — Isaiah       (Isa.1:1)
Jotham       —  "           (Isa.1:1)
Ahaz         —  "           (Isa.1:1)
Hezekiah     —  "           (Isa.1:1; 2 Chr.32:20)
Manasseh     —  "     (Killed Isaiah according to Josephus)
Josiah       — Hulda        (2 Chr.34:22)
               Jeremiah     (2 Chr.35:25)
Jehoahaz     —  "           (Jer.22:11)
  (also called
  Shallum)
Jehoiachin   —  "           (Jer.22:28)
Jehoiakim    —  "           (Jer.26:1; 36:4)
Zedekiah     —  "           (Jer.38:14)
```

**Q. 11:1-8** Where was the godly influence of Israel on Solomon's wives (cf. that influence on the Queen of Sheba, ch.10)? They were around for a long time where they could see and hear, yet they remained unmoved and committed to their gods.

**A.** As part of Solomon's harem, they probably lived in relative, if not total, isolation from the outside world. No real spiritual communication occurred between them and Solomon that would influence them toward God (but it <u>sure</u> flowed the <u>other</u> way!). Since their only contact with outside life was Solomon, and that basically for sexual relations, there was little external influence to change them. They had lots of time on their hands, so they turned to what they knew best, their idolatry, and probably badgered Solomon to build them shrines in which to worship. He probably did this first to please them (or escape their nagging—he said something in Proverbs about a whining and complaining wife!), but then gradually got drawn into that worship himself, and ended up doing some horrible things.

**Q. 12:4** With all of Solomon's fantastic wealth accrued from outside the country, what need did he have to levy heavy taxes on the people?

**A.** Realistically, none. But wealth begets the desire for more wealth, increasing the need to spend more and more as one's desires grow, thus creating the need for more wealth in order to "cover ever greater expenses" (Eccl.2:4-9). According to Eccl.2: 10, Solomon didn't deny himself anything he wanted. So, the wealthier he became, the more expenditures he had, thus requiring new and more constant sources of income—the people.

**12:10,11** Pride and a life of ease robbed these young men of wisdom, and hence the kingdom. So what they wanted to gain for themselves, they ultimately lost—and even more.

**12:15** "Was from the LORD." God didn't cause Rehoboam to answer in this way. That was already in his heart. God just let it happen without interfering as he would have done had Solomon been faithful to the end. Without God's intervention, the natural bent of our hearts would quickly lead us astray (cf. Rom.3:9-18).

## CAPITAL CITIES OF ISRAEL

**12:25**   Shechem  – 1ˢᵗ capital of Israel (Jeroboam to Nadab)
(15:21)  Tirzah    – 2ⁿᵈ capital of Israel (Baasha to Zimri)
(16:24)  Samaria   – 3ʳᵈ and final capital of Israel (Omri to the dispersion)

**12:26,27** Jeroboam had no faith in God's promise to him. Here he set his policy which was carried out (12:31-33) and overruled faith in spite of clear warnings from God (13:4-6,33).

**13:33** Policy overrules faith (cf. 12:27) even as that which we <u>really</u> believe overrules Scripture!

**14:14-16** To whom much is given (the Temple) much shall be required (heavier judgment).

**15:4,5** Our obedience can have a lasting affect even upon those who never knew us (cf. 1 Ki.11:12,32,34; 2 Ki.8:19)!

**17:9,14-16** With the Lord's command comes the Lord's provision.

**17:15** Faith produces obedience. The amazing thing here is that this widow had no idea who Elijah was, yet she responded in faith to what he said. Perhaps it was more fatalistic than faith at this point. "I may as well do this. We're going to die anyway, so what's the difference?" Was she in for a surprise!

**18:10** "Divine blindness."

**18:17** Wrong perspective!

**18:22-24,30-39** Power encounter of the first order! Elijah against the 450 prophets of Baal.

**18:37** God revealed himself to Ahab several times to turn him to the truth, but he refused to yield (see also 1 Ki.20:13,28 below; 21:20).

**18:40** Not a difficult task since Baal's prophets had been considerably weakened by their loss of blood (vs.28) and their day-long frenzied dancing (vs.26-29). By evening they must have been thoroughly exhausted.

**19:7,8** Journey of approximately 250 miles at 40 days = 6.5 miles per day—far enough for one day's walk in the desert! And Elijah wasn't exactly in a hurry anymore.

**19:11** Elijah went out of the cave to stand on the mountain, but the ferocity of the wind evidently drove him back inside for shelter since, when he heard the whisper of a voice, "he went out and stood at the mouth of the cave" (vs.13).

**19:16** Elijah was from the tribe of Manasseh.

**19:21** Evidently Elijah had dismissed his servant at Beersheba (19:3), thinking he would have no more use for him as Elijah would probably die. But later Elisha, more than just a servant, became Elijah's aide and eventual heir to his position (vs.16).

**20:13,28** Not only was God trying to teach the Syrians a lesson about himself, he was also trying to reach Ahab, but in vain (21:20).

**20:30** "Wall collapsed on them." Commentaries indicate that the city was too small for this event to actually happen—but that the city walls did collapse, leaving these soldiers defenseless.

Since no earthquake is mentioned, there has to be some reason why the whole wall fell and how its falling killed all these soldiers. If these 27,000 soldiers were on top of the wall, it could be that the vibrations from the activity and weight of so many armed men caused many structurally weak areas of the wall to give way, hence bringing down the entire structure and most of the 27,000 soldiers to their deaths.

**20:34** Had Ahab executed Ben-Hadad, he could have had all these things and more. This treaty limited what he received and allowed a man whom God destined for death to live. So Ahab lost both ways, but was still unrepentant (vs.43).

**21:27-29** The Lord rewards even the slightest hint of repentance. However, Ahab's repentance, or humbling of himself, was basically in response to announced judgment and his feelings about <u>that</u> rather than remorse over his sin leading to a change of character and deeds. He continued in his opposition to God and his ways (22:8).

**22:4-30** A study in hypocrisy and "prophecy-fixing."

vs. 8   Ahab hates Micaiah because all his prophesies are negative.

vs.13   Micaiah ordered to conform his prophecy to agree with the others.

vs.15b Micaiah "does so," but obviously with a mocking tone of voice.

vs.16   Ahab "scolds" him for Jehoshaphat's benefit.

vs.17   Micaiah then replies seriously.

vs.18   Ahab: "There, didn't I tell you that he never prophesies good about me?"

vs.30   But Ahab was worried that Micaiah's prophecy <u>might</u> be true after all, so tried to "outwit" the Lord and put Jehoshaphat in mortal danger. Some "friend"! One would have thought that Jehoshaphat would have picked up on this too.

**22:23** Micaiah's statement that "the Lord put a lying spirit in the mouths of all these prophets" doesn't mean that the Lord actively did so. He permitted it to happen, but also revealed to Ahab that it was indeed happening. [This had to be an evil spirit since the angels cannot sin, and all lies proceed from Satan, the father of lies— Jn.8:44.] But even in the face of truth, the unbelieving heart will choose the lie, the only alternative to hearts that refuse to submit to the Lordship of Jesus Christ.

**Q. 22:32,33** Jehoshaphat cried out—what?

**A.** Whatever it was, God used it to convince the chariot commanders that this wasn't Ahab (2 Chr.18:31,32). Either it was his dialect as he issued commands to his soldiers or he called out to the Lord God of Israel, whereas if he were Ahab, he would have called down curses on the chariot commanders in the name of Baal. In the heat of battle, dialect wouldn't be that noticeable, but many would hear the content of what was said, so I tend to believe it was the latter that turned the enemy away from Jehoshaphat.

# THE DESTRUCTION OF JEHOSHAPHAT'S FLEET

**22:48,49** with **2 Chr.20:35-37**    Sequence of events:

1. Jehoshaphat and Ahaziah wanted to increase their wealth, so agreed together to build a fleet of ships to gather gold from Ophir as Solomon had done.

2. However, the LORD disapproved of this unholy alliance and sent a prophet to declare the destruction of the fleet.

3. Jehoshaphat was alarmed at this turn of events, so refused to let Ahaziah's sailors go with his. He reasoned that the Lord would be pleased at the separation and thus bless his efforts.

4. Jehoshaphat, however, was wrong. It was the alliance with Ahaziah that displeased the Lord, not just this expedition.

5. Ahaziah interpreted Jehoshaphat's action as "backing out of a deal in order to take all for himself," so his men evidently trashed and burned the ships right on the spot.

# 2 KINGS

**God of the Impossible (cont.):**

125. He sent fire to consume the two captains and their 50's (1:9-12).
126. He split the Jordan River so that Elijah and Elisha could cross on dry ground (2:8).
127. He took Elijah up to Heaven in a chariot of fire (2:11).
128. He split the Jordan River again for Elisha (2:14).
129. He healed the water source in Jericho (2:19-22).
130. He brought out two female bears which killed the 42 young men who cursed Elisha (2:23-26). (The majority ostensibly <u>should</u> have been able to run away, but couldn't.)
131. He provided water where there was none (3:16,17,20).
132. He delivered the Moabites into Israel's hands (3:18,19,24,25).
133. He kept the jar of oil full until all the jars were filled (4:5-7).
134. He gave the Shunammite woman a child (4:16,17).
135. He raised the Shunammite woman's son from death (4:32-37).
136. He cured the poisonous stew (4:38-41).
137. He multiplied the barley loaves (20) and grain for 100 men (4:42-44).
138. He healed Namaan from his leprosy (5:14).
139. He transferred Namaan's leprosy to Gehazi (5:27).
140. He caused the ax head to float (6:5-7).
141. He revealed to Elisha the counsels of the Syrian king (6:8-12).
142. He struck the Syrian host with blindness then restored their sight (6:18-20).
143. He caused the Syrian army to hear the noise of a great army— and flee (7:6,7).
144. He brought to pass his word re: Jehu's descendants (15:12).
145. He governs kings and their fate (19:7).
146. He governs the victories of armies (19:25-28).
147. He preserves people against impossible odds (19:29-34).
148. He slew 185,000 soldiers in one night without a weapon (19:35).
149. He added 15 years to Hezekiah's life (20:6).
150. He made the shadow on the sundial reverse its direction (20:11).

\* \* \* \*

**Q. 3:26,27** Why did this act of the king of Moab cause great indignation against Israel?

**A.** Perhaps Judah's anger arose against Israel for invading Moab in a battle that resulted in their seeing such a repulsive act. (But there is no way such a thing could have been foreseen.) Whatever it was, the Moabite king surely interpreted the results as an answer from his god, Chemosh.

**4:3** Since a "company of prophets" usually lived in one place (cf. 2 Ki.2:3; 9:1), her neighbors were probably the wives of other prophets.

**5:11-14** God doesn't work according to our preconceived notions but accomplishes his purposes in surprising or unexpected ways.

**5:15-27** Gehazi's descent into sin:
He saw (vs.15)
He coveted (vs.20—because of personal ambition—vs.26)
He lied (vs.22)
He took (vs.23)
He hid the things (vs.24) then acted as if everything was fine (vs.25)
He lied again (vs.25)
His motive uncovered (vs.26)
His judgment: all is lost (vs.27)

**6:17** The Lord opened the eyes of Elisha's servant to <u>see</u> the heavenly army, and opened the ears of the Syrian army to <u>hear</u> the heavenly army (7:5,6)!

**6:19** Picture Elisha leading several thousand Syrian soldiers, each holding another's hand in one long, snaking line, for the 10 mile walk from Dothan to Samaria. How did they think they would still capture Elisha and take him back to the king in Damascus, all of them being blind? This episode becomes increasingly humorous the more you think about it.

**6:22,23** A good illustration of Romans 12:20.

**Q. 6:25** "...a quarter of a cab of seed pods..." or "...a quarter of a cab of dove's dung...." This measurement is about ½ pint (N.I.V. note). Why these totally different renditions of the same Hebrew words? Which is correct?

**A.** One possible explanation is that Hebrew was first written without
vowels. So it is possible to have several Hebrew words written
with the same consonants, but with different meanings depending
upon what vowels were inserted. Context made the original meaning
clear; but removed from that context, we have trouble deciding
which meaning was intended. For example: "bbbl"—is this English
word "babble," "bobble" or "bubble"? "bttl" —is this "battle" or
"bottle"? In considering the context, translators must choose which
word makes the better sense and use that one.

Since the context here deals with food, "seed pods" would make
more sense to us. However, if they used dove dung for fuel to cook
their food, then the second translation could be the correct one. But
½ pint of fuel is too little to cook anything (unless it is just stating the
price of a unit of this kind of fuel, which would require the purchase
of a number of units in order to cook). So, on this basis, I would
have to go along with the "seed pod" translation.

But "dove's dung" and "seed pods" are two completely different
Hebrew words, so no linguistic misunderstanding is possible:
סילרייךח "doves' dung"; צרזז "seed pods." Thus the first explanation
won't explain the differing translations. Then I read in another
commentary that, in historical context, dove's dung was eaten in
times of extreme famine. If that is true, then "dove's dung" should
be the preferred translation in this verse, causing the "seed pod"
explanation to fail.

**6:33** Apparently Elisha had told the king to wait for the Lord's
deliverance, but this situation seemed beyond hope and the king
blamed Elisha (vs.30,31) for the continuing distress. Again, misplaced blame!

**7:17** The mad, headlong rush of the starving people makes me
wonder if not more than just the king's officer got trampled to death
that day.

**Q. 8:1** Seven-year famine. Is there a cyclical pattern to these fam-
ines?

(Joseph in Egypt—another 7-year famine.)

(Ruth 1:1 Famine severe enough to cause some families to
move.)

**A.**

**8:4** This situation had to have taken place earlier during the reign of Jehu (see N.I.V. note) who had little contact with Elisha, rather than Joram, for two reasons:

1. Joram was far more familiar with Elisha than was Jehu (see vs.4,5).

2. Had Gehazi been leprous at that time (see 5:27), he could not have entered the city, much less the king's presence (see also 7:3).

**8:18,27** These verses demonstrate the great influence a wife can have on her husband, for good or for evil. Advice for young men: "Be careful whom you marry!" (cf. 1 Ki.21:25,26)

**9:11** "You know... ." Jehu probably thought that his fellow officers had sent the prophet to anoint him so that he would lead a revolt against Joram. The rapidity with which they paid homage to Jehu (vs.13) indicates their great discontent with Joram and their current situation.

**9:24-37; 10:10,30** Jehu recognized the word of the Lord, but it seemed to have had no further effect on him (10:28,29,31).

**9:27** Ahaziah, king of Judah, also fell under God's curse on Ahab and his family since his mother was Ahab's daughter. What Jehoshaphat thought was politically expedient, turned into disaster for his own family as well as Judah (cf. 8:18,27; 9:8). Jehoram's marriage to Athaliah introduced Judah to Israel's idolatrous practices from which they never recovered (2 Ki.17: 18-20).

**11:13,16** Probably Athaliah's first and only trip to the Temple. So it was the perfect hiding place for Joash. Her death brought the final and complete end to Ahab's family.

**13:2,4-6,14-19,22,23** How often the Lord helped Israel and delivered them, but the king still refused to follow him (14:24-28).

**14:25** Jonah was from the tribe of Zebulon.

**16:2-4,12-16** Ahaz mixed everything together. Evidently God was just one more god to him. He maintained the form of worshipping him, but without faith. He violated the symbolism of the bronze altar by substituting a heathen altar in its place and violated the function of the altar by reducing it to a tool of divination. His total disregard for the Lord was phenomenal (see vs.17,18).

**17:27,28** But what did this exiled "priest" teach the people of Samaria? Obviously not much since they just mixed that form of worship with their own (vs. 29-34).

**17:40** "They" refers to the Samaritans, not to Israel.

**19:35,36** The sudden and mysterious death of 185,000 of his troops should have given pause to Sennacherib to reconsider the God of Israel (vs.19), assuming that the message of verses 21-28 was passed on to him, though likely not, but given only as an encouragement to Hezekiah. Either way, the threat to Jerusalem was totally eliminated.

**20:7** Evidently Hezekiah had a general systemic infection from the boil.

### Josiah's Personal History
(Based on 2 Kings chs.23,31,36)

    8 when he began to reign (22:1).
    12,13 when he married Zebidah, and Hamutal shortly after.
    14 when Eliakim (Jehoiakim) was born (23:36).
    16 when Jehoahaz was born (23:31).
    26 when the Book of the Law was found, the Temple
        repaired, reforms carried out and the Passover held
        (22:3-23:23).
    29 when Mattaniah (Zedekiah) was born (24:18).
    39 when he foolishly fought against Egypt and was killed in
        battle (22:1 with 23:29).

**21:1** N.I.V. note says that Manasseh was born <u>after</u> Hezekiah's illness (placed at 702 B.C.—N.I.V. note on 20:6), including a 10 year co-regency with his father (697-686 B.C.).

**Problem:** If he was 12 years old when he began to reign, that would put his birth at 709 B.C., 7 years <u>before</u> Hezekiah's illness. Otherwise he would have been only 5 years old when he began his co-regency, not 12, making him 15 or 16 (not 22) when his father died and he assumed the throne.

On the other hand, Hezekiah knew exactly how long he had to live, so could have brought his son into kingly duties at an early age so as to have him adequately trained by the time he died. But this still does not answer the age discrepancy that the N.I.V. note introduces.

So I conclude that if it is clear that Manasseh was 12 when he began to reign, and that he reigned with his father for 10 years, beginning in 697 B.C., then his birth had to have occurred in 709 B.C., <u>before</u> Hezekiah's illness in 702 B.C.

**Q. 23:10** How did Josiah desecrate the Valley so that no one would ever again use it for human sacrifice?
**A. 2 Kings 23:14,16** It is not said, but this verse indicates one way in which this could have been done: by scattering human bones throughout the area.

**23:24** Hilkiah the priest, who had discovered the Book of the Law, probably was Jeremiah's father (Jer.1:1).

**23:24-26** There comes a time when goodness and obedience cannot "undo" the damage done (see also 24:2-4).

**23:25** I suspect this verse refers to kings of the divided kingdom rather than going back to David.

**24:4** Whereas the Lord was not willing to forgive the nation of its sins (which occasioned their destruction), he <u>did</u> forgive Manasseh when he humbled himself and repented (cf. 2 Chr.33:12-16).

### Jehoiachin's Personal History

18 when he began his reign of three months (24:8).
18 when he surrendered to Nebuchadnezzar and imprisoned in Babylon (24:12).
55 when he was released from prison in Babylon (25:27).

**25:12**  Sometimes it pays to be poor!

**Q. 25:13-16**  What happened to all the gold and silver and bronze that Solomon had gathered?  Where did it all go?

**A. TO ISRAEL** —Jehoash, king of Israel, denuded the Temple of all its treasure.

**TO EGYPT** —During the 5th year of Rehoboam, Shishak carried off the treasures of the Temple and palace plus the gold shields Solomon had made (1 Ki.14:25,26; 2 Chr.12:9).

**TO SYRIA** —Anything left in the Temple and palace treasuries was sent to Ben-Hadad to make a treaty with Judah (King Asa–1 Ki.15:18; 2 Chr.16:2).

**TO ASSYRIA** —King Ahaz evidently melted down the side panels, the bronze basins and bronze bulls in order to pay tribute to Tilgath-Pileser (2 Ki.16:17).

**TO BABYLON** —Nebuchadnezzar carried off the Temple articles (2 Chr.36:7,10); then later returned and burned down the Temple and the royal palace (2 Ki.25:9).  The assumption would be that any remaining gold, silver and bronze melted in the fire and was also carried off.  He then broke up the bronze pillars, moveable stands, the bronze Sea, and took away all remaining Temple articles and implements (2 Ki.25:13-17; 2 Chr.36:18,19).  Absolutely nothing more was left of Solomon's wealth.

# 1 CHRONICLES

## God of the Impossible (cont.):
### 1,2 CHRONICLES

151. He sent fire from heaven to consume David's sacrifice (1 Chr.21:26).
152. He has the power to grant wisdom, knowledge, riches, wealth and honor (2 Chr.1:12).
153. He sent fire to consumed the burnt the burnt offering (7:1-3).
154. He caused Shishak, king of Egypt, to subdue Judah (12:1-9) but stopped him short of destroying them (vs.7).
155. He gave Abijah and Judah victory over Jeroboam's hosts (13:14-18).
156. He gave victory to Asa and Judah over the army of Ethiopia (14:11-15).
157. He caused the nations around Judah to fear coming against them in war—so there was peace (17:10; 20:29,30).
158. He saved Jehoshaphat from certain death (18:30-32).
159. He delivered Israel from the hands of Ammon, Moab and Mt. Seir without them having to shoot one arrow (20:22-24).
160. He raised up adversaries against Jehoram of Judah (21:8-10,16,17).
161. He struck Jehoram with an incurable intestinal disease (21:15,18-20).
162. He brought destruction upon Ahaziah because he also was part of the house of Ahab (22:7).
163. He intervened to save David's line when Athaliah would have destroyed it entirely (22:10-12).
164. He delivered the large Judean army into the hands of a much smaller Syrian army as punishment for forsaking him (24:24).
165. He delivered Amaziah into Joash's hands (25:20-22).
166. He struck Uzziah with leprosy when he presumed upon the office of the priests (26:16-20).
167. He brought Judah low because of the unfaithfulness of Ahaz and his wickedness (28:19).
168. He brought Manasseh to the place of repentance (33:10-16).

* * * *

**2:9** The sons of Hezron are listed in order of birth, Jerahmeel, Ram and Caleb, yet their descendants are listed by importance rather than by birth: 1st Ram, who was the ancestor of David, King of Israel, then Caleb, father of Bezalel (who figured greatly in the preparations for the Tabernacle), then Jerahmeel whose descendants did not distinguish themselves.

**Q. 2:13-15** How is David here the 7th son of Jesse whereas in 1 Sam. 16:8-11 he is the 8th?

**A.** (N.I.V. note) Here David is mentioned as #7, enabling him to occupy the favored place of the 7th son. So it's a matter of prestige—his privilege as over against his actual place. Understanding this difference eliminates the apparent discrepancy.

**2:13-17** David's relationship to Joab was uncle to nephew; Joab to Amasa of cousin to cousin. David was also uncle to Amasa.

**Q. 2:18,42; 4:15** The mystery of the 3 Calebs: who are they? Are the two Calebs of chapter 2 the same person as both are said (or implied) to be the brother of Jerahmeel? Yet their wives' and sons' names are totally different in most cases (1 Chr.2:9,25,42).

| **A.** 1 Chr.2:18 | 1 Chr.2:42 | 1 Chr.4:15 |
|---|---|---|
| Caleb son of / | Caleb bro. of / | Caleb son of |
| Hezron | Jerahmeel | Jephunneh |
| Wives: Azubah | — | — |
| Ephrath[ah] | | |
| Concubines: Jerioth (?) | Ephah | — |
| | Maacah | |
| | | |
| Sons: Jesher, Shobab, | Mesha, Haran, Moza | Iru, Elah, Naam |
| Ardon, **HUR** | Gazez, Sheber, | |
| (vs.19,50) | Tirhanah, Shaaph | |
| Daughter: | **ACSAH** (vs.49) | **ACSAH** |
| | | (Josh.15:16) |
| Older bro: — | Jerahmeel (vs.9,25,42) | |
| Younger bro: — | — | Kenaz (Josh.15:17; |
| | | Judg.1:13) |

### Caleb's Genealogy from Judah

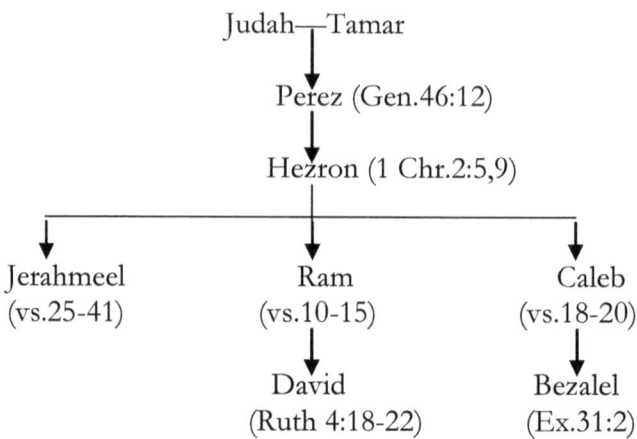

Judah—Tamar

Perez (Gen.46:12)

Hezron (1 Chr.2:5,9)

| Jerahmeel (vs.25-41) | Ram (vs.10-15) | Caleb (vs.18-20) |

David (Ruth 4:18-22)     Bezalel (Ex.31:2)

**Tentative conclusion:** From the context of 1 Chronicles 2:9,10,18,19, 25,42 and 50, the first two Calebs are the same man. This conclusion is helped <u>if</u> the two Hurs mentioned are the same man (vs.19,50; 4:1-4). Verse 50 and 4:1-4 definitely are the same. But the Hur of verse 19? His mother's name is Ephrath (vs.19). In verse 24 we find a place name, Caleb Ephrathah where Hezron died. <u>If</u> this "Ephrathah" is derived from Ephrath's name, then she could be the same as mentioned in verse 50 and 4:4, though it would seem to be most unusual, but not impossible, for a man to be said to be the firstborn of a woman (cf. Luke 2:7).

Then the Caleb of 1 Chronicles 4:15 is a different Caleb, Caleb the Spy. So Hezron, father of Caleb and Jerahmeel is the same Hezron. Jerahmeel, son of Hezron and older brother of Caleb is the same. Acsah (1 Chr.2: 49; Josh.15:16), daughter of both Calebs, seems to be different women with the same name.

**Q. 3:5-8** What's going on with the names of David's sons born to him in Jerusalem?

| 2 Sam.5:14-16 | 1 Chr.3:5-8 | | 1 Chr.14:4-7 |
|---|---|---|---|
| Shammua | Shammua | by | Shammua |
| Shobab | Shobab | Bath- | Shobab |
| Nathan | Nathan | she- | Nathan |
| Solomon | Solomon | ba | Solomon |

| 2 Sam.5:14-16 | 1 Chr.3:5-8 | 1 Chr.14:4-7 |
|---|---|---|
| Ibhar | Ibhar | Ibhar |
| Elishua | Elishua | Elishua |
| | *Eliphelet | *Eliphelet |
| | *Nogah | *Nogah |
| Nepheg | Nepheg | Nepheg |
| Japhia | Japhia | Japhia |
| Elishama | Elishama | Elishama |
| Eliada | Eliada | Beeliada (Eliada) |
| *Eliphelet | *Eliphelet | *Eliphelet |

**A.** From Irwin's Bible Commentary, p.128: "From comparing these lists, it seems likely that the first Eliphelet and Nogah died in childhood."

(From Jamieson, Fausset and Brown, p.458, note on vs.1-9)

Two sons with the same name, either

1. two sons of different mothers, differentiated by some title, or
2. the first died and his name given to another child.

It would seem to me that Irwin's comment and the second one offered by J,F&B give us the best explanation for the differences.

**Q. 4:10** Which is the correct translation of this verse?

| NKJV | N.I.V. |
|---|---|
| "O that You would bless me indeed, and enlarge my territory, That Your hand would be with me And that You would keep [me] from evil, That I may not [cause pain]!" | "O that you would bless me and enlarge my territory! Let your hand be with me, and keep me from harm so that I will be free from pain." |

**A.** The ESV and The Holy Scriptures (THS) in accordance to Jewish tradition support the N.I.V. translation rather than that of the NKJV: "Oh that you would bless me and enlarge my border, and that your hand might be with me, and that you would keep me from harm so that it might not bring me pain!" (ESV)

"Oh that thou wouldest bless me indeed, and enlarge my border, and that thine hand might be with me, and that thou wouldest keep me from evil, that it may not grieve me!" (THS)

**4:30** Interesting that Ziklag belonged first to Simeon. The Philistines later took it, then gave it to David (1 Sam.27:6).

**Q.** How does the list of David's men differ from 1 Chr.11:10-47 and 2 Sam.23:8-39?
**A.** See The Bible Knowledge Commentary, p.478, for a complete listing.

**12:23-37** Two other possible views on this passage, since the large numbers seem to be a problem for the N.I.V. note-makers.
  1. From 2 Samuel 5:1,3 "When all the elders of Israel had come." It could be that these elders represented the large number of fighting men mentioned in 1 Chronicles so that it was "as if" they were there.
  2. Yet the context (esp. vs.38-40) supports the entire number as reported. So I see no reason to try to figure out something else.

**13:11** David angry. Anger results from a blocked goal. David was doing the right thing with all his heart and soul, but in the wrong way (cf. 1 Chr.15:13). When God blocked his intentions (death of Uzzah), David became angry.

**Q.** Why would God do such a thing when he was bringing the Ark of God back?
**A.** Because a higher principle had been violated, the principle of
  God's holiness when they disobeyed his direct command (Num. 4:15). Even the priests had to take care not to touch the ark lest they die!
  Then David's anger turned to fear of God and frustration: "How can I ever bring the Ark of God to me?" (13:12). He canceled his plans, putting the Ark in Obed-Edom's house. Through this experience, he gained a new appreciation of God's holiness in his relationship to Israel. Through God's blessings to Obed-Edom over the next three months, David gained clearer insight into God's character: just because God is unbending in his demand for holiness and relating to him in the right way (see 2 Sam.6:12-15; 1 Chr.15:1,2), does not mean that he is harsh, demanding and capricious.
  We often want to serve God (the right thing) in our own wisdom (the wrong way), and end up violating his principle of holiness, then wonder why he isn't blessing—perhaps even becoming angry about it. In frustration (discouragement) we cancel our plans, suddenly

"unsure" of who our God really is.

Then, through his Word (Num.4:15) and the testimony of others (2 Sam.6:12), we gain new insight as to who he is and how he wants us to proceed with his work. If we have a willing and teachable heart, like David, the end will be blessed and our original desire to serve God will be fulfilled.

So, even those whose hearts are after God's own heart, have lessons to learn—sometimes the hard way. The change of fortune in Obed's household, assuming him to be a foreigner (see Q & A following), was even greater proof to David of God's mercy than it would have been had the Ark been in a Levite home. David may have thought, "If God is this gracious to a foreigner, then surely he will be just as gracious to his own people." So he was emboldened to resume his original plan to bring the Ark to Jerusalem (2 Sam.6: 12), this time in the correct way.

**Q. 13:13** Who was this Obed-Edom the Gittite?

**A.** Gittites are only mentioned three times in Scripture: Goliath (2 Sam. 21:19); Ittai (2 Sam.15:19-22, where David refers to him as a foreigner and an exile from his own place); and Obed-Edom.

1. So it would seem that this Obed-Edom was, at the least, a Philistine who had come to live in Israel, or, at the most, a proselyte. (But see the following **Q.**)

2. The later Obed-Edom was a Levite, appointed to be a gatekeeper for the Ark (1 Chr.15:17,18,24).

3. A third Obed-Edom, son of Jeduthun (1 Chr.16:38), also a Levite, was a harp player (1 Chr.15:21; 16:4,5) to help in the Temple music and also serve as a gate-keeper.

4. (2 Chr.25:24) The original Obed-Edom, guard of the Treasury, (yet by this time the treasures he had guarded were long gone).

5. Possibly a generic name in ref. to the "Order of the Gatekeepers of the Temple Storehouse" (see 1 Chr.26:15).

[NOTE: The special statement of God's blessing on Obed-Edom in 1 Chronicles 26:15 and 1 Chronicles 13:14 may serve to tie these two Obed-Edoms together, yet circumstantial evidence seems to "untie" them instead.]

**Q. Another problem:** <u>If</u> Obed-Edom was indeed a Philistine, why would David put the Ark of God in his house? This action would make more sense if Obed-Edom were a Levite, a "proper" custodian for the Ark.

**A.** 1. Perhaps his house was by the tragic site and expediency drove David to get the Ark off his hands as quickly as possible. The words, "he took it aside" seem to imply this possibility.

2. Perhaps he reasoned that God would be more forgiving toward a foreigner than toward an Israelite in terms of his Ark. For no doubt the Philistines had handled the Ark and didn't die for doing it (cf. 1 Sam. 6:8), whereas 70 of the Beth Shemeth people died because they had looked into the Ark (they had to touch it to do so—1 Sam.6:19).

I inclined to choose the first reason as it was a "spur of the moment" situation. David wouldn't have sat down to think through the second reason <u>unless</u> it was already on his mind.

**16:37-40** Interesting to note that although David brought the Ark of the Covenant into a special tent in Jerusalem (vs.1), the Tabernacle remained at the high place in Gibeon where the morning and evening sacrifices continued to be offered.

**Q.** Why did David remove the Ark from the Tabernacle, thus, in a sense, "remove" God's presence from the place of sacrifice and intercession?

**A.** David had such a yearning for God's presence that it only makes sense that he wanted him (hence the symbol of his presence, the Ark) as close to him as possible. Gibeon was just "too far away" (8 km. or 4.8 mi.). It was then just a matter of time and comparison (tent versus palace) when David conceived the idea of building a Temple to the Lord in which the Ark could reside (1 Chr.17:1,4).

**Q. 16:39,40** Whatever happened to the Tabernacle?

**A. 2 Chr.5:4,5** The Levites brought it up along with the Ark of the Covenant (from its tent) and evidently stored it away somewhere in the Temple.

**21:17** "What have they (Israel) done?" Obviously something (cf. 2 Sam. 24:1), otherwise the Lord would not have taken this kind of action against them.

**Q. 21:20** How is it that Ornan saw the angel and just continued on threshing the wheat while his four sons hid for fear?

**A.** He was threshing before the Angel came ("Now Ornan was threshing wheat"): I believe that it is a mistranslation in the NKJV. He would have hid himself along with his sons.

**Q.** Why did God refuse David's desire to build the Temple?

**A.** The emphasis in God's answer was on the differing characteristics of war versus peace and rest. Though David was a man after God's own heart **(22:8-10)**, God refused to let him build the Temple because he had "shed much blood and...fought many wars." "You have shed much blood on the earth in my sight. But you will have a son who will be a man of peace and rest...He will be the one who will build a house for my Name." God wanted to be known among the nations as a God of peace and rest, not of warfare. So it was important, symbolically, that the one who built the Temple also be a man of peace and rest.

**22:9,10** This information adds to what we find in 2 Samuel 7:11b-13 and 1 Chronicles 17:10b-12, which seems to put David's desire to build the Temple and God's declaration that it be one of his own sons to do it (whom we know to be Solomon) <u>before</u> David's affair with Bathsheba!

**Q. 25:1** What is the meaning of the word "prophesy" in this verse?

**A.** Even though Asaph, Jeduthun and Heman are elsewhere called "seers" (1 Chr.25:5; 2 Chr.29:30; 35:15), in this verse it is their sons whom David appointed to prophesy and were supervised in their prophesying. The context of this verse (vs.1-8) seems to link prophesying with the ministry of music. A regular prophet is not said to be "under the supervision" of any man, but speaks when moved by the Holy Spirit. In the ministry of music here mentioned, the sons of Asaph, Jeduthun and Heman were appointed by David (vs.4), not by God, and were under David's and their fathers' supervision (vs.2,3,6). "All trained and skilled in music for the LORD."

**Q.** A second question arises from the first: Would this use of the word "prophesy" throw some light on the "gift of prophecy" given to the Church, indicating special ability in music with which to praise the Lord?

**A.** Paul's use of the word "prophesy" in 1 Corinthians seems to carry
with it a different meaning, emphasizing the clarification of God's
Word for the edification of the listeners. Music does not necessarily
do this though it <u>can</u> help through reinforcement of truth.

**27:2-15** These 12 commanders were from The Thirty of 2 Sam.23:8-
39.

[**Note:** The 1st month of the Jewish sacred year begins in our month
of April (15th) - May (14th). So their first month is April-May, 2nd
May-June, and so forth until their 12th month March-April.]

| | | | |
|---|---|---|---|
| 1st Tishri (Ziv) | April/May | ("Leap Mo." Veadar, 7 x in 19 yrs.) | |
| 2nd Heshvan | May/June | 7th Nisan | Oct./Nov. |
| 3rd Chislev | June/July | 8th Iyar | Nov./Dec.. |
| 4th Tebeth | July/Aug. | 9th Sivan | Dec./Jan. |
| 5th Shebat | Aug./Sept. | 10th Tammuz | Jan./Feb. |
| 6th Adar | Sept./Oct. | 11th Ab | Feb./Mar |
| | | 12th Elul | Mar./Apr. |

(See <u>Nelson's</u>, p.48 for a more complete description of the Jewish
calendar.)

**27:30** Interesting that Obil the *Ishmaelite* was in charge of David's
camels.

**29:27-28** David was 70 when he died. He was 30 when he began his
reign of 40 years (2 Sam.5:4).

# 2 CHRONICLES

**1:3,4** It is interesting to note that the Tabernacle was still around (at Gibeon) but the Ark had been moved to another tent in Jerusalem that David had prepared for it. Ever since the Philistine wars, the Ark had not been in the Tabernacle, but evidently the sacrifices and other services had continued there (vs.5,6).

**1:7** Just a thought. If God ever came to you in a dream and said, "Ask for whatever you want me to give you," for what would you ask? It might be worth pondering for a while, then asking yourself why you chose what you did. If your desires are Scriptural and your motives pure, then go ahead and ask God for it. He just might be waiting for your request!

**1:14** Solomon's was a kingdom of peace, therefore he had no need of so many chariots and horses.

**3:2** Solomon began building the Temple on or around April 17, 966 B.C. [in the month of Ziv (April-May) on the second day which would be about April 17].

**Q. 3:8,9** What is the present-day value of these items?
**A.** Gold-----600 talents X 75 lbs. = 45,000 lbs. (720,000 oz. + 25
   oz. nails at $1,520/oz.) = $1,094,438,000.00 ($1 billion!)
   Silver-----17,000 talents = $ 437,835,000.00 (at $34.34/oz.)
   Bronze----18,000 talents = $ 86,400,000.00 (at $4.00/oz.)
   Iron-------100,000 talents = $ ???

**4:1** The size of Solomon's bronze altar of burnt offering is astounding. Twenty cubits long, 20 cubits wide and 10 cubits high, translates into 30 feet long, 30 feet wide (900 sq. ft.!) and 15 feet high! Picturing a ledge around the altar upon which the priests would stand to offer the sacrifices seems ludicrous because they would only be able to serve at the perimeter of the huge altar. The large number of sacrifices offered could not have been done on a single altar in any brief period of time. The more I thought about it, the more I wondered if Solomon's altar didn't appear more like a waffle iron on the top with many offering places so that many sacrifices could be offered at the same time. The priests could mount the altar by the ramp, then walk in among the places of sacrifices on the top. Presumably, there could have been as many as 25 places for sacrifice there if they measured 2.5 feet sq. with 4 feet of clearance around each one.

**Q. 5:9** If Ezra was the author of 1 & 2 Chronicles (see Introduction to 1 Chronicles), then this verse is definitely a problem, for the Temple had been destroyed and the Ark of the Covenant lost 70 years before.
**A. 2 Chr.9:29** answers this problem as Ezra, in quoting these sources, would write, "as it is this day" meaning when the sources were written.

**6:32,33** Answered prayer—a graphic difference between Jehovah and the gods of the nations.

**8:11** This verse bothers me: first that Solomon would purposely marry women who would "defile" the holiness of God by their presence; second, that he seemed to make no effort to apply his missionary vision (6:32,33) to his own home.

**9:25; 11:11** No fortification (or army) is strong enough to withstand the Lord's hand (cf. 2 Chr.12:2-4; Isa.45:1,2).

**11:1,13,16** In reality, the Kingdom of Judah consisted of 3½ tribes: Judah, Simeon, Levi and 1/2 Benjamin, plus a scattering of people from every other tribe. (Cf. 1 Ki.11:35,36 where 10 tribes were promised to Jeroboam, leaving three for Rehoboam since there were 13 tribes in Israel.) 2 Chronicles15:9 says that large numbers of people from Ephraim, Manasseh and Simeon also came over to Judah during Asa's reign, effectively giving the Southern Kingdom six tribes! But it seems that they assimilated into Judah and Benjamin rather than retaining their separate tribal identities (2 Chr.17:14,17).

**Q. 11:20** Rehoboam married Maacah, daughter of Abishalom (1 Ki. 15:2), or Absalom (2 Chr.11:20), or Uriel of Gibeah (2 Chr.13:2). 2). So whose daughter was she?
**A.** Since Absalom, David's son, had no sons (2 Sam.14:27; 18:18 — three sons were born to him, but must have died early), and Tamar lived as a desolate woman in Absalom's house (I'm assuming

by this statement that she never married), then the Absalom of 2 Chronicles 11:20 must be a <u>different</u> Absalom than David's son. It also seems reasonable to assume that this Absalom is a shortened form of Abishalom. If so, then these two names refer to the same person.

The notes in my N.I.V. Bible say that Maacah was Uriel's granddaughter. Since they have better sources than I, and since "son" or "daughter" are frequently used to mean "descendant of" (i.e., "Jesus, son of David," etc.), "granddaughter" could be the meaning here. So she'd be the daughter of Abishalom and grand-daughter of Uriel of Gibeah.

**18:1** "Jehoshaphat allied himself with Ahab by marriage." A smart move politically to finally bring some peace between the two kingdoms, but disastrous spiritually as it introduced a spiritual and political time bomb in Judah (Athaliah—see 2 Chr.21:4-6; 22:2,3,10).

**18:15** Hypocrisy—"false righteousness" for Jehoshaphat's sake, no doubt.

**18:18-22** It would seem from these verses that the Lord sometimes uses lies to accomplish his purposes. But even here, that is not the case since the Lord very clearly reveals to Ahab what was going on and Scripture states very clearly that God <u>cannot</u> lie (Heb.6:18).

**18:31** Ahab the coward—hedging his bet against Micaiah's prophecy by purposely exposing Jehoshaphat to danger. But God overruled Ahab's wicked scheme (vs.31,32) and accomplished his purpose on Ahab (vs.19,33).

**20:1-7** In facing impossible odds, Judah sought the Lord. The following day they had to go against the enemy and do everything but fight: march out [fit for battle], take your [battle] positions, and stand firm (cf. Eph.6: 11,13,14 where we are "to stand" firmly in our position—the battle is the <u>Lord's</u>).

**20:9** Jehoshaphat recalling Solomon's prayer.

**20:17** Judah had to do everything but fight.

**20:21** Only <u>faith</u> could justify this "foolishness." Whoever heard of a choir preceding an army into battle?!

**21:4,16,17** with **24:7** Jehoash first killed all his brothers, no doubt at the urging of his wife, Athaliah, to eliminate any political rivalry (see also 2 Chr.22:10), then the Lord raised up the Philistines and Arabs who killed all but one of his sons. What one sows, he also reaps. Athaliah not only ruined him, but ruined his sons as well. In 24:7 we read that they broke into the Temple, no doubt with Athaliah's approval, and used its sacred objects in their Baal worship. So the Lord judged them on the merits of their own sins.

**25:17** The challenge to Jehoash, King of Israel, may have been the result of the killing and plundering of Judean towns by Israel's soldiers (vs.10, 13).

**Ch.27ff** It's amazing to me that Jotham, a godly king (27:6), had such a wicked son (Ahaz—28:22), who had such a godly son (Hezekiah—29:2), who had such an extremely wicked son (Manasseh—33:2-9). He repented (33:12), yet had a very wicked son (Amon—33:22,23) who had a very godly son (Josiah—34:3).

**Q. Chs.28,29** Ahaz was 20 years old when he began to reign, and he reigned 16 years (28:1). Hezekiah was 25 years old when he began to reign, and he reigned 29 years (29:1). Do the math! Ahaz died when he was 36 years old. Hezekiah took over the throne at 25 years of age. 36-25 = 11! So Ahaz would have had to be married when he was just 10 years old so that his wife could have Hezekiah when he was 11. Somehow, I don't think so! How can this conundrum be reconciled? Commentaries don't help here.
**A.**

**29:36** "Done quickly," (i.e., within 17 days of his assuming the throne—vs.3,17,20)!

**32:12** Sennacherib demonstrates a cultural misunderstanding here and makes a "logical assumption" based on his misunderstanding of who Israel's God was (vs.13-16,19).

**33:17** The people's spiritual compromise made it that much easier to return to idolatry when the climate was right.

**Q. Ch.34** Interesting change of order of events from that of 2 Kings 22 and 23. Which is right?

**A.** N.I.V. note and commentaries are no help. From the internal evidence it would seem that the events happened in this order:

| 2 Chr.34 | 2 Ki.22 |
|---|---|
| vs.3 **8th yr.** Josiah began to seek God (without a copy of the Law around! He must have had a godly spiritual counselor). | |
| vs.3 **12th yr.** He <u>began</u> to purge Judah and Jerusalem, going so far as Manasseh, Ephraim, Simeon and Naphtali (2 Chr.34:3,6). [**NOTE:** Simeon was within Judah; Manasseh and Ephraim were neighbors; Naphtali a bit more removed.] | |
| vs.8 **18th yr.** He ordered the Temple cleansed and repaired. The Book of the Law found; Josiah humbles himself and covenants to keep the Law. He makes a clean sweep of every remaining vestige of idolatry in Judah and Jerusalem (finishing what he began in his 12th year.) He calls to for keeping of the Passover. | 22:3 —same— <br><br> 23:4 Ordered the cleansing of the land <u>after</u> the Law was read to him. |

## Josiah's Family Tree
(Superscript numbers indicate the order of their reigns)

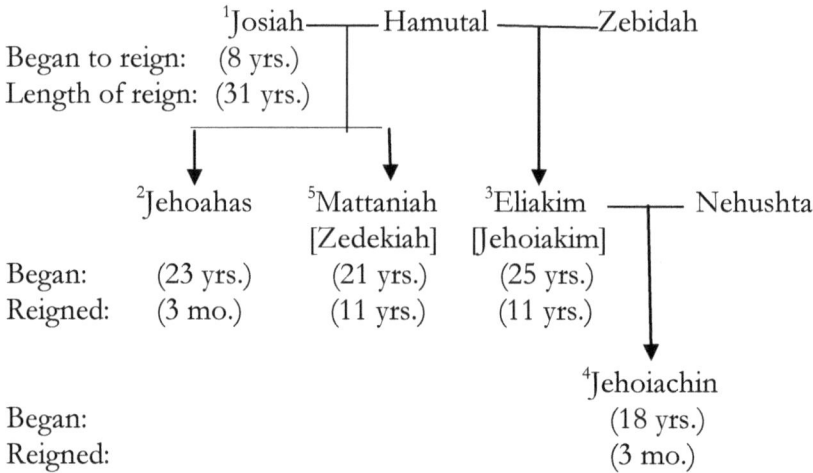

|  | ¹Josiah — Hamutal — Zebidah |
| Began to reign: | (8 yrs.) |
| Length of reign: | (31 yrs.) |

|  | ²Jehoahas | ⁵Mattaniah [Zedekiah] | ³Eliakim [Jehoiakim] — Nehushta |
| Began: | (23 yrs.) | (21 yrs.) | (25 yrs.) |
| Reigned: | (3 mo.) | (11 yrs.) | (11 yrs.) |

|  |  | ⁴Jehoiachin |
| Began: |  | (18 yrs.) |
| Reigned: |  | (3 mo.) |

**34:6** Josiah seemed to have some authority over the inhabitants of former Israel as well as Judah. According to the N.I.V. notes, this may have become possible because of the decline and fall of the Assyrian Empire about that time and Josiah's desire to resurrect the Davidic Kingdom, religiously and politically. From verse 9 it would seem that his authority had expanded somewhat over Manasseh and Ephraim. "The entire remnant of Israel" may indicate an even wider authority (see verse 33 also where the implication is of territory much bigger than Judah alone).

**Q. 36:5-7** N.I.V. notes say that Jehoiakim died <u>before</u> the Babylonian army arrived to besiege Jerusalem. 2 Kings 24:5-12 would seem to support this view. Yet 2 Chronicles 36:6 clearly states that Jehoiakim was bound with bronze shackles to be taken to Babylon. ???

**A.** Jehoiakim reigned from 609-598 B.C.

Nebuchadnezzar's first attack on Jerusalem came in 605 B.C.

Jehoiakim was his vassal for three years, then rebelled (602 B.C.) At that time he evidently was bound and taken to Babylon. The commentary says that he either escaped or was later released since he died in Jerusalem in 598 B.C. Escape is highly unlikely as the whole area was still under Babylonian control. But there is no indication of an interim king (8 months round trip to Babylon at the least—cf. Ezra 7:9), or his resumption of his rule (as with Manasseh), so restoration after a period of time in Babylon is not too likely.

Putting 2 Chronicles 36:6 with Daniel 1:1,2, I come up with a different scenario. 2 Chronicles 36:6 says he was bound "<u>to</u> take him to Babylon." However, Daniel 1:1 says that only the articles of the temple were carried off at this time (and, verse 3, some from the royal family).

To me, a much more reasonable answer is that Jehoiakim was bound, and Nebuchadnezzar was planning to take him to Babylon, but for some reason changed his mind. Jehoiakim was released at or near Jerusalem and continued as king until his death in 598 (see Jer.22:18,19). The siege described in 2 Kings 24:10-12 took place in 597, 3 months and 10 days after Jehoiakim's death.

## The Last 61 Years of the Kingdom of Judah

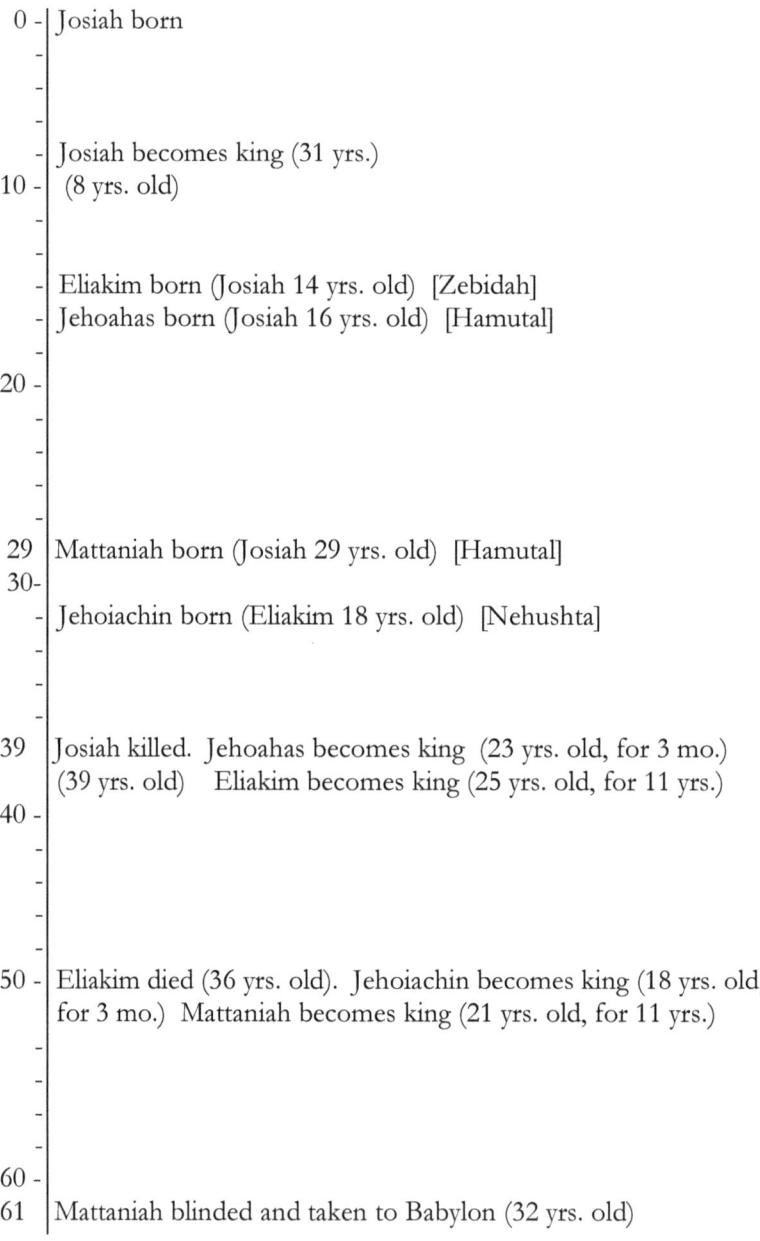

```
 0 -| Josiah born
   -
   -
   -
   -| Josiah becomes king (31 yrs.)
10 -|  (8 yrs. old)
   -
   -| Eliakim born (Josiah 14 yrs. old)  [Zebidah]
   -| Jehoahas born (Josiah 16 yrs. old)  [Hamutal]
20 -
   -
   -
   -
29 | Mattaniah born (Josiah 29 yrs. old)  [Hamutal]
30-
   -| Jehoiachin born (Eliakim 18 yrs. old)  [Nehushta]
   -
   -
39 | Josiah killed.  Jehoahas becomes king  (23 yrs. old, for 3 mo.)
   | (39 yrs. old)   Eliakim becomes king (25 yrs. old, for 11 yrs.)
40 -
   -
   -
   -
50 -| Eliakim died (36 yrs. old).  Jehoiachin becomes king (18 yrs. old,
   | for 3 mo.)  Mattaniah becomes king (21 yrs. old, for 11 yrs.)
   -
   -
   -
60 -
61 | Mattaniah blinded and taken to Babylon (32 yrs. old)
```

**God of the Impossible (cont.):**

169. He worked his desire for Israel in the hearts of heathen kings (1:1-4; 6:22; 7:27,28).

\* \* \* \*

**Q. Ezra 2** with **Neh.7** and **1 Chr.9.** The numbers don't tally up, neither with each other nor with the totals given in each chapter. Same event. What's going on?

**A.** Apart from "numerous scribal errors" which commentary and N.I.V. notes say caused these discrepancies (see comments in the last paragraph below), one source says the larger total may include women and children. Numerically, that would mean that most of the male returnees were bachelors. If each one was married, the total of 29,818 added in Ezra would have had to be doubled to 59,000. They certainly would have had one or more children which would at the least have added another 29,000 to the total, giving us a figure somewhere around 88,000, almost double the 49,000 total recorded. "Northern Jews" joining the company is the more likely reason for the larger totals than numbers recorded.

However, having said this, verses 64 and 65 talk about the "whole company besides men servants and women servants," came to 42,300 people. That sounds to me like it <u>includes</u> women and children in that figure, the totals under each man's name <u>not</u> being total heads of families but the total number of descendants (men, women and children) from that man.

Differences in numbers and totals is a problem and probably is left to the area of conjecture to figure out. Scribal error? Independent census taken: one by Ezra, another by Nehemiah? No, since Nehemiah's record was taken from previous records, not his own (Neh.7:5). Inclusion of "northern Jews? Other "hangers-on" — unlikely, given the nature of the case. Somehow the total neared 50,000.

**Q.** What about the differences in the amounts of gold, silver and priestly garments (Ezra 2:69 and Neh.7:72)? Again, scribal errors in the ciphers? Counting from a different perspective? (100 priestly

garments [Ezra 2:69] versus 69 [Neh.7:72]. Perhaps a difference in individual items counted? Or garments for whom? [Priests and helpers versus only priests?] The differences in the totals of silver and gold given could be as simple as counting them at different times, but...? I'm very uncomfortable with "scribal errors" as being the cause of so many numerical differences. One or two differences perhaps, but 20% would show great carelessness somewhere which is totally out of character for the super-meticulous Jewish scribes (cf. Ezra 8:26-29, 33,34). No, there is something else going on here to which we are not privy, and will take some deeper sleuthing to discover.
**A.**

**4:1** It is interesting to note that, at the division of the Kingdom and afterwards, the southern kingdom is often referred to as Judah and Benjamin—the two tribes from which came Israel's, then Judah's kings (see also Ezra 10:9).

**4:1,12-16,24** Interesting that the Jews were being accused of rebuilding the city, whereas they were only rebuilding the Temple at this time. But this false accusation accomplished its purpose and brought the Temple construction to a standstill.

**6:22-7:1** The book of Esther comes here (cf. Esth.1:3 with Ezra 7:7).

**7:10** An illustration of Psalm 119:97-100. Ezra devoted himself to studying and obeying God's Word. The results were obvious to everyone, even to a pagan king (7:25)! He had a passion for God that would put him in the same class as David.

**7:(12-26),27,28** Artaxerxes was Xerxe's son (probably the son of Vashti). I wonder how much of his attitude here reflects the influence of Mordecai and Esther? Under Xerxes, Esther, his queen, had much influence and Mordecai reached a pinnacle of power and influence that was far-reaching. It certainly was not lost on Artaxerxes who showed great sympathy to the Jewish people (as a result? – Neh.2:1-8).

**Q. 8:26,27** What is the approximate value of the items listed?
**A.** Silver: 650 talents ~ 25 tons = 800,000 oz. X $34.34 =
$ 27,472,000

Silver articles: 100 talents ~ 3¾ tons = 120,000 oz. X $34.34 =
$ 4,120,800

Gold: 100 talents ~ 3¾ tons = 120,000 oz. X $1,520 =
$182,300,000

20 gold bowls valued at 1,000 darics = 19 lbs. =
304 oz. X $1,520 = $ 462,080

2 fine articles of polished bronze (as precious as gold) = $ ???
$ 214,454,880

**8:36-9:1** Nehemiah 8-10 falls between these verses.

| Day | Month | Happening | Reference |
|-----|-------|-----------|-----------|
| 1 | 1 | Ezra leaves Babylon. | Ezra 7:9 |
| 1 | 5 | Ezra arrives in Jerusalem the seventh year of King Artaxerxes. | Ezra 7:8,9 |
| 1 | 7 | Ezra read the Law. | Neh.8:2 |
| 20 | 9- | The issue of mixed marriage... | Ezra 10:9 |
| -1 | 1 | ...dealt with over a period of three months. | Ezra 10:16,17 |

**9:1,2** The Israelites again took foreign, unbelieving wives. Twelve years later, they did it again (Neh.10:30), and again 30 years later (Neh.13:23). This was a very potent weapon in Satan's arsenal in an attempt to corrupt God's chosen people.

**Q. Chs.9,10** Out of approximately 14,000 heads of households, only 113 (17 priests, 10 Levites and 86 others) had taken foreign wives, a seemingly insignificant number, eight tenths of one percent! Wasn't Ezra's reaction far out of proportion to the offense committed?
**A.** No—for two reasons:
1. Because of Ezra's devotion to the Law of God, he had a heightened sense of God's holiness and the awfulness of sin in his presence. Any sin had to be dealt with thoroughly because any sin is an affront to a holy God. Example: Achan was only one man out of perhaps 3 million (0.00003%), yet his one sin condemned the whole nation to defeat!
2. Paul says in 1 Corinthians 5:6 that a little yeast works through the

whole batch of dough (see also Gal.5:9). If this sin went unchecked, it wouldn't be long before there would be mass intermarriage along with reintroduced idolatry and a returning of God's severe judgment as the nation once again proved unfaithful in departing from him.

**Commentary:** Freedom from the Law and living under Grace has made the Church very careless in its attitude toward sin. We do not realize, or refuse to recognize, how the sin of one or two can affect the entire congregation. (This is clearer in a group-oriented culture.) Our culture looks at the individual, not the group, not realizing how thoroughly the one influences the other. The only way I know how we can gain a heightened sense of God's holiness and the awfulness of sin is to do what Ezra did, devote ourselves to the study of God's Word with the intent of obeying it.

# NEHEMIAH

**God of the impossible (cont.):**

170. He caused Nehemiah's life to be spared when he was sad in the king's presence (2:1-3).
171. He enabled the Israelites to rebuild the walls of Jerusalem in 52 days against incredible odds (6:15).

**\* \* \* \***

**1:6,7** The reason that Nehemiah, Ezra (Ezra 9:6,7) and Daniel (Dan. 9:5-11) could identify with the sins of the nation ("we have done…") is that they had a corporate identity as a nation, a group-oriented culture, where the sins of the few were looked on as bringing corporate guilt on all. We do not have that consciousness in our culture which makes corporate identity for us far more difficult.

However, we <u>are</u> a single body as the Body of Christ, and when one member suffers (1 Cor.12:25-27), all suffer with it. Excepting Nehemiah 1:6 (and that only in general), Ezra, Nehemiah and Daniel never identified themselves with the sins of the empires in which they lived, but <u>only</u> with the sins of God's people.

In parallel, perhaps we don't need to personally identify with the sins of our nation, but only with those of God's people, the Church. (Even on this level our platter may be overloaded!)

**Ch.3** Four lessons learned:
1. Everybody doing a little bit gets the job done in a short time (52 days—6:15).
2. Everybody worked, even if "wall-building" wasn't their "gift" (cf. vs.31,32).
3. Enthusiasm for the task often brings in outside help (vs.2,5,7,15-19,26,27).
4. Some didn't just stop with their own part, but helped in other sections as well (cf. vs.4,21, Meremoth; vs.1,28, the priests; vs.5,27, the Tekoites; vs.4,30, Meshullam).

**Q. Ch.3** Is it possible to approximate on a map where each group worked?
A. Yes. See the ESV Study Bible, p.827.

149

**5:8** The Jewish nobles and officials really had a thing going, charging interest on loans to their countrymen, foreclosing on their lands and houses, then selling those who couldn't pay as slaves to the Gentiles, only for Nehemiah to buy them back!

**Q. 6:18** Is this Meshullam the same as in Ezra 10:15,29?
**A.** I believe so, though there is no concrete evidence to prove it. But putting all the passages referring to him together, an interesting story evolves. Meshullam was a leader in Israel.
1. He was opposed to getting rid of foreign wives (20th day of 9th mo.—Ezra 10:15).
2. He himself was guilty of having a foreign wife (Ezra 10:29).
3. He was under oath to Tobiah the Ammonite (Neh.6:18) whose son had married Meshullam's daughter. This explains his reticence to agree to the marriage order. It would really mess things up with his family socially and politically.
4. Yet two months earlier he had signed his agreement to keep the Law (Neh.10:20). Evidently he signed it without much thought as to the implications to his family—or else signed under community pressure to do so—for not signing would have separated him from the community of Israel—an even worse fate to him than his potential family and political disruption.

**6:15,16** God allowed all sorts of opposition to the building of the wall in order to demonstrate his power to Jew and Gentile alike in helping Nehemiah and company to complete it in just 52 days. Consider the opposition Nehemiah faced:
1. Personal opposition — fear (2:1-3).
2. Psychological opposition — mocking and ridicule (2:19; 4:1-3).
3. Internal opposition—some Jews refused to work (3:5), plus distracting social injustices (5:1-13).
4. Physical opposition — threat of attack (4:7-9,11-15).
5. Material opposition — too much rubble, workers tiring (4:10); so … the Lord slowed them down by one-half (because of #4) to conserve energy and keep them working (4:16-18).
6. Strategic opposition — to get Nehemiah away from the work (6:1,2).
7. Harassment — to wear Nehemiah down (6:3-9).
8. Intimidation — to make Nehemiah look like a rebel/criminal (6:10-13,19).

**9:16,17** When faced with change, and certain discomforts because of that change, the urge to return to the old and comfortable (familiar) at times can be overpowering, even if the new way is far better.

**9:36** Irony of history. In wanting to return to slavery in Egypt, Israel's progenitors planted the seeds for Israel's eventual return to slavery in their own land!

## God of the impossible, (cont.)

172. He orchestrated the people and events which led to the Jews'
     deliverance from Haman's wicked plot against them.

* * * *

**Q. 1:12** Why did Vashti refuse the king's command?
**A.** (See N.I.V. note on 1:9.)  If this note is correct, then she was preg-
     nant and not exactly in the "best of shape" to be put on public
display.  Her sensitivity as a woman made it impossible for her to obey
the king's command.

**3:4**  Evidently the royal officials held Mordecai in great respect, for it
was some time, and after much urging, before they reported his actions
to Haman.  If Haman hadn't noticed this "dishonor" it was probably
because he was holding his head high and didn't deign to look at those
whom he passed by.  Now, however, he "saw" and became enraged
(3:5; 5:9,10).

**Q.** The N.I.V. note on 3:1 states the probability of Haman's descent
     from Agag, the Amorite king (1 Sam.15:20), one reason for his
hatred of the Jews.
**A.** However, in light of the fact that archaeology has found a province
     of the Persian Empire named Agag (The Bible Knowledge Com-
mentary), it is far more likely that Haman came from that province
rather than being a descendent of King Agag.  Also, there were no
Amorites left for Haman to descend from (1 Sam.15:8,33)!

**3:5,6**  Haman obviously had a deep hatred toward the Jews (as
obviously did many others—9:12,15,16).  Mordecai was only an excuse
for him to act.

## THE SIGNIFICANCE OF THE SCEPTER

**5:2**  Whether planned or unplanned, the story of Esther brings out an
interesting illustration of Christ as the Scepter (Num.24:17).  In Esther

4:8-14, Mordecai persuades her to go before the king to intercede for her people. She replied, "All the king's officials and the people of the the royal provinces know that for any man or woman who approaches the king in the inner court without being summoned, the king has but one law: that he be put to death. The only exception to this is for the king to extend the gold scepter to him and spare his life" (Esth.4:11). She went in, and the king extended the golden scepter to her.

We find this same principle or law operative for anyone presuming to enter God's presence on his own and unbidden; there is but one law for him: "You cannot see my face, for no one may see me and live" (Ex.33:20). In Hebrews 10:14 we read that Christ has made us perfect [our position in him] and thus fit to come into God's presence: "Because by one sacrifice he has made perfect forever those who are being made holy" (our practice on earth, not perfect yet, but moving in that direction: equals Christian growth!). And we read in Hebrews 12:10 that "God disciplines us for our good so that we may share in his holiness." He thus "extends" to us the Scepter of Righteousness, Jesus Christ himself, for us to "touch." Having "touched" him, we are accepted by the Father and permitted to enter his presence and live.

**6:1,4** "Divine insomnia." The Lord was one step ahead of Haman!

**6:13** Hatred makes everything that is good fade into oblivion as it increasingly centers our focus on the object of our hatred.

# JOB

## God of the impossible, (cont.)

173. He totally limits what Satan can do (1:12; 2:6).

* * * *

**1:9** False accusation: *God pays Job to follow him.*

**1:12; 2:6** Satan's actions restricted. He cannot pass beyond God's limit placed upon him.

**1:15-19** Satan's true character is quickly revealed. All he desires to do is to kill and destroy (2:3; cf. Jn.10:7-10).

**1:20** Job's heart is centered upon <u>God</u>, not his possessions.

**2:4** False assumption: *Man's life is more precious to him than his faith.*

**3:14** The kings and counselors of the earth built "ruins" for themselves. This demonstrates the transitory nature of life.

**3:25,26** Again Satan's hand reveals who he really is, for he brought upon Job what Job greatly feared and dreaded. (His goal was to cause Job to curse God [2:5,9]; he does not seek Job's good.) Job probably had seen others suffer terribly with boils, and recoiled from it, dreading the possibility that he might suffer with boils someday. Satan would afflict us all terribly if God did not set limits on him.

[**NOTE** the contrast with God's intentions when he afflicts (5:17,18 with Heb.12:5-11). Also, in 42:10, God accuses Job's friends of not speaking what was true about him as Job did. Among other things, God declared Job a righteous man who feared God and shunned evil (1:8; 2:3). They were accusing Job of exactly the opposite, which, in essence, was calling God's evaluation of Job untrue! It's not good to call God a liar (knowingly or unknowingly)! I wonder how Job felt being so falsely accused by his friends. They were saying of him just the <u>opposite</u> of what was reality in his life!]

**5:17-27** Everything Eliphaz says about what happens to those who truly follow the LORD is opposite from Job's experience. Thus he implies that because of what Job is suffering, he <u>must</u> be a great sinner!

**8:4** Bildad's allegation here is that Job's sacrifices for his children were ineffective (see 1:5)!—a direct and inexcusable attack on Job's faith. And the fact that he is suffering so is evidence that he has greatly sinned. Such suffering doesn't come without cause (8:8-22).

**8:6,7** The "Prosperity Gospel" is nothing new.

**Ch.9** "God, you are so awesome, so strong, so overwhelming—there is no way I can make my defense before you. Since you have already determined and pronounced my guilt, what more can I say?" Job figures that he must have done something to deserve all this misery, but for the life of him, he can't figure out what. "Purposeless misery" leads one to despair. That's why we need the clear goal of Romans 8:28,29 to help us through the hard times.

**12:5** Job's evaluation of his friends' observations: "Those who are at ease find it easy to be judgmental of those who aren't."

**12:7-12** Job appeals to all creation to prove that God does what he pleases—that he does not use a person's piety as the sole basis for granting freedom from affliction (N.I.V. note). Then God continues this same argument from creation to "put Job in his proper place" (chs.38-41).

**14:12** No reincarnation!

**19:3** "Ten times"—actually only five up until now. But this phrase seems to mean "enough and more" (cf. Gen.31:7).

**26:5-14** (vs.14) What we see and know of God's power are but a faint whisper of the awesome, ear-splitting, rock-cracking thunder of his might.

**31:23** The basis of Job's godliness: fear of God's judgment and awe (fear) of his majesty/splendor.

**Q. 32:2** "Elihu…of the family of Ram."  Is this the same Ram as in the genealogy of David (Mat.1:4; Lk.3:33 N.I.V. note)?

**A.** No, because it's not the same time frame.  The Ram in Jesus' gene-alogy came <u>after</u> Judah; the Ram in Job's time lived before or during Abraham's time.

**32:2,3,12** is the basic summary of Job 1-31.

**38:1** Interesting how Elihu describes God in terms of a thunder storm (chs.36,37) and God answers Job "out of the storm."  This would seem to be God's confirmation that what Elihu said about him was true.  This assumption is further supported by the fact that God only reprimanded Job's three friends (42:7,8), not Elihu, for speaking falsely about him.

**38:2** In terms of 42:7, it would seem that God is not rebuking Job here, but reminding him that he cannot "explain" God nor fully understand his ways.  Job got the message loud and clear (42:2-6).  This was a gentle "putting Job in his place" while at the same time being tremendously pleased that he "passed the test."  Overall, Job grew in his knowledge of God.  Hopefully, his three friends did too.

**Q. 40:15** What animal is the behemoth?
**A.** <u>The Bible Knowledge Commentary</u> makes a good case for a giant hippo.

**Q. 41:1** What animal is Leviathon?
**A.** <u>The Bible Knowledge Commentary</u> suggests a giant crocodile known in the Jordan River at earlier times.

**Overall Thought:** Satan caused Job's distress in order to destroy him.  God permitted Job's distress in order to reveal more of himself to him (42:5) as well as to prove a point to Satan!  Job's response was to humble himself and repent from the presumptuous words he had spoken to and about God in his suffering.

### Synopsis of Job, chs.1-42

**1,2** <u>Satan</u>: "Job only worships you because you have 'bribed' him.

Take away all he has, and he will curse you to your face!"
Job continues to worship God but …

**3**   <u>Job</u>:   …curses instead the day he was born. Better to be dead and at peace.

**4,5** <u>Eliphaz</u>:   "God blesses the righteous and curses the unrighteous. He's disciplining you for something" (5:17,18).

**6,7** <u>Job</u>:   "What have I done wrong to be afflicted in this way?"

**8**   <u>Bildad</u>:   "Your children got what they deserved. They sinned, and you have sinned. Plead for mercy and God will restore you."

**9,10** <u>Job</u>:   "God is so awesome, I cannot plead with him. What could I say? Nothing will change his mind from what he intends to do. No, I desperately need a mediator, someone to plead my cause for me."

**11**  <u>Zophar</u>:   "Admit it—you've sinned. God is actually punishing you less than you deserve! Confess it and you will prosper again."

**12-14** <u>Job</u>:   "I am innocent! Quit trying to make me out to be what I am not! God, if you are afflicting me because of sin, show it to me. There is a resurrection (14:14-17) where grace covers all sin."

**15**  <u>Eliphaz</u>:   "Job, you're a worse sinner than I thought! You have no fear of God! The wicked have nothing but trouble and you are in deep trouble! Therefore, you must be very wicked!"

**16,17** <u>Job</u>:   "Even though I am innocent, both God and men have turned against me."

**18**  <u>Bildad</u>:   "The wicked have nothing but trouble and disaster, just like you are having now."

| | | |
|---|---|---|
| 19 | <u>Job</u>: | "For some reason, God has become my enemy. Pity me, don't judge me!" |

| | | |
|---|---|---|
| 20 | <u>Zophar</u>: | "Listen, Job, it's the <u>wicked</u> who are punished!" |

| | | |
|---|---|---|
| 21 | <u>Job</u>: | "Not so! I have seen the wicked prospering and free from trouble to the day of their death. Stop speaking nonsense!" |

| | | |
|---|---|---|
| 22 | <u>Eliphaz</u>: | "The proof of your great sin is your suffering. You need to repent and turn to God." |

| | | |
|---|---|---|
| 23,24 | <u>Job</u>: | "If only I could talk with God face to face, we could get things straightened out. But he's elusive. Who can know his ways? Where is the day of reckoning? It will surely come in time." (His ultimate faith remains unshakeable, even though he cannot understand why he is suffering.) |

| | | |
|---|---|---|
| 25 | <u>Bildad</u>: | "No man is righteous before God; neither are you!" |

| | | |
|---|---|---|
| 26-31 | <u>Job</u>: | "God is utterly magnificent in all his works. What we see and hear is a mere whisper of his power. |
| 27 | | "Though he has denied me justice and made me taste bitterness of soul, I will still maintain my integrity as the fate of the wicked is even worse. |
| 28 | | "True wisdom cannot be found anywhere or purchased. It is the fear of God and the shunning of evil. |
| 29 | | "Oh if I could only return to the days gone by when I lived under God's favor. |
| 30 | | "I had helped others in their affliction, but now when I am afflicted, they mock me and attack me on every side. Even God is against me! |
| 31 | | "If I have purposely sinned in any way, then let God's curses come upon me. I have nothing more to say." |
| 32-37 | <u>Elihu</u>: | "I can't contain myself any longer. I must speak. |
| 33 | | "Your concept of God as your enemy is wrong. *Your claim to be without fault is also wrong.* |
| 34 | | "God does not punish for no reason. He is not capricious. He is omniscient, omnipotent and totally just. |

| | |
|---|---|
| **35** | "Whether we sin or do what is right, God is God and will not be influenced by what we do. |
| **36** | "God will punish the wicked and reward the righteous. He will also deliver those who suffer in their affliction. |
| **37** | "The awesomeness of God is seen in the storm with which he punishes or blesses men. God is so majestic, how could you even consider trying to make your case before him?" |

**38,39** <u>God</u>: takes up where Elihu left off, speaking out of the storm, posing unanswerable questions about creation (38:4-38), personal power (40:6-14) and zoology (38:39-39:30; 40:15-41:34) .

**40:3-5** <u>Job</u>: "I have nothing to say."

**40:6-14** <u>God</u>'s challenge: "Will you condemn me to justify yourself? Can you array yourself like me or show the same power as I have?"

**40:15-41:34** God poses more unanswerable questions about zoology to Job.

**42:1-6** <u>Job</u> "I know who I am and who you are. I despise myself and repent."

**42:7,8** <u>God</u> reprimands Job's three friends for misrepresenting him.

**42:9** <u>Job</u> prays for them. Test over and passed.

**42:10-16** <u>God</u> blesses Job with twice as much as he had before (and Satan slinks off with his "tail between his legs," <u>still</u> not understanding Job's faith and integrity, and how he could not but curse God for all his troubles.)

## God of the Impossible (cont.):

174. He knows the number of stars and has named them all (147:4).

**\* \* \* \***

**1:1** Blessed...
1. are those chosen as his inheritance (33:12; 65:4; 144:15).
2. are those whose sins are forgiven (32:1,2).
3. are those who are of righteous character and action (1:1; 32:2; 41:1; 106:3; 119:1,2).
4. are those who delight in the LORD (1:2; 112:1; 119:2).
5. are those who are disciplined by the LORD and taught from his Word (94:12).
6. are those who fear and obey him (112:1; 115:13-15; 119:1; 128: 1,4).
7. are those who enter and walk in God's presence (65:4: 84:4; 89: 15).
8. are those who trust and take refuge in him (2:12; 34:8; 40:4; 84: 12; 146:5).
9. are those who find their strength in him (84:5; 146:5).
10. are those who worship him (84:5: 89:15).
11. is the family of the righteous (37:25,26; 112:2; 127:5).

**1:2b** "And on his law he meditates day and night."

## Question:

What do you think about when you have nothing to think about? Do your thoughts immediately turn to God's Word or to inconsequential things? The person God blesses is the one who is meditating/thinking on his Word during his "down times," not filling his thoughts with what is unimportant and unfruitful.

**8:1,9** "O LORD, our Lord, how excellent is your name in all the earth!"

# HOW EXCELLENT IS YOUR NAME

O LORD, our Lord,
How excellent is Your name in all the earth!
O LORD, our Lord,
Our mouths shall declare the greatness of Your worth.

For you have set Your glory high Above the heav'nly sphere;
The skies tell forth Your praise, Their voice not heard by ear.
You have made Your power known On land and foaming sea.
Wherever man may roam Your glory there shall be.

For You have set the starry host And called them all by name;
The course for sun and moon That man can never tame.
You have set the bounds of earth, Of every tribe and race,
The borders of the sea, For every one its place.

For You have weighed the mighty wind,
And every hill and plain.
You've counted every cloud And droplets of the rain.
You have measured sea and sky, The tears of those who cry;
You know the heart of man, His every step and plan.

Refrain:
O LORD, our Lord,
How excellent is Your name in all the earth!

R.J.L. — 1/31/88 (Revised 4/15/20)

**Q. 10:3,4** Why does the Lord seem to let the wicked go on and on in their wickedness without restriction or other judgment?
**A.** 1. To further his purposes for his people (Rom.8:28,29).

2. To extend his grace to them. Earth is the only "heaven" they will ever know. In his grace, God gives them as much time as possible to enjoy it (as such) before the eternity of hell envelopes them.

3. To allow them only the "rewards" this life offers (Ps.17:14a).

**11:3** "When the foundations are being destroyed, what can the righteous do?" They can do 2 Chronicles 7:14! Humble themselves, pray, seek God's face and turn from their sin!

**12:1,2,8** Commentary on U.S. politics and society.

**12:6; 18:30** indicate the inerrancy of God's Word. If the Bible is indeed his Word, then it <u>has</u> to be flawless—inerrant, otherwise it is <u>not</u> his Word.

**12:8** "vile" = pornography, etc.

**13:1,2** "How long...?"

## HOW LONG?

How long before we hear Your trumpet call?
How long before the nations quake and fall?
How long before the skies are rent in twain
And Jesus comes to earth again to reign?

How long e'er Satan's power be destroyed?
How long e'er Heaven's power be deployed?
How long must evil hold its foul sway?
"Until the filth of earth be swept away."

Oh come, Lord Jesus! Sweep Your threshing floor,
This world of chaff. Oh cleanse it to the core.
Renew this earth and all who in it dwell.
Set up Your Kingdom, then all will be well.

R.J.L. — 3/21/93

**17:3** "Even at my most secret personal times, you will find nothing unrighteous in me." What we think about and/or do in our bedroom before sleeping is a good indicator of the true condition of our hearts. Psalm 63:6 gives us the cure for secret problems.

**18:1-9** The Lord "moves heaven and earth" to help his own.

**19:1-14** Knowledge of the God of Creation (vs.1-6):
The Creation of God turns us to the God of the Word (vs.7-11);
The Character of God leads us to the God of the Heart (vs.12-14) and the confession of our sins to him.

**23:6** For some reason the N.I.V. has chosen to translate the Hebrew word as "love" rather than "mercy." In the Septuagint, **ἔλεός** (el-ĕ-**OS**) is translated **"mercy,"** "compassion"; and in the Interlinear Hebrew, Greek, English Bible, it is translated "mercy." The two words perhaps are similar in Hebrew, but give two very different meanings in English. "Love" implies a tender relationship between two people; "mercy" implies one showing good to an undeserving person. If the word "mercy" isn't acceptable, then "compassion" (an alternate meaning) would still be better than "love" as it includes the concept of "mercy."

**27:6c** "I will sing and make music to the LORD."

### I WILL SING AND MAKE MUSIC TO THE LORD

I will sing and make music to the Lord.
For He is worthy to be praised.
He is loving and faithful to His word.
To Him my hands will be upraised.

I will gaze upon the beauty of the Lord,
And seek Him in His holy place.
He will shelter me within His fold
Where I'm protected by His grace.

I will shout with the sacrifice of joy,
For He has set me up on high.
All my enemies He shall destroy;
My victory He will supply.

Chorus:

Sing to the Lord! O magnify His name!
Sing to the Lord! Proclaim abroad His fame!
O worship our God! And tell of His Worth!
O worship our God! Proclaim Him to the earth!

R.J.L. — 1/3/1990

**29:9** "Glory!"—probably the equivalent of "Ah-h!" as people instinctively duck when a streak of lightning hits close with an immediate roar of thunder.

**38:3,4** When a Christian sins, he's in "double trouble," for sin brings along its own consequences and the Holy Spirit adds to them by his own work of conviction. Misery twice over until confession is made!

**40:12** Sin blinds spiritual perception and brings its own discouragements.

**44:9-19 (esp. vs.17-19)** In terms of God's promise to bless Israel if they obeyed him, this turn of events is totally incomprehensible to them. Perhaps he was testing their faith to see if they would remain faithful to him in spite of their circumstances. Abraham and especially Job were tested like this.

**46:10** "Be still and know that I am God."

## BE STILL AND KNOW THAT I AM GOD

Be still and know that I am God In the quiet of your heart.
I'll be exalted among the nations, I'll be exalted in the earth.
Come rest upon Me, My yoke is easy.
Lay your burdens at My feet.
　　There you'll find new strength and comfort given,
　　And your joy be made complete.

Be still and know that I am God!
There is naught too hard for Me.
I'll be exalted among My people, I'll be exalted in the earth.
Come, trust Me fully, My pow'r is for thee.
Large petitions to Me bring.
　　There you'll find such peace and mercy given
　　That will cause your heart to sing.

RJL — July 2,1989

**Psalm 49** This could be called "Job's Psalm." When the righteous suffer, and sin doesn't seem to be the precipitating cause, then we can be sure that God is doing something else for some other reason in their lives. The larger picture is found in Romans 8:28,29 as he is using those adverse circumstances to conform them to the image of Christ. For example, Christ loved his enemies, forgave them, and gave himself for them. Part of our being conformed to his likeness is having those experiences that will help develop these same attitudes in us that Christ had for his enemies, and so on.

**49:7-9** Why we cannot possibly be saved by works.

**Psalm 51** Such a contrast between David and Saul when confronted with sin. David admits it, and pleads for mercy and forgiveness. Saul denied responsibility and tried to pass on the blame to others, responding in anger when God wouldn't let him off the hook.

**Q. 51:16-19** David says that God doesn't delight in sacrifices (vs.16) and that righteous sacrifices and whole burnt offerings are a delight to him (vs.19). So which is right?

**A.** <u>Both</u> are. The change arises from the worshippers' attitude of heart (vs.17). Verse 16 deals with "form" in which the their heart is unrepentant; verse 19 with the "substance" in which their heart is broken and contrite because of their sins.

So the key to God's acceptance of our worship is our attitude of heart.

**55:4-8** In the face of difficult circumstances, David wanted to "crawl into a hole" somewhere and close it behind him.

**55:12-15,20,21** One of the hardest experiences of life is betrayal by a close friend.

**59:14-16** The difference between the songs of the wicked and those of the righteous is that of a dog's howl compared with the most beautiful of melodies.

**65:8** Papua, Indonesia, could qualify for this verse. "Thank you, Lord, for reaching out to these people, saving them, and giving them songs of joy."

**69:6** Our actions directly reflect on other believers in the public's eyes.

**Q.** If David was "a man after God's own heart," how could he pray things like "may my accusers perish in shame, may they never know your salvation" (69:27; 71:13). The Jews in Babylon added their two cents' worth by praying, "Blessed is he who dashes your children upon the rocks" (Ps.137:8,9).

**A.** David walked with God, worshipped him, knew him, and trusted him implicitly. But David lived in the context of the Law where righteousness was rewarded and wickedness judged (cf. Ps.73: 2-14). His psalms/prayers reflect this view. This is why Asaph was so greatly troubled when it seemed that the wicked were prospering and the righteous were being punished.

But David does not go out on his own seeking to wreck vengeance on his enemies. He asks God to deal with them according to the Law and God's righteous judgments. He asks for justice: "As they have done to others, so let it be done to them" (cf. Ps.109:17-20). David was also a man of war, and his warfare mentality influenced his attitude toward his enemies.

**69:28** If this book of life is the same as mentioned in Revelation 3:5, then what Jesus said makes sense. Those who do not "overcome" (cf. 1 Jn.5:4,5) are those who do not have faith, hence unsaved, and their names are erased from the Book of Life (when they die). If this is true, then it means that everyone's name is written in the Book of Life and only erased when all opportunity to repent has passed. I assume this would occur at death.

On the other hand, the NKJV translates the term as the "book of the living" which would put an entirely different slant on things, making possible two or even three different books:

1. one for all the living from which their names would be erased at death;
2. one for the citizens of the Kingdom of Israel from which names could be erased either upon death or after having reached some spiritual point of "no return"; and
3. one especially designated for the righteous (saved Jews and Gentiles).

According to Revelation 13:8 and 17:8, those who worshipped the beast never had their names written in the Book of Life—from the creation of the world. So their names could never have appeared with those who are saved in order to be erased. Yet God told Moses in Exodus 32 that those who sinned against him would have their names blotted out. So a different book has to be in view here, one from which names could be erased. In the immediate context of

Psalm 69, I would have to conclude that the book here mentioned must be something like a list of the citizens of the Kingdom (Israel). Then the book of life mentioned in Revelation and other N.T. passages must be exclusively for the saved, the "overcomers" (cf. 1 Jn.5:4,5) and from which their names could never be expunged.

**73:9** The ungodly make high-sounding promises to take advantage of the gullible and profit at their expense!

**74:10**
**Q**: "How long will the enemy mock you, O God?"
**A**: "Until the times of the Gentiles be fulfilled." (cf. Rom.11:25-27)

**75:3** Mankind, if left to themselves, would utterly destroy everything. Only God holds things together to accomplish his purposes.

**75:7,8** Preview of the Tribulation period.

**78:31,32** Judgment and miracles will not convince the heart of unbelief. Both are explained away in terms of natural causes or paranormal phenomenon. Faith comes by hearing the Word of Christ (Rom.10:17). So instead of Christians saying/proclaiming that "this is God's judgment on America for such-and-such a sin," they should rather be proclaiming the Word of Christ that deals directly with the sin issue and living in such a way as to give their message credibility.

**83:2-9** All of these nations (except the Hagrites, Gebal, Philistia, Tyre and Assyria) were descendants of Abraham and Lot! These are the Arab nations of today. Nothing like having your own "relatives" trying to wipe you out!

**Psalm 88** A poem of despair, feeling deserted by God.

**Q. 107:10-16** Is this passage describing suffering and release from depression?
**A.** The description could very well describe the inner feelings of the depressed with the encouragement that the Lord will deliver them when they turn to him. This deliverance may include medical help and/or counseling.

**107:6,13,19,28** The purpose of trials, for whatever other reason, is to turn our eyes toward God.

**112:6-8** Those who know who their God is can have great confidence and peace of heart no matter the circumstances (cf. Ps.119:165; Rom.8:28,29; Phil.4:6,7; 1 Thes.5:18 with Dan.3:16-18).

**115:16** I suspect that what was said of mankind at the Tower of Babel (Gen.11:6) that "nothing they plan to do will be impossible for them," could also be said of man's plans for space travel. On the basis of this verse, I also suspect that these plans, too, will be thwarted—or at least not be fulfilled. I believe that the Rapture will come before any serious space activity can take place. The vast destructions of the world during the Tribulation will put an immediate end to space ventures of any kind.

**Q.** If this is so, then how can Matthew 24:31 be explained? For this verse seems to imply the gathering of God's elect from all over the universe.

**A.** The context of this verse is the Second Coming of Christ. At that time he will be accompanied by the Elect, descending to the earth to reign for 1,000 years. The Elect on earth and the Elect in Heaven will be called together from wherever they are ("from the four winds"—on earth and "from one end of the heavens to the other"— in Heaven) to meet him when he comes (Mat.25:31-34) or accompany him from Heaven to the earth (Rev.19:14).

Another thought that may answer the "heavens" question is,

**Q.** Where is heaven?

**A.** "Up there." But what is "up" to us is "down" or "sideways" to others depending upon where they live on this earth. Heaven can't be "up" for everyone...<u>unless</u> Heaven is a 4th dimension existence that literally encompasses the earth <u>and</u> the universe. <u>Then</u> it would be "up there" for everyone, and God's elect could be said to be gathered "from one end of the heavens to the other," because, in the 4th dimension, they can be. Notice also that there is no mention anywhere of sinners being gathered from one end of the heavens to the other. This omission indicates to me that there probably will be no space travel. Something to ponder at any rate. (For further discussion, see p.309, Hebrews 11:5.)

**118:22** with **1 Pet.2:6,7** Jesus is called the "capstone." In verse 6 the "cornerstone." Both are different, yet perform a similar function. The cornerstone ties the building together at the foundation; the capstone ties the building together at the top of the wall. This pictures Christ as the Alpha and Omega, the Beginning and the End, the First and the Last. What he starts, he finishes, and everything is held together by his presence and power (see Col.1:17).

**119:3** Those who obey God's Word do nothing wrong <u>in that obedience</u> because they are doing what is good and true, that which comes from a God who can do no wrong.

**119:9-11,167** Abiding in the Word and loving it will keep us from sin, for as we love his Word we will also be doing it (Jn.14:15).

## PSALM 119
### (Based on the NKJV)

The many times I have read Psalm 119 have left me wondering just what the Psalmist was after? What was he trying to say? Is there some thread running through this Psalm that ties it together in a logical sequence? I think there is, and the following is my attempt to demonstrate it.

### THE DESIRE FOR OBEDIENCE – vs.1-8

vs.1 "There is blessing in the way of obedience. It purifies me...

vs.2 ...but it takes effort to get there,...

vs.3 ...however, the results are worth it.

vs.4 Lord, you have commanded me to obey you and work at it;

vs.5 I wish I could! Because then...

vs.6 ...I wouldn't feel guilty or ashamed when I compare myself with your Word;...

vs.7 ...and I could praise you with an upright heart because I know [and do] your righteous laws.

vs.8 So...I promise to obey you, but I need your help!"

## THE PROCESS OF OBEDIENCE – vs. 9-16

*Question:*
vs.9a "How <u>can</u> I cleanse my life?"

*Answer:*
vs.9b "By heeding your Word,

vs.10 by seeking you with my whole heart,

vs.11 by memorizing and hiding your Word in my heart,

vs.12 by you teaching me your ways,

vs.13 and by repeating your lessons to others.

*Results?*
vs.14 Genuine joy which gives me...

vs.15 ...motivation to further meditation;

vs.16 delight in your lessons [because they work!]; retention of your Word [It's a part of me now and I obey it instinctively]."

## THE PLACE WHERE OBEDIENCE IS LEARNED – vs.17-24
### (in the Lord's classroom where he is my teacher)

*Preparation:*
vs.17 "I'm ready to study, Lord; prepare your lessons for me,...

*Enlightenment:*
vs.18 ...then help me understand them.

*New Student:*

vs.19  I feel like a new student in your classroom,...

vs.20  ...but I have a great desire to learn.

vs.21  I see you rebuking the proud who think they don't need your instruction; but I want to be taught so that...

vs.22  ...I won't have the stigma of being uneducated.

vs.23  Others criticize me for not being 'properly' educated,...

vs.24  ...but that's O.K.  I get what really counts from you."

## STUDENT STRUGGLES – vs.25-32

vs.25  "Lord,...I've messed up.  Let's try again.

vs.26  I've asked you questions, and you answered them,

vs.27  but I need further clarification so that I can think them through better.

vs.28  Lord, sometimes it gets a bit discouraging.  ...Could we try again?

vs.29  You're so patient; help me to learn what is true.

vs.30  That's what I really want, so that's why I have your Word spread out before me.

vs.31  I'm really counting on your help so that I won't fail."...

vs.32  "Practice teaching?  O.K., I'll do it since I know you'll help me."

## YEARNING TO LEARN – vs.33-40

vs.33  "But first, Lord, teach me what you want and I will do it.

vs.34 Help me understand your lessons and I will keep them with all my heart.

vs.35 Give me direction in applying them because they make such good sense!

vs.36 Keep my motivation pure, and...

vs.37 ...help me not to be distracted [from the truth] by worthless things.

vs.38 Show me how these lessons will work out, because I am determined to obey you.

vs.39 Lord, I dread making stupid blunders that will discredit you.

vs.40 I don't want to. So please, help me live out these lessons as you have intended."

## HOPE IN WHAT HAS BEEN LEARNED – vs.41-48

vs.41 "Lord, I'm trusting for good results from your lessons.

vs.42 Then I'll be able to answer those who dispute with me.

vs.43 Don't take away from me what I have already learned, for I have no other resources.

vs.44 My intent is to follow your teachings always...

vs.45 ...for in them I find true freedom.

vs.46 I will even share them with presidents, if I have the opportunity, and that without shame...

vs.47 ...because I love your teachings and delight in doing them.

vs.48 What's more, I want to study them and meditate upon them even more than I have up to now."

## OPPOSITION – vs.49-56

vs.49 "Lord, I'm counting on the principles you've taught me to work.

vs.50 This is my hope when my circumstances fly in the face of all I've learned...

vs.51 ...and others mock me for following your Word when it appears totally stupid to do so.

vs.52 Yet I remember previous lessons learned, and see how your principles worked out in the end, and so I'm encouraged to keep on in spite of my circumstances.

vs.53 Now it's <u>my</u> turn to get really peeved with my mockers because they purposely ignore your laws.

vs.54 Sometimes I feel like putting your Word to music, for a melody seems to follow me wherever I go.

vs.55 Even at night, when I wake up, my first thoughts are of you and your Word.

vs.56 Guess that's because I'm so intent on obeying you."

## THE LORD'S MERCY – vs.57-64

vs.57 "You are my inheritance, Lord. That is why I said I'd obey you. [You are all I have.]

vs.58 That is the reason why I so earnestly pled with you for mercy.

vs.59 I knew my way was wrong, so I turned to your truth.

vs.60 And that I did quickly once I recognized it.

vs.61 Though I am often strongly tempted, I will not forget the principles for living that you have given.

vs.62 Even in the middle of a sleepless night, I will rise and give thanks to you because of them.

vs.63 I have also chosen as my friends all those everywhere who fear and obey you.

vs.64 That shows that the whole earth is full of your mercy [since they, too, have come to know you]. So, Lord, teach me more about your ways."

## THE LORD'S DISCIPLINE – vs.65-72

vs.65 "Lord, thank you for dealing with me according to the lessons from your Word.

vs.66 That way I see how they operate, will learn to trust them, and learn good judgment from them.

vs.67 Before you disciplined me, I didn't know a thing. But now I know your Word and keep it.

vs.68 [Your discipline] proves that you are good and do good, which gives me confidence that what I'm learning from you is good.

vs.69 The proud try to discredit me [in my pursuit, but that's their problem]. As for me, I will keep your Word with all my heart.

vs.70 Your truths slip away from them [like a greased pig], but they bring deep joy to me.

vs.71 I'm glad you disciplined me, because it got my attention and taught me how practical your lessons are.

vs.72 They are worth more to me than all the riches of the world."

## THE LORD'S ENABLEMENT – vs.73-80

vs.73 "Because you made me, you can also help me understand your Word.

vs.74 Then others, who also fear you, will be encouraged when they see what you've done in my life.

vs.75 I know, Lord, that the principles you've taught me are right and that you are molding me according to them.

vs.76 But some of them are kind of hard. May your love comfort and encourage me...

vs.77 ...so that I won't be overwhelmed by them. I really <u>want</u> to learn them, [but it's going to take time].

vs.78 Those who don't want to study have slandered me for meditating on your Word [because it doesn't make any sense to them]. Lord, make them ashamed as they see <u>their</u> way not working.

vs.79 But I need friends from among those who know your Word and obey you.

vs.80 Then I will be strengthened so that I won't disobey you and bring shame on myself."

## PERSECUTION – vs.81-88

vs.81 "Lord, help! I'm desperate! I need the assurance of your promises,...

vs.82 ...but I can't find anything from your Word that helps me or comforts me.

vs.83 I feel like a dried and cracked wineskin choked in smoke, yet I am trying to remember your laws.

vs.84 But how long must I wait before you send relief? When will you deal with my persecutors?

vs.85 At every turn they wait to trap me. They couldn't care less about your Word.

vs.86 Yet all your laws are trustworthy. Help me, LORD! They're persecuting me when I haven't done a thing to them!

vs.87 They've nearly killed me [several times]; even so, I'm still committed to your laws.

vs.88 Encourage me in your love so that I'll have the motivation to continue obeying you."

## GOD'S SOVEREIGNTY – vs.89-96

vs.89 "Lord, there is nothing that can shake your Word; it is fixed for eternity.

vs.90 Your faithfulness is the same; so is your creation: the earth continues on.

vs.91 They all continue and serve you to this day because of your decrees.

vs.92 If I hadn't known these things, I would have given up under my trials.

vs.93 I will never forget your laws because they have strengthened and renewed my life.

vs.94 Save me [from my persecutors], Lord, for I am yours and have sought your laws.

vs.95 They are planning again to kill me, but I will take courage from your promises.

vs.96 I have seen the limits of perfection here on earth, but your commandments are infinite."

## THE AWESOMENESS OF GOD'S LAWS – vs.97-104

vs.97 "Oh how I love your Law! I think about it all day long,...

vs.98 ...and through it gain more wisdom than my enemies [because your commandments are always in my thoughts].

vs.99 They give me more insight than my teachers because I constantly meditate upon them.

vs.100 Obeying them also gives me more understanding than the elders.

vs.101 Lord, I have purposefully avoided sin so that I can be free to keep your Word.

vs.102 And that I can do because you yourself have taught me.

vs.103 [Oh Lord! What more can I say?] Your Word is sweeter to my taste than honey!

vs.104 It gives me understanding of what is true and makes me hate everything that is false."

## FIRM RESOLUTION — vs.105-112

vs.105 "It lights the way before me and guides me in the way that I should go.

vs.106 So I have vowed and solemnly promised that I will obey every aspect of your Word.

vs.107 But because of this, I am persecuted over and over again. Lord, encourage and strengthen me by...

vs.108 ...accepting my worship and teaching me more of your ways.

vs.109 My life is in constant danger, yet your laws are with me. So...

vs.110 ...even though the wicked have laid a trap for me, I have not retaliated in kind.

vs.111 Your promises are my eternal inheritance.  Because I love them...

vs.112 ...I have determined to obey you forever [—well, at least until the end of this life]."

## SECURITY – vs.113-120

vs.113 "I hate inconsistency, but I love your law [because it does not change].

vs.114 Therefore you are my security and your Word is my hope.

vs.115 Get away from me, you who hate God's Word! for I will keep it [regardless of your efforts to make me do otherwise].

vs.116 Lord, I'm trusting the principles of your Word to work as you have said they would.  Don't let me wake up in the morning and find them just a dream.

vs.117 Put your arms around me, Lord, and I shall be safe and continue to obey you.  [Lord, do this because I see how...]

vs.118 ...you reject those who disobey you.  They think they know better, but are deceived.

vs.119 You wash them away like slag from molten metal, which makes me love your promises even more [as I see how they separate the good from the bad].

vs.120 On the other hand, seeing this happen makes me terrified of you and your judgments [for I realize what could have happened to me!]"

## CONFLICT BETWEEN GOOD AND EVIL – vs.121-128

vs.121 "Lord, I have tried to live according to your Word.  Do not let the wicked gain the upper hand over me.

vs.122 Be my guarantee for good, for the proud determine evil against me [unless you stop them].

vs.123 As evil grows, I become discouraged looking for your way out of it all.

vs.124 O LORD, be merciful to me and teach me;...

vs.125 ...show me what is going on from your perspective so that I may understand how your laws are working [when they don't seem to be].

vs.126 From my perspective, it's time for you to intervene, for our nation has declared your Law null and void.

vs.127 LORD, I value your laws more than vast wealth in pure gold.

vs.128 They apply to every situation in life; they are just and right, making me hate everything that isn't."

## SOLD ON GOD'S WORD – vs.129-136

vs.129 "Your laws work; that's why I keep them.

vs.130 They enlighten the mind and give understanding even to slow learners.

vs.131 I rush back to you [after the busyness of the day] because I long for your Word.

vs.132 LORD, look upon my circumstances and be merciful to me as you are toward all those who love you.

vs.133 Guide me with your Word so that no sin will rule over me.

vs.134 Deliver me from my persecutors so that I can give my full attention to your laws.

vs.135  I long for your approval.  Teach me your ways [so that I'll know what pleases you].

vs.136  It grieves me much that others don't share my desire to obey your Word."

## THE CHARACTER OF GOD'S LAWS – vs.137-144

vs.137  "LORD, you are righteous, and your laws reflect that.

vs.138  So do your promises: they are righteous and totally trustworthy.

vs.139  I'm worn out trying to convince my enemies of the truth of this fact, for they have willfully neglected your words.

vs.140  Yet your Word has been thoroughly tested, [proven and not found lacking in any way whatever].  Therefore I love it [as something of great value].

vs.141  Even though I am of little account in the sight of others, I will not forget your rules for living.

vs.142  They are as true as your eternal righteousness.

vs.143  They are my delight even when I'm stressed out and troubled.

vs.144  There is no limit to the righteous character of your promises. LORD, help me understand them, for they give me life."

## A DESPERATE PLEA FOR HELP – vs.145-152

vs.145  "O Lord, I call to you with my whole heart; answer me and I will obey you.

vs.146  I plead with you to deliver me, and I will keep your laws [in gratitude].

vs.147 I rise before daylight to cry for your help; I have no other hope than what your Word gives me.

vs.148 I even go without sleep so that I can meditate on your promises.

vs.149 O LORD, if you love me, hear me and preserve my life from...

vs.150 ...those who plot wickedly [against me] and violate your laws.

vs.151 Yet you are even nearer to me, O LORD, and all your commands are true...

vs.152 ...and changeless, just as I have learned long ago."

## IN COURT – vs.153-160

vs.153 "LORD, I have been wrongly accused. Consider this fact and deliver me. [I'm bold to ask this of you] because I have not broken your law.

vs.154 Be my defense and bring about my acquittal so that I can have a fresh start, even as you have promised.

vs.155 There's no hope of acquittal for the wicked, for they don't even try to obey your laws. [They are guilty beyond question.]

vs.156 You are compassionate, LORD. Renew my life according to your laws.

vs.157 I have many enemies who accuse me of breaking your laws [even as they do]; yet I will not stop living by them.

vs.158 Those people are treacherous, LORD, and I loathe them because they totally disregard your Word.

vs.159 But I love it. Consider my attitude, LORD, [in your dealings with me,] and grant me renewed life according to your love and mercy.

vs.160 Your Word is truth from start to finish. Therefore your right-eous laws will never change [because they don't need to]."

## THE BASIS FOR OBEDIENCE – vs.161-168

vs.161 "Even those in authority unjustly accuse me, but I'm more 'afraid' of your Word than I am of them.

vs.162 I rejoice in it as one who has discovered great wealth.

vs.163 I love your law [because it is truth], which makes me recognize and hate every form of falsehood.

vs.164 LORD, I keep praising you all day long because your laws are good.

vs.165 They give me, along with others who love them, great peace and stability.

vs.166 My hope for salvation is rooted firmly in you, LORD. That is why I obey you,...

vs.167 ...not only outwardly, but inwardly as well. [I also obey you because] I love your laws.

vs.168 [There's a third reason why] I obey you: you know me inside out [and still love me. For that you deserve my obedience!]"

## FINAL PLEA TO BE TAUGHT – vs.169-176

vs.169 "LORD, once again I earnestly beg you to give me understand-ing of your Word.

vs.170 Heed my request, and grant it to me according to your prom-ise.

vs.171 You will find me a very willing student, LORD, as you teach me,...

vs.172 ...then I will teach your righteous commands to others.

vs.173 But I'm counting on you to help me because I've chosen to teach nothing but your laws.

vs.174 [There is an 'occupational hazard' to all this, though.] Being so involved in your Word makes me spend time in longing and dreaming for the day of your salvation [when you will order this world according to your Word].

vs.175 With the help of your laws, I shall live and praise you.

vs.176 In the past, I have wandered from your laws like a lost sheep. But keep me in your fold, LORD, so that I won't forget what you have said."

**\* \* \* \***

**128:1** General thought: "The fear of the Lord," positively, is to obey him (128:1); negatively, is to hate evil (Pro.8:13).

**130:3,4** The fate of the wicked in Revelation 20:11-13 is that God has kept a record of their sins, and they cannot stand before him. But of the righteous there is no record of their sins for the blood of Christ has erased them completely (cf. Heb.10:14; 1 Jn.1:7)!

**137:4** There is no "song" outside of the will of God.

| **138:8** | Verse | Commentary |
|---|---|---|
| | "The LORD will fulfill his purpose for me." | The firm hope of a trusting heart. |
| | "Your love, O LORD, endures forever." | The basis for this hope. |
| | "Do not abandon the works of your hands." | God's character will cause him to work. |

**139:13-15** Abortion terminates the process of God's creative activity in the womb.

**Q. 139:19-24** After extolling God's omniscience (vs.1-6), omnipresence (vs.7-12) and omnipotence (vs.13-18), David then goes into an imprecatory exclamation against his enemies and ends with a plea for God to search his own heart. What's the connection between the first three sections and the last two?

**A.** "Lord, let nothing from the outside (vs.19-22), nor anything from the inside (vs.23-24) distract me from who you are."

**141:3** "Set a guard over my mouth, O LORD; keep watch over the door of my lips." Combating troubled thoughts, I prayed: "Set a guard over my mind, O LORD; keep watch over the treasury of my thoughts" (cf. Mk.7:21-23 and 2 Cor.10:5b).

**Psalm 148:1** "Praise the Lord from the heavens."

## PRAISE THE LORD FROM THE HEAVENS

Praise the LORD from the heavens,
Praise Him from the heights above!
Praise the LORD, all you His angels,
Praise Him, all His heavenly hosts!
    Praise Him, sun and moon and shining stars!
    Praise Him, in the heav'ns above!
Praise the LORD from the heavens!
Kings of earth, exalt His name!

Praise the LORD from the heavens,
Praise Him from the earth below!
Praise the LORD, all hills and mountains!
Praise Him, lightning, wind and snow!
    Praise Him, creatures in the sea and air!
    Praise Him, creatures great and small!
Praise the LORD from the heavens!
Young and old, exalt His name!

RJL — June 5, 1984

# PROVERBS

(The whole book of Proverbs provides a wealth of story lines / script ideas for books, short stories and films.)

**1:7; 8:13** Fear of the Lord (hatred of evil) is the beginning of knowledge (vs.7a) in that it "clears one's mental slate" from a lot of cluttering garbage that only confuses and hinders learning (sin blinds us to truth, vs.7b) and takes up "mental bytes" that could be used for storing better things.

**4:1-13,20-27** Any Christian father should be able to say these things to his children. Unfortunately it seems that many of them are not even living it themselves. But what a change there would be if they were!

**Chs.5,7-9** Interesting that Proverbs always presents the prostitute as a married woman. Evidently in the culture of that day there were no single women as no doubt they were all spoken for by the time they had reached puberty. Yet at the same time there were many widows because of warfare, though most of them probably married soon afterwards because they had no means of support otherwise.

**5:22** Sin has its own way of keeping its victims captive.

**8:6-9** "Faultless to those who have knowledge." Those who have knowledge perceive the truth in what Wisdom says. To those who don't have knowledge, Wisdom's advice seems foolish and full of fault (cf. 1 Cor.1:18).

**8:19** Wisdom's fruit is better than silver and gold in that money cannot give guidance in how to live right. One can be wealthy and still have a miserable life (cf. 15:16 and Eccl.7:12).

**8:34** "Watching daily"—Since wisdom comes from God's Word, this is a good plug for a daily Quiet Time.

**10:16** The wages of the righteous bring them life, but the income (wages) of the wicked (sinful) brings them punishment (death).

## EXAMPLES OF SOME PROVERBS:

**11:2a** Miriam (Num.12:10)

**11:2b** David

**11:7** Nabal

**11:8** Daniel & his accusers
(Dan.6:18-24)

**11:10** Mordecai & Haman,
Athaliah (2 Ki.11:20)

**11:16a** Ruth

**11:16b** Nabal

**11:25** Gaius (3 John)

**17:13** David with Bathsheba
(2 Sam.12:9-10)

**20:25** Jephthah (Judg.11:30,31)

**27:6** Judas Iscariot (according to
Zvi Kalisher—Friends of Israel)

**28:13a** Saul

**28:13b** David

**11:16** In the end, respect is far better than wealth. Good relationships are better than material gain with hatred.

**17:16** In other words, don't waste money trying to educate a fool because he has no interest in learning.

**19:3** God often gets blamed for our troubles even though the chief cause lies at our doorstep! Man does not want to accept responsibility for his own actions nor for the consequences that result from them, so blames God for them all!

**21:3** with **Matt.5:23,24** In essence, the Lord is saying, "Your relationship with others is more important to me than your worship. Get the first straightened out, then I will accept the second!"
**Q.** How can this be so?
**A.** Because unresolved relational problems (that we cause wrongfully) are sins that come between us and God (as they break the second Commandment of loving our neighbor as ourselves) and, thus "defiled," there is no way he can accept our worship. We can only come before him to worship with pure hands (cf. Ps.15; 24:3,4. As a contrast, see Pro.21:27; 28:9).

**22:7** "The borrower is a servant to the lender" in that he is never free from the lender's pressure to pay back what he owes. Everything he does is influenced by his need to pay back the loan. The lender assumes the role of "God" in his life since the whole focus of the borrower is turned to paying back his debt—thus having nothing for God, which results in blessings robbed from himself. Borrowing is the sure road to spiritual poverty!

**22:20** Thirty sayings of the wise (chs.22-24):

| Ch.22 | Ch.23 | | Ch.24 | |
|---|---|---|---|---|
| 1. vs.17-21 | 7. vs.1-3 | 14. vs.15,16 | 20. vs.1,2 | 26. vs.13,14 |
| 2. vs.22,23 | 8. vs.4,5 | 15. vs.17,18 | 21. vs.3,4 | 27. vs.15,16 |
| 3. vs.24,25 | 9. vs.6-8 | 16. vs.19-21 | 22. vs.5,6 | 28. vs.17,18 |
| 4. vs.26,27 | 10. vs.9 | 17.vs.22-25 | 23. vs.7-9 | 29. vs.19,20 |
| 5. vs.28 | 11. vs.10,11 | 18.vs.26-28 | 24. vs.10 | 30. vs.21,22 |
| 6. vs.29 | 12. vs.12 | 19.vs.29-35 | 25. vs.11,12 | |
| | 13. vs.13,14 | | | |

**28:13** Three ways in which one who conceals his sin doesn't prosper:

1. God knows all and won't let him get away with it.

2. Guilt over that sin clouds his judgment so that he can't make wise decisions.

3. Sin sets in motion its own consequences that militate against prospering.

**29:27** The righteous detest the dishonest because dishonesty is an offense to honesty; the wicked detest the upright because the lives of the upright show them up for what they are—wrong.

**31:25** "She can laugh at the days to come"—optimistic because of adequate preparations for the future.

# ECCLESIASTES

## "The Emptiness of Everything apart from God."

**1:14**  All that man can do is not enough.

**2:18,19**  It's not our place to worry about what will come or be done after us, but God's place to order the future.

**2:22**  Answer: "Reward in Heaven."

**3:15-17** w/ **1 Cor.11:29,30**  God's judgment.

**5:4-7**  Ending of vs.7…"Therefore stand in awe of God" [and keep your mouth shut (vs.2)] !

**5:8,9**  When there is corruption in the lower ranks, look first at the upper ranks.

**5:10**  Ex. A rich person was once asked: "How much money would you need to be completely happy?"  Answer: "Just a little more."

**10:20**  What you say has a way of coming back to you!

# SONG of SOLOMON

# ISAIAH

## God of the Impossible (cont.):

175. He grants or withholds protection (5:5).
176. He commands the clouds to withhold rain (5:6).
177. He governs the fate of nations (7:7,8).
178. He caused a virgin to conceive and bear a son (7:14).
179. He killed 185,000 Assyrian soldiers in one night (37:36).
180. He caused the sun's shadow to fall back 10 degrees on the sundial of Ahaz (38:8).

**\* \* \* \***

**1:2** The LORD knows the broken hearts of parents whose children rebel against them.

**1:4-10** In spite of discipline and severe judgment, Israel stubbornly persisted in her rebellious ways (see 26:10). Since their hearts were of "clay" and not of "wax," the fire of God's judgment only hardened them even further.

**1:10-15** Hypocritical worship is a stench in the nostrils of God. Worship from a willfully sinning heart is an abomination to him (cf. Matt.5:23,24 for this principle in the N.T.).

**1:21-26** Jerusalem—faithful city—harlot—judgment—righteous and faithful, full of justice.

**2:6-8** Growing similarity to American Christianity and culture. Materialism displaces the object of our faith from God to things (our "idols"—i.e., whatever we substitute for God in our lives).

**2:18** Total destruction of everything worshipped by man.

**4:5** Return of the Shekinah Glory Cloud and Pillar of Fire over Mt. Zion (the Millennial Jerusalem)!

**5:26** with **7:18,19** When the Lord "whistles," the nations obey.

**6:3** "Holy, holy, holy is the LORD Almighty; the whole earth is full of his glory."

**Q.** Since "holy" can imply sinlessness as well as separateness, which of these two meanings is implied in this passage?

**A.** By context, it is God's uniqueness (separate from everything else) as illustrated in creation. Hebrew parallelism supports this view. God is unique in his being and unique in his work.

**Q.** Secondly, how is the earth full of God's glory? It is full of violence, wickedness and all sorts of evil. How are these things a glory to God?! Not by a long shot!

**A.** However, consider a painting. We look at it, admire it, and ask a question: "Who painted this picture?" Then we look in the corner to see the signature of the artist. This picture reflects the artist's glory, or is a glory to the artist.

As we look at the earth/sky/nature, we ask a question: "How did all of this get here? Who made it?" Then we look for the "signature" that is found in Romans 1:20 and Psalm 19:1-4: "God." His <u>creation</u> reflects his glory, and thereby "the whole earth is full of his glory."

Now, what is it called when someone tries to change the signature on a painting? A forgery! The theory of evolution is Satan's attempt to "change the signature," to take away that glory from God and take it to himself.

So, in summary, we could say: *The signature of creation, according to the Bible, is* **"God."** *The signature of creation, according to evolution, is* **"Chance."** Something to think about.

**7:(3-6)7-9** with **Lam.3:37** "The head of Damascus is <u>only</u> Rezin" (a mere man).... "The head of Samaria is <u>only</u> Remalaiah's son" (not worthy enough to have his name even mentioned!). Both men are totally insignificant in God's sight: a real Divine put-down (cf. Isa.40: 23,24)!

**Q. 7:9b-13** Isaiah gave Ahaz an opportunity to exercise and strengthen his faith but he refused. Why?

**A.** From verse 9 it seems to have been an issue of faith and obedience.

If Ahaz had asked for a sign (faith), he would have incurred, as a result, the responsibility to obey the Lord (obedience), which he obviously was <u>not</u> prepared to do, and about which the Lord was pressing him. Thus his "pious" refusal (vs.12) rang hollow and only emphasized his determination <u>not</u> to obey the Lord.

**7:18,19** "Flies" (Egyptian army )— a nuisance; "bees" (Assyrian army)—the serious problem. There will be no escape from either one.

### The King of Assyria is pictured as:
**7:20** a razor.

**8:7** mighty flood waters, "reaching up to the neck" (vs.8—i.e., right up to Jerusalem).

**8:8** a giant bird.

**10:15** an ax.

**10:15** a saw.

**10:5,15** a rod, club.

**33:1** a destroyer, and

**33:1** a traitor.

**8:3** It's interesting that Isaiah's wife is referred to as a prophetess, either because she was the wife of a prophet or she may have had some kind of ministry too.

**8:19,20** Old Testament test of orthodoxy.
  (New Testament test of orthodoxy—cf. 1 Jn.4:1-3).

**9:6,7** with **11:1-5** The first passage declares Christ's position; the second the character of his reign and how he will carry it out.

**Q. 9:7** To what time does the phrase "from that time on" refer?
**A.** Probably, from verse 6, to the time when "the government will be on his shoulders," (i.e., when Christ assumes the rule of the world at his Second Coming).

**11:1** A shoot from the roots of Jesse. Jim Showers (Friends of Israel Gospel Ministry, Dec.2016 letter) sheds an interesting light on this verse. He writes: "Most people are not aware that olive trees don't come from the pits found inside olives. To reproduce, the root of an olive tree must send up a shoot, called a *netser* in Hebrew. The shoot is like a small branch; and it must be severed from the tree, along with a small portion of the root, and replanted for a new olive tree to grow.

  "Nazareth derives its name from the word *netser*. But what does that have to do with the birth of Jesus Christ, which took place in Bethlehem about 100 miles to the south?

"Speaking of the coming Messiah more than six centuries before his First Advent, Isaiah prophesied, 'There shall come forth a Rod from the stump of Jesse, and a Branch shall grow out of his roots' (11:1). The word we translate as 'branch' is the word *netser.*"

If only the Scribes and Pharisees were willing to pay attention to the details!

**11:3,4**   Christ will not judge by appearances nor on the basis of compelling, heart-wrenching stories.  He knows the hearts of plaintiff and defendant, and will judge accordingly in righteousness (the standard of his judgments), in truth (according to what really happened), and in justice (the judgment exactly fitting the situation).

**11:9**   "My holy mountain"—a reference to Mount Zion (vs.9a), which stands for his entire Kingdom (vs.9:b), just as Washington, D.C. often stands for the entire U.S.A (a "metonymy" in English grammar).

**13:22**   "Her time is at hand, and her days will not be prolonged."   Yet Babylon was not destroyed for another 200 years!   Obviously, God's timing is not our timing.

**14:4,12-15** with **Ezek.28:11-19**   Satan described in context of the king of Babylon (in Isaiah) and the king of Tyre (in Ezekiel).

Q.19:6  Are these "brooks of defense" the large and deep canals the Egyptians built between Egypt and the land of Israel?
**A.**

**21:11,12**   "No change in present conditions."

**22:12-14**   The LORD called Judah to repentance, but they completely ignored him to their everlasting destruction.

**22:22**   Picture of complete authority (cf. Rev.3:7).

**23:17,18**   Illustration of Proverbs 13:22.

**24:5**   "The earth is defiled by its people"—moral and environmental pollution.

**24:10** Picture of desolation, chaos and anarchy.

**24:18-20** (vs.20b) "It falls...never to rise again." The final death knell for this present world system. The earth itself will be renewed, but its present system will never be heard from again.

**25:7** The "shroud"—what blinds people to the knowledge of God (cf. Heb.8:11; Isa.11:9; Hab.2:14)—will be taken away so that everyone will know him.

**26:8a** Active, not passive, obedience...
**26:8b** ...while waiting for the Lord to work.

**26:10** A sad commentary on the perversity of people's hearts. They will continue to do evil even when they see a better way.

**26:18** Isaiah's declaration of Israel's failure in its God-given mandate to be a light to the nations.

**28:10,13** An illustration of Proverbs 26:5, the Lord answering Israel's foolishness in kind.

**28:17** Hail...knocking down outer defenses/shelter; Water...searches out and seeps into every hidden crack and crevice. "No hiding place down here."

**29:6** A picture of how the Lord delivers Israel in Ezekiel 38:22,23.

**29:11,12** What is sealed to the literate and illiterate will later be revealed to the deaf and blind. The Pharisees claimed to have spiritual sight, but the Lord declared them blind (the scroll was "sealed" to them). But the Gentiles, considered "blind" by the Pharisees, were the ones to "see" and believe as the contents of the scroll were revealed.

**30:26** No night there! Or perhaps a picture of an entirely new order of things.

**34:2-7** Judgment of God upon the nations pictured in various ways.
**Q.** What is the meaning of verse 4 in this context?

**A.** Probably a metaphorical expression of political, economic and social chaos (such wording used many times in Scripture—cf.
Ezek.32:7,8).

**Q. 36:1** Where was Hezekiah and his army while all this was going on?
He surely must have heard that his country was being attacked and
that his cities were falling. Why was he not out defending them?
**A. 36:8; 37:27** The implication of this taunt/offer is that Hezekiah
basically had no army to fight with. Furthermore, the LORD
withheld power from the Judean cities so that they could not resist the
Assyrian army. Destruction of these cities was probably God's
judgment for their continued idolatry. They had to know that their
gods could not deliver them.

**36:7,18** Sennacherib reveals a misunderstanding of the Jews' faith and
the God whom they worshipped.

**37:7** The reason Sennacherib returned home at this report of the
approaching Egyptian army was not that he was afraid of them; he
wasn't. But he had no army left with which to fight them (37:36,37)!

**38:6,7** Chronologically, vs.21 and 22 belong between these two verses.

**38:7,8** Hezekiah believed God and was given a sign without asking.
Ahaz didn't believe God and was commanded to ask a sign from him
which he refused to do (Isa.7:10-14).
**Q.** Why this difference?
**A.** Because if God could do whatever Ahaz asked, then Ahaz would
have to believe him and acknowledge who he is. Perhaps this is
why he refused to ask for a sign.

**38:15** "I will walk humbly all my years." Hezekiah forgot this
resolution as soon as he became well. He was greatly humbled by the
Lord's healing, but his heart was still full of pride (cf. 2 Chr.32:24,25).
We can be humbled by one experience and another, yet still be
basically proud in our general outlook. Feeling humility at one point
does not guarantee a humble spirit from then on.

**40:12** "Who...with the breadth of his hand marked off the heavens
...?" The Hubble Telescope has "seen" a galaxy 44 billion light years

from earth. This distance translates into 258,090,625,000,000,000,000, 000 [258 sextillion, 90 quintillion, 625 quadrillion] miles! A bit far to walk in one day!

**40:22** I am hypothesizing here a bit, and may be way off the mark, but...if this verse is not poetical language (which it very well may be), then it would seem that Heaven is actually in close proximity to earth (earth is called God's footstool in Isaiah 66:1, and a footstool has to be in close proximity to the chair/throne!). So it could be construed from all of this that the earth is actually at the center of the universe, and however "far" it is out there, it's just as far the other way! *Even flying at the speed of light for an entire lifetime, one would not even be close to exiting our own galaxy!* The vastness of the universe is incomparably staggering! (See also Amos 9:6.)

**40:26** with **Psalm 147:4** God has determined the number of the stars and calls them each by name!

**42:2** Where public demonstrations are our right, it seems that that was never Christ's way. Rather than crying out against Rome's oppression, he quietly taught about the Kingdom of God to all who would listen. Could it be that a quiet witness, in the end, is more powerful than a shouted word with upraised fist? I suspect we may have our priorities (methods) turned around from what Christ would do were he here now. The Apostle Paul said the same about his ministry (Acts 24:17,18).

**42:25** Announcing "God's judgment" on America, vis-à-vis natural calamities, etc., is essentially wasted breath. Unbelievers will not understand nor take it to heart, no matter how true it might be. We need to get back to our personal witness that will change lives and bring God's blessings. Then there will be no need to "announce" his judgments.

**45:8** A very captivating picture! Oh that it would happen today.

**45:15,16** "God, the Hidden One"—"hidden" in the sense of being invisible as compared with idols which are very visible but powerless to do anything.

**47:8**  In her pride, Babylon took to herself God's very words about himself, "I am, and there is none besides me."  This harkens back to Lucifer's prideful statements in Isaiah 14:13,14.

**54:4-6**  Compare:

| God as Husband to Israel in the O.T. | Christ as Husband to the Bride in the N.T. |
|---|---|
| Isa.62:4,5 | John 3:29 |
| Hos.2:16-20 | Eph.5:25-27 |
| Jer.31:32 | Rev.21:2 |

**54:7**  In terms of eternity, 70 years is even less than a nanosecond. Even the years since 70 A.D. to the present could be considered less than a brief moment.

**57:1,2**  One reason the righteous die "before their time" is to spare them from coming evil and give them peace.

**58:1-9** with **2 Chr.7:14**  The Church may pray and worship for nothing if there is no change of heart and attitude toward sin.

**60:2,3**  God's intent for Israel was to be a bright light (his glory) in gross darkness to draw all nations to himself even as a lamp, at night, attracts every bug in the neighborhood.

**60:12**  This is not an ethnocentric statement to boost Israel's national pride.  At this time, Christ himself will be ruling.  So any nation not serving him will be judged.

**61:10b**  "...For he has clothed me with garments of salvation and arrayed me in a robe of righteousness."

### FORGIVENESS

*I was out on the hillside, alone and afraid.*
*I was cold, clad in garments all threadbare and frayed.*
*Then Jesus came softly, all dressed in pure white,*
*His garment all shining and glistening bright.*
*He tenderly raised me, and what do you know!*
*He gave me His garment, His eyes all aglow.*

*No cold wind could reach through its tightness of weave.*
*I was warmed with more comfort than I could believe.*
*I glanced up to thank Him, and to my dismay,*

*His robe was now threadbare, and rotting away.*
*But it seemed so familiar, each seam and each line.*
*And I knew as He stood there, that garment was mine.*

--Edith G. Leland
September 1997

**66:9** "Do *I* say something and fail to accomplish it?"
"Do *I* promise something, then put obstacles in the way to keep it from happening?" (cf. Jer.1:12b).

# JEREMIAH

**God of the Impossible, cont.**

181. He promised deliverance from all threats on Jeremiah's life (1:8).

\* \* \* \*

**2:19** Sin has its own built-in punishments.

**2:22** Outward (ritual) cleansing does nothing in purifying the heart. Self-purification can never erase the stain of guilt.

**2:29** The one guilty brings charges against the victim! Nothing new!

**Q. 3:6-11** How is it that Israel was considered "more righteous" than Judah in her unfaithfulness to the Lord?
**A.** Because Israel rejected the Lord and made no bones about it. Judah

rejected the Lord but pretended they hadn't. Israel was honest in her rejection; Judah was hypocritical. Therefore Israel was "more righteous" than Judah. Strange as it may seem, outward sin is more bearable to the Lord than hypocrisy!

**4:1,2** The result of true repentance is a heart for missions.

**4:23-26** This, in context, is not a statement about the original earth, destruction and re-creation, but a lament in hyperbole over the total desolation of Judah.

**4:27** implies that the land has not always been desolate as today.

**5:22,23** The sea faithfully keeps to its boundaries, but God's people, Israel, do not. (cf. Jonah where nature obeyed the Lord, but Jonah wouldn't until forced to!)

**7:4** The Temple reduced to a fetish in the minds of the people.

**7:24,26,27; 25:3** "Jeremiah, you may as well know right now that nobody's going to listen to you, because they won't listen to me" (cf. Jn.15:20).

**12:5** "Jeremiah, if you are weary now, you haven't seen anything yet! Gear up and move out. Remember, I am with you; they will not overcome you" (Jer.15:20,21).

**13:23** Sin is its own trap...
**16:10-12** ...and anesthetizes the sinner!

**16:18** "Pay double for their sins"
    1. Sin carries with it its own wages and suffering.
    2. Then comes God's judgment as well.
So, in that sense, those who sin receive "double" for their sins.

**17:1** They even had diamond-tipped writing instruments at that time! As their sin was engraved deeply in their hearts, eventually God will write his law on their hearts in sin's place (31:33).

**20:1,2** First recorded outright persecution of Jeremiah. He really felt it as indicated in verses 7-10,14-18, even though he tried to encourage himself in the Lord (vs.11-13).

**Q. 22:15,16** How is it that defending the cause of the poor and needy is what "knowing God" means?

**A.** Because it is doing what he would do, responding to them as he would if he were here, implying a knowledge of his heart (i.e., "knowing him").

**24:4-10** Sometimes what we consider "the worst" is actually God's "best" for us. The "worst" thing for the Jews was to be separated (exiled) from Jerusalem. Those remaining thought themselves to be "most blessed." Yet it was the exiles that lived and were blessed and those left in Jerusalem who were cursed to destruction. Like Isaiah 57:1,2 (in principle), "The righteous perish [in this case, taken away]...to be spared from evil."

**25:14** Indication that in the day of judgment there will be degrees of punishment (cf. Rom.2:6; Rev.20:12).

**26:16-19** In spite of everything, there was still a believing remnant, even among the leaders of the land (also vs.24). The Lord used these

men to fulfill his promise to Jeremiah of protection (1:8,19—see also 38:7-10).

**27:9,10; 28:15; 29:8,9,17-19,21-23,31** Wherever the truth of God is given, Satan tries to counteract it with as many lies as possible.

**28:9** Theological test of a prophet: what he says <u>must</u> come to pass. If not, he is a false prophet and deserves to die as he purposely misrepresents God to the people. Hananiah died two months later (vs.16,17).

> **34:(11),15,16** In the stressful siege, the Israelites freed their slaves. ("Of what use are they if the city falls shortly? Better to let them go than to be responsible for them.") What they did pleased the Lord (even if their motives were wrong), and evidently he caused Nebuchadnezzar's army to withdraw (vs.22—see Jer.37:5 as to why his army withdrew). With the threat gone, and the prospect of continuing

on in the city after all, suddenly the loss of all these servants loomed very large indeed on the economic horizon, and they were once again pressed into servitude. The Lord hates it when people go back on their promises (vs.18-20).

**35:4** Even though Jeremiah was very much alone in his ministry and rejected by the people, there are hints here and there of a godly remnant. Here it is Igdaliah, the man of God; Baruch, Jeremiah's scribe (36:4); Elnathan, Delaiah and Gemariah (government officials— 36: 25); Ebed-Melech (38:7; 39:15-18). [Another reading may reveal more names.]

**35:7** Jonadab had the "sojourner" mentality that the heroes of faith shared in Hebrews 11:13-16.

**35:18,19** The Lord places a real premium on obedience to those in authority over us. The willingness of the Recabites to obey their forefather, Jonadab, in everything he commanded them very likely indicates a similar willingness to obey the Lord, hence the promise given to them.

**36:30** Jesus was "descended" from Jehoiachin (Jeconiah of Matt.1:11, through Joseph) who was eventually honored in Babylon (2 Ki.25:27-

30), and directly descended from Nathan through Mary (Luke 3). Thus the prophecy against Jehoiakim was fulfilled.

**40:1-3** Interesting commentary on the part of the commander of the imperial guard. He probably heard of Jeremiah's prophecies from Jews who had gone over to the Babylonians. How much he actually believed it at this point is another question.

**42:2,3,7-12,19-22** The Jews were willing to do what God wanted as long as he agreed with their plans!

**43:7-13** The Jews' flight to Egypt was the same as "jumping from the frying pan into the fire!"

**44:22** Even the Lord has a limit to his patience.

**52:2,3** Zedekiah had an "attitude." He rebelled against the Lord and against Nebuchadnezzar—definitely <u>not</u> a good combination!

**52:3** The Lord knows what it feels like to "kick someone out of the house." It is not necessarily an unbiblical action (see Hos.9:15).

**52:11** What happened to Zedekiah is a vivid illustration of Proverbs 13:9; 20:20 and 24:20.

**52:28-30** with **Rom.9:27-29** "Unless the Lord has left us a remnant"—from over 3,000,000 to 4,600! (Possibly 10,000 more from other deportations—but that still is not much.)

**Q. 52:28** with **2 Kings 24,25** Jeremiah 52:28 says that only 4,600 people in all were carried away into Babylon by Nebuchadnezzar. 2 Kings 24:14 says that he took 10,000. How can these figures be reconciled?
**A.** Several possible answers:
   1. There is a one year discrepancy between the two accounts:
     2 Ki.24:12 "eighth year"; Jer.52:28 "seventh year."
     2 Ki.25:8 "19$^{th}$ year"; Jer.52:29 "18$^{th}$ year."
This inconsistency indicates a different means of computing regal years, <u>or</u> there were actually minor deportations in the earlier years.

   2. In the 8$^{th}$ (7$^{th}$) year deportation, 10,000 people were taken: 7,000 fighting men; 1,000 craftsmen and artisans; leaving about 2,000 others. Jeremiah's figure of 3,023 seems to be an exact count of the "extra 2,000" whereas the 2 Kings account appears to be rounded off.

   3. <u>Or</u>, more likely, there were six different deportations: 3 major ones (2 Kings) and 3 minor ones (Jeremiah).

# LAMENTATIONS

Lamentations forms a Hebraic chiasm:

Ch.1  Confession of sin
Ch.2  God's great anger against sin
Ch.3  God's judgment tempered by his great love for Israel
Ch.4  God's great anger against sin
Ch.5  Repentance from sin

## God of the Impossible, cont.

182. He totally annihilates the Russian and Arab allies attacking Israel (chs.38,39).

\* \* \* \*

**General Comment:**

| | |
|---|---|
| Isaiah saw God's holiness and his own defilement, feeling <u>totally undone</u> (Isa.6:1-5). | Ezekiel saw God's glory and was <u>totally</u> <u>overwhelmed</u> (1; 3:12-15,23; 8:1-4; 9:3; 10:1-5,18,19; 11:22,23; 43:1-5; 44:4). |

**3:5,6** The Lord knows all probabilities of what would have happened <u>if</u>..., (i.e., all the possibilities of alternative actions; all that <u>could</u> happen under different circumstances).

**3:7** If we do not listen to the Lord, we will not listen to his messengers. If we are unprepared to follow him, we will not follow his servants either.

**4:1-5:4** Ezekiel had to have been a good mime artist (12:3-7,17,18). He <u>had</u> to mime since he could not speak unless the Lord gave him something to say (3:26,27). See also 24:27 ("at that time") and 33:22 ("that time") when the Lord restores his speech.

**Q. 4:14,15** (vs.14) "Not so, Sovereign LORD!" (vs.15) Ezekiel given permission. (Acts 10:14) "Surely not, Lord!" Peter rebuked (Acts 10: 15). Both Ezekiel and Peter said "No" to the Lord. The Lord acquiesced to the first but rebuked the second. What was the difference?

**A.** Ezekiel: God's picture of judgment on Jerusalem.

Peter: Evangelism of the Gentiles.

Ezekiel: Physical, public defilement.

Peter: "Defilement" only in his vision—just between him and the Lord.

Ezekiel: The "drama" would not be significantly altered by the use of different "fuel." The message of judgment would still be clear to the people—who would not pay attention to it anyway. So whether Ezekiel used human excrement or cow dung as fuel to cook his food, the end result would be the same. So Ezekiel would become defiled for what, in the end, would make no difference anyway. Thus God permitted the change.

Peter: He felt revulsion for the same reason—personal defilement that would result from eating unclean animals. But this was in a vision, not literally to be eaten before others to cause physical defilement. And the Lord's intent was different; it was to convince Peter that the Gentiles were not to be treated as "unclean" [dogs] but to be accepted because God has provided for their cleansing through Christ. Peter's objection therefore would have stopped the Gentiles from coming to Christ; Gentiles, who, not like the Jews of Ezekiel's day, would have heeded the Gospel and repented. Thus God's rebuke.

Q. 5:2,12; 6:12 (sword, famine, plague). In judgments, the Lord here deals in thirds as in Revelation. Why thirds? What is their signifycance?

**A.** According to E. W. Bullinger (Number in Scripture, Kregel Publications, 1980, p.116), the number 3, among other things, stands for the completeness of God's judgment. Without enlightenment from any other source, I'm left to my own devices to suggest an answer. If the number 3 indicates the completeness of God's judgment, then 1/3 must indicate his grace to a fallen world, meting out a severe enough judgment to get people's attention, but not enough to bring total destruction and, hopefully, to move them to repentance.

**7:27b** Israel was so wicked that God could thoroughly judge them by their own standards and condemn them!

**11:17-20** Without the sovereign intervention of God, none of us ever seek
him or even try to obey him (cf. Eph.2:8; Rom.3: 10-12,18)!

**14:1-8** Idolatry in one's heart is just as abominable to the Lord as the outward worship of idols/images, etc.

**14:3** Idolatry begins in the heart and ends up in the worship of idols.

**14:4-10** The context of these verses demands "false" prophets. The Lord would never deal with his prophets in the manner described here.

**16:9-15** with **28:12-17**

a. As <u>Satan</u> fell because of his beauty,…

b. …so <u>Israel</u> fell because of hers!
   Both described as being prosperous and wealthy and putting their trust in their riches rather than God.

c. Since the "Prosperity Gospel" emphasizes wealth and health in this world, it is setting <u>the Church</u> up for trusting in itself rather than God (since that seems to be a rather consistent result of health and wealth). The consequences of this misplaced trust are catastrophic.

d. <u>Tyre</u> fell (29:4,11) because of the same — her great wealth (28:5), synonymous with her great "beauty" (28:17).

e. <u>Assyria</u> fell for the same reason (31:8-12).

f. <u>Egypt</u> also (31:18).

"Lord, save us from 'health and wealth' that we might always place our full trust in you rather than in ourselves as we would do if we were too healthy and too wealthy" (cf. Prov.30:7-9).

**16:14,15** Israel was in the perfect position to reveal God's glory. God sovereignly put her there. But Israel used her position for self-gratification rather than ministry, and proceeded to become even more wicked than the nations around her or that preceded her (16:27,47-52)! In fact, she made them "righteous" by comparison! *Pride* was at the core (16:56).

**17:16,19,20** Zedekiah despised not only his oath and treaty with Nebuchadnezzar, but also despised God's covenant with Israel. He wanted to be his own man in every way, and lost.

**18:30** Repentance doesn't necessarily involve tears and emotion, but is an active choice to turn away from sin.

**20:25,26** I see three ways God works among his people to draw them to himself:

    1. <u>Grace</u>—Exercising his will by direct intervention (11:17-20; 20:39,40; 36:25-27).

2. Active discipline—Exercising his will through discipline to effect correction (20:32-38; Heb.12:5-11).
3. Passive discipline—Exercising his will by letting the sin they've chosen to commit work its own grief, thus turning their eyes back to him (20:25,26).

**20:32-34,42**  The impossibility of Israel to assimilate into other nations.  God will force them to leave those nations with outpoured wrath (anti-Semitism) and to return to Isrel.

[**NOTE:** The Lord had to force them <u>out</u> with great wrath and has to force them <u>back</u> again with great wrath!]

**Q. 20:33-38**  Is this a judgment of Israel at Christ's Second Coming?
**A.**

**21:9,10**  Compared with the sovereign sword of the Lord, the scepters of earth's kings are but sticks in their hands!

**21:27**  Zedekiah was the last Israelite king until the Messiah comes.

**27:1-36**  Tyre is a type of Babylon in Revelation, both in its worldwide prosperity (vs.1-26a) and in its destruction (vs.26b-36).

**Ch.29**  To this place (Egypt) the remnant of Judah went to escape death (see Jer.42:15-22; ch.46).  "There is a way which seems right to a man [even when God opposes it], but its end is the way of death" (Pro.16:25).

**29:17-20**  Why God told the Judean remnant <u>not</u> to go down to Egypt (see also 30:13,14,16,18 and Jer.44:1).

**32:7,8**  "Cover the heavens, darken their stars, cover the sun, moon not give its light, darken the shining lights in the heavens, darkness on your land"—all seem to be a figurative language for "You've <u>had</u> it!" (cf. Isa.34:4).

**Q. 33:10-20**  Do the life and death in this section refer to this world only, or to the life to come?

**A. 2 Sam.7:12-15**   Re: Solomon.  He ceased from doing right and began to worship idols later in his life, yet the Lord promised that his love would never be taken away from him as it was from Saul.  There will be discipline in this life for the wrong doing (7:14), but the implication is life in the world to come.

**33:30-32**  Even today, people love to have good preaching but most don't take it beyond the church door.  It warms their hearts, but seldom penetrates their will.  They are hearers of the Word, but not doers of it (see Jas.1:22-25).

**Q. Chs.38,39** When does this battle take place?

Pre-trib?  Beginning of the Tribulation?  Mid-trib?  Post-trib?  Post-Mill?

**A.**  Post-Mill doesn't fit since that is a worldwide rebellion led by the Devil.

Post-trib doesn't fit since the Battle of Armageddon involved armies from the entire world.  This one is just Russia and her allies.

Mid-trib (or sometime during the first half of the Tribulation period) doesn't fit because, even though Israel is living in a guaranteed peace, as long as Islam is around, they would never be able to rebuild a Temple on or near the Muslim holy site on the Temple Mount.

Pre-trib doesn't fit because Israel's peace has to be confirmed, and that won't happen until the Antichrist is on the scene.

The beginning of the Tribulation period seems to make the most sense in that it would allow the Jews to rebuild the Temple on the Temple Mount without any further Muslim resistance.

I see the Antichrist coming in and confirming the previous peace accords (Camp David, Oslo, etc.) putting them into effect, which, until now (2022), has not been done.  He is Israel's guarantor of peace, so they breathe a sigh of relief and begin to live in safety.  The Muslim world goes ballistic with this development, and, with Russia's help, decides to end the Jewish question once and for all.  They invade Israel and suffer nearly 100% casualties.  With the Arab and Russian forces decimated, there is no power left to prevent Israel's rebuilding of the Temple.

**Q. 38:10-14** When does Israel dwell like this?

**A.** I believe Israel does under the 7 year confirmation of the peace accords by the Antichrist. In exchange for his guaranteed peace,
Israel probably largely disarms herself.

**38:22** The "plague" could be natural (but governed by God), supernatural, or the result of "germ" warfare.

**39:9** If the wooden weapons are burned for seven years, and this
invasion occurs at the beginning of the Tribulation, then there would
be enough wood for fuel in Israel during the entire seven-year period.

**Q. 39:9-16** When would the defeat of Gog allow for these events to
happen, and what might that defeat look like?
**A.** I believe it will be at the beginning of the Tribulation for the reasons mentioned above under Ezek.38,39 and might look like the
following scenario:

## RUSSIA'S DEFEAT ON THE MOUNTAINS OF ISRAEL

**Setting:**
Allies: Russia, Iran, Libya, Turkey, Sudan, N. Ethiopia, Ukraine, and
others (See **NOTE**[1], p.211. Nice pincer movement!) This vast army
invades Israel.

Meteorological and Geographical events: A great earthquake. The Rift
Valley fault line runs right up the Jordan River valley. If the
earthquake happens at night, along with thunder, lightning, torrential
rain and hail stones, it is no wonder that the northern army turns upon
itself in total confusion (vs.21), thinking themselves under attack. The
earthquake also gives rise to volcanic eruptions. Burning sulfur, the
same as rained down upon Sodom and Gomorra, rains down upon the
armies of the north revealing God's great wrath.

**Scene 1:** Night. The thunder and lightning of an approaching storm
mix with the thunder and flashes of big guns. The storm hits with
sudden fury, blasts of wind, blinding rain, lightning bolts crisscrossing
the sky and striking the ground "at random" driving the soldiers to
whatever shelter they can find. Some bolts find the fuel and
ammunition dumps causing great explosions. Soldiers panic amid zig-
zagging missiles and exploding shells. There is nowhere safe to hide!

**Scene 2:** Then a gigantic earthquake hits! Mountains slide wholesale into the valleys. Walls crumble, buildings collapse, tents disappear under rubble or fall flat, some ripped apart by the earth's movements or by shrapnel from exploding ordinance. Fissures split the earth open everywhere with fire, ash, dust and lava thrown high into the air. Dust particles gather freezing moisture and quickly descend as huge hailstones. Molten lava, not thrown as high, descends with the hail as a rain of fire. Panic turns to pandemonium, and all appearance of military order and command evaporates.

**Scene 3:** With the shaking ground, noise and tumult of storm and explosion, fire, rain and hail falling, darkness, miserably wet and thoroughly frightened soldiers stagger in drunken disorientation, their warfare mentality unable to take in what is really happening. They think that they are under direct attack and that the enemy has penetrated their defenses. Someone starts shooting at a suspected enemy who returns fire suspecting him to be the enemy. Soon everyone is shooting everyone else in the mass confusion. …Suddenly all is deathly quiet except for the tumbling water, raging fires, aftershocks and the occasional detonation of ammunition.

**Scene 4:** Morning light reveals barren mountains, broken land, clogged valleys, fires, smoke, steam, crumbled ruins, dead bodies everywhere—charred, mutilated, crushed—and birds, vultures of every description, descending upon them to gorge themselves in the deadly quiet of the land. A few survivors return to their own lands, so crazed and troubled with recurring nightmares of the conflagration that they wish they had died with the others.

**Scene 5:** Israelites gathering and burying the bones of the dead; gathering also the wooden war implements to use for firewood; praising God for his deliverance from certain national annihilation.

**39:9,10** The reason Russian army is using wooden weapons and riding on horses (38:4) is because of the collapse of their economy by that time (38:10-13). Wooden weapons[2] indicate severe economic distress and the disintegration of steel weaponry through rust or plain wear-and-tear. By sheer weight of numbers, the Russians and their allies think that they could literally overwhelm Israel, even with great losses.

Another reason that Russia is willing to attack Israel, even with wooden weapons, is the probability that the Antichrist's guarantee of peace for Israel, and resulting disarmament, will leave Israel basically defenseless.

Judging by Russia's Muslim allies in this battle, the religious element must also be considered: to eliminate Israel from the face of the earth so that Islam might reign supreme over the whole Mid East.

Nevertheless, in the end, they suffer total defeat!

[NOTE:

1. According to Google Search, the potential allied military manpower for this army could reach a little over five million soldiers.

2. Years ago I read somewhere where Russia was already experimenting making weapons out of lignite, "a brownish black coal intermediate between peat and bituminous coal: especially one in which the texture of the original wood is distinct" (Webster's Seventh New Collegiate Dictionary). Lignite is purportedly harder than steel and thus would serve very well for guns of all kinds. With the disasters of the Tribulation and the destruction of Russia's economy, it is not inconceivable that these kinds of weapons, using modern technology, could be made. Unfortunately, I can't back this up, but it might be worth a thought anyway.]

**Q. Chs.40-44**  What was the significance of this description of the Temple (apart from recorded "tedium")?
**A.** 1. To assure the Jews that they would indeed return to their land; God was not through with them as a nation.
   2. (Ezek.43:10,11)  To give them a blueprint to follow in building the post-exilic Temple.

**Comment:** I had always thought of this passage as dealing with the Millennial Temple, but the context seems to imply the post-exilic Temple. However, God's comment in 44:2,3 seems to imply both. It is amazing how the Eastern Gate of the Temple complex has been preserved until now.

**40:2 w/**  Ezekiel saw the New Temple from a very high mountain.
**Rev.21:10**  John saw the New Jerusalem also from a very high moun-
**and**  tain.
**Deut 34:1**  Moses saw the entire Promised Land from a high mountain.

(It would be interesting to do a study on "Mountaintop Events" in Scripture to see what other events occurred on mountaintops. See **APPENDIX VII** for a start.)

**41:18** The Cherubim in this passage have <u>two</u> faces: of a man and of a lion.

**Q.** Could this be a symbolic representation of Christ as Savior (Son of Man) and Messiah (Lion of the Tribe of Judah)?—a symbol that the Jews totally missed?

**A.** I believe it could very well be.

**43:2,4,5**  The glory of the Lord <u>returns</u> to the Temple (see 9:3; 10: 4,18; 11:23 for stages of its departure).  It departed to the east and returns from the east.

**Q.** What is the significance of "east" in Scripture?  (<u>Eastern</u> gate now closed, awaiting entry by the Messiah—see also 43:17).

**A.** In Revelation 22:16, Jesus describes himself as "the Bright and Morning Star" that rises in the east—*the harbinger of a new day.* In Revelation 1:16, his countenance is described as "the sun shining in all its strength" which also rises in the east—*the reality of a new day.* So, generally speaking, the "east" in Scripture seems to symbolize a "new day" coming in which righteousness reigns and God's blessings flow unhindered.

**Q. 44:22**  Do these marriage regulations apply in principle to pastors in the Church today?  (Marry only virgins or widows of priests [other pastors?] —not other widows nor divorced women?)

**A.** The emphasis of the O.T. Law was on holiness.  The officiating priests had to be ceremonially holy in order to serve.  Anything that would violate that ceremonial holiness would also exclude them from serving.

In the N.T., we are free from the ceremonial laws of the O.T., but are <u>not</u> free from the command to be holy (1 Pet.1:15,16).  2 Corinthians 6:14-18 gives us God's guidelines for our relationships with others, and 1 Corinthians 7:39 talks about the parameters of marriage. The marriage of a pastor should be determined on a case-by-case basis, keeping in mind that his holiness as a servant of God, and his ministry as a result, must not be compromised.

# MILLENNIAL SACRIFICES

**Q. 45:18-46:15**  Why are sacrifices commanded to be offered in the
Millennium?  Wasn't Christ's sacrifice of himself sufficient for all
time?"

**A. Short Answer:**

Leviticus 15:31 says, "Thus you shall separate the children of Israel
from their uncleanness, lest they die in their uncleanness when they
defile my tabernacle that is among them."  In the Millennium, God's
very presence is in the Temple.  Thus the presence of unbelievers
would defile the Temple (unholiness cannot coexist with holiness) and
atonement has to be made for them, or else God would have to destroy them.

**A. Long Answer:**

The answer to the second part of the question, "Wasn't Christ's
sacrifice of himself sufficient for all time?" is, "Yes."  So then, what
about the first part?  Why are sacrifices necessary/commanded to be
made in the Millennium?  Perhaps the answer lies in Leviticus 15:31
which says, "Thus [with these sacrifices] you shall separate the children
of Israel from their uncleanness, *lest they die* in their uncleanness when
they defile my tabernacle that is among them" (italics mine).

That verse gives us a possible clue to the answer.  In the Millennium, God is present in a physical way as signified by the presence of
the Temple.  There will be unbelievers in Israel specifically and in the
world in general (children from the original body of believers who
entered the Millennium in their physical bodies), who are not covered
by the blood of Christ, being unsaved.  The blood of the sacrifices
offered on their behalf keeps them from being destroyed by God's
presence among them, even as it kept the Israelites in O.T. times from
being destroyed by his presence among them.  This may be a primary
purpose for the sacrifices.

It may be, too, that these sacrifices will become an "evangelistic
tool" which clearly illustrates Christ's sacrifice for us, thus helping
unbelievers understand the principle of Substitutionary Atonement and
come to him.

**47:2**  Interesting that in the vision, the angel led Ezekiel out through
the north gate and around to the east gate.  The east gate could only be
used by the Prince — and the Lord honored that even in Ezekiel's

vision.

**47:12** In the Millennium people will still have physical bodies, and as such, be subject to injury and sickness even though the curse will be lifted. The leaves of these trees will be a literal pharmacy available to bring healing whenever applied: blessing to the believer and grace to the unbeliever.

**48:30** A very minor sidelight: The new capital city of Jerusalem in the Millennial Kingdom is only half the size of Oak Park, IL where I grew up (2.5 sq. mi. compared with 4.5 sq. mi.), so could have a population of up to 33,000 people (Oak Park's being 66,000).

**48:30-35** No doubt this earthly, millennial Jerusalem is a miniature of the New Jerusalem, for there are many parallels:

| Ezekiel | Revelation |
|---|---|
| 1. City 4-square (48:16,17) | City 4-square (21:16) |
| 2. River flowing out giving life (47:1,8-10) | River of Life (22:1) |
| 3. Trees on either side: fruit for food; leaves for healing (47:7,12) | Tree of Life (22:2) |
| 4. River proceeded from the Temple (47:1) | River from the throne of God (22:1) |
| 5. The faithful are there | His servants (22:3,4,14) |
| 6. Holy (48:12) | Holy (21:27) |
| 7. Name: THE LORD IS THERE (48:35) | The LORD is there (21:22,23) |
| 8. 12 gates (48:30-34) | 12 gates: tribes not named, but generally mentioned (21:12,13) |

**48:31-34**

| Gates' location around the City: | Tribes' location around the Tabernacle (fr. Num. chs.2,10): |
|---|---|

| Reuben Judah Levi | | | Dan Asher Naphtali | | |
|---|---|---|---|---|---|
| Naphtali | | Joseph | Benjamin | | Judah |
| Asher | | Benjamin | Manasseh | Levi | Issachar |
| Gad | | Dan | Ephraim | | Zebulon |
| Zebulon Issachar Simeon | | | Gad Simeon Reuben | | |

**Q.** Why are these locations listed differently?
**A.**

# DANIEL

**God of the Impossible:**

183. He blessed Daniel's faithfulness by causing simple food to be more nourishing than the King's fare (1:11-16).
184. He revealed the King's dreams to Daniel (2:19; 4:19).
185. He reveals what is to come (2:29).
186. He gave Nebuchadnezzar everything he had (2:37,38). He also took it away (4:28-33) and gave it back to him again (4:34-37).
187. He rescued Shadrach, Meshach and Abednego from the fiery furnace (3:24-28).
188. He produced writing on the wall announcing Belshazzar's judgment (5:5).
189. He rescued Daniel from the lions' den (6:21,22).

\* \* \* \*

**2:1** If the first year of Nebuchadnezzar was 605 B.C. when he carried Daniel and company off to Babylon, and he had his image dream in his second year (604 B.C.), then Daniel was still probably in his first year of training to serve the king (cf. 1:5,18). This would have made his interpretation of the king's dream even more astounding since his training period was not yet completed. Somehow Daniel and his three friends were also included on the king's "hit list" (2:13,18). Evidently Nebuchadnezzar lost faith in the whole system and wanted to rid himself of it entirely.

**Q. 1:18-20** and **2:48,49** seem to conflict since 2:48,49 takes place
during the first or second year of Daniel's training. Daniel 1:19 says the four men entered the king's service at the end of three years. Daniel 2:48,49 would have them in elevated position far before that time, by the end of the first year or a bit into the second. (???)
**A.** During Nebuchadnezzar's second year, he had dreams that troubled
him. Evidently it was a recurring dream since Daniel gave only one interpretation. If the dream came numerous times to Nebuchadnezzar over a period of time, and his inquiries of the wise men also took some time, two years of Daniel's training could easily have passed. By that time, his skills were well-known and his elevation to governor of the Province of Babylon could have been made while he yet had one more year of training to go, after which they would "formally" enter the king's service.

**1:8-20** For whatever reasons, the other young men were not concerned about adhering to God's dietary restrictions, hence defiled themselves and placed themselves outside of God's blessing. In the end, they lost not only any testimony they might have had for the God of Israel, but also any places of high responsibility in the government (vs.18) like Daniel and his three friends were given. God honors those who honor him (vs.20).

**Q.** Since Daniel and company no longer had sacrifices available to
them for the forgiveness of sins, how were they saved? (cf. Ezek. 14:16,18).
**A.** By their righteousness (cf. Ezek.14:14,20; 18:5-9) which demon-
strated their faith (see Hab.2:4). The LORD said that he desired obedience (mercy) rather than sacrifice (Hos.6:6). So it would seem that if people responded to God by faith and obedience (demonstrating their faith), they would be saved even when the sacrifices were not possible.

**2:14,24** Daniel must have had great influence in the government since he put the King's edict to full stop. Because of his faith, he saved not only himself and his three friends, but also all the wise men of Babylon!

**2:47; 3:28; 4:2,3** Nebuchadnezzar's journey in his knowledge of God:
1. He is one among many (2:47; 3:14,15).
2. He is chief among all gods (3:28,29).
3. He is the *only* God (4:2,3,17,34,35,37), righteous, sovereign, etc.

**6:7** "all agreed"—Obviously the king thought that Daniel had too since he was one of the three royal administrators (vs.2). Darius was greatly distressed because of Daniel's situation; he was probably, at the same time, angry with himself and furious with impotent rage at the insidious deception of the other two administrators and satraps and his inability to do anything about it (vs.14,15,18-20), which paved the way for their prompt execution when Daniel was delivered (v.23,24).

**7:9,10** a. From the throne of God flowed a fiery river.
  b. From the throne of God flowed a river of life (Rev.22:1,2).
  From the context, the "fiery river" occurs at Christ's Second Coming (cf. vs.25-27 with Matt.25:31-33 and Rev.19:19,20).
  Ezekiel 47:1-12 also gives another picture of a life-giving river—but this one flows out from the Temple.
  These two rivers picture God's holiness that totally consumes (fire) what is not holy, but gives life (water) to what is. The character of the river depends upon our relationship with God.

**7:11,12** Evidently the remnants of these kingdoms (as represented by believers from those nations) will be obvious in the Millennium. But nothing will be left of the Roman Empire.

**Q. 8:9,10** If the "host of the heavens" refers to believers, and "the starry host" refers to the same, then how does this imagery and its interpretation affect similar imagery in Revelation when it speaks of stars?
**A.** It doesn't. The star imagery in Revelation has to be interpreted in its own context, especially in light of the fact that the word "star" in Revelation has at least eight different meanings! (See comments on the various meanings of the word "star" on pp.330,331).

**8:13,14** "2,300 days" (See The Bible Knowledge Commentary, Old Testament, p.1358; 8:23-25, for a fuller commentary on these verses.)

**9:21** Gabriel appeared to Daniel at the time of the "evening sacrifice" (3:00 p.m.), or the ninth hour (when Jesus also died as our sacrifice).

**9:25** (From Dr. David Jeremiah's sermon, "The Herald," 3/22/20.) King Artaxerxes of Persia began his reign in 465 B.C. He issued a decree to restore and rebuild Jerusalem on March 14, 445 B.C. Exactly 173,880 days later (April 6, 32 A.D.) Jesus rode into Jerusalem on the donkey!

**10:7** with **Acts 9:7** Selective visions where only the person involved saw anything. Those accompanying them knew something was happening, but didn't know what.

**10:13,20,21** Prince of the Persian Kingdom
Prince of Greece
Michael, your prince (Israel's—cf.12:1)
one of the chief princes (10:13)
the great prince (cf.12:1)
head of the heavenly forces (Rev.12:7)
Angel of the Bottomless Pit (Rev.9:11)—king of demons
Angel in charge of the waters (Rev.16:5)
Angels in charge of the wind (Rev.7:1)
Angel in charge of fire (Rev.14:18)

From this brief window on angelic responsibilities, some general observations can be made, and conclusions drawn which can shed greater light on the angelic world.

1. Each country of the world has its own demonic prince (10:13, 20,21).

2. Israel has an angelic prince (12:1). Had there been a correspond-ing angelic prince of Persia, Michael would not have had to come to help the angel sent from God to Daniel. Yet, perhaps this angel is that angelic prince as in hinted at in Daniel 11:1, but needed outside help.

3. Knowing the administrative hierarchy of both angels and demons (cf. Col.1:16; Eph.6:12; Rev.9:11), it could be a reasonable conjecture to conclude that there could be angels/demons over

continents, countries, provinces or states, counties, townships, cities, villages and hamlets. Whatever the human government, I suspect in some way it has its angelic/ demonic counterpart.

4. There is also a military aspect to the angelic/demonic activities. Michael is called the great prince (first among the chief princes? Dan.10:13) who also is the commanding general of the angelic army (Rev.12:7). Satan is his counterpart. This equality of position makes me wonder if Michael has been appointed to Satan's original position.

5. There also appears to be angelic responsibilities over the elements: wind (Rev.7:1), fire (Rev.14:18) and water (Rev.16:5) are mentioned specifically.

6. I suspect that for everything happening in the visible world, there is a corresponding occurrence in the spirit world. Said another way, the happenings on earth are a reflection of the activities in the spirit world (Dan.10:20).

7. Our greatest weapon to effect change is *prayer* (cf. Dan.9:23; 10:12-14; Lk.22:31,32; Eph.6:18). In answer to our prayers, the powers of Heaven are loosed and the powers of darkness are restrained. So it's no wonder that prayer is such a struggle for so many Christians and that Satan opposes it so strongly.

**11:1** The angel speaking to Daniel supported and protected Darius the Mede, an unbelieving king, yet a servant of God's purpose (see 6:25-27). Thus when God sets up a king or puts down a king, it seems that the angels have a direct role to play in the process.

**Q. 12:1** Does this verse mean that only believing Jews will make it through the Tribulation alive?
**A.** Possibly. Revelation 12:6,13-17 would seem to indicate this.

However, there is said to be a judgment upon Israel at Christ's coming (Ezek.20:34-38 with Matt.25:1-30) which would necessitate a believing and an unbelieving element present. If this is so, then there will be both believing and unbelieving Jews who will live through the Tribulation period.

**12:1b,3** The 144,000 of Revelation 7 fit in this context. If so, then their ministry indeed will be that of world evangelism.

## Daniel 4:15,16,33 Contrasted with Daniel 7:4

An interesting contrast between Daniel 4:15b,16,33 with Daniel 7:4.

| Daniel 4:15,16,33 | Daniel 7:4 |
|---|---|
| **Nebuchadnezzar** | **Babylon** |
| Went from two feet to "four" | Went from four feet to two |
| Given the mind of an animal | Given the heart of a man |
| Driven away from his people | Wings torn off |

For both the change from what they were was humiliating and their power was taken away.

### Time Line for Daniel 1-6 / Daniel's Personal History

| | | | Daniel's Age |
|---|---|---|---|
| **Nebuchadnezzar** | 605-562 = 43 years | | |
| 3rd yr. of Jehoiakim | | | |
| Daniel + 3 deported | | | ~ 15 years |
| App'ted by Neb. to | | | |
| serve in his court | 602-562 = 40 years | | 18 – 58 |
| Judah deported | 586 | (21 yrs. later) | 36 |
| **Evil Merodach** | 562-560 = 2 years | ⎫ 9 yrs.be- | 58 |
| **Neriglissar** | 560-556 = 4 years | ⎬ tween Neb. | 62 |
| **Labashi-Marduk** | 556-553 = 3 years | ⎭ and Bel- | 65 |
| | | shazzar | 65 |
| **Nabonitus** ⎫ | 553-539 = 14 years | | 79 |
| **Belshazzar** ⎭ | | | |
| **Daniel** made 3rd ruler | 539 | | 79 |
| (lasted only for | | | |
| several hours) | | | |
| **Darius the Mede** | 539-525 = 14 years | | 80's |
| **Cyrus the Persian** | 559-530 = 29 years | | |
| Captured Babylon (Oct.539) | | | |
| Orders the rebuilding | | | |
| of the Temple | 539 (His 1st yr. as king over Babylon) | | |
| 1st Return | 539 = 66 years after the 1st deportation. | | |

Therefore, approximately a 70-year captivity.

[Note: Since the final deportation occurred **21 years** after Daniel and friends were deported, that left **45 years** until the foundation of the new Temple was laid. Thus those who remembered the first Temple could have been quite a few (cf. Hag.2:3 and Ez.3:12).]

# HOSEA

**3:1,2** Evidently Hosea was a single parent for a time (N.I.V. note on vs.2).

**5:4,5** Sin has its own peculiar way of blinding its followers, then "pushing" them to make them stumble!

**5:7** "Illegitimate children"—born because of sexual ritual in Baal worship. "New Moon festivals"—Baal worship ceremonies. "Devour them and their fields"—judgment will destroy both because of their unfaithfulness to the Lord.

**5:15** The purpose of judgment/punishment: that we might earnestly seek the Lord and admit our guilt.

**6:6** Our character and actions are more important to the Lord than our worship (cf. Matt.5:23,24)! If the first are not right, then our worship is defiled and unacceptable to God (Isa.59:2).

**Q. 8:1** Could this "eagle" reference be referring to Rome in days to come?
**A.** Probably not. Both the NKJV and N.I.V. notes say that the reference is to Assyria. The immediate context would support that view.

**8:11** Worship perverted!

**9:7** The present situation in America is not unique! Because of their sins, they make God's servants out to be fools and crazy people, dangerous to the State, a threat to national security.

**10:4** Litigation proliferation is not a new thing!

**10:5** "Fearing *for* one's god" equals placing one's faith in something <u>weaker than man</u>. "Fearing *God*" equals placing one's faith in Someone <u>stronger than man</u>.

**12:4** Jacob's first personal encounter with God evidently was at Bethel.

**12:8** The wealthy are seldom convicted. Again nothing new. They can most always buy themselves out of trouble.

# JOEL

**NOTE:** Joel seems to be a kaleidoscope of end-time events:

**2:28,29** Pentecost
**2:30,31** Tribulation
**2:32** Second Coming
**3:1** Millennium
**3:2-14** End of the Millennium (Great Rebellion)
**3:15,16** Defeat of the final rebellion
**3:17-21** The eternal state

**2:2** Probable reference to the 200-million-man army from the East coming to Armageddon—or the demonic invasion of the world (Rev.9) from the Abyss—or just figurative language for a large invading army (2:25). Verse 11 may support the demonic invasion since the human army is numbered. So...

**Q.** Which is the more likely interpretation?

**A.** Probably the second, since Revelation 9:13-19 speaks of this army killing 1/3 of the world's population. An invading army from the East wouldn't go about killing everybody in its path (people from its own countries) on its way to the Middle East. In order to kill 1/3 of the world's population, it would have to wage warfare in a much broader scale than it would take for them to merely move against the Antichrist in Israel.

But a "200-million-man" army of demons, moving worldwide, would have no problem slaying 1/3 of the world's population.

It is interesting to compare the descriptions of this army with that of the locusts in Rev.9:1-11:

| Joel | Revelation | | |
|------|-----------|---|---|
| 2:4 | 9:7 | Looked like horses | = fearsome, powerful |
| 1:6 | 9:8 | Teeth of a lion | = vicious |
| 2:5 | 9:9 | Noise of chariots | = well-equipped and numerous |
| 2:6 | 9:4-6 | Nations in anguish | = fear and despair |

**2:25** reflects 2 Corinthians 4:17 and Psalm 90:15.

**Q. 2:30,32**  What is the prophetic significance (meaning) of the sun turning to darkness and the moon to blood?

**A.** It would seem to be <u>a metaphor for distress, suffering, defeat</u> (3:15), and <u>spiritual darkness</u> (2:2,10).

That being said, with all the debris thrown into the atmosphere by earthquakes, volcanoes, and smoke from fires all over, the sun will literally be darkened and the mood become blood-red. We have already seen this effect to a degree during dry seasons in Indonesia.

(See also: <u>Amos</u> 5:18,20; 8:9; <u>Joel</u> 2:1,2,10, 30,31; 3:15; <u>Isa</u>.13: 10; 5:30; 8:22; 9:1-5 [which gives insight as to spiritual darkness]; 24:23; 34:4; 50:3; <u>Jer</u>.4:23; 13:16; <u>Ezek</u>.30:3,18; 34:12; <u>Zeph</u>.1:15; <u>Mic</u>.3:6,7 [spiritual darkness]. The opposite is found in <u>Isaiah</u> 30:26 as to the brightness of the sun and moon, indicating victory, prosperity and spiritual enlightenment.)

# AMOS

**2:4**  Features of Protestantism today.

**5:10-13**  A chiasm:

| | | |
|---|---|---|
| A | vs.10 | Truth despised in court |
| B | vs.11a | Injustice toward the poor |
| C | vs.11b-12a | Judgment upon the judges |
| $B^1$ | vs.12b | Injustice toward the poor |
| $A^1$ | vs.13 | The prudent keep silent |

**9:1-4**  "No hiding place down here!"

# OBADIAH

# JONAH

## God of the Impossible (cont.):

190. He brought a terrible storm on the sea (1:4).
191. He prepared a large fish to swallow Jonah (1:17).
192. He kept Jonah alive for three days in the belly of the fish (1:17).
193. He caused the fish to spit Jonah up on the beach (2:10).
194. He convinced the Ninevehites to repent (3:5-10).
195. He caused a gourd to grow up to shade Jonah (4:6).
196. He caused a worm to destroy the gourd (4:7).
197. He prepared a vehement cast wind to blow (4:8).

**\* \* \* \***

**1:17-2:10** A chiasm:

| | | |
|---|---|---|
| A | 1:17-2:1 | Jonah swallowed by the fish |
| B | 2:2 | Jonah prays in distress |
| C | 2:3,4 | Jonah hurled into the deep |
| D | 2:5 | Jonah sinks to the bottom |
| C¹ | 2:6 | Jonah brought back up |
| B¹ | 2:7-9 | Jonah prays in distress |
| A¹ | 2:10 | Jonah vomited out on land by the fish |

**1:3,10** In order for Jonah to flee "far from God," he had to assume that God was a local god (like the gods of the other nations), whose place was in Jerusalem, but <u>not</u> in Spain. This shows his basic lack of understanding of God's omnipresence, etc. He should have read Psalm 139!

**1:17** What must have gone through Jonah's mind when he saw that big fish coming at him with its mouth wide open? "What a way to die! But at least I won't have to go to Nineveh!" [Guess again, Jonah!]

# MICAH

**4:10** God may not be mentioned in Esther, but here his actions for Israel while in Babylon are prophesied. (Esther is the visible expression of the invisible hand of God.)

**6:16** Some testimony!

**7:13** Results of the Tribulation.

# NAHUM

# HABAKKUK

**1:2-4** "How long, O LORD ...?" [See "How Long?" under Psalm 13:1,2, p.162.]

**2:18-20** The contrast between dead idols and the living God. Idol worshippers continually exhort their idols to live and work; God tells us to be silent and let <u>him</u> work! (see 1 Ki.18:25-29; Ecc.5:1-3; Matt.6:7,8 with Phil.2:13).

# ZEPHANIAH

**3:5,13** As the Lord in Jerusalem does no wrong, even so the remnant who are in Jerusalem (the redeemed) will do no wrong.

**3:9** The curse of Babel lifted (?)

**Q.** Does this indicate the return to one universal language?

**A.** Not necessarily. Note the similar imagery in Isaiah 6:5-7 where the purifying of one's lips has to do with sin rather than language.

**Q.** But will there be one language or many languages in Heaven?

**A.** Some have postulated that each nation will retain its own language in Heaven through which God will be praised and glorified. However, we will automatically understand whoever is speaking, even though recognizing their language as French, Italian, Japanese, etc. Somehow I doubt that, for the following reasons:

1. The confusion of languages, in the first place, was a judgment of God upon man's rebellion. In eternity all memory of this world will be erased. So why would God perpetuate a sign of judgment that he would always have to "remember"?

2. Multiplicity of languages flies in the face of the unity Christ prayed for in John 17, since diversity of language is a sign of disunity. The Trinity has its own form of communication, and if we're like Christ in Glory, I suspect we will share in that method in union with the Trinity.

3. How would we know there is more than one language if we could equally understand them all as being heard as our own? God's "glory" in the multitude of languages would be for his ears only, which would "rob" him of our worship and praise that should come because of this unusual phenomenon.

4. The clincher for me is in Isaiah 65:17. God will create new heavens and a new earth; the former ones will not be remembered nor come to mind (i.e., no holdovers from the old system: everything new and fresh, including, I believe, our heavenly language).

5. On the other hand (and there always seems to be an "other hand"!), God often takes the wrath (sins) of man to ultimately bring glory to himself. Could he not just as easily take the multiplicity of languages, in which he can be praised, and cause them to become something glorious and eternal?

He could just as easily take away from us the memory of "which languages those are [were]" so that their differences would be of no importance to us. I'm still holding to 1-4 above, but number 5 must also be considered as a possibility.

# HAGGAI

**1:12-14** The leaders and people chose to obey God. <u>Then</u> he stirred up their spirits to do the work. The Temple of God, his place of worship, has to be rebuilt in our hearts. It's a <u>relationship</u> he's looking for, not a building (cf. Rev.21:22).

**2:6,7**
1st fulfillment: An "earthshaking" event rather than a literal shaking.
2nd fulfillment: At the end of the Tribulation is a literal shaking as there will be many and great earthquakes.
3rd fulfillment (2:21,22): Political upheaval and warfare.

**1:15** Nineveh taking to herself the character and uniqueness of God (see N.I.V. note).

**Q. 3:4** Is this angel who says, "I have taken away your sin," actually the Lord Jesus? No angel could do that <u>unless</u> it is a symbolic gesture (taking off the dirty clothing, at the angel's command, thus symbolizing the removal of his sin that God himself had already cared for). So the angel could say, "I have taken away [the symbol of] your sin."
**A.** However, 3:1,2 make clear the angel's identity: it *is* Christ (see 1: 11,12).

**4:1** Evidently Zechariah drifted off in "day dreams" of that glorious coming day until the angel talking with him got his attention again.

**9:9** with **Matt.21:6-9** Israel's King, the Messiah (see below for the list of Christ's kingly titles.)

**12:10-14; 13:1,7-9** The mechanism by which Romans 11:26,27 will be fulfilled, God pouring out upon Israel the Spirit of grace and supplication while in affliction.

**Q. 13:8,9** What is the significance of thirds?
**A.** (See Ezekiel 5:2,12, p.205, for a possible answer.)

**14:9** Perspectives on Jesus as King over all the earth:

## HE IS THE KING

### The Believers' Perspective

| | | |
|---|---|---|
| The Everlasting King | (Mic.5:2; Isa.9:7; Lk.1:33) | — Eternal |
| The Prince | (Acts 5:31) | — The Chief Leader |
| King of Glory | (Ps.24:7,10) | — Exalted in praise, honor or distinction |
| King of Righteousness | (Isa.32:1 with Heb.1:8) | — Just and right |

## REGARDING ISRAEL:

### The Gentile Perspective

King of the Jews (Mat.2:2) — the people

### The Jewish Perspective

The King of Israel (Jn.1:49) — the nation
King of Zion (Ps.2:6) — the place of his rule
Governor/Ruler (Mat.2:6) — how he will rule

## REGARDING THE EARTH:

### The World's Perspective

King of kings (Rev.19:16) — Authority over all
The Prince of Kings (Rev.1:5) — Leader over all
King over all the earth (Zech.14:9) — Jews and Gentiles
King over the Gentiles/nations — Non-Jewish nations
(Rom.15:12)

## REGARDING THE CHURCH / BELIEVERS:

King of Saints (Rev.15:3, NKJV)
King of the Ages (Rev.15:3 N.I.V.)
King of the Nations (Rev.15:3)—Gk. word, ἐθνῶν, used.
The Scepter (Num.24:17 with Esth.4:8-14; 5:2)—Symbol of the king's authority and supreme power (see p.152; 5:2).
The Prince of Life (Acts 3:15 with Jn.10:28)—Author, Beginner, Sustainer and Example of life.
The Prince of Peace (Isa.9:6 with Jn.16:33)—Author/Giver of peace, taking the lead in establishing peace.
The Servant (Isa.52:13-53:12; Mat.12:18a with Jn.13:13-15; Mat.20:25-28, Phil.2:7)—a servant heart, serving his people.

# MALACHI

## God's Contending with Israel

Malachi reveals a contentious, doubting Israel, contesting every statement God makes:

| God's Statement | Israel's Response |
|---|---|
| **1:2** "I have loved you." | "How have you loved us?" |
| **1:6** "Where is the honor due me?" | "How have we shown contempt for your name?" |
| **1:7** "You place defiled food on my altar." | "How have we defiled you?" |
| **2:9,10** "You have not followed my ways, but have shown partiality in matters of the law." | "Why do we profane the covenant of our fathers by breaking faith with one another?" |
| **2:13** "The... LORD ...no longer... accepts your offerings." | "Why?" |
| **2:17** "You have wearied the LORD with your words." | "How have we wearied him?" |
| **3:7** "Return to me and I will return to you." | "How are we to return?" |
| **3:8** "You rob me." | "How do we rob you?" |
| **3:13** "You have said harsh things against me." | "What have we said against you?" |

Israel was in a dreadful state:

**1:2** Doubting God's love.

**1:6-8,13,14** Showing contempt for God's name by placing defiled food on his altar.

**1:12** Profaning God's name in defiling their worship and calling it a burden.

**2:2** [The priests] refusing to listen to the LORD.

**2:8** [The priests] turning from the way and leading many to stumble; they
   also violated the covenant with Levi.

**2:9** Showing partiality in matters of the law.

**2:11** Mixed marriages with non-Israelites.

**2:14** Unfaithfulness in marriage: divorce, family violence (vs.16).

**2:17** Perverting the sense of right and wrong; doubting God's justice

**3:5** Sorcery, adultery, perjury, fraud, oppression of widows and fatherless, aliens deprived of justice, no fear of God.

**3:7** Turning away from God's decrees.

**3:8** Robbing God of his due.

**3:13,14** Speaking harshly against God: "It is futile to serve God. What gain is it to us to do his bidding?"

**3:15** Calling the arrogant blessed: evil doers prosper and those who challenge God escape.

**4:5,6** The ministry of John the Baptist was more critical than the Jews knew.

* * * *

Looking over the prophets, it is interesting to notice their style of writing and possible "place in society" (if it's not explicitly stated). Consider the following possibilities:

| Prophet | Style | Place in Society |
|---|---|---|
| Isaiah | Poetic | Poet |
| Jeremiah | Prosaic (Weeping) | Pastor |
| Ezekiel | Pictorial | Actor |
| Daniel | Political | Statesman |
| Hosea | Pathetic | Dysfunctional Family |
| Amos | Pastoral | Shepherd |
| Obadiah | Prophetical | Common Man |
| Jonah | Pouter | Patriot |
| Micah | Protester | Social Activist |
| Nahum | Comforter | Counselor |
| Habakkuk | Ponderer | Traditionalist |
| Zephaniah | Poetic | Royalty |
| Haggai | Reconstructionist | Builder |
| Zechariah | Revivalist | Priest |
| Malachi | Prosecutor | Lawyer |

Conclusion: Whoever we are, whatever we are, there is always something we can say to others about God and our relationship with him.

# NEW

# TESTAMENT

# MATTHEW

## God of the Impossible (cont.):

198. He caused a special star to shine (2:2).
199. He enabled the wise men to leave without Herod's knowledge (2:12).

\* \* \* \*

**1:11** Though Christ was descended from Jeconiah (Solomon's line) <u>through Joseph</u>, he could not claim David's throne from this descent because of the curse put on Jeconiah (Jer.22:30), plus the fact that he was not Joseph's physical son. His claim to the throne came <u>through Mary's lineage</u> from David's son Nathan (Lk.3:31). Therefore, the Shealtiel and Zerubbabel in both genealogies have to be different men.

**Q. 2:4-6** Why didn't the Jewish religious leaders go to Bethlehem to see for themselves what was going on?
**A.** Because they were afraid of Herod's wrath and edict that if he were to be killed, so would they! (Herod wanted to be sure that there was mourning at his funeral!)

**Q. 4:8,9** In Christ's temptation, Satan led him to a high place, showed him all the kingdoms of the world, and said to him, "I will give you all their authority and splendor, for it has been given to me and I can give it to anyone I want to." In light of Romans 13:1, Matthew 28:18, Luke 10:19 and John 19:11, is Satan, the father of lies, making a bold-faced lie here, or does he actually have the power he claimed? Evidence in Job shows that he could exercise his power only as far as God gave him permission to.
**A.** Satan's power is "legal" power, received from Adam when he surrendered it to him at the Fall (one of the results of sin that Adam hadn't counted on!). God is the Greater Power over all, but he gave Adam delegated power to rule over creation. Satan only acquired that "delegated power" from Adam, so God is <u>still</u> the Greater Power. Adam was free to administer that power in any way he wished — so can Satan — but only within the confines of what God

has permitted. So Satan wasn't lying (notice that Christ didn't contest what he said). He <u>could</u> have given all the kingdoms to Christ, but but *that is where I see the deception.* If Christ surrendered to Satan as Adam did, then that would be the surrender of the Greater Power to Satan. Once Satan had <u>that</u> power, do you think for a moment that he would let Christ continue as King of the Nations? Hardly. He would have eliminated him (as a potential threat), and begun to rule the nations himself as the Prince of Darkness, raining upon them all the destruction that is inherent in his nature. (Shudder!)

But Christ came to destroy Satan and all his works (1 Jn.3:8) and take back that authority that was originally given to Adam, in which *he* will rule the nations as the Prince of Life, raining upon them all the blessings of his righteousness and grace. What a difference! And in him, we also have the final victory over Satan. As the Apostle Paul wrote, "But thanks be to God who gives us the victory through our Lord Jesus Christ!" Whew! That story has a *good* ending!

**Q. 4:23** What is the difference between the Gospel of the Kingdom that Jesus preached, and the Gospel of Grace that we preach now?

**A.** The Gospel of the Kingdom was God's offer to Israel of the Kingdom in which Christ would reign as the promised Messiah. "Gospel" means "good news" and can cover much more territory than just "salvation." So Christ went about preaching the "good news" about the Kingdom and offering it to the Jews. It is <u>this</u> gospel that will be preached once again during the Tribulation period (Mat.24:14). That is the <u>emphasis</u> during the Tribulation time though the Gospel of Grace will no doubt also be preached since people will still have the Bible and will be saved during that time.

Christ could not have preached the Gospel of Grace because he had not yet died. So the time for the "good news" of Grace had not yet come.

During this "Age of Grace," the Gospel of Grace, the basis of our salvation, is preached. But once this age is over, and God resumes his program for Israel (according to Daniel's 70 Weeks; see Dan.9:24-27), then the Gospel of the Kingdom will be reintroduced to prepare Israel for entrance into the Kingdom seven years hence.

**Q.** Had the Jews accepted Christ as the Messiah and hence received the Kingdom, what about his death for our sins, etc.?

**A.** According to Renald Showers (<u>Israel My Glory</u>, Oct./Nov. 2000, p.31), "Even if Israel had believed the gospel of the Kingdom and repented, Christ would have died for the sins of the world. If Israel had believed and repented, the nation would have acclaimed Christ as its king. The Roman government would have regarded this action as the beginning of a revolt and undoubtedly would have crucified him. Then Christ would have risen from the dead, crushed and removed Satan and his kingdom (including the Roman Empire), and established God's theocratic Kingdom on the earth."

**Q. 4:24** Is there anything significant about these listed afflictions? Why were these mentioned specifically and others not?
**A.** They are listed in the context of "various diseases" among which these would probably be considered the most severe. There wasn't any affliction (demon possession) or disease of mankind over which Christ didn't have control.

**5:20** Key verse for all that follows.

**5:23,24** Reconciliation is more important than worship! (cf. Pro. 21:3).

**Q. 8:28** with **Mk.5:2** and **Lk.8:27.** Mark and Luke say that Christ was met by one man; Matthew says two. Which is it?
**A.** (Fr. Robert J. Little, Radio Pastor of WMBI [1963 letter] in response to my question) "With regard to the discrepancy in the number of the men mentioned in Matthew 8:28 and in Mark 5:1 and the parallel passage in Luke 8:26, the fact is simply, that there were two men as Matthew states. The references in Mark and Luke make mention of only one, not as denying that there was another, but simply using the case of one for the purpose of their narrative. There are various other examples of this in the Bible and it is in keeping with the way the Bible is written.

"...We must compare one passage with another to get the entire story, and the full meaning of the Scripture."

**8:29** The demons know that the time for their judgment is set. So they know they have lost the war. Satan is also aware of that set time—and the awareness of the nearness of it greatly increases his wrath (Rev.12:12). His ship is going down, so he unleashes the greatest salvo possible to destroy as much of the "coast" as he can before his last gun falls silent beneath the waves of God's wrath.

**Q. 10:7** with **Acts 28:23**   Is there a difference between:
1. "the Kingdom of heaven" and "the Kingdom of God"?
2. "the gospel of the Kingdom" (Mat.24:14),
   "the eternal gospel"         (Rev.14:6,7)
   "the gospel of Jesus Christ" (Mk.1:1; 2 Cor.4:4);
   "the gospel of grace"        (Acts 20:24),
   "the gospel of God"           (Rom.15:16), and
   "the gospel of peace"        (Eph.6:15)?

**A.**  1. No. "Heaven" is a euphemism for "God" in Jewish expression, so the two expressions mean the same thing.
2. On the other hand, there is a difference in the various "gospels" listed. The word "gospel" means "good news"; so here we have good news about several things:

  a. The Gospel of the Kingdom is the good news given to the Jews that the Kingdom of Heaven was near. I take that to mean that since the Messiah had come, the Kingdom was being offered to the Jews, but they rejected both.

  b. The Eternal Gospel is offered to the earth-dwellers during the Tribulation period to fear God, give him glory and worship him because the hour of his judgment has come. The good news, in this case, God is still in control, the time of tribulation is near its end and that people could still turn to him if they would. Unfortunately, most of them, by this time, have made their decision not to.

  c. The Gospel of Jesus Christ is the good news that a Savior has come through whom we can receive forgiveness of sins.
   1) The Gospel of God is another name for the Gospel of Jesus Christ in that it originated with God in order to redeem mankind to himself.
   2) The Gospel of Grace and the Gospel of Peace are subcategories of the Gospel of Jesus Christ, emphasizing the means by which we receive salvation and its results.

**10:23** Persecution is one means God uses to spread the Gospel (cf. Acts 8:1,4).

**11:20-24** God knows all possibilities even though they never happened. Miracles do not guarantee results, but demand greater responsibility. Jesus said that if the miracles performed in Capernaum (vs.23) had been done in Sodom, they would have repented. But that wasn't the time for miracles. However, the Canaanites <u>had</u> a witness to the truth: Noah's son, Seth (perhaps from a distance), Abraham (journeyed all over Canaan), Melchizedek (a long time in Jerusalem), Job, his three friends and obviously others on the other side of the Jordan, and even Lot who lived in Sodom (albeit a rather doubtful witness). Had the Canaanites <u>wanted</u> to know the truth, it was right there among them!

**12:9-13** The Lord expanded the Pharisees' question from healing on the Sabbath to doing good on the Sabbath. <u>Not</u> what they wanted to hear (vs.13).

**13:12** could be translated: "Whoever has [God's revelation] will be given more, and he will have an abundance. Whoever does not have [God's revelation] even what he has [the O.T. revelation] will be taken from him." This certainly was true of the Pharisees, among others.

**13:28,29** Probably because the root systems intertwined.

**13:30,49** At the end of the age the angels come to separate the wicked from among the just, whereas the Rapture (1 Thes.4:14-18) is a "severing" of the just from the wicked. If a Post-Trib Rapture occurred, there would be no just persons left for the wicked to be separated from!

**14:6-23** When Jesus heard about John the Baptist's death, he wanted to get alone in a solitary place—no doubt to grieve, meditate and pray. But the crowds came. In compassion he put aside his grief for the day and ministered to them. At the end of the day, he dismissed them (they were satisfied), then went up on a mountainside to finish his personal grieving over John and to pray.

**17:20** with **1 Jn.5:14,15** "The bridge between submitting to God's will ('Thy will be done') and persevering in prayer ('knocking down Heaven's door' as it were) is <u>knowing</u> God's will in that particular circumstance." (Michael McMahon—ACTI trainee, 1996)

**18:1,4** The disciples ask <u>who</u> is greatest in the Kingdom of Heaven and received a different answer than what they were expecting. (Note all the times they argued among themselves as to who among <u>them</u> would be greatest: Matt.20:20-28; Mk.9:34; Lk. 9:46; 22:24). Christ answered, "Whoever humbles himself like this child is the greatest, and only those who do will enter the kingdom of heaven." In other words, <u>everyone</u> in the Kingdom is equally the "greatest." The disciples were asking the wrong question!

**20:20-24** The 10 were indignant because <u>they</u> wanted those positions themselves!

**25:5,19** and **13:39,49** In these passages are statements from Christ which indicate that it will be sometime before he returns: "The bridegroom was a long time in coming." "After a long time." "At the end of the age," etc. (Luke 12:45; 19:12; 20:9; 21:8-28).

**Q.** In light of these statements, how could the early Church believe in an imminent return?
**A.** The words "a long time" are actually part of the parable story and <u>*not*</u> the main intent of the parable. Parables are given to teach <u>*one*</u> main truth, not many. Therefore, we cannot take these time phrases out of context in order to glean additional truth regarding the Rapture.

**25:46** There is nothing mentioned in Scripture about another resurrection of the just at the end of the Millennium. This verse gives us the reason: there will be no deaths among the righteous; they receive eternal life as their *possession* at the point of entering the Millennium (while still in their <u>earthly bodies</u>) but will only *experience* it when they receive their <u>resurrection bodies</u> at the end of Millennium.

**Q.** Since <u>only</u> believers enter the Millennium, from where comes the mass of unbelievers who rebel at its end and the need for Christ to rule with a rod of iron during the Millennium?

**A.** These have to be the descendants of the original inhabitants of the Millennium who could only have progeny if they entered the Kingdom in their physical bodies.

It stands to reason then that all the Millennial believers will receive their resurrection bodies at the end of the Millennium, even as we who are alive at the coming of the Lord (the Rapture) will receive ours. This change will probably occur at the time of the Great Rebellion since at that point, <u>all</u> unbelievers are destroyed (Rev.20:9), the devil (and his angels) are thrown into the Lake of Fire (Rev.20:10), and the earth and heavens are totally vaporized (2 Pet.3:10-12). Then comes the Great White Throne Judgment. The Millennial believers would <u>have</u> to have their resurrection bodies by that time.

**Q. 27:3-8** with **Acts 1:18,19** Matthew says it was the Pharisees who bought the field. In Acts, Peter says it was Judas who bought it. Who is right?

**A.** Actually both! Even though the Pharisees made the actual purchase, it was bought with Judas's money and for his "benefit" (since it seems he was probably buried there, too). So, by extension, Peter could say that Judas bought it. This principle is often seen in Scripture. "David slew 10,000 men in the valley" does not mean that he did it himself, but that his army did it. So "David" here stands for his army, though by extension he gets the credit. Since Judas and the Pharisees were one in their betrayal of Christ, what the Pharisees did could easily be said to have been done in Judas's name, hence, "Judas bought the field."

**27:6** Thus they "strain at a gnat and swallow a camel." No problem in planning to murder Jesus, but they greatly worry about "impure" money defiling the Temple!

**27:25** "Let his blood be upon us and our children." Little did they realize what they were really saying. His blood was required of them all in 70 A.D. when Jerusalem was destroyed by Rome.

**27:46** On the cross, Jesus suffered God's desertion so that we would <u>never</u> have to (cf. Matt.28:20; Heb.13:5).

**Q. 27:46-50** What was the order of Christ's 7 last words? (see also <u>The Bible Knowledge Commentary, New Testament</u>, p.88).

**A.** Right after he was crucified: 1. "Father, forgive them." (Lk.23:34)
To the thief on the cross:  2. "Today you will be with
 me in Paradise." (Lk.23:43)
To Mary and John:  3. "Dear woman...your son;
 here...is your mother."
 (Jn.19:26,27)
At the ninth hour:  4. "My God, why have you forsaken
 me?" (Mk.15:34)
 5. "I thirst!" (Jn.19:28)
 6. "It is finished." (Jn.19:30)
 7. "Father, into your hands
 I commit my spirit." (Lk.23:46)

**27:65,66; 28:2-6** Something has to be said about the total futility of man's attempts to thwart God's working, but I'm not sure just how to say it. Well, Psalm 2:4a is a good start: "The One enthroned in heaven laughs." Also Proverbs 21:30: "There is no wisdom, no insight, no plan that can succeed against the LORD."

**28:1-6** Jesus actually rose *before* the stone was rolled away. The reason the stone was moved was to show that he was *already* gone.

**Q. 28:10** Why Galilee?
**A. Jn.21:1-19**
 a. The disciples, and mainly Peter (vs.2,3), had to make a final break with their old way of life and make a new beginning. That had to be done in Galilee.
 b. Also, there were many people in Galilee (cf. 1 Cor.15:6) who needed to see Jesus alive; people Jesus had ministered to and needed this final encouragement to believe.
 c. On the purely human side, might Jesus not have desired to "see" his home town and area of ministry one last time before leaving it? (Nostalgia? I don't think so...but...maybe.)

**Q. 28:8-10,16-20** What were the actual chronological appearances of Jesus to the disciples and others?
**A.** From considering the four Gospels, Acts 1 and 1 Corinthians 15: 1-7, I would suggest the following sequence:

1. Four women: Mary Magdalene, Mary the mother of James, Salome and Joanna, prepare to take spices to the tomb and leave while it is yet dark (Jn.20:1), arriving at the tomb just after dawn, only to discover that the stone had been rolled away (Matt.28:1; Mk. 16:2)!

2. Shocked, Mary Magdalene turned heel, leaving the other women, and ran to report to Peter and John about the missing body (Jn.20:2).

3. Peter and John came running to the tomb, John stopping short of going in, but Peter entered right in to see for himself. "Right, no body" ("Him they did not see" — Lk.24:24). And he left, puzzled (Jn.20:3-9).

4. Mary stood weeping at the tomb's opening (Jn.20:11). Looking inside, she saws two angels who asked her why she was crying (Jn.10:12). She told them her assumption, then turned around and left before they could reply, whereupon she met Jesus (Jn.20:13-17).

5. Meanwhile, Peter was on his way back to Jerusalem when Jesus appeared to him (Lk.24:34; 1 Cor.15:5) after seeing Mary (Mk.16:9). Peter reported his seeing Jesus to the others, but they evidently did not believe him (see #9 below).

6. As Mary returned to the tomb to tell the other women that she had met Jesus, they all saw the angel who confirmed what Mary had just seen. "He is risen, and will be going ahead of you to Galilee. Go quickly and tell his disciples to meet him there" (Matt.28:7).

7. On the way, Jesus met them all, encouraged them, and told them to tell the disciples to go to Galilee where he would meet them (Matt. 28:8-10).

8. The women, along with several others (Lk.24:10), went to tell the disciples that his body was *not* taken away, but that *he had risen* (Jn.20: 18; Mk.16:10,11)! But the disciples refused to believe them (Lk.24: 11).

9. Meanwhile, late that afternoon (Lk.24:28,29), Jesus appeared to Cleopas (Lk.24:18) and his friend (wife?—Jn.19:25, KJV, alternate

spelling?) on the road to Emmaus (Lk.24:13-16; Mk.16:12,13), after which they hurried back to Jerusalem to report his appearance to the disciples (Lk.24:33-35), and confirmed Jesus' appearance to Peter. Evidently they too had been there when Peter reported his meeting Jesus, but didn't believe him either. Now they <u>did</u>.

10. While they were still speaking about these things, Jesus stood among them (Lk.24:36; 1 Cor.15:5) and proved that it was indeed he himself (Lk.24:37; Jn.20:19,20). Thomas was not there at the time (Jn.20:24,25). Then he taught them the same things he told the two on the Emmaus Road (Lk.24:44-46—Thomas missed all that!), and gave them an abbreviated Great Commission (Lk.24:47,48).

11. After that, he led them out to the vicinity of Bethany where he blessed them and ascended to Heaven (Lk.24:50,51).

12. A week later (Jn.20:26), he once again appeared to his disciples, Thomas with them, who finally confessed his belief in Christ's resurrection (Jn.20:27-29).

13. Evidently the disciples then left for Galilee, but Peter, seeing Jesus leave, still had no idea what to do. So he decided to return to what he did know: fishing (Jn.21:2,3), and invited the others to come along.

14. Jesus suddenly appeared to them (Jn.21:4-6) and was recognized by John (Jn.21:7-9). He dealt specifically with Peter and his doubts (Jn.21: 10-19).

15. After that, Jesus came and went among his disciples for the remainder of the 40 days of his appearances (Acts 1:3), at one time appearing to a group of over 500 people, likely in Galilee (1 Cor.15:6), then, at some point, specifically to James (1 Cor.15:7).

16. Evidently Jesus told his disciples to return to Jerusalem (Acts 1:4) where he appeared once again to them (1 Cor.15:7) and gave them his final instructions and blessing, after which he ascended to Heaven, from the Mount of Olives (Acts 1:12,) for the final time (Acts 1:4-12).

# MARK

**Q. 4:11,12** Verse 12 is still a puzzle (cf. Isa.6:9,10; Matt.13:14,15; Lk.
8:10). If the Lord knew these people could turn and be forgiven
— why didn't he open their eyes and ears to the truth?
**A. Matt.13:14,15** makes this situation more clear. The people themselves closed their ears and eyes and hardened their hearts to the
truth. Had they <u>not</u> done this, they would have gained spiritual
perception and forgiveness. Had Christ given them understanding,
and they still persisted in their hardness of heart, they would have
been even more responsible for the truths they heard and rejected
and would have added judgment to themselves. So, in part, it was
grace that withheld understanding from them.

**Q. 6:13** When the 12 went out, they healed the sick, but anointed
them with oil first. Jesus is never shown doing this. Why the dif-
ference?
**A.** Oil is the symbol of the presence and power of the Holy Spirit.
The disciples, not divine, needed this symbol of divine power.
Jesus, divine, didn't.

**6:43** Twelve baskets full of leftovers from perhaps nearly 15,000
people are not that much! No caterer could come nearly that "close"
to figuring out how much that many people would eat. <u>But</u>, the
emphasis has to be on *full* baskets: everyone had enough, there was
no lack, and there was plenty to go around again if necessary. The
Lord's provision is enough and exceeds enough if that is what is
needed.

**8:17-21** "Familiarity breeds contempt." The disciples were so used to
seeing miracles by now that they had ceased to be impressed or
moved by them. So they began missing the lessons that the Lord
intended for them to receive. How much of our faith do we take for
granted because we're "so used to it," and thereby cease to be awed
by what God has done—or be instructed by it? Thus many truths,
commands and lessons from God's Word slip by us unnoticed.

What is the remedy for this situation? I think there is <u>only</u> one
way— by meditating on God's Word during which time our minds
and hearts are quieted from the distractions around us and the Holy
Spirit can show us "new" things that will amaze us and keep us

appreciative of what God has done and is doing.

**Q. 8:22-26** How would the blind man, now seeing, know where his home was?

**A.** My guess is that he had to find it first with his eyes closed! He would have felt very foolish asking people where it was, that he was lost, now that he could see! On the other hand, if he had friends with him, he no doubt asked them to show him the way home, about which they must have had a good laugh.

**10:35,47** (From my sister, June Wiegert) "To both people Jesus said, 'What do you want me to do for you?' One request was denied, but the other gladly granted. The request denied (vs.35ff) was for power and prestige, based on pride, given as a demand, demonstrating a desire for power, and was for the purpose of making <u>them</u> great. The second request, gladly granted (vs.47ff), was for mercy and healing, based on humility, presented as a request for mercy; the desire was for wholeness, and the granting of it would be a display of *Jesus'* power and bring *him* glory."

**12:43,44** God evaluates by percentage, not by amount, for the percentage is the measure of one's heart. All the others gave only 10%; the widow gave 100%. In Jesus' opinion, she gave more than all the others put together!

**14:60-62** with Isa.53:7; Matt.26:62-64; 27:11-14; Mk.15:2-5; Lk. 22:66-70; 23:3, 8-10; Jn.18:4-8,20-23,33-37; 19:10,11 and 1 Pet.2: 23. During his "trials," Christ never answered an accusation made against him; he only responded to acknowledge the truth.

**14:63-65** When the opposition has it in mind to condemn you, no amount of truth will change their minds.

**15:26** Pilate didn't necessarily believe that Christ was actually the King of the Jews, but it was probably his means of getting a "dig" at the Jews for forcing him to crucify an innocent man. He knew it would gall them but that they wouldn't do anything more since their will had been accomplished.

# LUKE

**God of the Impossible (cont.):**

200. He gave Elizabeth, barren, a child (1:36).
201. He gave Mary, a virgin, a son, Jesus (1:35).

* * * *

**1:5,6,18-20** Even the upright and blameless can have trouble believing at times. Zechariah questioned the possibility; Mary, on the other hand, questioned the method (vs.34 with 38,45).

**1:20** Zechariah was probably not deaf (Gk. σιωπῶν [seeōPŌN], indicates "silence," not able to speak). But because he could not talk, the normal reaction of others was not to speak, but to communicate through signs also. Totally unnecessary, but a natural response.

| **3:8  "Lessons from the Stones"** | **Pharisees' Problem:** |
|---|---|
| 1. John the Baptist told the Pharisees (Matt.3:7-9) that God was able to raise up children for Abraham "out of these stones." | Pride of descent |
| 2. When Christ entered Jerusalem and the disciples were praising him, the Pharisees objectted. Christ answered them: "If they keep quiet, the stones will cry out" (Lk.19:40). | Religious embarrassment Pride of power/influence (Jn.11:47,48; 12:19) |
| 3. When Peter and John appeared before the Sanhedrin (Acts 4:1-21), Peter accused them of rejecting Jesus, God's capstone. | Pride of position |
| 4. Peter also said that they stumbled over this Stone… …(1 Pet.2:8) because they disobeyed the message, not believing it. | Pride of knowledge —unbelief: rejection… …of truth |

247

| **"Lessons from the Stones"** | **Pharisees' Problem:** |
|---|---|
| 5. Then the Pharisees (Sanhedrin) used stones to kill Stephen (Acts 7:58). | Pride in religion—murder in their hearts |

**4:5-7** (vs.7) "If you worship me, all will be yours." A bold-faced lie. If Christ worshipped Satan that would complete the handover of world power to him forever, making Christ subservient to him and thus eliminating the threat of coming judgment.

**4:22-29** There is nothing as wild, blind and unpredictable as religious bigotry; it can change at a moment from total acceptance to total rejection.

**Q.** What "tone of voice" might be indicated in these passages? Mockery? Fear? Anger?
**A.** 4:34,35 (Mk.1:23-26)  _____
    4:41 (Mk.1:34)  _____
    Mat.8:29-31  *Fear*
    Mk.3:11,12  _____
    Mk.5:6-8 (Lk.8:27-29)  _____

**5:22** The fact that Jesus knew what they were thinking in their hearts should have arrested their attention and proved that someone greater than man was among them.

**6:7-10** Prejudice blinds the eyes to truth and keeps one from appreciating anything good that happens apart from his own frame of reference.

**6:10,11** The Pharisees were more concerned about keeping their laws than they were about showing mercy to those in need. They willfully ignored what God said in Hosea 6:6, "For I desire mercy, not sacrifice, and acknowledgment of God rather than burnt offerings" (cf. Lk.11:42).

**7:28** Christ seems to be saying here that John the Baptist was actually greater than Moses and the prophets! Yet the Jews didn't react to this statement as at other times. Had they understood this to be Christ's meaning, surely they would have rioted.

**8:18** can be illustrated by Hebrews 10:26 in this way: "Whoever has [faith in God's sacrifice] will be given more; whoever does not have [this faith], even what he thinks he has [forgiveness through the O.T. sacrifices] will be taken from him" (70 A.D.—the Temple destroyed—all sacrifices ended—no sacrifice left for those who refused Christ's sacrifice).

**Q. 8:40-50** Why did Christ make such an issue over the woman who touched him and was healed? Is there any significance to the fact that Jairus' daughter was 12 and the woman had suffered for 12 years?
**A.** Jairus' faith was about to be severely tested (vs.49), thus the woman became an immediate object lesson to him of Christ's power to heal if he would believe. Perhaps the similarity in years of the woman's suffering and Jairus' daughter's age served as a strong tie in Jairus' mind between what the Lord did for the woman and what he will do for his daughter. Thus his attention was even more riveted upon the woman and what Christ did for her.

**9:9** Herod heard about Jesus and tried to see him, but somehow never succeeded until the time of his crucifixion (Lk.23:8-12).

**9:33-36** Moses and Elijah disappeared in the cloud.

**10:8-12** Sometimes, God's message comes to us in unexpected ways. If we do not "receive" his messenger, we do so to our own peril.

**10:16** When we are sent by Christ to others, and they listen to us and receive our message, they listen to and receive Christ. But if they reject us, they not only reject Christ, but also the Father! This is an awesome truth, and puts upon us the responsibility to represent Christ before the world in the best way possible. If, by our attitudes and actions, we cause others to reject us, we cause them to reject Christ. "Lord, help us be faithful to you in every way."

**10:23,24** God chose to reveal to the disciples what was not revealed to the prophets and kings! This is 1 Corinthians 1:26-31 exemplified even within the body of believers.

**10:25-28** The answer to those who feel they must <u>do</u> something to be saved.

**11:20**  The main purpose of Christ's miracles was to announce the Kingdom of God.

**11:39-54**  Quite a dinner speech!  The Pharisees and guests must have quickly lost their appetites.  Obviously they weren't impressed (vs.53,54).  After Jesus' scathing rebuke, they had nothing left but to fiercely oppose him and try to discredit him in some way so as to restore their image and justify their position.  No one likes to be told, "You're wrong!"

**Q. 12:9**  What is the power of the word "disown/deny" in this verse? What are its implications?

**A.** Since Jesus says that those who disown him he will disown, it <u>has</u> to be in reference to unbelievers.  No true child of God would ever disown Christ in this way.  What's more, Christ promised that he will <u>never</u> cast out those who come to him.  Since those who disown him (as in this verse) are also disowned by him, they are rejected, cast out by him, thus proving that they were never his to begin with.

**12:35-38**  There will be one more time when the Lord serves—at the welcome feast in Heaven.  I don't believe that this feast could be the marriage supper of the Lamb (Rev.19) as the roles are different then.

**12:47,48**  There will be gradation of punishment as well as gradation of reward (see Lk.19:16-19).

**Q. 13:31**  In light of Luke 9:9 and 23:8-12, could this be true, or were the Pharisees just making it up?

**A.** From the sound of these verses, and in light of the others, I assume they were just trying to give Jesus a hard time.

**16:31**  Faith does not need miracles in order to believe.  Miracles do not engender faith (Jn.12:37), but the hearing of the Word does (Rom.10:17).  The use of miracles only validated the message being given (Lk.11:20—cf. Lk.22:51) and confirmed faith already there (Jn.3:1,2).

**Q. 17:5** What is the difference between faith and presumption?
**A. Faith** says, "God can."
Presumption says, "God must."

**Faith** is centered on God and his will.
Presumption is centered on us and our will.

**Faith** is acting on what we know to be God's will, even when it
appears unreasonable to do so (cf. Lk.17:12-14,19; Jn.2:7,8).
Presumption is acting upon the assumed will of God, even when
it appears unreasonable to do so.

**Faith** claims God's promises as we fulfill their conditions.
Presumption claims the fulfillment of the promises without meeting their conditions.

**Faith** submits and patiently awaits God's timing.
Presumption demands that it be done now.

**Faith** believes because God said so.
Presumption puts words in God's mouth.

**Faith** believes and plans until God shuts the door.
Presumption keeps knocking after the door is shut.

**17:34-36** Indirect proof that the world is round, since at Christ's
coming some will be sleeping at night, just fixing their daily food, or
working in the fields (cf. Isa.40:22).

**17:37** "Where, Lord?" "Where there is a dead body, there the vultures
will gather."
**Q.** How do dead bodies and vultures figure in what Christ was saying
about his coming?
**A.** The issue here is judgment. The Greek word παραληφθήσεται
(paralāfTHĀsetai) implies the taking away to judgment. The
implication of Christ's final statement then would be, "Where there is
a dead body [unbeliever], there the vultures [judgment] will gather
[fall]."

**19:8,9** Zacchaeus—a good example of how faith produces good works (1/2 to the poor) underline{including} restitution. He felt responsible to make right his past wrongs toward others. That in itself proved his genuine repentance and change of heart, for anyone not truly repentant wouldn't even think about restitution let alone restitution at 400%! That must have pretty well wiped him out financially.

**19:30** A colt which no one has ever ridden.
**23:53** A tomb in which no one had ever been laid.
**Q.** Is there any significance to these statements? If so, what?
**A.** I believe we can take a cue from Exodus 20:25 where God says, "If you make an altar of stones for me, do not build it with dressed stones, for you will defile it if you use a tool on it." Fashioning an altar with tools implies human effort which would make the stones "second hand" rather than "original" and impure because of human involvement. So the colt and the grave had to be "original" rather than pre-used by someone, totally unsullied by human use.

**21:36** Here seems to be the promise of escaping all that is about to happen on the earth and to stand before the Son of Man. For Christ's audience, that could have meant: 1. physical removal from the area; or 2. death preceding the event.

As we extend the words to our time (double-fulfillment principle), it could mean for us: 1. physical removal from earth (Pre-Trib Rapture); 2. adequate provision and protection during that time; or 3. death preceding the event (Isa.57:1).

**22:44** There is a well-believed myth about this verse that I believe should be put to rest. It is promulgated by the familiar hymn, "My Savior's Love," written by Charles H. Gabriel, verse 2: "He took my sins and my sorrows, He made them His very own; He had no tears for His own griefs, But underline{sweat drops of blood} for mine" (underlining mine).

First of all, grammatically, this musical verse ignores the *simile* in verse 4 which says, "and his sweat was *like* drops of blood falling to the ground" (emphasis mine). Saying that something is *like* something else doesn't mean that it *is* that something.

Secondly, it is a well-known medical fact that under extreme duress, a person's capillaries under the skin could burst, and he would "sweat blood." But if Christ had sweat blood like that, think for a moment what effect that would have had on his disciples. Here they were, sound asleep, and suddenly awakened by a bloody specter. They would have been terrified—but no such response is evident. There was nothing unusual about Jesus' appearance that caused them alarm.

So let's continue to enjoy the general message of this song, but with the awareness, according to my understanding, that the last part of the second verse is hermeneutically and Biblically incorrect.

**22:49-51** So much for Peter's willingness to go to prison and die with Jesus (cf. Jn.18:10)! Jesus' miracle obviously had no effect upon the hardened hearts of his captors, but it <u>had</u> to have had some influence on Malchus.

**23:23** Perversion of justice for the sake of peace. "He who shouts loudest wins."

**23:47** Jesus' attitude and words were in such contrast to what the centurion usually saw and heard from those crucified that he had to confess that Jesus was a righteous man. No other explanation could account for the difference between him and all the others. Jesus' example should be instructive to us when enduring persecution.

**24:33** Emmaus to Jerusalem was probably about 7 miles. At a brisk walk, one can do a mile in 15 minutes. Walking and running, the two could have covered the entire distance in a little less than two hours.

**Q.** By the way, was it two men, or a man and his wife on the Emmaus road?

**A.** I had always thought it to be two men, since the famous "Emmaus Road" picture shows two <u>men</u> with Jesus. However, the fact that only one man is named in the context, and it says that they urged Jesus to stay with them (in their home), points to the possibility of the other person being Cleopas's wife, Mary (see Jn.19:25).

**24:45** A key verse for a teacher. He can teach, but only the Lord opens the minds of the students to receive what is taught. The same can be said for a preacher or anyone sharing the Word with someone.

# JOHN

## QUESTIONS JESUS ANSWERED

**Q.** Reading through the Gospel of John, I was struck by how many questions Jesus was asked and puzzled by his answers. It seemed that from his answers, he was either ignoring the question or not in tune with what was being asked (not likely!). So what was going on?

**A.** Jesus knew the underlying motives for the questions and answered them according to the need, not according to the words spoken. This explains why some of his answers seemed so far removed from the questions asked. I have recorded 62 questions asked in the Gospel of John, 49 of which were directed to Jesus. Here are his replies along with questions he asked [in brackets] to Nicodemus, the disciples (4x), the Jewish leaders, the blind man, the High Priest, the Temple officer and Peter (4x):

**1.** 1:38   **Q.** (Andrew, vs.40) "Rabbi, where are you staying?"
     1:39   **A.** "Come and see."

**2.** 1:48   **Q.** (Nathanael) "How do you know me?"
     1:48   **A.** "Before Philip called you, when you were under the fig tree, I saw you."

**3.** 2:18   **Q.** (Jews) "What sign do you show us, since you do these things."
     2:19   **A.** "Destroy this temple, and in three days I will raise it up."

**4.** 2:20   **Q.** (Jews) "Will you raise this temple up in three days?"
            A. <u>No answer</u> required to their scoffing question.

**5.** 3:4   **Q.** (Nicodemus) "How can a man be born when he is old?"
**6.** "         "Can he enter a second time into his mother's womb and be born?"
     3:5-8   **A.** "One needs to be born of water and the Spirit to enter enter the Kingdom of God."

7. 3: 9 **Q.** "How can these things be?"

[  3:10 **A.** "Are you a teacher of Israel, and do not know these things?"]

  3:11-21  (Explanation of spiritual birth: belief/faith in the Son.)

8. 4: 9 **Q.** (Woman at the well) "How is it that you, being a Jew, ask a drink from me, a Samaritan woman?"

  4:10 **A.** "If you knew who it was asking 'Give me a drink,' you would have asked him, and he would have given you living water."

9. 4:11 **Q.** (Woman) "Sir, where then do you get that living water?
10. 4:12  "Are you greater than our father Jacob who drank from this well?"

  4:13, **A.** "Whoever drinks from this water will thirst again, but
  14  whoever drinks of the water I shall give him will never thirst again."

11. 4:33 **Q.** (Disciples) "Has anyone brought him anything to eat?"
  4:34 **A.** "My food is to do the will of him who sent me, and to finish his work."

12. 6:9 **Q.** (Andrew) "What are [these five barley loaves and two small fish] among so many?"

  6:10,11 **A.** No answer but to pray and distribute the food.

13. 6:25 **Q.** (People) "Rabbi, when did you come here?"
  6:26, **A.** "You seek me not because of the signs but because you
  27  ate and were filled.   Do not labor for food that perishes, but for food which endures to everlasting life."

14. 6:28 **Q.** (People) "What shall we do, that we may work the works of God?"
    (The real question: "How can we do miracles like you do?")

  6:29 **A.** "This is the work of God, that you believe in him whom he sent."

15. 6:30 **Q.** (People) "What sign will you perform then, that we may see it and believe you?"

**16.** 6:30,31  "What work will you do?  Our fathers ate manna in
the desert."

6:32-40 **A.** "I am the bread of life from heaven… ."

**17.** 6:41, **Q.** (People) Murmured—"[He's not from heaven]; is not
42    this Jesus, the son of Joseph, whose father and mother
we know?

**18.**    How is it he says, 'I have come down from heaven'?"

6:43 **A.** "Do not murmur among yourselves. [Appearance is
not always what it seems.] I am the living bread which
came down out of heaven.  And the bread that I shall
give is my flesh which I shall give for the life of the
world."

**19.** 6:52 **Q.** (Jews) "How can this man give us his flesh to eat?"
[Jewish leaders began to argue the point literally,
intellectually and academically according to the Law,
totally missing the point.] Jesus answers them according to Proverbs 26:4,5 by extending his metaphor.

6:53, **A.** "Not only do you have to eat my flesh, but you also
54    have to drink my blood[!] if you want to abide in me
and me in you." [This answer really blew them away.]

**20.** 6:60 **Q.** (Disciples) "This is a hard saying; who can understand
it?"

[  6:61 **A.** "Does this offend you?] It is the Spirit who gives life.
The flesh profits nothing.  The words that I speak to
you are spirit, and they are life."

[  6:67 **Q.** (Jesus) "Do you also want to go away?"]

6:68 **A.** (Peter) "Lord, to whom shall we go?  You have the
words of eternal life."

**21.** 7:15 **Q .** (Jewish leaders) "How does this man know letters,
having never studied?"

7:16-18 **A.** "My doctrine is not mine, but his who sent me."

**22.** 7:20 **Q.** (People) "Who is seeking to kill you?"

[  7:23 **A.** "If people are circumcised on the Sabbath, why are
you angry with me if I heal a man on the Sabbath?"]

7:25,26—They understood by this answer that it was the Jewish leaders who wanted to kill him.

**23.** 8:19 **Q.** (Pharisees) "Where is your Father?"

8:19 **A.** "There is no way for you to know because you do not know me."

**24.** 8:22 **Q.** (The Jews) "Will he kill himself, because he says, 'Where I go you cannot come'?"

8:23, **A.** "You are from beneath; I am from above. You are of

24 this world; I am not of this world. If you do not believe that I am he, you will die in your sins" [hence cannot come to heaven where I am going].

**25.** 8:25 **Q.** (The Jews) "Who are you?"

8:25, **A.** "Just what I have been saying to you from the begin-

26 ning. I am your Judge and the Father's Ambassador to the world."

**26.** 8:33 **Q.** (The Jews) "We have never been in bondage to anyone. How can you say, 'You will be made free'?"

8:34- **A.** "If you commit sin, you are a slave of sin. A slave

36 doesn't stay in the house forever, but a son does. Therefore if the Son makes you free [i.e., no longer a servant of sin but a son of the Father], you shall be free indeed."

**27.** 8:48 **Q.** (Jews) "You are a Samaritan and have a demon, no?"

8:49 **A.** "I do not have a demon; but I honor my Father, and you dishonor me. I do not seek my own glory; there is one who seeks and judges. If anyone keeps my word, he shall never see death."

**28.** 8:53 **Q.** (Jews) "Are you greater than Abraham, who is dead? And the prophets are dead. Who do you make yourself out to be?"

8:54- **A.** "I am the Son of my Father, of whom you say that he is

56 your God. Yet you have not known him, but I know him and keep his word. Your father Abraham saw my day and was glad."

**29.** 8:57 **Q.** (Jews) "You are not yet 50 years old, and have you seen Abraham?" (That wasn't what Jesus said. He said that Abraham saw *his* day and was glad; not that he saw Abraham. But he answers them anyway, saying,)

   8:58 **A.** "I tell you, before Abraham was, I AM" (i.e., I AM the Yahweh of the O.T.).

**30.** 9:2 **Q.** (Disciples) "Rabbi, who sinned, this man or his parents, that he was born blind?"

   9:3-5 **A.** "Neither this man nor his parents sinned, but that the works of God should be revealed in him."

[ 9:35 **Q.** (Jesus) "Do you believe in the Son of Man?"]
**31.** 9:36 **Q.** (Man born blind) "Who is he, Lord, that I may believe in him?"

   9:37 **A.** "You have both seen him and it is he who is talking with you."

**32.** 9:40 **Q.** (Pharisees) "Are we blind also?"

   9:41 **A.** "If you were blind, you would have no sin; but now you say, 'We see.' Therefore your sin remains" (see following **NOTE**).

[**NOTE:** Jesus came to give spiritual sight to the spiritually blind. But because the Pharisees claimed to already possess spiritual sight, they refused to come to Jesus for it, so remained in their spiritual blindness (i.e., in their sin).

**33.** 10:24 **Q.** (Jews) "How long do you keep us in doubt? If you are the Christ, tell us plainly."

   10:25, **A.** "I told you, and you do not believe...because you are
   26      not of my sheep."

**34.** 11:8 **Q.** (Disciples) "Rabbi, lately the Jews sought to stone you, and are you going [to Judea] again?"

[ 11:9, **A.** "Are there not 12 hours in the day?] If anyone walks in
   10      the day, he does not stumble, because he sees the light of this world. But if one walks in the night, he

stumbles because the light is not in him." (In other words, "As long as I am walking in the appointed time, there is no danger.")

35. 12:5 **Q.** (Judas Iscariot) "Why was this fragrant oil not sold for 300denarii and given to the poor?"
12:7, **A.** "Let her alone; she has kept this for the day of my
 8    burial. For the poor you have with you always, but me you do not have always."

36. 12:34 **Q.** (The people) "We have heard from the law that the Christ remains forever; and how can you say, 'The Son of Man must be lifted up'? Who is this Son of Man?"
12:35 **A.** "A little while longer the light is with you. Walk while
 36    you have the light, lest darkness overtake you; he who walks in darkness does not know where he is going. While you have the light, *believe in the light, that you may become sons of light."

*[**NOTE:** Faith is the issue here (vs.37). For those who already believe in him, they <u>knew</u> that he was the Son of Man. So the answer to the people's question lay in their faith. If they would believe (walk in the light), then they would know the answer to their question.]

37. 13:6 **Q.** (Peter) "Lord, are you washing my feet?"
13:7 **A.** "What I am doing your do not understand now, but you will know after this."

38. 13:25 **Q.** (John) "Lord, who is it [that is going to betray you]?"
13:26 **A.** "It is he to whom I shall give a piece of bread when I have dipped it."

39. 13:36 **Q.** (Peter) "Lord, where are you going?"
13:36 **A.** "Where I am going you cannot follow me now, but you shall follow me afterward."

40. 13:37 **Q.** (Peter) "Lord, why cannot I follow you now? I will lay down my life for your sake."
[    13:38 **A.** "Will you?...] The rooster shall not crow till you have

(14:3,4)      denied me three times...I go to prepare a place for you and will come again to take you there. And where I go you know, and the way you know."

41.  14:5  **Q.** (Thomas) "Lord, we do not know where you are going, and how can we know the way?"

    14:6  **A.** "I am the way, the truth, and the life. No one comes to
    16:5      the Father except through me. ...But now I go away to him who sent me."

42.  14:22 **Q.** (Judas, not Iscariot) "Lord, how is it that you will manifest yourself to us, and not to the world?"

    14:23- **A.** "The Father and I will indwell you, and the Holy Spirit
     26     will you and remind you of everything I have said to you." (A guarantee for the inspiration of the Gospels.)

43.  16:17, **Q.** (Disciples) "What is this he says to us, 'A little while, and will not see me; and again a little while, and you
     18     will see me'; and 'because I go to the Father'? What is this that he says, 'A little while'? We do not know what he is saying."

    16:19- **A.** (He clarified, in principle, the resurrection, and that
     28     he was leaving the world to go to the Father.)

44.  18:19 **Q.** (High Priest) (He asked Jesus about his disciples and his

            doctrine.)

    18:20, **A.** "I spoke all things openly and nothing in secret. So why
[    21     ask me these things?] Ask those who heard me."

45.  18:22 **Q.** (Officer striking Jesus in the face) "Do you answer the High Priest like that?"

[    18:23 **A.** "If I have spoken evil, bear witness of the evil; but if well, why do you strike me?"]

46.  18:33 **Q.** (Pilate) "Are you the King of the Jews?"
  18:34-37 **A.** "Yes."

**47.** 19:9 **Q.** (Pilate) "Where are you from?"
       **A.** (No answer.)

**48.** 19:10 **Q.** (Pilate) "Are you not speaking to me? Do you not
              know that I have power to crucify you, and power to
              release you?"
    19:11 **A.** "You could have no power at all against me unless it
             had been given you from above. Therefore the one
             who delivered me to you has the greater sin."

    [21:15, **Q.** (Jesus) "Simon, son of Jonah, do you love me more
    16,17     than these?"]
       **A.** (Peter) "Yes, Lord; you know that I love you."

**49.** 21:21 **Q.** (Peter) "But Lord, what about this man?"
    21:22 **A.** "If I will that he remain till I come, what is that to you?
            You follow me."

**\* \* \* \***

**1:1** with **2 Cor.3:17,18** re: the Trinity
  A. John 1:1    Christ and the Father are one,
  B. 2 Cor.3:18  Christ and the Spirit are one,
  C. Therefore:   the Father and the Spirit are one.
  **Conclusion**: If A is true and B is true, then C is also true.

**Q. 1:45-50** Jesus testified that Nathanael was "a true Israelite, in
   whom there was nothing false" (vs.47). Nothing like this was ever
said about any of the other disciples, yet Nathanael was not chosen to
be in Christ's inner circle! Impetuous Peter and angry James and John
("Sons of Thunder") were chosen instead. Why was this?
**A.** The Lord, in his sovereignty, chose them for this position rather
   than Nathanael, for his own purposes. Perhaps their leadership
abilities were different than Nathanael's. Perhaps Nathanael didn't
require the "tender, loving care" that the others did in order to make
them into what the Lord desired.

**3:5-8** The parallelism of verse 6 demands the "physical birth"
explanation for verse 5. "Born of water" hence must refer to the
waters breaking before the physical birth takes place.

**4:14** "Spring of water welling up to eternal life" equals overflowing with an ever-increasing knowledge of God and Christ (cf. Jn.17:3).

**Q. 6:16,17** (Capernaum) with **Mk.6:45** (Bethsaida). Bethsaida was where Jesus fed the 5,000 (Lk.9:10). How is it then that he told the disciples to get into their boat and go ahead of him to Bethsaida?
**A.** There seems to have been another Bethsaida, Bethsaida of Galilee, by Capernaum. That is not unusual: there are three Woodlands in the state of Maine only differentiated by their zip codes!

**6:63** A very clear statement against the idea of "transubstantiation."

**7:41,42** They obviously had not done their homework (cf. vs.53).

**7:48,49** Yes! Joseph of Arimathea and Nicodemus believed, though secretly.

**7:49** The attitude of the Pharisees toward their own people is nothing short of bigoted, religious pride, assuming them cursed because they didn't know the Law (Whose fault was that?), and themselves blessed and in God's favor because they did (even if they didn't obey it!).

**Q. 8:3-9** What was it that Jesus wrote on the ground that caused the woman's accusers to leave?
**A.** There is really no way to know for sure, but, judging from their re-action to what he wrote, I would speculate that it was the names of women they had lusted after or had had affairs with!

**8:31,32** Jesus' statement indicates that we move from truth to experience, not from experience to truth. The fundamental flaw in our society today is the attempt to establish truth (if it is even acknowledged) by one's experience. "This is what I experienced, therefore it must be true."

**8:44** "There is no truth in him [Satan]." Satan cannot recognize the truth if it hit him in the face. He will always put his own spin on whatever happens so as to justify himself and bolster his position. Think for a moment of Revelation 12:10. He accuses us day and night before God, and day and night he is defeated by Christ's intercession for us. You'd think he'd catch on after 2,000 years!

I suspect the same is true when he is released after the Millennium. For 1,000 years he applies all his wiles to free himself from the Abyss, but to no avail. Finally, God sends an angel down to unlock the door to the Abyss. "But quietly, and leave it closed," he says. Once again Satan approaches the door, and this time it opens for him! "I've won! I've set myself free! I <u>knew</u> God couldn't keep me captive forever!" And in his final act of pride, he leads a mass rebellion which he is <u>sure</u> he'll win this time—but goes down to his final and eternal defeat, kicking and cursing, but sure that he will yet come up with something to "set things right."

**9:16** Because Jesus did not conform to the Pharisees' spiritual box, they concluded that he could not be from God (vs.24). Yet they could not explain how he could work such miracles if he were not from God. It just didn't compute. Therefore "he must have received his power from Satan!" (Matt.12:24).

**9:27** The Pharisees generally were unable to perceive the truth, proving who their real father was (cf. Jn.8:44; 9:39).

**9:28** "We don't even know where he comes from." Willful ignorance! If they really wanted to know, they could easily have found out. The uneducated man, healed, knew (vs.33); the highly educated were blinded to the truth, holding to their opinion that the "common" people were cursed and knew nothing (vs.34; 7:49).

**11:2** Mary, sister of Lazarus, poured perfume on the Lord and wiped his feet with her hair. There are four references in the Gospels to a woman doing this.
**Q.** Are they all the same woman?
**A.** No. <u>Matthew 26:6-13</u> and <u>Mark 14:3-9</u> take place at the home of Simon, the leper, in Bethany. There, a woman anoints Jesus' head with perfume.

      <u>John 12:1-8</u> also takes place at Bethany, but does not say where, only that Martha served at a dinner held in Jesus' honor, and Mary anointed his feet with pure nard. John 11:2 also refers to this same event. The similarity of Jesus' and the disciples' responses to this act, as recorded in these three above passages, lend support that it was one event in which Mary did the anointing.

The fourth passage, Luke 7:38, occurred at the home of a Pharisee in Nain (or nearby that town), and was done by a "sinful" woman (Mary doesn't qualify for that reputation). The disciples said nothing, but the Pharisee thought much! So this woman had to be someone else.

**11:45-53** The Pharisees and chief priests would have made good Baptists! Jesus raised Lazarus from the dead and they "called a meeting" to decide what to do about it (end of comparison). Their conclusion defies logic (Jn.12:9,10) but is consistent with religious pride and rejection of truth which will "kill" anything good.

**12:6** Jesus knows what it's like to have a dishonest treasurer!

**12:9-11** The Pharisees had murder in their hearts which proved Christ's words to them in John 8:44,45 as to who their real spiritual father was.

**14:1-3** Christ is describing to his disciples how he will return in terms of the Jewish marriage custom.

1. The Bridegroom (Christ) first goes to the Bride's house (earth) to settle the bride price (his own blood) with her father (God), and pay for it (his death on the cross).

2. The betrothal ceremony takes place (when we accept Christ as Savior) at which time they are legally considered husband and wife.

3. The Bridegroom (Christ) leaves instructions with his Bride (Great Commission) as to how she should prepare herself for his return (Rapture). Meanwhile, he will go to build them a house (Christ ascends to Heaven to build the New Jerusalem).

4. The Bridegroom returns to his father's house to build his house onto or adjacent to it. The Bride has no idea as to when he will be finished and return ("Imminent Return"), so always has to be ready to meet him, no matter what time of day or night he comes. (Christ urged his followers always to be watchful for his coming.)

5. Upon completion of the house, the Bridegroom (Christ) returns to the house (the earth) of his bride (the Church), stands outside (in the sky) and calls her out (Rapture). He does not enter her father's house (i.e., does *not* descend *to* the earth).

6. They both immediately return to the house he has built and enter into the wedding chamber for seven days. The wedding guests (O.T. believers and martyred Tribulation saints) are outside taking part in the seven-day wedding feast. (Christ and his Bride hidden" in Heaven for seven years — years of tribulation on earth, while the friends of the Bridegroom feast in Heaven, celebrating the wedding.)

7. At the end of seven days, the Bridegroom brings his bride out to the wedding guests to introduce her to them. (At the end of the seven years of tribulation on the earth, Jesus brings out his Bride to "introduce" her to the O.T. and Tribulation saints: his Second Coming.)

8. After that, life returns to normal, and the newly married couple establish their home (Millennial Kingdom followed by eternity in a new heaven and a new earth with the New Jerusalem as their home.)

**A thought** regarding the Post-Trib Rapture position:

It seems to demand belief in no Millennium (A-Mill position) because there wouldn't be anyone left to repopulate the earth, nor people to rebel at the Millennium's end when Satan is released. All the unrighteous will be judged (Matt.25:46) and all the righteous will go immediately into eternal life. So those who hold to this position are forced to reinterpret Revelation 20:1-10.

**14:9** Jesus said to Philip, "If you have seen me, you have seen the Father" (i.e., "Everything the Father is, I AM").

**15:1-8** The context of this chapter is fruit-bearing, not salvation (15:2,4-8, 16 also supports this). Notice that verse 6 is a *simile*, "he is *like* a dried-up branch that's destined to be thrown out and burned" (i.e., useless). 1 Corinthians 3:12-15 describes this kind of Christian.

**Q. 16:7** Why did Jesus not stay on earth?
**A.** For at least five reasons:
1. Because he would only be able to be in one place at a time, limited by his body. His Spirit could be everywhere, indwelling and empowering all believers to do God's bidding.

2. Christ had to enter the heavenly "Holy of Holies" (Heb.9:12,24) in order to fulfill the O.T. typology of his ministry as our High Priest and Intercessor.

3. Also, Satan is continually before the throne of God accusing the saints (Rev.12:10), and Christ, as our High Priest, has to be there to intercede for us (Rom.8:34).

4. He also went to build a "house" for us (Jn.14:1-3) and fulfill the Jewish picture of the Bridegroom.

5. He had to go so that he could come again as the Scriptures had prophesied.

**17:4,22** We glorify God by:
1. completing the work he has given us to do (faithfulness).
2. having the same oneness between one another as exists between God and Christ (oneness of "family" and character).

**Q. 20:23** Since only God has the ultimate right to forgive or not to forgive sins, what is Christ saying here to his disciples? And what is the connection to this with their receiving of the Holy Spirit (vs.22)?
**A.**

**20:16,17** It is vital for us to cling to Jesus (Ps.37:4; Matt.5:6) in close fellowship because only he has the answers to life's questions. Knowing him helps us understand what our role is to be in this world and where we "fit" in the scheme of things.

**21:15-17** What is lost to us here is Jesus' and Peter's words for "love" (see **NOTE** on p.267). Jesus uses AGAPE (ah-GAH-pay); Peter uses

FILEO (fi-LEH-o). The first is the love of choice for the sole benefit of the one loved; the second is the mutual love between friends—a reciprocal love of mutual benefit and affection.

In light of Peter's denial of Christ, Christ asks him three times if he loves him:

1. "Peter, do you love (AGAPE) me?"
   "Yes, Lord, you know I love (FILEO) you."
2. "Peter, do you love (AGAPE) me?"
   "Yes, Lord, you know I love (FILEO) you."
3. "Peter, do you love (FILEO) me?"
   "Yes, Lord, you know I love (FILEO) you."

Peter refused to acknowledge AGAPE love for Christ, claiming rather their mutual love. Finally Christ comes down to Peter's level and asks, "Peter, do you even love me with that mutual love [FILEO]? After all, you denied me three times, hardly the proof of mutual love!" Peter got the point (vs.17b) and it grieved him.

[**NOTE:** There are at least four Greek words for "love," only two of which** are found in the New Testament:

AGAPE** = the love of choice for the benefit of the one loved; nothing more.

FILEO** = brotherly love, mutual/reciprocal love ("You scratch my back, I'll scratch yours").

STORGE (STOR gay) – familial love, the love of a parent for a child.

EROS = physical love (proper within marriage; "lust" outside of marriage); or self-love: desiring the other person to satisfy one's own desires, whatever they may be.]

Matthew 22:34-37 commands us to love (AGAPE) the Lord our God with all our hearts, souls and mind, and our neighbor as ourselves.

**Q.** How can we love God for his benefit since he is totally complete in and of himself?

**A.** 1. Our love brings delight to his heart (as a child to his father — Ps.147:11).

2. Our love must be unconditional, not dependent upon what God does or does not do for us. "Though he slay me, yet I will trust him" (Job 13:15). This demonstrates our utter trust in him,

which pleases him (Heb.11:6).

3. Our love ministers to him as he accepts what we do to fellow believers as being done directly to him, positively (Matt.25:40) or negatively (Matt.25:45; Acts 9:5).

4. Our love prompts us to sacrifice our desires and ourselves for what is important to him (Rom.12:1,2; Mk.8:34,35; Matt.10:37-39). Done in the context of AGAPE love, any sacrifice doesn't really seem to be a sacrifice at all, but we are eager to do it (cf. 2 Cor.8:2-5)!

5. Our love for God is expressed also as we in respond to him in the character of AGAPE love as described in 1 Corinthians 13:4-7. AGAPE love can be expressed in two directions: horizontally toward our fellowman and vertically toward God (see the closing comment on 1 Corinthians 13:4-7, p.282).

**Q. 21:15** "Peter, do you love me more than these?" More than these what?

**A.** It couldn't be "these men" because how could Peter know the answer to this question since he couldn't see into the hearts of the other disciples? The context is fishing, and they had just finished eating fish with many leftovers. When Peter announced that he was going fishing (vs.3), he was essentially "closing the book" on the last three years. "Jesus has left us in the lurch. I don't know what to do now, so let's go back to our fishing—what we <u>do</u> know."

In uncertainty, we always want to return to the familiar where we feel secure. So I suspect that Jesus' question was directed at Peter's comfort zone, "Peter, do you love *me* more than these [fish, i.e., more than your old way of life]?"

**21:20-23** We need to concern ourselves only with our own "race," not the "race" of others (cf. 2 Tim.4:7; 2 Cor.10:12 and Heb.12:1). God is looking for faithfulness wherever he has placed us.

**21:22,23** "Rumor spread among the brothers"—not "the disciples"—so it seems the belief that John wouldn't die before the Lord returned was generally held by all the early believers.

# ACTS

## God of the Impossible (cont.):

202. He enabled the 120 disciples to speak in languages they did not know to communicate the Gospel to pilgrims in Jerusalem (2:7,8).
203. He raised Jesus from the dead (2:24).
204. He enabled the Apostles and others to work miracles (4:30).
205. He whisked Philip away from the Ethiopian eunuch (8:39,40).
206. He released Peter from prison, saving him from execution (12:6-10).
207. He struck Herod with worms so that he died (12:22,23).
208. He got Paul to Rome in spite of Satan's six attempts to stop him (23:12; 24:27; 25:9; 27:14,42; 28:3; 28:16) .

\* \* \* \*

**1:5**  Baptized with the Holy Spirit.  We receive the Holy Spirit at salvation (Acts 2:38) who, at that time, baptizes us into the body of Christ (Jn.1:12; Acts 5:32; cf. 1 Cor.12:13).

Joel 2:28  I will pour out my Spirit on all people.

1 Corinthians 12:13  We were baptized by one Spirit into one body.

Baptism, for the Jew, meant immersion into an element (cf. Matt. 3:11 where Jesus will baptize with the Spirit and with fire. "Baptism in fire" always means total immersion in whatever trial we may be experiencing).

So the baptism of the Holy Spirit would seem to be a total immersion in him as he is poured out upon us, hence filling us (Acts 2:4), the result of the baptism.

Where his presence is always with us (Jn.14:16), his filling* is a repeatable occurrence (Eph.5:18—"be filled ['be being filled'— Greek present tense] with the Holy Spirit") having to do with his control over our lives in answer to our submission to him.

[*NOTE: There is no command to be baptized by the Spirit, but there is a command to let ourselves be filled by the Spirit, which is a

269

repeatable experience for those who are baptized by the Spirit (Acts 2:4; 4:8,31; 6:3,5; 7:55; 9:17; 13:9,52).]

**1:16,17** Judas Iscariot shared in the ministry of the disciples (cf. Matt.7:21-23). Even unbelievers can have an effective ministry if they are teaching what is true because truth *always* works (cf. Isa.55: 10,11; Matt.7: 21-23; Acts 10:1,2)!

**Consider:**
**3:2** A man crippled from birth.
**Jn.9:1** A man blind from birth.
**14:8** A man lame from birth.
**Q.** Any significance between these three?
**A.** (From my brother-in-law, Roger Jardine) "From birth we are infected with sin. The men, then, become an object lesson of this truth to all on-lookers."

**4:13-18** When confronted by miraculous truth, rather than examine its source, which would have forced them to confront their own sinfulness and the claims of Christ, the Sanhedrin once again tried to deal with the "symptoms" in order to avoid personal discomfort because of their "disease." People will reject clear, incontrovertible truth in order to avoid admitting their sin and guilt. The basis of their actions is <u>pride</u>.

**5:17-40** The Lord kept giving the Sanhedrin opportunities—and they kept hardening their hearts against the truth. Yet a large number of priests <u>did</u> believe (6:7).

**5:28** Ironic that the Sanhedrin is accusing the Apostles of trying to make them feel guilty for Christ's death, since the Jews very plainly said earlier, "His blood be upon us and upon our children" (Matt.27:25).

**Q. 6:15** Stephen's "face was like the face of an angel." What kind of appearance was that?
**A.** Not only strong, confident and peaceful, but probably glowing / radiant, reflecting Christ's glory.

**Q. 7:22 with Ex.4:10**   If Moses was so well educated, how could he say to God that he was "slow of speech" and ineloquent? Stephen claimed that Moses was powerful in speech and action.
**A.** He very likely was powerful and fluent in Egyptian, but not in Hebrew.   But once God got hold of him, it was a different story! With God's call comes God's enablement!

**7:51-58**   Once again, when confronted with truth from their own Law, the Sanhedrin became furious and full of uncontrollable rage.

**8:4-23**   The danger in being baptized too soon.   This situation was outside the context of godly Jews who <u>could</u> be baptized immediately upon their confession of faith (Acts 2:38) because they had the background to understand what was going on and what that baptism meant.

**11:1-3**   Culture dies hard!

**11:18**   In light of the Great Commission, this "amazing conclusion" is unbelievable.   What other conclusion could there possibly be?   Verse 19—they evidently interpreted the Great Commission as meaning "the Jews of every nation!"

**Ch.12**   All of this happened while Barnabas and Paul were in Jerusalem.   No doubt they were also at that prayer meeting in John Mark's house.   After some days, when they had finished their mission, he went with them to Antioch (12:25-13:1).

**Q. 12:6**   How could Peter sleep so soundly the night before his trial?
**A.** He was sleeping in faith that he would be released since the Lord specifically told him that he would die in old age (Jn.21:18—from Mel Szto, director of the Asian Cross Cultural Training Institute, Singapore, Fall of 1996).

**13:13**   If John Mark left Barnabas and Paul while things were going well, what would he have done in the face of such hostile persecution that later befell them?   (Interesting that John Mark was also Barnabas' cousin—Col. 4:10).

**14:17**   Illustrations of God's common grace toward mankind.

**14:19** Now Paul knew how Stephen felt! Perhaps it was at this time the experience he tells of in 2 Corinthians 12:1-4 took place.

**16:7** Paul and Silas were forbidden to enter Bithynia and Pontus to preach the Gospel. But that didn't stop those people from coming to know the Lord. Aquila was a native of Pontus (Acts 18:2), and no doubt there were many others.

**22:21-23** The response of the Jews to the word "Gentiles" shows not only their religious bigotry but also their hatred for anyone not Jewish (racial bigotry). Anti-Semitism, not to justify it, is but the natural response to the Jewish attitude toward everyone not Semite.

    This whole Jewish attitude shows the necessity of the doctrine of Election and God's Effectual Call, for without those, <u>none</u> of them would ever believe and be saved. (Again, see comments from John 11:45-53, p.268 ; Acts 4:13-18, 5:17-40, p.275 and 7:51-58, p.276).

**23:6-10** What's more, the Jews fought each other with the same amount of venom when one differed from another (as on the topic of "The Resurrection")!

### SATAN'S ATTEMPTS TO STOP PAUL
### FROM GOING TO ROME

**23:11** God's plan for Paul. He had to go to Rome to testify. In spite of Satan's attempts to thwart this plan, he got there (Acts 28:14).
1. 23:12, Forty-plus Jews bound themselves with an oath to kill
       13    Paul —*defeated* (23:16).
2. 24:27  Lengthened imprisonment of over two years.
3. 25:9    Attempt to get Paul to return to Jerusalem—both 2 and
       3 *defeated* by Paul's appeal to Rome (25:11).
4. 27:14  A hurricane on the sea—*defeated* (27:23,24,43,44).
5. 27:42  Soldiers planned to kill all prisoners—*defeated* (27:43,44).
6. 28:3    Paul bitten by a viper—*defeated* (28:5,6)

[**NOTE:** The number 7 is the number of perfection/completeness.

    The number 6, the number of man, one short of perfection. Satan his best (6 times) to stop Paul from getting to Rome, but it wasn't enough. He has no power to overturn what God has sovereignly declared is going to be done (Acts 28:14).]

**23:27** "Rearranged truth."

**24:4** [Tongue-in-cheek] "But in order not to weary you further [with our flatteries]...."

**24:6,7** "The pot calling the kettle 'black'."

**Chs.23-25** The whole of Paul's imprisonment was a travesty of justice for he was held for two years, not convicted, with absolutely no proof of wrongdoing. It was purely political, but put Festus in a bind as how to present Paul to Caesar since there was nothing to write against him (25:25-27). Justice would have demanded Paul's immediate release and put a stop to this political pussyfooting.

**26:31,32** Agrippa said that Paul was innocent and could have been set free had he not appealed to Caesar. Festus knew this all along, but wanted to please the Jews to keep the peace (Acts 25: 9)—so sacrificed justice to achieve that goal.

**27:4** "Winds were against us" — a hint of what was to come.
**27:7** "Wind did not allow us to hold our course."
**27:13,14** "Gentle south wind deceived them." A hurricane-force wind from the northeast soon hit them.
**27:27** A two-week storm! Satan really pulled out the stops on this one. Storms just don't last that long.

**Q. 27:30-32** Why did Paul say that unless the sailors stayed with the ship, the centurion and soldiers could not be saved?
**A.** If all the sailors left the ship, there'd be no one left to operate it, to run it near enough to land the next day for everyone to make it to shore. They would all remain stranded beyond help. (God's promises still demand that we act responsibly.)

**28:1 Take note:** Where Satan tried his utmost to destroy Paul and the others with him, all his efforts accomplished were to move them on their way toward Rome! Whatever God allows Satan to do in our lives will only serve to move us closer to our ultimate goal: to become like Christ (cf. Rom.8:28,29).

## Assumptions in the Book of Acts:

| | |
|---|---|
| **1:6** | That Jesus was going to set up the Kingdom of Israel at that time. |
| **2:13** | That the disciples were drunk. |
| **3:13-15,17** | That Jesus was a man, a blasphemer, and had to die. |
| **4:13** | That Peter and John were well-educated. |
| **5:1,2** | That the disciples would never know Ananias and Sapphira's deceit. |
| **7:54-8:1; 9:1,2** | That Christians were heretics and had to be put to death. |
| **8:18-20** | That the gift of God could be bought with money. |
| **9:26** | That Saul was really not a believer, but was trying to infiltrate them for his own purposes. |
| **10:34,35** | That Gentiles are unacceptable to God. |
| **12:15** | That Peter was actually an angel in Peter's guise. |
| **14:11-13** | That Paul and Barnabas were gods. |
| **14:19** | That Paul was dead. |
| **15:38** | That John Mark was useless for the ministry because of past unfaithfulness. |
| **16:27** | That all the prisoners had escaped. |
| **21:29** | That Paul had brought Trophimus, a Gentile, into the Temple area. |
| **21:38** | That Paul was the Egyptian who led 4,000 terrorists. |
| **28:4** | That Paul was a murderer. |
| **28:5,6** | That Paul was a god. |

# ROMANS

**3:1-12**  Were it not for God's sovereign intervention in our lives (see Eph. 1:4,5), not one of us would be saved nor would we ever want to be!

**3:25**  "He had left the sins committed beforehand unpunished" (i.e., if a person sinned and offered a sacrifice, the penalty of his sin was <u>suspended</u> on the basis of Christ's death as pictured by that sacrifice). That Christ had to die showed that the penalty for sin had <u>not</u> been <u>removed</u>, just transferred from the sinner to himself. The sins of Old Testament believers were thus "covered" but not taken away until the final sacrifice once for all time (see Heb.9:28).

**4:5**  "God who justifies the wicked."  An incredible thought!  To justify means to pronounce them guiltless—just as if they'd never sinned!  Peace, God's response to the wicked who believe in him (Rom.5:1).  Then he makes them new creatures in Christ and sinless in him (their <u>position</u>, but not their <u>practice</u>—cf. Heb.10:14).

**4:25**  Christ "was delivered over to death for our sins and was raised to life for our justification."  The first part shows that the penalty of our sins was not removed; the second part shows how God justified the wicked—by Christ's resurrection from the dead.  Once the penalty is paid, the law is satisfied, and there is no need of anything more.  So the guilty one leaves the presence of the Judge free.  The law has no more claim on him.  He is <u>as if</u> he had never broken it— as if he had never sinned!

**5:1**  The "pearl" of the New Testament.

**5:17-21**  The "four kings" of Romans 5:
<u>Death</u> through the trespass of one man
<u>Sin</u> reigned in death ⟶ eternal death
<u>Righteousness</u> through Jesus Christ
<u>Grace</u> reigned through righteousness ⟶ eternal life

**Chs.5,6**  The difference between Law and Grace is that…
1. the Law demands the death of the offender, whereas
2. Grace provides a substitute for the offender.

**8:29,30** *Foreknew, predestined, called, justified, glorified* are <u>all</u> in the Greek aorist tense meaning an act done and completed <u>in past time</u>. So the whole process of our salvation is <u>already completed</u> in God's sight. Hebrews 10:14 supports this truth even stronger where Christ "has made [us] perfect forever." "Has made" is in the Greek perfect tense meaning an act done and completed in time past with its effect continuing right on to the time of the speaker, and hence, according to this verse, on into eternity ("forever"). We cannot undo what God has already done and finished! <u>Nothing</u> can separate us from the love of God in Christ Jesus (vs.38,39).

**8:31-34** Only God could successfully accuse us (vs.33), but it was he who justified us! Only Christ could condemn us (vs.34) but it was he who died for us. So there is <u>nothing left</u> that can separate us from God!

**9:6-18** must be understood in the context of Romans 3:9-18 and 9:29, remembering that <u>none</u> of the ones chosen by God would have come to him in any other way—nor would have desired to do so. The basis of God's choice (vs.15) is hidden in his own heart.

**9:17** Pharaoh was raised up to show forth God's glory. It was Pharaoh's choice as to how that would be done, through his belief and obedience to God or through his unbelief and rebellion against him. Pharaoh chose to go his own way (Rom.3:11,12) according to the condition of his heart apart from God's intervention.

**9:19-21** According to Rev. Ray Pritchard, my former pastor and founder of Keep Believing, the first law of the Christian life is, "he is God and we are not." There are things we simply have to leave in his hands because there is no way we could understand them. God uses the unbelievers to demonstrate his wrath, power and patience (already demonstrated in that we all were under his wrath and headed for Hell), just as he uses the righteous to demonstrate the riches of his glory and mercy through his rescuing those whom he chose to deliver them from their ultimate destination. We need to remember that mankind was not created to demonstrate God's wrath, but to have fellowship with him. This situation changed only when sin entered the scene, and they turned away from him. As in all other things, God took that "turning" and incorporated it into his eternal plan in order to reveal the whole spectrum of his character from wrath to love.  God knew from beforetime what would happen (cf. Matt. 13:35; 25:34; Lk.11:50; Jn.17:24; Eph.1:4; Heb.4:3; [9:26]; 1 Pet.1:20; Rev.13:8; 17:8), but went ahead with creation anyway. Knowing these things, why did he do it?  Unless someone has a special revelation from God, we will have to wait until we're in Heaven to learn that answer.

Meanwhile, we need to remember the corollary to Pastor Pritchard's statement: "We are human, and God is not."  There are things about God that we cannot possibly understand—but our faith in him is not determined by those things; our faith in him is determined by what we <u>do</u> understand about him: his love, his grace, his mercy, forgiveness, compassion, holiness, his wrath against sin, his role as the just Judge of all creation.  Knowing that God is holy, just and loving, and that he cannot violate his own character (2 Tim.2:13), then we can be assured that whatever he does among us is totally consistent with his righteous character.  Since we cannot see the whole picture, and because we are influenced by sin, there is no way we can understand fully what is going on or why.

So there comes that time when we've exhausted our resources to understand something, and still come up with more questions than answers.  It is at that point where, based on the knowledge of God's character, we have to simply trust him—that he will do what is just and right in that situation—and leave it there.

**9:22,23** I read recently, but cannot remember where, an opposite take on these verses—a perspective from a different angle that throws these oft-questioned verses in a totally new light and, perhaps, better said than what I tried above.  Because of man's sin, God's wrath and power already had a venue for their full expression; but he also wanted to fully express his love, mercy and forgiveness, so chose those among the damned upon whom he would express these qualities.  Apart from that, we, as sinners, would only know a God of wrath and vengeance upon sin and know nothing about a God of love, mercy and forgiveness.

**11:11** In a similar way, Israel was raised up to show God's power in salvation before the nations.  It was their choice as to how this would be done.  Unfortunately, they also made the wrong choice.  Their rejection of the Gospel necessitated a full-scale evangelistic effort directed toward the Gentiles (see Acts 13:44-48).

Hopefully, as the Jews saw the Gentiles responding to the Gospel and attaining to the righteousness of the Law through faith, which they sought by works, they would be struck with envy, repent and be saved as well.

Unfortunately, Gentile Christians throughout history have responded to Jewish unbelievers in the same way as Jewish believers have responded to Gentile unbelievers—with hatred and a spirit of exclusivism, which only served to drive the unbelievers farther away from God. [Chalk one up for the devil!]

**Q.** A general question from the above passage: "Why does God choose to work through failures?"

**A.** 1. So that the glory for what is done may be more obviously his (1 Cor.1:27-29).

2. So that the devil and his minions might understand that God reverses their sponsored failures into his sovereign victories (cf. Gen.50:20).

3. Because the believing remnant make all his efforts worthwhile (Heb.12:2).

**Ch.11 Commentary:** The Jews, <u>as a nation</u>, were in <u>the place of privilege</u> (those who believed along with those who did not) in which a special relationship with God was made available to them. Those who did not believe were broken off (removed from their place of privilege) and that <u>privilege</u> was given to the Gentiles. If the Gentiles respond in faith, they will continue in this place of privilege, even as the believing Jews. But those who fail to respond by faith, will also be "broken off and thrown away," losing their privileged position. This situation has nothing to do with salvation, but everything to do with being in the environment which enables them to know God if they so choose (cf. 1 Cor.7: 14).

**Q. 12:14** What does it mean to bless someone?

**A.** Well, to curse someone is to wish something bad upon them. So, to bless them must be to wish something good upon them. Practically, it's returning good for evil (vs.20,21).

# INDEBTEDNESS

**Q. 13:8** God's statement on indebtedness: "Let no debt remain outstanding," or, as in the NKJV, "Owe no man anything." Why?
**A.** For two reasons:
1. Proverbs 22:7 "The borrower is servant to the lender."
2. Matthew 6:24 "No man can serve two masters."

**Comment:** So when we are in debt to someone, <u>that person becomes our master</u>—dictating the use of our time, money and energy to pay off our debt. Stories abound about people wanting to serve the Lord, but cannot because they are shackled with debt.

3. Psalm 37:21 "The wicked borrow and do not repay."

**Comment:** Payment of loans from family or friends is usually put off in favor of paying off loans to others. Since there never is enough left to repay them, we look to their good graces to let us off the hook, even though we solemnly promised to repay them. For the Christian, to promise to do something and not do it is sin. Borrowing from someone with the promise to repay them, then not doing so, is what I call "stealing with permission." They gave to you with the expectation of getting it back, but you had little or no intention of giving it back. Among other things, this situation violates the Second Commandment of loving (AGAPE) our neighbor as our self (see Rom.13:9,10).

4. Matthew 6:33 Indebtedness is a "slap" in the face of God who promised to meet all our needs if we put his Kingdom and his righteousness first in our lives. Indebtedness shows that we believe in man more than in God. How do you feel when someone calls you a liar when all you have spoken is the truth? Can God feel any differently when, after he has promised to meet all our needs, we turn away from him to look to others to meet them and thus fall into debt?

**14:14,20** "No food is unclean in itself." (cf. 1 Tim.4:1-5; Mk.7:18,19; Gen.9:3 with Acts 10:6-15).
**Q.** If this is so, then why were the Israelites forbidden to eat certain kinds of animals? (cf. Lev.11)

**A.** It was not that these animals could not be eaten, but these forbidden animals served as living illustrations of the need for holiness (Lev.11: 44,45). For instance, the pig is an animal that loves the mud, is dirty in its habits, and very destructive as it roots up gardens and land owned by others. Thus it pictures everything that holiness is not (see further discussion under Leviticus 11).

**Q.** Then why are not these same animals forbidden today?
**A.** 1. Because both the Lord and other Scriptures very clearly say that they are not (Mk.7:18,19; 1 Tim.4:1-5; Rom.14:14,20b).
2. Because we have Christ himself who fulfilled the Law and the Prophets (Matt.5:17), so became himself our example of holiness that God used the forbidden animals to exemplify for Israel. In other words, "When the reality has come, there is no more need for the picture of that reality."

**15:31** The answer to this prayer is seen in Acts 21-28. He <u>was</u> delivered from the unbelievers in Judea. So the prayers of the Roman Christians had their effect in far-off Judea.

**15:32**
**Q.** Is this trip of Paul's to Jerusalem the same as referred to in 2 Cor. 8:1-7?
**A.** Perhaps not, since 2 Corinthians refers to the "service to the saints" in general and has no reference to Paul's going to Jerusalem. Also, 2 Corinthians was written in 55 A.D. and Romans in 57 A.D. Evidently this giving from the Macedonian believers occurred at a later time than what is referred to in 2 Corinthians 8.

**16:23** From the sound of this verse, I would surmise that this Gaius is the same man as the Apostle John addressed in 3 John. If so, at the writing of Romans, he was probably living in Corinth (see N.I.V. note on vs.23) and was baptized by Paul (1 Cor.1:14).

# 1 CORINTHIANS

**Q. 1:17** In light of Matthew 28:19, how can Paul say this? He was in Corinth for 1.5 years (Acts 18:11), baptizing a few believers only (1 Cor.1:14), but generally leaving it to be done by others (Acts 18:8).

**Further discussion:** In Christ's appearance to him on the Damascus road, and through Ananias who came to him three days later, Paul was commissioned to be Christ's witness to the Gentiles (cf. Acts 9:15; 22:14,15; 26:15-18). Christ did not say anything about baptizing. Paul evidently assumed from this that his main ministry was to be evangelism, leaving the baptizing to others. How could his assumption be correct in light of the Great Commission?

**A.** The Great Commission was given to the Church, not to individuals (i.e., the whole of the Great Commission is fulfilled by the combined efforts of the individuals within the Church exercising their spiritual gifts): Ex.
  1. "Go into all the world"—but not <u>everyone</u> goes. Some stay behind to support those who do.
  2. "Baptizing them..."—not <u>everyone</u> baptizes new believers, even though all <u>could</u>, given the opportunity. (The Apostle Paul baptized only a few people, emphasizing rather his ministry as an evangelist.)
  3. "Teaching them..."— not <u>everyone</u> teaches (as a teacher), even though we all must "teach" by example (cf. Deut.6:6,7 — God's command to parents regarding their children).

**Q. 5:5 (1 Tim.1:20)** What does it mean to hand someone over to Satan?
**A. 1 Cor.5:13** To expel him from among the believers. Outside the shelter of other believers, he is particularly susceptible to Satan's attacks which God uses as discipline to bring the erring one back to himself.

**8:6** God is the Originator ("from whom...") and ultimate goal ("...for whom") of all things, but Christ is the vehicle through whom all things came and by whom we live.

**8:12** Sinning against our brother is sinning against Christ (cf. Matt. 25:40, 45; Acts 9:4,5).

**Q.** What was Paul's reward, actually?

**A.** It was God supplying his needs apart from the people to whom he ministered so that he would not have to "charge" for his services.

**Q. 10:21** and **11:26,27**  According to the marriage customs of the Jews in which the bride and groom drink from the same cup, then smashing it—or do they smash a different cup?

**A.** They drink from a silver cup, then smash a crystal cup in a cloth, symbolizing, among other things, the destruction of the Holy Temple in Jerusalem.  Another possible meaning is that the marriage could not be broken, as it would be as difficult to put it back together as it would be to reassemble the shards of glass.

**11:19**  "God's approval."  Those "blessed" economically evidently boasted of God's "approval"—the seeds of the "Prosperity Gospel" of today.

**Q. 12:14-20**  "Why didn't the Lord create us with four hands?  Then we could do a lot more jobs much easier!"  Put another way, "Why did God create us with limitations?"

**A.**  So that we would need each other!

**13:4-7**  Personal check list—How do I measure up to this standard in my daily living?

**Comment:** The word "love" in this chapter is AGAPE in the Greek, meaning *the love of choice*.  "I choose to love you for your benefit, period."  It is unconditional love.

| LOVE IS: | LOVE IS NOT: |
|---|---|
| patient | envious |
| kind | boastful |
| rejoicing with the truth | proud |
| protecting | rude |
| trustful | self-seeking always |
| hopeful | easily angered |
| persevering | a record-keeper of wrongs |
| never failing (always there) | delighted with evil |
| greater than faith and hope(!) | |

How is your "love quotient"?  Horizontal relationships are "easy" to figure out. But how about your vertical relationship with God? "How is our AGAPE love toward him expressed by these character- istics?" For example:

Are we patient to wait for him when he doesn't answer our prayers *the way* we think he should or *when* we think he should?

Are we easily angered when he doesn't do something the way we want him to?

Are we boastful, taking credit to ourselves for what he has done?

I'd encourage you to go through the list and think of each characteristic of AGAPE love in terms of your relationship with God. The results might be surprising and enlightening.

**13:8-12** Nowhere in the discussion of spiritual gifts is there a clear division between "sign" gifts and "practical" gifts (cf.Rom.12:3-8; Eph.4:7-13). These two divisions seem to come from the theologians or commentators. In these passages, all the gifts are freely mixed.

**Q.** Since all the gifts were given for the common good (12:7), and since our needs are the same as the needs of the early Church, why would some of these gifts be withdrawn and others left?

**A.** Some say that the statement "when perfection comes, the imper- fect disappears" (13:10) means that at the completion of the canon of Scripture, all the "sign" gifts disappeared. But does this reasoning agree with the context of these verses? I have some questions about that.

First of all, this context is dealing with only three of the gifts: prophecy, tongues and knowledge: communication gifts between God and us. No mention is made of the other gifts or the division of other gifts.

Secondly, this reasoning fails the test of the context. When will we know, even as we are known? When will we see face to face? All commentators agree that this is referring to our being in God's very presence. At this point, the three communication gifts are no longer needed, and so will pass away. When the canon of Scripture was completed, did we know ourselves even as God knows us? True, we can know ourselves better, but that is not "fully." Do we now see God "face to face"? True, we know him better through his Word, but still it is but a "poor reflection" of who he really is.

Thirdly, it seems to fail the practical test of ministering to one another. To take as one example, the gift of healing. Is it no longer needed among us since the completion of the canon of Scripture? Are Christians no longer sick and in need of healing? To withdraw such a life-giving and vital gift from God's people, when it is still so badly needed, would seem to me to be a very cruel act indeed.

When we first entered the Citak (CHEE-tuck) tribe in Papua, Indonesia, we went in with medicine and set up two clinics both to minister to the people's physical needs and to demonstrate our love for them. We did this also in order to gain a hearing for the Gospel. Now, once they heard and believed the Gospel, and accepted Christ as their Savior, then there was no more need for us to prove our love for them, etc., so what would you think if we then closed the clinics and refused to treat their illnesses anymore because now they are Christians? They knew that we loved them, that God loved them, and that was enough. Then we concentrated on preaching and teaching doctrine. How do you react to this line of reasoning? ...Then in all simplicity, I ask, "If we react like that to this kind of 'uncaring' attitude, would God react any less to the same? Would he say to us, 'Now that you have my completed Word, you know that I love you, so now you no longer need healing; I'm going to take back that gift from you'"?

Is there, then, no place for those arbitrarily designated "sign" gifts in our lives today, which so ministered to the early Church? I think we need to make a serious reexamination of these gifts to properly understand their functions and their need in the Church today. We are paupers in our ministry to others because nearly a third of the gifts, intended and given by God to the Church for the building up and mutual service of the Church are not recognized nor used today.

**Q. 14:34,35** What are the meanings of the words "silent" and "speak" in the Greek?

**A.** "*silent*"—σιγάτωσαν (siGAtōsan) pres. act. imperative 3 per. pl.—"stop talking" (absence of all noise).

"*speak*"—λαλεῖν (laLEIN) pres. act. infinitive—"to be speaking, talking, saying; to be preaching, proclaiming."

The context of these first two words seems to indicate that women should refrain from interrupting the service with questions about things they don't understand. Rather, they should ask their husbands [or someone else] for clarification at another time.

"*speak*" (fr. 1 Tim.2:11,12) — **λαλεῖν** (laLEIN) — silence of worship (reverence, devotion).

"*silence*" — **ἡσυχίᾳ** (hesuCHIa) dative sing. fem. — in the context of teaching or exerting authority over men. [See additional comments under 1 Tim.2:11,12.]

**Q. 15:8** What is the meaning of the phrase "abnormally born"?
**A.** Greek **ἐκτρώματι** (ekTRŌmati) = "abortion."

**15:57,58** "He gives us"—Gk. pres. participle **διδόντι** (diDŌNti) "He is giving us"—a present daily reality.

# 2 CORINTHIANS

Purpose and litany of Paul's sufferings:

| | |
|---|---|
| 1:6-11 | Comfort and encouragement for those in Achaia. |
| 2:4 | To demonstrate his love in his concern for the Corinthian Church. |
| 4:8-11 | God's power to be demonstrated in Paul and his fellow workers through persecution in general. |
| 4:16-18 | Future reward for suffering and persecution. |
| 6:4,5, 8-10 | An example for others to follow in general persecution. |
| 7:5,6 | Comfort when harassed, troubled, afraid and discouraged. |
| 11:23-29, 32,33 | Proof of Paul's apostleship as seen in greater persecution. |

**Q. 2:12,13** If the Lord had given Paul an open door to preach in Troas, why did Titus not being there cause him to neglect this open door and move on to Macedonia? Was Paul wrong in making Titus's presence the determining factor for where he served?
**A.** That was only part of it. In Acts 16:8-10 we find Paul receiving the Macedonian vision. His unrest of spirit and the vision prompted him to leave immediately. Evidently he accomplished at Troas what the Lord intended for the short time he was there.

**3:2** The "Fifth Gospel," the lives of those whom we've won to the Lord.

**3:10,11** "What was glorious" — the Law of Moses — "was fading away."
"The surpassing glory" — the Gospel — that which "lasts."

**5:21** "made sin for us"—ἁμαρτίαν (hamarTIan—i.e., a sin offering).

**8:2-5** Amazing! The Macedonian churches were in <u>extreme poverty</u>—yet they asked nothing from Paul or anyone else for their own needs, but <u>urgently pleaded</u> for the opportunity to help meet the needs of others! The key to this kind of attitude is in verse 5 where they <u>gave</u> themselves first to the Lord, then to his servants. They were <u>totally</u> the Lord's in heart and in service, thus they were more

286

concerned for others than for themselves.

**Q. 8:18,19,22** Who was this "brother"? (2 Cor.12:18)
**A.** [There probably is no way to know.]

**9:2,6,11-14** Results of giving:
- vs.2 — Others will be encouraged to give.
- vs.6 — Much fruit accredited to us.
- vs.11,12 Thanksgiving to God from those helped.
- vs.13 — Praise to God for our obedience to the faith we profess.
- vs.14 — Prayer for us from those who have been helped. A bond of love and fellowship between us and them, which will prompt them to meet our needs when they arise (8:14).

**9:14** "The surpassing grace God has given you... ." There are various references to the surpassing greatness of our God (Ps.150:2) as seen in:
1. His love that surpasses knowledge (Eph.3:19),
2. His peace which transcends (surpasses) all understanding (Phil. 4:7),
3. His foolishness which is wiser than man's wisdom (1 Cor.1:25),
4. His weakness which is stronger than man's strength (1 Cor.1:25),
5. The heavenly body of surpassing glory which he's prepared for us (2 Cor.3:10),
6. His position which surpasses John the Baptist (greatest of men —Jn.1:15,30),
7. His grace which surpasses all other grace (2 Cor.9:14),
8. The knowledge of Christ which surpasses all earthly value (Phil. 3:8), and
9. His great, incomparable power (Eph.1:19).

**11:4,19,20** Even in the face of truth, people will believe anything if it is forcefully enough presented.

# GALATIANS

**1:11** Hermeneutical basis for all of Paul's letters and why they are regarded as God's Word (cf. 2 Pet.3:15,16; Eph.3:3).

**4:1-7** Forms a chiasm:

    A  vs.1,2  heir
    B  vs.3    children/slavery
    C  vs.4a  God sent his Son
    D  vs.4b  under the Law
    $D^1$ vs.5a  under the Law
    $C^1$ vs.6   God sent the Spirit of his Son
    $B^1$ vs.7a  Slave/son
    $A^1$ vs.7b  heir

**4:15** "torn out your eyes" equals "cut off your right arm," (i.e., the Galatians would have made any sacrifice necessary in order to help Paul). This verse does not necessarily support the idea that Paul had serious eye trouble, though it could have been that (see Gal.6:11).

**4:21-31** Illustration of Hagar and Sarah.
(Follow this diagram as you read the text.)

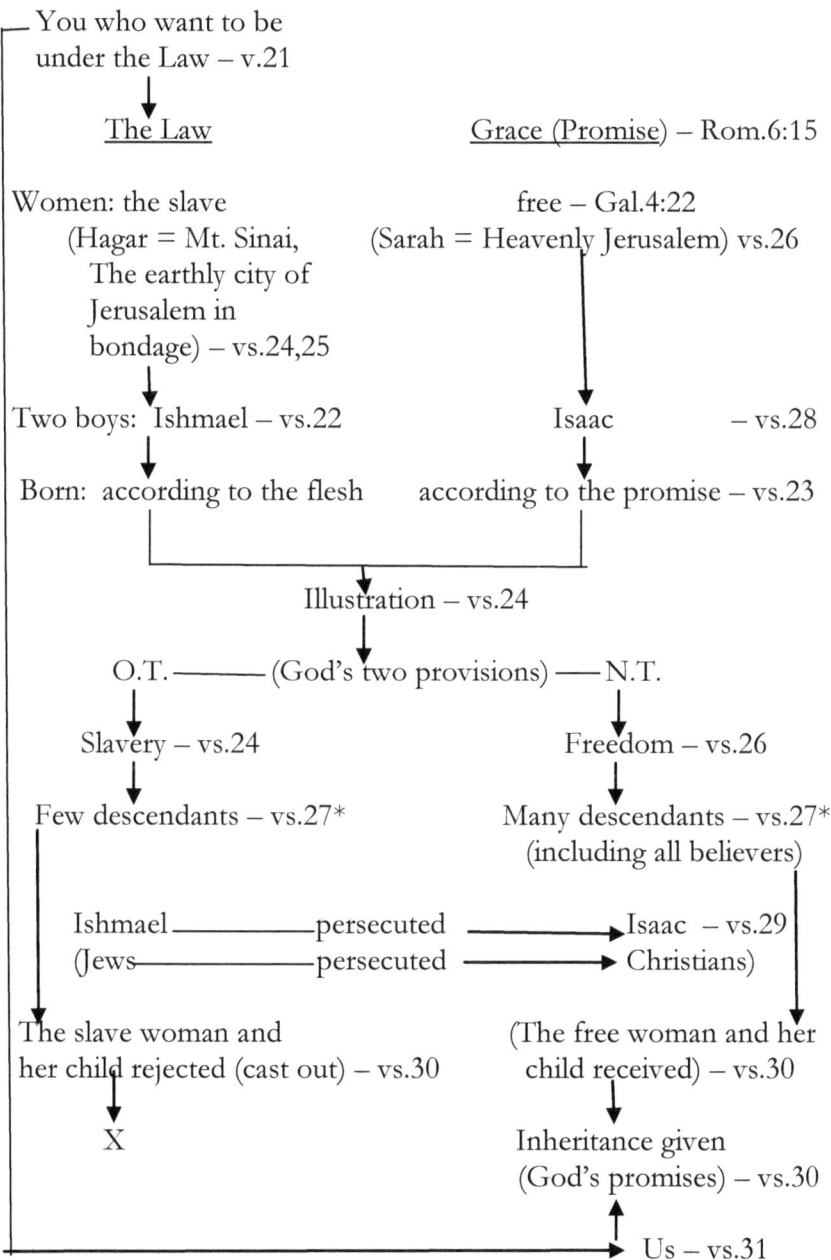

[**\*NOTE** on vs.27. The primary interpretation of this verse has to do with Israel. Before her expulsion to Babylon, she was as God's wife. In Babylon, she was as left by her husband, or barren.

"More are the children of the desolate woman" pictures Israel in the Millennium in her final "married" state.

Paul used a prophecy to show the difference between Sarah and Hagar. Sarah, who was barren, is in the condition as being without a husband. But finally, the Lord will give her many more physical and spiritual descendants than Hagar (4:26).]

**6:4,5** with **2 Cor.10:12** Comparing ourselves with other Christians will always work us woe. It is not wise, for it will either so discourage us that we quit, or make us so proud (Lk.18:9-12) that we become useless. It's like the hand trying to compare itself to the foot. It really can't because the form and functions of both are so different. So it is in the Body of Christ. We need to concentrate on our function (spiritual gift[s]) and walk with the Lord in our own spiritual race, and be faithful in that. The Lord will judge us on our own merits (Rom.14:4,12), not by the merits of others.

## God of the Impossible (cont.):

209. He unified Jewish and Gentile Believers by the blood of Christ (2:13-16)

* * * *

**Q. 4:8** How does this verse play in Christ's taking the residents of Paradise

up to Heaven and his "announcing" to the spirits in prison (1 Pet.3:19, 20; and also Col.2:15)?

**A.** First of all, this verse is a quote from Psalm 68:18 where the King ascends his throne after victorious battle.

In this procession are the Lord's people, his army (Psalm 68:17b, 24-27); nothing is said here about an actual procession of captives, though captives are mentioned as a result of several of David's wars (2 Sam.8:2; 1 Chr.18:3,4; 20:1-3).

Technically, all enemy cities occupied by David could be considered his "captives," even though they probably didn't follow him in procession as such every time.

So...after the cross and his resurrection, Christ ascends to his throne in Heaven, his enemies conquered (1 Pet.3:19,20; Col.2:15). From the context of Psalm 68, I would assume that he was also accompanied by the redeemed hosts as his "army." The only group that qualifies for this are those in Paradise, waiting to be taken up into God's presence after the final and complete sacrifice for sins has been made. My assumption is that they could not have come into his presence prior to this time since their sins were only <u>covered</u> by their sacrifices, not erased. God's holiness demands erasure, sinlessness, which could only be accomplished by Christ on the cross (see Heb.10:14). It would stand to reason, then, that he would take these saints, now made perfect, with him into God's presence, just as we, made perfect by his sacrifice, go directly into his presence when we die (see Phil.1:22,23).

Since the wicked dead and the imprisoned spirits remain in their respective places until the Day of Judgment (Rev.20:12,13; 2 Pet.2:4,9), they cannot be said to have literally followed Christ to Heaven as captives "in his train." So I take this statement as symbolic for Christ's victory over them.

291

**4:9** "…descended to the lower, earthly regions?" with the comma added, is an interpretation implying just a descent to the earth from Heaven. But translated literally, it is the "lower parts (Genitive case) of the earth?" 1 Peter 3:19,20 supports this literal translation as Christ went to "proclaim" (Gk. ἐκήρυξεν [eKĀruxen])—not "preach" (Gk. εὐανγγελίσατω [euanggeLIsato])—[his victory] to the imprisoned spirits (assumed to be evil angels since the normal qualifier indicating spirits of humans is not used here. See comments on Genesis 6:1-5 for more details).

**4:13** "Until we all…[attain] to the whole measure of the fullness of Christ." None of us individually can reach this point on earth, but collectively we can express the fullness of Christ.

**4:15** The key to effective ministry: "Speaking the truth in love, we will in all things grow up into him who is the Head, that is, Christ."

**Observations:**
    1. Truth almost always fails when it conflicts with the falsehood that someone really believes (see 2 Tim.4:3,4).
    2. We don't need to apologize for proclaiming the truth. Because it works, it is its own best proof. So we can proclaim it boldly and challenge our listeners to examine the results for themselves.

**6:10-18** can be outlined as follows:

| | |
|---|---|
| vs.10 Our Position | vs.16 exercise (faith |
| vs.11 The Promise | vs.17a possess (salvation) |
| vs.12 The Problem | |
| vs.17b use (sword of the Spirit) | |
| vs.13 Our Provision | |
| *What you:* | *How you:* |
| vs.14a know (truth) | vs.18a prepare (by prayer) |
| vs.14b do (righteousness) | vs.18b persevere (in prayer) |
| vs.15 communicate (the Gospel) | |

**6:14** Acting (righteousness) on what you know (truth) equals what you believe.

# PHILIPPIANS

**1:29**  (Aug.7,1997—from my diary) "I have been praying diligently for relief from various physical afflictions, thinking about ready medical help available elsewhere and that all my problems would have been cared for by now were I there.  But eight months later, the problems are still with me with little hope of alleviation without great expense and time going to where medical help is available.  I have struggled greatly over the money and time issues: the money expended could be much better used in ministry, and the time expended—I need to use in the classroom.  So I have delayed the decision to go anywhere.

"Last night Goliat (theological college student) referred us to Philippians 1:29 which states that it has been granted to me not only to believe on Christ, but also to suffer for his sake.  Here that means being where there is no ready medical help and having to go far afield to seek it when the need arises.  That changed my attitude toward my physical afflictions.

"Then Tandi Randa's message (president of the theological college) included a reference to 1 Peter 1:6,7 which says that even though we suffer grief in all sorts of trials, these have come to prove the genuineness of our faith—which is of far greater value than gold (money) that perishes.

"In these trials that demand money for travel and medical help, money is not the issue with the Lord, but the proving, perfecting of my faith, which is far more valuable than money."

**1:22** We are free from accusation (cf. Rom.8:33,34), therefore Satan's accusations against us are futile (Rev.12:10).

**3:1-3** This verse reflects the security of the believer not only in regard to his salvation, but also in terms of his daily living. Not only are we in Christ, who is in God, but the Holy Spirit is in <u>us</u>. So before anything can touch us, it has to go through God, then Christ, and once it gets to us it meets up with the Holy Spirit! That is why we can be said to be more than conquerors through Christ who loves us (Rom.8:37). Pictured, it looks like this:

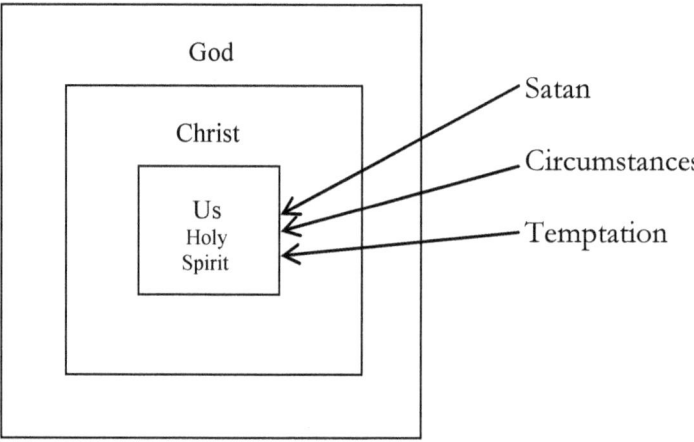

Whatever God allows to touch" us, it is for the purpose of conforming us to the image of Christ (Rom.8:28,29). For that we can legitimately be thankful, even when it hurts.

# 1 THESSALONIANS

**1:3** parallels vs.9,10 and 5:8

   1:9,10                                           5:8

     faith ⟶ turned to God from idols (vs.9) ⟶ breastplate

     love ⟶ to serve the living and true God ⟶    "

     hope ⟶ to wait for his Son from heaven (v.10) ⟶ helmet

**1:3** Faithfulness and endurance are handmaidens:

      <u>Faithfulness</u> is sticking to the job until it is done.

      <u>Endurance</u> is getting through the tough places on the way.

**Q. 5:23** Is man a tri-partate (trichotomy) or bi-partate (dichotomy) being?

**A.** This may ultimately be an unanswerable question. There are all sorts of arguments both ways from the Hebrew and from the Greek depending upon one's point of reference. My answer is "Yes" to both!

We have a <u>material</u> part which we call our body and we have an <u>immaterial</u> part called soul/spirit. Two parts. But the immaterial is of necessity divided into two parts: soul and spirit as indicated by the difference between humans and animals, thus giving us three parts!

My reasoning is this: What is the difference between humans and animals?

    1. We have a body—they have a body.

    2. We have a soul (life principle)—they have a soul (life principle).

    3. We have a spirit (God-consciousness, cf. Rom.8:16)— they do not.

Since we have one additional part to us that the animals don't have, simple mathematics says that $1 + 1 + 1 = 3$! So we have two parts (material and immaterial) that make us what we are, but the immaterial also made up of two parts (soul—life principle) and spirit—God-consciousness), thus giving us three parts.

However, in the end, it becomes a matter of perspective and semantics that are not worth arguing over.

# 2 THESSALONIANS

**2:6-8** "What is holding [the lawless one] back" (vs.6) I believe is a reference to the Holy Spirit's restraining evil through the Church. When the Church is raptured, that restraining influence is "removed," but the Holy Spirit himself does not leave. He also is omnipresent and will continue his convicting work among mankind (otherwise we wouldn't see Rev.7:9). People will be saved in the Tribulation period just as they were in the O.T.—by faith.

**2:9-12** Some say that those who have heard the Gospel before the Rapture but didn't accept Christ will have no further opportunity to be saved during the Tribulation because God will send them a delusion that they should believe the lie and be condemned.

But these verses don't support that view. They clearly state that those who are deluded and believe the lie are the ones who are "perishing," (i.e., "on their way to hell," not of the elect), because they "<u>refused</u> ...and...have not believed the truth but have <u>delighted in wickedness</u>" (underlining mine). This attitude indicates a purposeful rejection of truth and a delight in wickedness that is not characteristic of the majority of the unsaved. It is not unlike Pharaoh who hardened his heart six times before the Lord stepped in and continued the process. When the Holy Spirit ceases his work in the hearts of these people, the only thing left to them is the lie which they will readily enough believe having rejected the truth.

As for the rest who put off salvation for whatever reason, I believe that the Rapture will be their "wake-up" call and that many of them will be saved, knowing that the Tribulation period is ahead of them. Others who have never heard will hear and have opportunity to be saved (as indicated by Rev.7:9; 14:6,7 and Matt.24:14).

# 1 TIMOTHY

**1:13** The fulfillment of John 16:2.

**Q. 1:18; 4:14; 2 Tim.1:6** What was this spiritual gift given to Timothy by the laying on of hands by the elders and Paul?
**A.** 2 **Tim.2:2,7** implies the ability to <u>teach</u> (see also 2 Tim.2:15; 4:2).
   1 Tim.1:3,4   implies <u>exhortation</u> (see also 2 Tim.2:14; 4:2)
   2 Tim.4:2,5   implies <u>pastor</u>
   2 Tim.4:5      implies <u>evangelism</u>

Whatever it was, he was fearful of using it (1 Tim.4:14; 2 Tim. 1:6,7; 2:1-7) so needed encouragement. My guess from 1 Timothy 1:3,4 (and assumptions following) is that he was afraid of confrontation. He already knew the Word and probably could teach it (2 Tim.3:14,15)—but the gift of exhortation was no doubt very difficult for him because he was young (1 Tim.4:12), not confrontational by nature, and afraid of those older than he. So he was ready to let that gift die on the vine and stick with being a pastor-teacher and evangelist. But this gift was absolutely essential at that time because of the proliferation of false teachers within the Church, and so it was conferred upon Timothy at the direction of the Holy Spirit to enable him to confront, derail and perhaps win over those false teachers (2 Tim.2:24-26).

**Q. 2:11-14** What is the real basis for Paul's injunction against women? He says it's because Eve "was deceived and became a sinner." But Adam's sin was the greater since he sinned by choice! Do the words "deceived" and "by choice" indicate something of that basis? If so, what? (See also 1 Cor.14:34,35 where there is also an injunction against women's participation in the public gatherings.)
**A.** There seems to be two issues Paul is dealing with in these two passages.
   1. <u>The issue of education</u>
   In 1 Corinthians 14:34,35 Paul seems to be dealing more with the woman's lack of education and presumed illiteracy. In general, though with some exceptions, the women of that day were uneducated. So their many questions about things they didn't or couldn't understand would take up a lot of time, and the teaching that was supposed to have taken place in the gathering, easily understood

by the men, would be severely limited, causing great frustration.

So the husband, who was educated and could understand these things, should answer all her questions at home where time is not a factor. Nowadays, most women are well-educated and very articulate, so their participation in these public discussions is no longer a problem nor a disgrace.

2. The issue of authority.

However, in 1 Timothy 2, the issue seems to be that of authority. Consider:

a. In most circumstances, it would be unusual for an uneducated woman to exert authority over an educated man. (However, in some situations, wisdom can supersede education!)

b. A woman exerting authority over a man (in family and church) violates the Lord's injunction in Genesis 3:16 in which he said that the woman's husband would rule over her.

So the real issue needing resolution is "what constitutes exerting authority over a man?" Teaching a mixed Sunday School class or seminar? Heading up a department in which there are men? Sitting on the Board of Elders or Board of Deacons? Teaching men in seminary or Bible school? Preaching from the pulpit? Preaching in a non-church setting? Sharing from the pulpit? Pastoring a church? Directing an outreach ministry? Directing a mission board? Discipling men (as Priscilla and Aquila did with Apollos)?

I suspect that there may be different answers to these questions from one culture to another. But each one has to answer the authority question from their understanding of authority, then live with it and minister accordingly.

However, there is one more very important consideration concerning the authority issue—1 Timothy 3:1-13, where we find the prerequisites for church leaders. Whom does God say should be leading the church? So where it may not be culturally unacceptable for a woman to pastor a church, if it violates Scripture, then the pastoral responsibilities must remain with the men.

**2:14** As indicated above, Eve was deceived when she sinned. Adam wasn't. So his was the greater sin and greater responsibility (cf. Rom. 5:12-19 where the entire responsibility for sin rests upon him!). But again, if Paul's injunction rests upon the uneducated woman, then she, like Eve, could be easily deceived and thus be used to lead others astray, especially if she were in a position of authority.

**2:15** Paul's reference to the woman being saved through childbearing may have reference to Genesis 3:16 where both that and the authority issue are dealt with. Obedience in the authority issue would result in safe delivery of children for the woman. We can all think of exceptions to this, but perhaps Paul was speaking from the viewpoint of Deuteronomy 7:12-14 where obedience guaranteed fertility and successful delivery of children.

**3:7** "The devil's trap" = pride (see Ezek.28:17).

**4:3,4** There is no unclean food for the Christian (see Mk.7:18,19; Gen.9: 3; Acts 10:9-15; Rom.14:14; and notes on Leviticus 11 as to why certain foods were forbidden for Israel).

**4:14** with **1:18; 2 Tim.1:6** It would seem from these passages that additional gifts can be received from the Holy Spirit for ministry, but only at his direction. When in my ministry I needed the gift of administration, he gave it to me in answer to prayer as long as I needed it, even though my main gift is exhortation.

**4:15,16** Even though the N.I.V. notes call "save" here as having to do with the salvation of our souls, the context calls for something else, for we cannot save ourselves and others by the "works" mentioned in these verses. I believe the salvation mentioned here is from false teaching from which good doctrine practiced will save both the teacher and those whom he teaches. The entire context of chapter 4 seems to support this view as the emphasis is upon false teachings successfully averted by godly living.

**5:11-13** A widow would take a pledge or make a vow to serve Christ from that time on. If she were young, the normal physical desires to remarry and raise children would seriously conflict with her promise to devote herself fully to the Lord's service. When her physical desires become too strong, she will have to choose either to break her vow or to serve in ministry. There is judgment for vow-breaking (vs.12) with serious consequences (vs.13-15). Paul wants to spare them this prospect (vs.14). As Ecclesiastes 5:5 says, "It is better not to vow than to vow and not pay."

**5:21** "elect angels." Like us, angels were also created as free moral agents and, at one point in time, had to make a decision whether or not to obey God. The "election-free will" debate could apply to them too. But the fact that they are said to be "elect" tells me that without divine intervention, all of the angels would have followed Satan, even as all mankind would have (Rom.3:9-18) had not God divinely intervened in their lives. Since they were in God's very presence, their choice was that of obedience rather than faith. Their decision, once made, was confirmed for eternity with no further "tests" required, even as we are "made perfect forever" (Heb.10:14) upon our confession of faith in Christ. Once in Heaven, sin will no longer be an issue for us. In other words, as it is now impossible for the elect angels to sin, so it will be impossible for us to sin after we are in God's very presence.

# 2 TIMOTHY

**Q. 2:12b** What does Paul mean when he says, "If we disown him, he also will disown us"? Is he talking about believers or mankind in general?

**A.** According to Matthew 10:32, Christ is speaking generally about those who acknowledge him and those who disown him. The first are received by him, the second rejected. The Greek word in both instances is the same, meaning to deny or totally disown.

Matthew 10:32

ἀρνήσηται (arNĀSātai)—aorist, middle, subjunctive, $3^{rd}$ pers., sing., deponent (-an + subjunctive) = "*If he denies*"

ἀνήσομαι (arNĀSomai)—future, middle, indicative, $1^{st}$ pers. sing. = "*I will deny*"

2 Tim.2:12b

ἀρνησόμεθα (arnāSOmetha)—future, middle, indicative, $1^{st}$ pers. pl. with ει (EI = "if") = "*If we shall deny*"

ἀρνήσεται (arNĀSetai)—future, middle, indicative, $3^{rd}$ pers., sing., deponent.) = "*He will deny*"

**Comments:**

Since it is impossible for God to disown his elect (as that would mean he erred in choosing those he would later "un-elect"), and since it is impossible for God's elect to disown him (otherwise their salvation would depend on them, not on God who intervened to save them in the first place), I conclude that only the unsaved (the "non-elect") will disown him (as in Romans 3:10-12). So Paul must be speaking about mankind generically when he says "we."

One further proof: verse 13 says that Christ cannot disown himself. If true believers are his Body, he could not disown any of them without disowning himself, which he cannot do. So only unbelievers will be disowned (as in Matt.7:21-23; 10:33; 25:31-33,41,46). We are secure in him!

**2:20,21** The kind of vessel we are in God's service is <u>our</u> choice (cf. 1 Pet.1: 22).

**Observation:**

Walking with the Lord is a conscious, daily choice. It won't continue today because of the choice I made yesterday. But yesterday's choice will make today's easier to make—or more difficult.

# TITUS

**2:1-10** Three vital reasons to live Biblically:
    1. vs.5   "<u>So that</u> no one will malign the word of God."
    2. vs.8   "<u>So that</u> those who oppose us may be ashamed
            because they have nothing bad to say about us"
            [i.e. us all together].
    3. vs.10 "<u>So that</u> in every way we will make the teaching
            about God our Savior attractive."

**Comment:** One reason that Christians are so vilified today is because they are not living in such a way as to make the Gospel attractive to others. We are so much like the world, that the world cannot see any difference between us and them. So our words ring hollow and we have no credibility because what we say is not backed up by what we do or how we live.

**2:14** "A people that are his very own" (1 Pet.2:9,10).

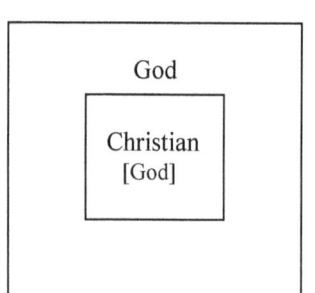

| | God is... | |
|---|---|---|
| Isa.48:17 | | before |
| Isa.30:21 | | behind |
| Ps.16:8 | at our rt. hand | |
| [NKJV—Job 23:9 | at our left hand] | |
| Ps.36:7 | | above |
| Deut.33:27 | | underneath |
| 1 Cor.3:16 | | within |
| | | ...us |

As God's possession, we are totally immersed in him!

# PHILEMON

**vs.6** We grow in understanding about what we believe as we witness and share the Word of God with others.

**vs.23,24** By this time (60 A.D.), Mark had proven himself to Paul and was accepted as a valuable fellow worker (see 2 Tim.4:11).

# HEBREWS

## O.T. Quotations in Hebrews

In the 13 chapters of Hebrews, there are 36 quotations from the Old Testament:

| | | | |
|---|---|---|---|
| Ch.1, 7 quotes | Ch.5, 2 quotes | Ch. 9, 1 quote | Ch.13, 2 quotes |
| Ch.2, 4 " | Ch.6, 1 quote | Ch.10, 7 quotes | [36 quotes, ex- |
| Ch.3, 2 " | Ch.7, 2 quotes | Ch.11 O.T. | cluding ch.11; |
| | | (illus. of faith) | ave. 3 quotes |
| Ch.4, 4 " | Ch.8, 1 quote | Ch.12, 3 quotes | per chapter.] |

## Christ is greater than:
1. the forefathers and prophets (1:1,2)
2. the angels (1:2-2:18)
3. Moses     (3:1-4:7)
4. Joshua     (4:8-13)
5. the High Priest (4:14-6:20)
6. the Levitical Priesthood (7:1-10:39; esp.8:6)
   a. Melchizedek was greater than Abraham (7:6-10)

   b. Christ as priest after the     Levites as priests after the
        order of Melchizedek        order of Aaron

   c. <u>Therefore</u> Christ is greater than the Levitical priesthood.

**1:2,3** The seven-fold work of Christ—completed:
1. Appointed heir of all things
2. Creator of the universe
3. Reflector of God's radiant glory
4. The exact representation of God's being
5. Sustainer of all things by his powerful word
6. Provider of purification for sin.
7. Seated [work finished] at the right hand of God

**4:15** "...tempted in every way, just as we are."

| Eve | Christ |
|---|---|
| *Lust of the flesh*: | |
| Gen.3:6 "good for food" | Matt.4:3 "stones become bread" |
| *Lust of the eyes*: | |
| Gen.3:6 "pleasing to the eye" | Matt.4:8 shown the world kingdoms |
| *Pride of life*: | |
| Gen.3:6 "desirable to gain wisdom" | Matt.4:6 "throw yourself down" |

[**NOTE:** Temptation is different from sin. We can be tempted and not sin. Sin results when we yield to temptation.]


## LOSS OF SALVATION?

**Q. 6:4-6** with **10:26,27**   Many commentaries I have read claim that these passages teach the possibility of the loss of salvation. But it seems that not one of them has interpreted these verses according to proper hermeneutical principles. They have all jumped into their interpretations making the application to us today rather than interpreting these verses in terms of the original recipients, then moving on to an application for today. So the question is, Do these verses teach loss of salvation, or do they teach us something else?
**A.** Perhaps my final answer will be no better than any others in the end, but at least I want to try by beginning with the original recipients and what this letter meant to them in their situation.

**People and situation.**   The original recipients of this letter were Hebrew Christians. They had just come out of the O.T. economy and were moving into the N.T. economy.   In other words, they were in a spiritual transition period unique to that time. "Last year" they were under the spiritual tutelage of the priests and Pharisees, and now they were being strongly opposed and persecuted by them as heretics or apostates from the true faith.

These believers <u>knew</u> that they were following the true God under the O.T. economy; they were blessed and experienced the things listed in 6:4,5. But they experienced these things under what Hebrews says was a shadow of what is in heaven (8:5), and an inferior system compared with what was to come (8:6).

Now that Christ had come, they were in a dilemma: to hold on to what they <u>knew</u> was true, or to move on to the <u>fulfillment</u> of what was true. But the severe reaction of their spiritual leaders gave many of them pause. "<u>Are</u> we doing what is right or are we following a false Messiah?"

The writer of Hebrews kept warning them, "Don't turn back!" What they had before was but a picture of the reality to come. They <u>must</u> accept the reality or be forever lost (10:26,27). It can be illustrated like this: If your hands are dirty, you can cover them with a <u>picture of a bar of soap</u> so that the dirt is not seen. But the picture is of no use to actually <u>clean</u> your hands; it merely shows you what <u>can</u> clean your hands so that you will recognize it when you see it. That was the function of the Old Testament sacrifices; they merely covered the believer's sins while foreshadowing that perfect sacrifice that was to come, which would provide the final cleansing from sin (10:1,4).

Would these Hebrew believers now move from the shadow to the reality? Would they <u>apply</u> God's "soap" to their hearts? Or would they continue to hold on to the <u>picture</u> that can only cover, but not take away sins? If they returned to the picture, rejecting its fulfillment, then the reality would be of no use to them. In essence, they would be saying, "Jesus deserved to die. He was a false Messiah. No Savior. We are still looking for the Messiah to come." And the writer of Hebrews says that those who arrived at that conclusion will have <u>no interest or inclination to repent after that</u> since they had categorically crossed Christ off. Having rejected *the* sacrifice for sins, there remained for them now *no more* sacrifice for sins (10:26). Having returned to the old economy, even *that* was soon to be taken away from them so that they did not even have that to hope in (70 A.D. when the Temple was destroyed and the whole O.T. system came to an abrupt end).

**Believers today.** So how do these verses apply to us today? There are several points that must be made first in order, hopefully, to come to a proper conclusion.

1. Many preachers and commentators say that these verses describe apostasy. Since an unbeliever cannot apostatize from what he doesn't believe, that leaves us with <u>believers</u>, those who <u>do</u> believe but turn away from the truth.

2. But are all "Christians" true believers? Paul made an amazing statement in Romans 9:6 that "not all who are descended from Israel are Israel." There were believing Jews and unbelieving Jews, even though all were of the same community. The same is true in the Church. Not all Christians are Christians. There are those who believe and those who do not, whom we call "nominal Christians," those who are Christian by religion, but not by faith.

3. Since God's blessings fall upon the community of believers, those who do not believe also share in those blessings. This is God's "common grace" in action. For example:

a. In Israel, when the king was godly, he was blessed, and so was the nation, even though the majority of the Israelites didn't believe.

b. Among the Lord's disciples, when they were blessed, Judas Iscariot was blessed along with them. He cast out demons, healed the sick, and did other wonderful works along with the rest. They could tell no difference, but the Lord called Judas a "devil" (Jn.6:70,71).

c. In 1 Corinthians 7 Paul talks about believing and unbelieving spouses, saying that the believing spouse "sanctifies" the unbelieving spouse, and also "sanctifies" the children. He is <u>not</u> saying that they are saved by being in the presence of the believer, but that they are placed in a special position of blessing, different from unbelieving families; for the blessings experienced by the believing person are shared by the rest of the family. And the family is in a much better position to receive Christ because of the presence of that believing member.

d. The "believers" in Matthew 7:21-23 claimed assurance of their salvation on the basis of fruitful ministry, but were rejected because they had not truly believed in Christ (cf. Jn.6:29). They had experienced many of the blessings genuine believers experience, along with the power of the Holy Spirit, <u>but were lost</u>. Truth (God's

Word) <u>always</u> works whether it is proclaimed by a believer or an unbeliever!

4. The issue of the security of the believer must also be addressed. Is it possible for a true believer to apostatize as stated in Hebrews 6? I do not believe so, for whatever "if" verses that are used to prove otherwise, there are too many other verses that are absolute in their meaning that those elected and chosen by God will be eternally saved. Consider…

**Ephesians 1:4** states that God "chose us in [Christ] <u>before the creation of the world</u> to be holy and blameless in his sight" (underlining mine).

We also read in **Romans 11:29** that "God's gifts and his call are irrevocable." He doesn't change his mind. He doesn't elect us now and "un-elect" us later because of something we did or did not do. His calling us is not based upon our works, but upon his mercy (cf. Rom.9:10-16).

**John 10:27-30.** In verse 28 Jesus says that his sheep will "<u>not ever</u> perish" [double Greek negative, very strong—underlining mine]. The Greek double negative indicates "no possible way for this to happen."

**Hebrews 10:14** states that Jesus, by one sacrifice, has made us perfect <u>forever</u>. "Has made perfect" is in the Greek perfect tense (τετελείωκεν—teteLEIoken), indicating an act completed in the past, but its effect continues right on to the speaker, and, in this case, forever (εἰς τὸ διηνεκὲς — EIS TOW diāneKES)! That is our <u>position</u> in him at salvation. Our <u>practice</u> is often much different but that is where "those who are being made holy" come into play. We are <u>not</u> perfect in our practice, but are in the process (Greek present continuous tense) of being made perfect so that our practice eventually will match our position.

**Romans 8:29,30** All five verbs in these verses (*foreknew, predestined, called, justified, glorified*) are in the Greek aorist tense which indicates an action <u>performed and completed in the past</u>. So, in God's eternal sight, we are <u>already glorified</u> and seated with Christ in the heavenly realms (Eph.2:6). As far as God is concerned, it is a "done deal." So, can true believers apostatize? According to these verses, it would seem they won't and can't; they can certainly backslide, but God will deal with them as sons or daughters and do what is necessary to keep them, protected by his very name in answer to Christ's prayer for us in John 17:11. (See also the discussion of this issue from 2 Tim.2:12b on p.301.)

**Conclusion:** So, who are those of Hebrews 6 that today experience the blessings listed there and turn away from them? I believe the only possible answer is **nominal Christians**, those who have been in the environment of truth, have experienced its blessings, then, for whatever reasons, turn back to the world. Having totally rejected the truth, they deliberately keep on in their sins (10:26) and have no desire to repent (6:6). According to 2 Peter 2:20-22, the false teachers who were in the Church knew the truth by experience but not by faith, and purposely turned from it for their own advantage because their character had never been changed (cf. 2 Cor.5:17 with 2 Pet.2:22).

**7:1-3** Some think that Melchizedek was a pre-incarnate Christ appearing to Abraham. I believe he was only a type of Christ. That he had "no genealogy" is not surprising since he didn't figure in Jewish lineage, so they would have no reason to research his family tree (see N.I.V. note for further comments).

**9:16,17** A will only takes effect when the author of it dies. In the O.T. it was not the Author who died, but animals symbolizing his death to come. Thus the O.T. was powerless to effect the removal of guilt and sin (cf. 10:1-4 along with 9:13). Only when the Author himself died did the provisions of his will take effect (9:14) and bring the cleansing that we need (see also 10:14).

**10:14** This is a very special verse as it helps us understand our position in Christ and our practice or condition here on earth. (See the discussion of this verse under Heb.6:4-6, p.311.) An important principle is seen in this verse as it demonstrates the difference between our position in Christ and our practice in this world. Many verses of Scripture must be considered and understood in light of these two concepts. Consider the following:

| Our Position in Christ | Our Practice on Earth |
|---|---|
| 1. Joint-heirs of all things | Possess nothing |
| 2. Citizens of Heaven | Pilgrims, wanderers |
| 3. Seated with Christ in the heavenly realms | Still on earth |

(cont.)

| Our Position in Christ | Our Practice on Earth |
|---|---|
| 4. More than conquerors in Christ | Often defeated |
| 5. Perfect | Unholy |
| 6. Justified | Blameworthy |
| 7. Kings and Priests of God | Nobodies |

**Q. 11:5** with **Acts 1:9-11** "Where is Heaven?"

**A.** "Up there." Jesus went "up" and the angels said that he was "taken up...into Heaven." That was Israel. How about Australia? "Where is Heaven?" "Up there." But "up" on one side of the world is "down" or "sideways" to other parts. So which is right? If Heaven is some specific location somewhere in the universe, then "up there" is the wrong direction most of the time, <u>unless</u> "up there" is taken symbolically. I suspect, though cannot prove, that they are <u>all</u> right. The spirit world is a 4$^{th}$ dimension existence, invisible to our eyes (cf. Heb.11:27). Is it possible that Heaven may actually surround the earth, that when Enoch was taken away by the Lord, perhaps, as they were walking along, a "door" into the 4th dimension appeared and they walked right out of this world and into Heaven? (For further discussion, see pp.168,169, comments following Psalm 115:16.)

**Q. 11:35-38** Why do such bad things happen to such "good" people?

First of all, that is not the right question, for, according to Romans 3, there are <u>none who are good</u>, there are <u>none</u> who seek after God. So the question really ought to be, "Why do such bad things happen to Believers?"

**A.** 1. Because the world does not understand who they are nor who their God is (cf. Jn.15:18-21).
   2. To remind them that they are pilgrims on this earth heading for a better world (cf. Heb.11:8-10; Col.3:1-3).
   3. To purify them from sin (1 Pet.4:1) and develop character (Jas. 1:2-4).
   4. To increase their joy at Christ's coming (1 Pet.4:12,13).
   5. To conform them to Christ's image (Rom.8:28,29).
   6. To increase their eternal reward (2 Cor.4:17).
   7. To teach them compassion toward others who suffer (2 Cor.1: 3-5).
   8. To have a platform for their witness (1 Pet.2:12; 4:19 with Matt. 5:16).

**Q. 13:7,8** What is the connection between verse 7 and verse 8? The one seems so disconnected with the other.

**A.** I think this paraphrase might be a help.

"Remember your leaders, who spoke the word of God to you. Consider the outcome of their way of life and imitate their faith [because] Jesus Christ, [whom they declare to you] is the same yesterday and today and forever."

Because Jesus doesn't change, neither does their message, which gives us confidence in what they are teaching and keeps us from being "taken in" by all kinds of strange teachings (vs.9).

# JAMES

**Outline:** The book of James is written as a CHIASM:  A,B,C,B¹,A¹

```
A   1:1-18     Trials and Temptations (suffering)
B   1:19-3:12  Listening and Doing
C   3:13-18    Two Kinds of Wisdom: Worldly and Heavenly
B¹  4:1-17     Listening and Doing
A¹  5:1-20     Trials and Temptations (suffering)
```

**2:17** True faith produces good works (cf. Eph.2:8-10 and Jas.2:22) just as a live birth produces bodily movement.  As a body without movement is considered dead, so faith without good works is dead (2:26).

**2:26** Since the mouth speaks from out of the heart (Matt.12:34,35) an uncontrolled tongue reflects an uncontrolled heart that is not submitted to the Lord.

**4:7** The key to victory in spiritual warfare.  In every case, before resisting the powers of darkness, we must submit ourselves to God, for it is his power, not ours, that makes the devil flee.

**Q. 5:15,16**  The question remains, "Why don't these verses <u>always</u> work? They seem like a cut-and-dried promise. Yet we all know of people who have followed the 'prescription' of these verses and remained sick or infirmed, or died anyway. Why were they not healed?"

**A.** First of all, it's not a matter of increased faith before God will act.

Paul prayed earnestly three times for his infirmity to be healed (2 Cor.12:8), but the Lord said, "No." Why? Verse 7 gives us the answer—to keep Paul humble and thus retain the fruitfulness of his ministry.

A close friend once told me, "Sickness can be a blessed ally and good health can be a deadly enemy." God's grace (2 Cor.12:9) enabled Paul to minister in spite of his infirmity.

Joni Earekson Tada was anointed for healing several times, but she remains in her wheel chair. Why? Not enough faith? No. God's grace to her as evidenced in her attitude (gratitude!) in her suffering and fruitfulness in her ministry that she would not otherwise have, is a daily source of amazement to others and a reminder to us of who our God is.

Victory in suffering is a much bigger victory than what is found in healing. But it is God's prerogative to choose which one we should receive.

Secondly, unless I am misreading these verses, they seem to be specifically dealing with sickness that has resulted from sin (vs.15-19). In that case, once the sin is cared for, the discipline of sickness is no longer needed, so the sinner recovers.

I think the key here is coming before the Lord in a spirit of submission rather than in a demanding spirit. He knows what is best for us and will do it. In the most trying of circumstances our hearts can be at peace, and actually filled with deep joy, if we trust him and submit ourselves to him. Romans 8:28,29 give us the assurance that even in these circumstances God is working to make us like his Son, and in that we can truly rejoice.

I don't want to be tedious in dragging out this discussion. But there is another thing to consider regarding sickness and infirmity. I see at least *nine reasons in Scripture as to why we get sick or suffer infirmity*:

1. Sin (John 5:14)
2. Demonic attack (Luke 9:42)
3. For the glory of God in healing or in the affliction (John 9:1-3)
4. That we might comfort others (2 Cor.1:3-5)

5. As a test and maturing of our faith (Jas.1:2-4)
6. Because of our fallen condition our bodies are naturally subject to disease and infirmity (Rom.8:22,23)
7. Because of hygienic carelessness (1 Tim.5:23)
8. So that the character of Christ can be formed in the lives of others as they minister to us (cf. Rom.8:28,29).
9. To keep us humble and depending upon God (2 Cor.12:18).

Since it is not always God's will to heal us, we need to be aware of these other issues so that we can respond to our situation properly, biblically, in faith and in submission to God.

**5:16-18** Some say, "I'm only one person. My prayers don't make a difference." Verse 16 says, "The prayer of a righteous man [person —singular] is powerful and effective." Ex. How many others prayed with Elijah so that it wouldn't rain? None! He was the <u>only</u> one— and it made a difference. Our individual prayers <u>are</u> important, even if we don't see the results this side of Glory. We can pray in faith that our prayers will accomplish what God intends, and pray boldly based on these verses.

# 1 PETER

**3:14b** "Do not fear what they fear; do not be frightened." A good word of comfort and encouragement during these troubled days.

**Q. 3:18-20** Who were these "spirits in prison" and what did Christ actually <u>do</u> there?
**A.** I believe that these were the imprisoned demons (since the word "spirits" standing by itself without an article always indicates spirit beings, not human beings) to whom Christ <u>proclaimed</u> something (Gk. ἐκήρυξεν—eKĀruxen—not <u>preached</u> which is another word in Greek—εὐανγγελίζω—euanggelĪdzō), no doubt his victory over them, etc. (See comments on Gen.6:1-5 for further identification of these demons.)

**4:1b** Again, infirmity can be a blessed friend, and health a deadly enemy! (cf. 2 Cor.12:7-10 where infirmity kept Paul from being proud, which he would have been had he not been afflicted.)

# 2 PETER

**1:10** "Make your calling and election sure" [for yourselves.— Gk. middle voice—ποιεῖσθαι—poiEISthai—which makes the subject the object of the verb]. In other words, we assure ourselves of our salvation as we obey the Word and live by it. These are the "good works" which are produced by true faith that James speaks about.

**2:1** "Denying the sovereign Lord who bought them." "Bought" in the sense of 1 John 2:2 where Christ is said to be the atoning sacrifice for the whole world. His death was sufficient for everyone; he bought mankind with his blood (1 Cor.6:20; 1 Pet.1:18,19). But provision made does not mean provision used. And in this case (2 Pet.2) it is not used. These false teachers knew the truth and experienced the truth in fellowship with God's people (2:20), but, in the end, denied that truth (2:21). Just as the nature of a dog and a pig cannot be changed, so their true nature was never changed. They never had that faith experience that would make them a new creation (2 Cor.5:17). The adjectives and "destructive" phrases used to describe these false teachers show their unregenerate state (even though they are in the church) and the judgment that awaits them (2:1,3,9,12, 13,17,19).

**2:19b** "For a man is a slave to whatever has mastered him."

| - Slave to sin (Satan) | + Slave to righteousness (God) |
|---|---|
| Compulsory (by force engendering hate) | Willingly (by grace, engendering love) |
| Forced to subjugate his desires in order to fulfill those of his master. | Willingly subjugates his desires in order to fulfill the will of his Master. |
| Motivated by fear | Motivated by love |

Types of Servitude:
If self has mastered us, we will sacrifice anything for self-gratification.

| If sex | " | " | to get it. |
| If golf | " | " | to play it. |
| If football | " | " | to watch it. |
| If business | " | " | to make it succeed and get ahead. |

313

If gossip <u>has mastered us, we will sacrifice anything</u> to hear it and
pass it on.

If eating          "                    "     to enjoy it to the full  as often
and as much as possible.

If T.V.          "                    "     to watch it.

If the Lord          "                    "     in order to
please him and have
fellowship with him.

<u>The Test of Servitude</u>: (to be considered positively and negatively)
   1. What do we think about the most?
   2. What can't we absolutely do without?
   3. What aggravates us no end when we're interrupted from doing
it?

   1 Corinthians 6:12 is Paul's general comment on servitude.

**3:8**  God dwells outside of time.  He introduced himself to Moses as
the I AM (Ex.3:14).  *HE IS*.  He is the "God of the eternal present
tense," (i.e., everything that happens in the course of world history is
happening <u>right now</u> in his sight.  See further comments under
Ex.3:14, p.35.)

**Q. 3:12**  How is it possible for us to speed up the coming of the Day
   of God?
**A.** One commentary says: "That day may be hastened by God's people as they speed up the accomplishment of his purposes."  Matthew 24:14 may support this view if "the end" refers to the
Tribulation period, and the "gospel of the Kingdom" refers to the
"gospel of Grace."  But if the "gospel of the Kingdom" is not the
"gospel of Grace," but a resumption of the 70th Week of Daniel, then
this verse has to refer to the <u>end</u> of the Tribulation and has nothing
to do with the Rapture as the "introduction" to the Day of God.
   Jewish thought regarding hastening the coming of the Messiah
was that "Jews can take certain actions that will speed up the process
of the Messiah's coming.  Thus, the Messiah's arrival is being delayed
by the poor behavior of Jewish people and can be brought about by
their obedience to God and his Torah" (from <u>Israel My Glory</u>,
Oct/Nov.1995, p.11).  So Peter is saying that we can speed up the

coming of the day of God by living holy and godly lives (vs.11,14).

    **(Q.)** So, is this a speeding up of the maturation of the grain, thus bringing on the "day of harvest" sooner (Matt.13:24-30)?

    **(A.)** Possibly.


**Q.** But what does the "gospel of the Kingdom" refer to?  And what is "the end"?

**A.** I believe that this phrase, the "gospel of the Kingdom," refers to the worldwide call to faith in preparation for the Millennial Kingdom, and once that gospel is preached throughout the entire world, the end of the Tribulation will come with Christ returning to destroy the Antichrist and the False Prophet, banish the Devil to the Abyss, and set up his 1,000-year reign on the earth.

The proof that this gospel will have been preached to the entire world at that time is found in Revelation 7:9 where we read that there was a great, innumerable multitude from every nation, tribe, people and language standing before the Throne.  Verse 14 says that they had come out of the Great Tribulation, which usually refers to the second half of the Tribulation period.

The context of Matthew 24:14 (vs.1-13) seems to deal with the Tribulation period that is coming.  Verse 13 especially seems to point to the end of that period saying that "he who stands firm to the end shall be saved."  Then verse 14 indicates when the end will be. Applying these verses to events occurring just prior to the Rapture (pre-Trib) makes me very uncomfortable hermeneutically.

**Q. 3:17** What does Peter mean when he says, "so that you may not be carried away by the error of lawless men and fall from your secure position"?  Does "secure position" refer to salvation or doctrinal soundness?

**A.** He cannot mean their "secure position" in salvation since in Christ our salvation is a "sure thing."  I believe what Peter is talking about here is their "secure position" <u>doctrinally</u>.  As Christians, we are secure <u>positionally</u> in Christ, but we also are secure <u>practically</u> in what we believe as long as it is the truth.  False teaching will mess up our doctrine, and with that our Christian life as we move further and further from our secure position in the truth.  The context here is one of error versus growth in grace and knowledge of Christ (see vs.14-18).

**Discussion:**

On the basis of Romans 8:29-31, Ephesians 1:4,5,13,14 and John 10:27-30 (among others) we understand that God chose those whom he would save, gave us to Christ, sealed us with his Holy Spirit, and is keeping us firmly in his hand until the Day of Redemption. Since we are already seated with Christ in Heaven (Eph.2:6), it is presumptuous of us to think that we can undo what God has already done, that by our own actions we can separate ourselves eternally from God after he has once saved us.

If the maintenance of our salvation depended totally on our works, how much would we have to do to maintain our status before God? How many sins would we have to commit before God would disown us? The Bible doesn't say, and we'd be in a constant state of anxiety about whether or not we're still saved.

In terms of works maintaining our salvation, following false teachings would mean that we have fallen away from our secure position (i.e., lost our salvation). But what Christian has not believed something false at one time or another? True believers can be deceived, but their being deceived doesn't make them any less children of God than a biological child can nullify his relationship to his birth parents by doing something stupid. No matter what he does or what he thinks, he is still and always will be the child of his parents. His actions will influence that relationship and bear certain consequences, but his being their child can never be undone.

So it is with those who are born into God's family. We will always be his children and nothing we can do will change that fact, ever!

In this light then, I would conclude that our "secure position" in verse 17 has all to do with doctrinal purity and practice rather than our salvation. And it has everything to do with the reception of our eternal inheritance or reward (1 Cor.3:10-15) which is dependent upon our works.

# 1 JOHN

**1:6,7,8-10** form two CHIASMS: so also do **2:3-6** and **9-11**

| **1:6,7** | **2:3-6** |
|---|---|
| A 1:6a Fellowship | A 2:3 Obey his commands |
| B 1:6b Walk in darkness | B 2:4 Disobeying his |
| C 1:6c We lie | commands |
| B¹ 1:7a Walk in light | A¹ 2:5,6 Obeying his commands |
| A¹ 1:7b Fellowship | |

| **1:8-10** | **2:9-11** |
|---|---|
| A 1:8 Claim sinlessness | A 2:9 Hatred = walking in darkness |
| B 1:9 Confession of sin | B 2:10 Love = walking in light |
| A¹ 1:10 Claim sinlessness | A¹ 2:11 Hatred = walking in darkness |

**2:2** Christ's blood was sufficient for the entire world's salvation, but only God's elect will take advantage of it.

**3:10** One sign of an unbeliever is continuance in a sinful life style regardless of his confession. Another sign is failure to love his brother. The Greek word for love here is ἀγαπῶν (agaPŌN meaning "loving"), from AGAPE, the love of choice that chooses to love someone else purely for their benefit, period. The unsaved are incapable of AGAPE love, for AGAPE love comes from the Father through the indwelling Spirit (cf. 4:19 and Rom.5:5). Those who do not have the Father also do not have his love that he expects us to show to others.

**3:16-18** The point here is that genuine love will compel us to give whatever our brother or sister needs, without a feeling of regret or sacrifice.

**3:24** John gives us several "assurances" of salvation—how we can know we are saved:
1. 1:6,7        If we are walking in the light.
2. 2:3          If we are obeying his commands.

317

3. 2:10            If we love (AGAPE) our brother (4:7).
4. 3:24            By the witness of the Spirit (4:13).
5. 5:11 with
    Jn.17:3         The ability/capacity to know God and Jesus.
6. 5:4,5           If we are overcoming the world (5:18).
7. 5:14,15        If our prayers are being answered.

**4:19** The best-kept secret in the universe is AGAPE love!

**5:6-11** Four witnesses that disprove the Gnostic and Docetist heresies which, among other things, deny the incarnation; believe that everything material is sinful and everything spiritual is sinless; so Jesus, sinless, could not have come in a physical body; and that the Christ descended upon Jesus (son of Joseph and Mary) at his baptism and left him at the crucifixion (see The International Bible Encyclopedia, Vol III, p.1713 for a fuller explanation of these two heresies):

| Witness | Testimony |
| --- | --- |
| 1. Water = baptism of Christ (you can't baptize a spirit!) | Spirit descends; God's voice (Matt.3:17) |
| 2. Blood = death of Christ (you can't kill a spirit) | God's voice (Jn.12:28); darkness, earthquake, rent veil. |
| 3. Spirit = dove | Internal witness in our hearts. External witness through the Word. |
| 4. God | Gives eternal life. |

**Q.** The first three witnesses were tangible; people could see, hear and feel them. But how can God giving us eternal life serve as a witness to us? Eternal life is a very intangible thing.

**A.** According to John 17:3, one definition of eternal life is "knowing God and Christ whom he has sent." Eternal life is not just living forever (quantity aspect of eternal life). We could live forever like zombies or robots in a vacuum with no meaning. What is it that gives eternal life meaning? Christ's second definition of eternal life provides the answer, the quality aspect of eternal life: the ability to know God.

The proof that we know Christ as our Savior and possess eternal life is the witness of God in our hearts which gives us the ability and the desire to know him. If that desire is not there, then God's witness is not there, and we are not his.

**Q. 5:16,17** What is this sin ("a sin") that leads to death, and that cannot be prayed for?

**A.** It would seem from Matthew 12:31 (blasphemy against the Holy Spirit), Acts 5:1-10 (lying to the Holy Spirit), 1 Cor.11:30 (misuse of the Lord's Table) and 1 Samuel 3:12-14 (willful sin) that there is not just one sin that leads to death. "Commit *a* sin" in verse 16 refers to any sin a person commits (see vs.17). Because of the above references showing several different sins that led to death, I would surmise that "there is a sin that leads to death" denotes any of several sins a person could commit, the results of which is certain death; so prayer would be of no value in those situations.

Another possibility: There is only one sin mentioned by Christ that will never be forgiven, and that is blasphemy against the Holy Spirit (Matt.12: 31). The Pharisees <u>knew</u> the truth (vis-à-vis Heb.6:4-6) but willfully denied it, attributing Christ's power to Satan rather than the Holy Spirit. This is the heart of apostasy, willfully and knowingly turning from the truth to embrace a lie. The truly saved (God's elect) can never do this. The unsaved (outside the church) can never do this as they have no truth to turn from. Only the nominal believer within the believing community can do this (and Jewish "believers" during the transition period from Law to Grace), and once having so thoroughly turned, will never repent again. There is therefore no use in praying for this person. Christ assured the Pharisees that they would <u>never</u> be forgiven of this sin—<u>ever</u> (Matt.12: 32).

**5:18** "Harm" ("touch" in the KJV) here is the Greek, ἅπτεται (HAPtetai) which means "to assault in order to sever the union," here between Christ and the believer (cf. Jn.10:27,28; Rom.8:38,39).

# 2 JOHN

# 3 JOHN

# JUDE

**vs.7** Jude 7 supports verse 6 in terms of the sexual impurity of these demons as seen in Genesis 6.

# REVELATION

## God of the Impossible (concl.):

210. He struck the earth with three series of coordinated judgments (chs. 6,8,9,15,16).
211. He preserved Israel from total destruction (12:6).
212. He created a new heaven and a new earth (21:1).

\* \* \* \*

My approach to studying Revelation is founded on the Hermeneutical Law which says that we should *take literally what can be taken literally, and what doesn't make sense literally, take figuratively.* If we try to figuratively interpret what already makes sense literally, then we open the door to all sorts of conflicting interpretations and could end up with a lot of nonsense.

## General Comment

This book is obviously full of mysteries and many things which are impossible for us to know. Yet there is much we <u>can</u> know, or can figure out with a bit of thought and prayerful study. I don't claim to have the final word on anything following, but hopefully some of my thoughts are on target, and others perhaps will cause you to stop to think, and maybe come up with different answers, or confirm what I have written. Whatever we think or may not think, let me urge you to be watchful, always, for the coming of the Lord draws near! We all need to be ready for that glorious event!

## General Observation

There seems to be a rather free mixing of imagery throughout Revelation, (i.e., one symbol can have multiple meanings depending on its context).
Ex. "star"
> = the messenger (angel) of the church (1:16,20)
> = Christ himself (2:28; 22:16)
> = hail reflecting sunlight (6:13)
> = asteroids, or meteors (8:10,11)

= literal stars (8:12)
= an angel (9:1; 12:4)
= either the 12 tribes of Israel or the 12 Patriarchs (12:1)
= demons (12:4)
"heaven"
= God's abode (4:1)
= the sky (12:1,4)
= the abode of birds (19:17)

## Symbols Identified Internally

| | | |
|---|---|---|
| **1:20** | seven stars | = angels (messengers) of the 7 churches |
| | seven golden lamp stands | = the 7 churches |
| **4:5** | seven lamps of fire | = the 7 Spirits of God (or the seven-fold Spirit) |
| **5:5** | Lion of the Tribe of Judah | |
| | Root of David | ⎫ = Christ himself |
| **5:6** | Lamb slain | ⎭ |
| | 7 horns and 7 eyes | = the 7 Spirits of God (or the seven-fold Spirit) |
| **5:8** | incense | = prayers of the saints (8:3,4) |
| **11:3,4** | two olive trees | |
| | two lamp stands | ⎱ = the two witnesses |
| **11:8** | Sodom and Egypt | = Jerusalem |
| **14:14-20** | sickle | = judgment |
| **17:1,18** | Harlot | = Babylon the Great (false religion that prostitutes the truth) |
| **17:8,11** | the Beast | = world government as seen in 13:1 |
| **17:9,10** | 7 heads | = 7 mountains = 7 kings |
| **17:12** | 10 horns | = 10 kings |
| **17:15** | waters | = peoples, multitudes, nations, tongues |
| **21:9,10** | the New Jerusalem | = the Bride, the Lamb's Wife |

## Three Series of Judgments
### (with parenthetical material)

## Seven Seal Judgments

**(General)**

1. **6: 1,2**   1$^{st}$ Horse  = psychological warfare (Antichrist)
2. **6: 3,4**   2$^{nd}$ Horse = warfare.
3. **6: 5,6**   3$^{rd}$ Horse = famine.
4. **6: 7,8**   4$^{th}$ Horse = death.
5. **6: 9-11**   Souls under the altar.
6. **6:12-17**   Great earthquake.
   **(7: 1-8**   144,000 sealed from the 12 tribes of Israel;
    **7: 9-17)**   and an innumerable multitude in Heaven.
7. **8: 1-5**   Silence in Heaven; noises, thunderings, lightnings,
          an earthquake.

## Seven Trumpet Judgments
**(Severe)**

1. **8: 7**      Earth:      Hail, fire and blood—1/3 trees and all grass
                              burned.
2. **8: 8,9**    Sea:        Like a great mountain of fire into the sea—
                              1/3 water becomes blood, 1/3 sea crea-
                              tures die, 1/3 ships destroyed.
3. **8:10,11**   Waters:     Great star burning—1/3 waters bitter—many
                              died.
4. **8:12,13**   Heavens:    1/3 sun, moon and stars darkened; 3 WOES
                              announced.
5. **9: 1-11**  (*1$^{st}$ WOE*) Mankind tormented by demons for 5 months
                              — cannot die.
6. **9:12-19** (*2$^{nd}$ WOE*) 200 million (demonic) army—great war—1/3
                              mankind killed.
   **(10: 1-11)**            The little scroll, the 7 thunders.
   **(11: 1-14)**            The two witnesses.
7. **11:15-19** (*3$^{rd}$ WOE*) Announcement of Christ's reign—lightnings,
                              noises, thunderings, and earthquake, great
                              hail.

## Parenthetical Material

**Ch.12**   Spiritual warfare in the unseen world: Satan cast onto the
earth.

**Ch.13** Its expression in <u>the seen world</u> [beginning of Great Tribulation].

> **NOTE:** the similarity between the great red dragon (12:3) and the beast rising up out of the sea (13:1; 17:3).
> **NOTE:** the parallels between 12:11,17 and 13:7; 15:2).
> **NOTE:** the patience of the saints (13:10 and 14:12).
> **NOTE:** the parallel between 14:17-20 and 16:12-16).

**14:1-5** The 144,000 seen again.

**14:6-20** The Everlasting Gospel preached to the entire world.
> a. Worship God.
> b. Babylon is fallen.
> c. Don't receive the mark of the beast.
> d. Final harvest of earth.

**15:1-8** Heavenly scene introducing the 7 Bowl Judgments (the contents of the **3$^{rd}$ WOE**).

## The Seven Bowl Judgments
### (Catastrophic / Complete)

| | | |
|---|---|---|
| 1. | **16:1,2** | Foul, loathsome sores. |
| 2. | **16:3** | The sea becomes blood. |
| 3. | **16:4** | Rivers and springs of water turned into blood. |
| | **(16:5-7)** | Paean of praise to the Lord God Almighty. |
| 4. | **16:8,9** | The sun scorches mankind. |
| 5. | **16:10,11** | Darkness over the kingdom of the Beast. |
| 6. | **16:12-16** | Euphrates River dried up; earth's armies gathered at Armageddon. |
| 7. | **16:17-21** | Greatest earthquake ever. "It is done!" |

### Hymns of Praise

| | |
|---|---|
| **4:8,11** | The four living creatures and 24 elders |
| **5:9,10** | The four living creatures and 24 elders |
| **5:12** | Angels |
| **5:13** | Every creature |
| **7:10** | A great multitude from every nation |
| **7:12** | Angels |
| **11:16-18** | The 24 elders |

(cont.)

| 15:3,4 | Victorious multitude in Heaven |
| 16:5,6 | The angel in charge of the waters |
| 16:7 | The altar in Heaven |
| 19:1-3 | A great heavenly multitude |
| 19:4 | The four living creatures and 24 elders |
| 19:6-8 | A great Heavenly multitude |

\*  \*  \*  \*

(From The Bible Knowledge Commentary:

**1:1** "His angel." "Some have surmised that this angel is Gabriel since he figures strongly in communicating God's word to man (Daniel, Mary and Zechariah. See Dan.8:16; 9:21,22; Lk.1:26-31)."

**1:10** "Lord's Day." "This expression is never used in the Bible to refer to the first day of the week. Probably John was referring to 'the day of the Lord,' a familiar expression in both Testaments."

\*  \*  \*  \*

**Q. 1:1** with **2:16; 3:11; 22:6,7,10,12,20** (cf. **Matt.24:27; Lk.17:24**)
   What is the time framework indicated here?
**A.** "Shortly" is "soon" (Gk. ἐν τάχει — en TAkei) means "with
   speed," meaning that the action will be sudden when it occurs, not
necessarily that it will occur immediately, yet for the seven churches,
verses 1-3 had immediate relevance.

**Q. 1:3** "The time is near." How can this statement and others like it
   (Jas.5:9; 1 Cor.7:29; Rev.2:25; 3:11; 22:7,10,12,20) be true?
**A.** In terms of the Jewish marriage customs, which pictures Christ's
   coming for the Church (see John 14:1-3, p.269), the bridegroom
was to be expected at any time, so the Bride had to live constantly in
an attitude of expectation of the bridegroom's return. In terms of 2
Peter 3:8, the Lord's return could be said to be "day after
tomorrow"—not a long time. In terms of eternity, and God's
"present tense" existence, the Rapture is happening "right now."
   So where nearly 2,000 years in time have passed, we need to look
at Christ's return in terms of the Jewish marriage customs (imminent)
and eternity ("now" in God's sight).

**Q. 1:7** Is this mourning the mourning over sin, etc., or mourning over a lost way of life caused by Christ's return?

**A.** Zech.12:10 Israel shall mourn in recognition of who Christ actually is (Matt.24:30). The tribes of earth shall mourn for the judgment that is upon them and their loss suffered because of it (cf. Rev.18:9ff).

**1:20** Seven golden lamp stands—all the same in shape, content and value. No difference between one church and another before the Lord.

**2:7** "To the churches." The reward for overcoming is given equally to all the churches, not just to the one addressed. So each of us can receive each promise given to the seven churches.

"To him who overcomes" refers to genuine believers who overcome the world because of their faith (in Christ—see 1 Jn.5:4,5). To them these promises are given.

**2:9** "Poverty" (Gk. πτωχείαν—ptōCHEIan means "extreme poverty" in contrast with πενία—peNIa, ordinary poverty from where we get the word "penury").

**2:10** "Ten days" indicates a limited period of time [Biblical evidence: Gen.24:55; Neh.5:18; Jer.42:7; Dan.1:12; Ac.25:6; Num.11:19; 14:22; 1 Sam.1:8; Job 19:3] or ten years of constant persecution under Diocletian or both.

2:16 "fight against them," (i.e., believers holding false doctrines).

**Pergamos:** Taken as a whole, the message is a warning against compromise in morals or teaching, and against deviating from the purity of doctrine required of Christians.

**2:17** According to Randy Alcorn, author of the book Dominion, p.91, the name each believer receives reflects one aspect of Christ's character, so that the sum total of our names reflects the totality of his character. I tend to think that it might be his special name just for us, just right for who we are. Either way, the name will "fit" us perfectly.

**Q. 2:25** "Hold fast...till I come." What did this mean to the read-
ers? Is it also a broader message to the Church in general down
to the end of time?
**A.** See the answer from 1:3 above. To the Church of that time, it
meant, "Be ready!" To the Church down through the ages it
means, "Be ready!" We just don't know when the Bridegroom will
come, so we must always be faithful and watchful.

**3:5** "I will not blot out his name from the Book of Life" does not
mean that he <u>would</u> for some reason, but that he <u>wouldn't for any
reason</u>. It is a statement employing the Greek double negative
meaning that he <u>absolutely will never under any condition</u> blot their
names out of the Book of Life (for those who overcome are true
believers—see 1 Jn.5:4,5). This statement could be called a *litotes*, a
figure of speech in which a positive is affirmed by stating an
impossible negative. Perhaps this statement is in response to false
teaching that claimed that Christ <u>would</u> blot out the names of the
"unfaithful."

In **3:12** several names are given to us. Perhaps like the following:
Our special name (2:17) + El [God] + Christ's new name (cf. 19:12).
The name of "the city of my God" could refer to the register of the
inhabitants of the New Jerusalem, like referring to a person as a
"Chicagoite"—not his personal name, but a name nonetheless
denoting his origin or place of residence. The full import of this
statement is that we will have full access anytime, anywhere to any
place in the entire expanse of the Lord's Kingdom!

**3:19** As many as he loves, the Lord rebukes and chastens.
　　　As many as we love, we hesitate to do anything!

**4:2,3** Jasper—a clear stone in contrast to the opaque jasper stones of
　　　　today;
　　　Carnelian (ruby and sardius) — ruby-red in color; the first and
　　　　last of 12 gemstones worn on the High Priest's breast-
　　　　plate.
　　　Emerald (green) rainbow enhancing the beauty of the throne.

**4:4** "crown" (Gk. στεφάνους—steFANus) = "victor's crown" to him
"who overcomes" (not the king's crown—διαδέμα—(diaDEma).

**4:7** Note the connection between the four living creatures and the first four Seal Judgments:

    1$^{st}$ creature like a lion (king) announcing the white horse (6:1)
        = psychological warfare, leading to world dominion.
    2$^{nd}$ creature like a calf (blood sacrifice) announcing the red
        horse (6:3) = war.
    3$^{rd}$ creature like a man (intelligence) announcing the black
        horse (6:5) = famine, the end-result of man's "wisdom."
    4$^{th}$ creature like an eagle (sovereignty) announcing the pale
        horse (6:7) = death that reigns supreme over all mankind.

**4:4-11** The four living creatures do not rest day or night praising God's holiness. Whenever the creatures worship (vs.9), the 24 elders also worship and cast their crowns before the throne.

**Q.** Is this scene literal or symbolic?

**A.** Since there is no night in Heaven, "day and night" cannot be interpreted literally, but must mean "continuously." If the 24 elders laid down their crowns at the feet of the Lamb every time the four creatures praised him, the scene would be like the American Dipper which bobs up-down, up-down, up-down on a rock in mid-stream (Google). However, if the four creatures with the four different faces (lion, ox, man, eagle) represent the entirety of creation (see **NOTE** below), and the 24 elders represent Old and New Testament saints, then there is constant worship going on day and night all around the world: nature praising God and his people praising him. Thus the continuous worship theme makes sense in that context (see 5:11-14).

[**NOTE:** Lion   = king of the animal kingdom
           Ox   = king of burden-bearing animals
          Man  = the pinnacle of God's creation
        Eagle = king of birds
    Hence, the entirety of the living beings of creation is covered.)

    There are two other possibilities:
      1. The four living creatures revealing the attributes of God:
      a. Covered with eyes = God's omniscience and omnipresence.
      b. Lion            = God's majesty
      c. Ox           = God's faithful labors and patience
      d. Man         = God's intelligence
      e. Eagle       = God's supremacy

2. The four living creatures represent Christ in the four Gospels:
    a. Lion   = Christ as the Lion of the Tribe of Judah (Matthew)
    b. Ox    = Christ as the Servant of Yahweh        (Mark)
    c. Man  = Christ in his incarnation as Jesus     (Luke)
    d. Eagle = Christ as the divine Son of God      (John)]

**Chs.4,5** The central point of these chapters is that God and the Lamb are worthy to be praised and worshipped. All else is secondary, literal or symbolic, depending upon one's point of view. And here it is difficult to separate the two.

**Q. 4:6; 5:6** "in the midst of the throne and round about the throne were four creatures" (cf. 3:21 "sit with me in my throne,...set down with my Father in his throne."). What kind of throne is this? Or is it the <u>concept</u> of shared power (5:10)?
**A.** If this vision of John is symbolic, then the four creatures could be anywhere that would show their connection to the throne and to God. As to sitting "in" someone else's throne, the simplest interpretation would be that of "shared power/authority" rather than literally sitting on the same throne as another.

**5:1; 6:1** The seven-sealed scroll.
**Q.** Were these seals
    1. seven in a row, closing up the scroll or
    2. affixed on the end of the scroll at intervals to allow gradual opening, or
    3. were they placed at intervals from the outside of the scroll to the inside, allowing only a certain portion of the scroll to be unrolled after the opening of each seal?
A. I believe it to be the first choice if the scroll is, as some say, Christ's title deed to the earth (i.e., <u>not</u> containing the written information about the judgments but the provisions of his inheritance); then all seven seals would have to be broken before the document could be read and acted upon. Hence with each broken seal comes a judgment in preparation for Christ's claiming what is rightfully his. Thus all seven seals, fastened in a row on the outside of the scroll, means that the scroll is absolutely sealed up until the rightful heir appears to open them.

**5:3,4** Not only was no one found worthy to open the scroll, and to read it, but no one was found worthy enough even to <u>look</u> at it! No hope! No wonder John wept.

**5:6** 7 horns = omnipotence
   7 eyes = omniscience
   7 Spirits into all the earth = omnipresence

**Q.** According to <u>The Bible Knowledge Commentary</u>, most of the events in Revelation 6 take place during the last half of the Tribulation since they contrast sharply with the relative "peace" that is to characterize the first 3½ years.

**A.** In Revelation 7:14, "the great tribulation" seems to refer to the second 3½ years (Matt.24:15-22 with Dan.9:26,27 and 2 Thes. 2:3,4). It is conceivable that everything from verse 3 on could take place in the Great Tribulation period, since the appearance of the great multitude before the throne takes place <u>before</u> the seventh seal is opened. It's something to think about.

**6:8** A "pale" ("pale green") horse. Death and Hades "were given power over a fourth of the earth to kill by sword, famine and plague, and by the wild beasts of the earth." Because of worldwide warfare, and resulting famine, animals of all stripes will "pack" together, attacking human beings in order to find something to eat. Imagine walking down the street and suddenly being set upon by a pack of 20 dogs, all wanting <u>you</u> as their meal!

**6:11** "White robes" given to the souls under the altar. <u>The Bible Knowledge Commentary</u> suggests that they (all believers) are given temporary bodies (since a spirit can't be clothed) that are later replaced by resurrection bodies at the time of the resurrection. A reasonable assumption.

**6:12,13** Literal effects of billions of tons of debris thrown into the atmosphere by such a large world-wide earthquake. As particles are thrown into the atmosphere, water accrues around them until it freezes and forms hail. The "stars in the sky" are not literal stars (for even a large asteroid would totally obliterate the earth!), but large hail stones falling from such a great height that they catch sunlight on the way down.

   "The sky receding like a scroll" could easily involve cosmic disturbance coinciding with the world-wide earthquake; or, with all the debris in the atmosphere, if there were a great wind dispersing it, it would appear as if the sky were receding as a scroll. This seems more probable since it's in the immediate context of the great earthquake.

Another possibility would be a display of the Aurora Borealis caused by all the debris thrown into the atmosphere and the electrical disturbances that it will cause.

Yet another possibility: I suppose that the stars "falling to earth" could be the "appearance of falling" as the stars "fell quickly" from their places in the sky—looking like they were falling to the earth. However, Revelation 8:12 refutes this view as all the stars are still obviously in their places at that time.

**6:16,17** Obvious, from this response on the part of unbelievers, it is clear to them who God is and why all this is happening. They fear him, yet hate him for his wrath and will not repent (cf. 16:11,21). This general knowledge of God evidently is the fulfillment of Matthew 24:14.

**7:1** "Wind should not blow on the earth, sea or on any tree." Smoke and smog would just sit there. Intense heat in the lowlands. No waves on the sea. Heat stroke and respiratory illnesses take an extreme toll. All wind-driven alternatives to electrical power shut down.

**Q.** What effect would "no wind" have on the sea?
**A.** It would cause the sea to cease most of its motion, greatly diminish the currents, and cause the water mostly to lie there and stagnate. Water temperature would heat up all over the world, causing vast ecological problems and the death of much sea life.

A secondary question related to this one:
**Q.** Are all currents caused by just the wind? How about the tides caused by the gravitational pull of the moon? Would currents be affected by this action?
**A.** Yes, but not to the same degree as with the wind.

**Q.** Why are trees singled out particularly here, as they would automatically be included in the "earth"?

**A.** Perhaps because they are the clearest indication of any kind of breeze. So the lack of any movement among the trees shows no wind at all.

**Q.** Does this verse correspond with 16:8,9 (cp. with 7:16)?
**A.**

**Q. Chs.7,14** Why are the 144,000 mentioned in chapter 7, then again in chapter 14?
**A.** Chapter 14 seems to be looking ahead to the end of the Tribulation when the Lord stands on Mount Zion at his Second Coming. Thus the appearance of the 144,000 at that point assures us that they will survive the Tribulation. Yet...verses 3,4 may point to their martyrdom...or...that they were the "firstfruits of faith" from among mankind throughout the Tribulation (?). I tend to think the latter.

**7:5-8** The Tribe of Dan being omitted from the list does *not* seem to be significant since in at least 30 different lists of the 12 tribes in Scripture, Dan appears 83% of the time. Levi, on the other hand, appears only 57% of the time. (For these listings, see Appendix II.)

**7:14** "These are they who have come out of the great tribulation." Perhaps many more Believers will suffer and die from warfare and natural disasters than will die as martyrs.

**8:3-5** It seems that the 7 Trumpet Judgments are in direct response to the prayers of the saints.

**8:6-9:21** What is awesome here is to think about the resulting effects of these judgments. One-third of the earth burned up would cause a lot of smoke and totally change the environment. A huge meteor falling into the sea (see **NOTE** below) would cause such a colossal tidal wave as to destroy 1/3 of all shipping as well as all coastal areas/cities, bordering the sea into which the meteor falls, etc. The immensity of that tidal wave is unthinkable.

[**NOTE:** I believe that "sea" here refers to the Atlantic Ocean which (according to Google) covers 41,100,000 sq. mi. or 29% (nearly 1/3$^{rd}$) of the total water surface of the world.]

These verses seem to combine the natural with the supernatural: hail, lightning and blood, etc.

**8:7** 1/3 of the earth burned up: not 1/3 as a slice of earth, but fire all over the earth (all the green grass) destroying a total of 1/3 of it. Hail and fire mingled with blood: perhaps a great worldwide storm.

**8:7-9** This could almost be a tremendous meteor shower (6:13), with smaller particles from the earthquake of 6:12 thrown high into the atmosphere, gathering moisture and turning to hail with meteor particles still burning as they strike the earth. One huge meteor strikes the sea, turning it to "blood" (perhaps some chemical reaction?), and the tremendous tidal waves destroy 1/3 of all the ships.

This would also account for Luke 21:25,26: "signs in the sun, moon and stars...men's hearts failing them from fear and expectation of those things which are coming on the earth" (as agrees with Revelation 8:12).

**8:10,11** "Star Wormwood" — a blazing meteor or asteroid either disintegrating as it enters earth's atmosphere or blown apart by nuclear tipped missiles, so that the debris from it falls onto 1/3 of the earth's surface, polluting 1/3 of all the fresh water.

**8:12** Light decreased by 1/3 and darkness increased by 1/3. This could be a supernatural darkening, but I think it could equally be the result of all the smoke in the atmosphere from the fires over 1/3 of the earth. I have personally seen clouds (as well as smoke—cf. 9:2) darken the day—one time as dark as night at 1:00 in the afternoon! With a third of the sun's light reduced, the earth would become colder and darker.

**9:1** "Star"—probably Satan. "Locusts" = demons.

**9:1-5** For five months (vs.5) the entire world order will come to a screeching halt. It will be up to the believers to keep things going until the five months are over.

**9:3,4** If this is indeed a demonic attack on human beings, then
    1. they cannot touch the believer;
    2. they have free access to non-believers who do not have the

seal of God in their foreheads.

**9:14** These "angels" must be demons for holy angels are never said to be "bound."

**9:17-19** The description here sounds like a first century attempt to describe tanks. However, it could also describe a demonic host that goes throughout the entire world.

**11:3** The two witnesses. There has been much conjecture as to the identity of these men. Some have put forth Enoch and Elijah since they are the only two men in the O.T. who never died. Based on Hebrews 9:27, they <u>have</u> to return to earth to die! What this view ignores is the Rapture in which all living believers will be changed and taken up to Heaven without dying. Thus Enoch and Elijah do not "qualify" for this verse. Other names have been put forth, but the bottom line is, we don't know and can't know who these two men are. They are probably two specially anointed ones near the midpoint of the Tribulation, appointed and supernaturally endowed for this particular task.

**11:13-14** The context of these verses would seem to place the two witnesses in the second half of the Tribulation since they die and are resurrected at the end of the 6th Trumpet / Second Woe. There remains only the $7^{th}$ trumpet to sound which introduces the seven Bowl Judgments which fall upon the earth in a matter of perhaps several weeks or, at the most, two or three months, followed immediately by Christ's Second Return (see 11:15-18).

**11:19** Revelation 15:1 follows immediately in this context. Chapters 12-14 are parenthetical, adding additional information that can be placed only on the basis of their context.
**Q.** What is the significance of the opening of God's temple (the Holy of Holies) at this time and thus revealing the ark of his covenant? Is there an analogy here to the tearing of the veil at the death of Christ? ["It is finished!" "The mystery of God will be accomplished" (10:7); "You have begun to reign" (11:17).]
**A.** It is as if God is saying, "This is the final act. Now my hand will be clearly seen as I bring things to a conclusion." (See also Rev.15:5 and 19:11 — Heaven standing open.)

**12:1** "Great sign"—see also 12:3; 13:13,14; 15:1; 16:14; 19:20.
"Sun" indicates Israel's future glory according to Isaiah 60:1-3, 20.
The woman is Israel (vs.5).

**12:3,4** "Great red dragon"—see Daniel 7:7,8,24 and Revelation 13:1. This beast represents Satan's control over the world empires in the Great Tribulation.

**Q. 12:4** What is the significance of 1/3 and divisions of three mentioned so often in Revelation? (See also 8:7-13; 9:15,18; 16:13,19.)
**A.** Perhaps it takes a judgment that big to get mankind's attention, but not so big as to destroy them all. (But see comments on Ezekiel 5:2,12 and 6:12, p.205. See also Zech.13:8,9, p.233.) As for the non-judgment instances ???

**12:4** Two views on 1/3 of the angels that Satan drew down to the earth:
1. The first, which most commentaries do not agree with, is that at the time of Christ's birth, Satan drew 1/3 of his angels from the atmosphere (their place of abode from which Satan got his title "Prince of the Power of the Air") and threw them down to earth to withstand Christ and oppose him at every turn. At the time of his ministry, there was a great outpouring of demonic activity which would seem to fit this context very well.
2. The second view is that when Satan rebelled and was thrown down to the earth (Ezek.28:17), he drew a third part of the heavenly angels with him in his rebellion. Most commentaries say that this statement in verse 4 is merely a general statement of something that happened in the past. Then, at The Fall, he gained power over the earth and the atmosphere.

**Commentary:** The Greek word for "heaven" here is **οὐρανοῦ** (ura<u>NU</u>) which can mean either Heaven, the heavens (universe) or the sky. The KJV, NKJV and ESV translate it as "heaven." The N.I.V. translates it as "sky." Translating **οὐρανοῦ** as "heaven" would lend credence to the second opinion; translating it as "sky" would lend credence to the first. If **οὐρανοῦ** refers to God's Heaven, then Satan literally drew 1/3 of the holy angels with him in his rebellion. If **οὐρανοῦ** refers to the sky (atmosphere), then he threw 1/3 of his resources to the earth to withstand Christ and his ministry. So, you could go either way with this one!

Verse 7 says that war broke out in heaven in which Michael and his angels defeated the Devil and his angels, throwing them down to the earth. But how could this be God's Heaven if Satan and his had already been cast out and down to the earth (Ezek.28:17)? Only the atmosphere makes sense to me where Satan is presently exerting his power (as well as on earth) and Ezekiel 28:17 foreshadowing this defeat. So then, linking verse 9 with verse 4, we have the rest of Satan's forces thrown down from the atmosphere to the earth. So I sense that the general context seems to support the first interpretation rather than the second in spite of the plethora of voices to the contrary.

**12:6** Israel fleeing (cf. Matt.24:16 and Mk.13:14).

Q. 12:6 with 12:14; 17:3 Where or what is "the wilderness" or "dessert"?

**A.** It could be one of two places: the Gentile nations (as 17:3 might
  indicate), or Petra, which could be inferred by 12:6,14. I believe it may be Petra on the basis of Daniel 11:41 where it is specifically said that the Antichrist could not control Ammon, Edom or Moab. That is amazing. He controls the whole world but <u>not</u> these three areas right at his doorstep. Why? Because God has reserved that area for sheltering the believing Jews, probably during the Great Tribulation (referred to in Daniel 11:41, 42).

**Q. 12:7-12** War in heaven resulting in the conquering of demonic
  powers (cf. Matt.24:29; Mk.13:25; Lk.21:26). Is "the powers of heaven will be shaken" a reference to this war in heaven or disturbance in the heavens? (See also Rev.6:13).
**A.**

**12:9** The other 2/3 of Satan's angels cast out of the sky (following
the commentary on 12:4).
   The great dragon = Satan himself.
   The ten horns = ten kings (see Dan.7:24) who also correspond,
I believe, to the ten toes of Nebuchadnezzar's image (Dan.2:42).

**12:10** Satan accuses the believers "day and night" (i.e., continuously) before God, and Christ is always there to intercede for us (Heb.7:25). After nearly 2,000 years of constant defeat, you'd think that Satan would quit trying. But he is blind to the truth even if it hits him in the face! (see Jn.8:44—no truth in him), so is incapable of recognizing it. There is always an "explanation" for the defeat, so he keeps on with complete assurance that "this time I will win," only to lose again!

**12:12-14** Satan is cast out and down to the earth at the middle of the tribulation period. This is also when the Antichrist breaks his treaty with Israel and sets himself up in the Temple as God. It is interesting to note Satan's "life history" of always being thrown out from wherever he is (see diagram on p.338).

1. Because of sin, he is thrown out of Heaven and onto the earth (Ezek.28:17) with free access to earth's atmosphere (he is called the Prince of the Power of the Air — Eph.2:2). He still has access to God's presence (Job 1:6,7; Rev.12:10) but cannot stay there as before.

2. Revelation 12:7 states that there is war in heaven (the sky/atmosphere). Through the Antichrist, Satan gains full control of the earth in addition to his full control of the atmosphere. From the context, it seems that Michael and his angels attack Satan and his angels to remove them from the atmosphere, throwing them down onto the earth.

3. In great wrath he persecutes the saints and Israel. At the end of the Tribulation, Christ comes through the atmosphere as he descends to the earth. Satan, through the Antichrist and the world's armies, tries to stop him, and thus regain the atmosphere. Again, he fails, is bound, and cast into the Abyss for a thousand years.

4. At the end of the thousand years, he is released (he probably assumes by his own machinations), returns to earth to gather a vast army to attack the Lord and restore the earth to himself through the Great Rebellion. His forces are destroyed and he is thrown into the Lake of Fire, never to be seen again, forever. His history is finished.

**Lesson:** Those who align themselves with the Devil align themselves with the losing side — downhill all the way!

## SATAN'S LIFE HISTORY

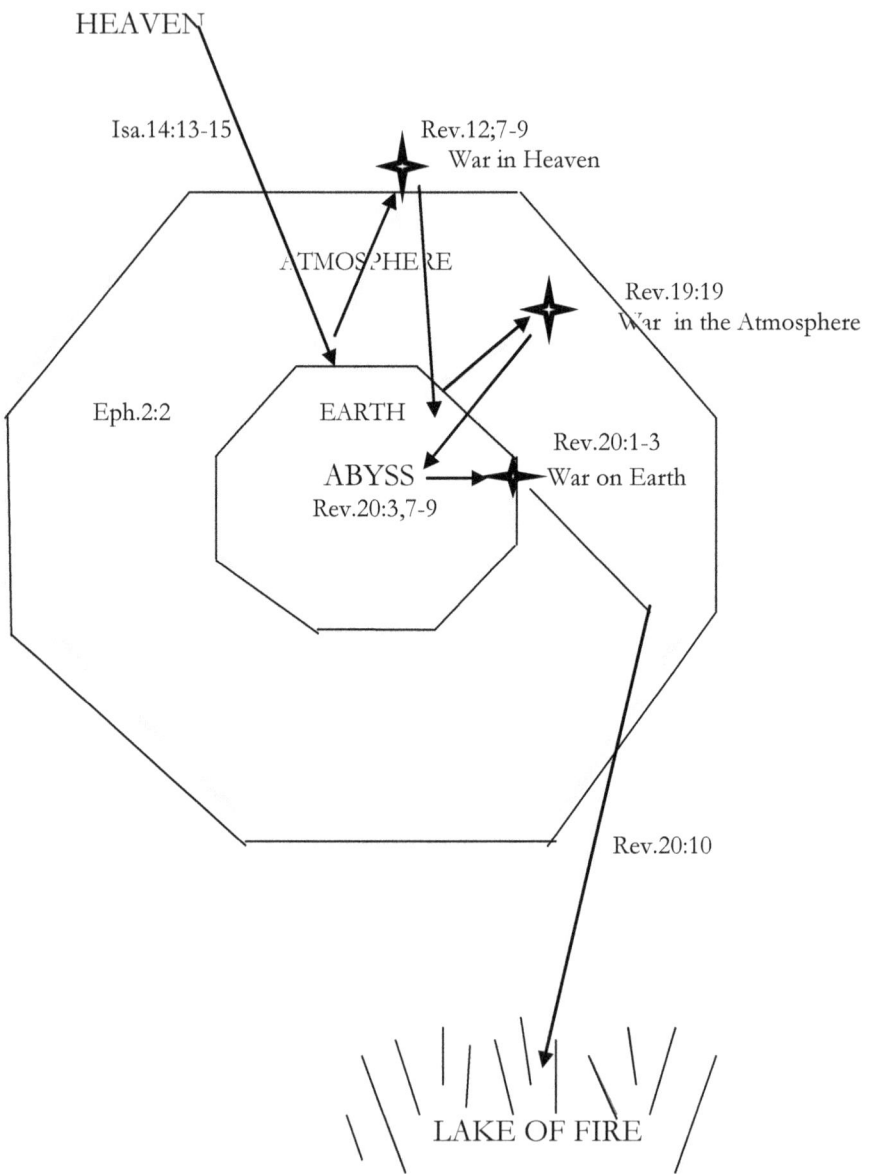

**12:16** with **Gen.4:10**   The ground "opened its mouth" to receive Abel's blood (i.e., Abel's blood was absorbed into the ground).

**Q.** How would this first mention affect the interpretation of Revelation 12:16 as well as its corollary in Numbers 16:30-32?

**A.** In Numbers 16 the earth is said to have split apart and swallowed Korah's men and all their possessions.   In Genesis and Revelation there is no mention of the earth splitting apart, but only opening its mouth to receive/swallow whatever.   So it would seem that the Dragon's massive effort to locate and destroy the Jews fizzles.   Too costly, too widespread, and too many people helping them stay hidden.

**12:17**   "Frustrated rage."   Satan can't believe that his plans have failed, so he strikes out in greater fury to prove to himself and everyone else that he has <u>not</u> lost his power, that he is <u>still</u> in complete control.

**Q.** Compare 12:3 with 13:1, heads, horns, crowns (17:3).
**A.**

**13:1**  Beast with 10 horns (see also Dan.7:7,8; Rev.13:3; 17:3,7).
"Sea" = the nations; therefore I assume from this that the Antichrist is probably a Gentile, not a Jew (cf. 17:15 and also <u>The Bible Knowledge Commentary</u>.)

**13:2**   The Beast gathers into one the symbolism of the three preceding empires: Greece (a leopard—Dan.7: 6), Medo-Persia (a bear—Dan.7:5), and Babylon (a lion—Dan.7:4).  The Dragon (Satan) gave him his throne, power and great authority (see 2 Thes.2:9).

**13:3**   "<u>seemed</u> to have."   Satan cannot give life, but works by deceptive appearances (cf. 2 Thes.2:9-11), but real enough to cause great astonishment.  The Antichrist will not die and be resurrected, but will appear to have done so.  And those who refuse to believe the truth will believe this deception also (cf. 2 Thes.2:11) to their own destruction.

**13:7**  The Beast becomes a worldwide ruler (cf. Dan.7:23).

**13:11** "earth" (Gk. γῆς—GĀS = "earth" [entire world])

**Q.** What is the difference between "sea" (13:1) and "earth" here?
**A.** The "sea" refers to the peoples of the world (see 17:15).
   "Earth" could have two possible meanings:
   1. "Israel," according to some;
   2. "The entire world," which the Greek seems to imply.

Depending on which meaning chosen, the interpretation of other aspects will be influenced. For instance, choosing the first will make the False Prophet Jewish in origin. Choosing the second will allow for some other prominent world religious figure to assume that role, etc.
   Now, having said that, verse 12 seems to clarify the meaning of GĀS: "And he [the False Prophet] made the earth (γῆν—GĀN) and its inhabitants worship the first beast." On the basis of this verse, "earth" (GĀS) then would mean "the inhabited <u>world</u>" whereas the "sea" refers specifically to the <u>peoples</u> of the world.

**14:1** It would seem that the 144,000 are still intact as a group at Christ's return.

**GENERAL OBSERVATION:** The elect in the Tribulation, for whatever reason, while still in unbelief, will not receive the mark of the beast. Specifically to Israel, I suspect the mark is never offered since the Beast breaks covenant with them and attempts to destroy them.

**Q. 14:4a** "Not defile themselves with women." Does this statement indicate celibacy or the refraining from immorality?
**A.** Since God created the family, and Paul declares that anyone who marries has not sinned (1 Cor.7:28), and since defilement indicates the presence of impurity—the two cannot be equated. Marriage does not equal defilement. So I would say that this defilement has to do with sexual impurity, immorality, marital unfaithfulness. One can keep himself pure in the marriage relationship by being faithful to his spouse.
   On the other hand...this statement must be understood from the Jewish perspective since God here is dealing with Jews. What would this statement mean to them?

In Leviticus 15:18, sexual intercourse makes both the man and the woman ceremonially "unclean till evening." But is "unclean" the same as being "defiled"? I don't think so. Being defiled results from unfaithfulness and sin (as in worshipping idols, participating in heathen practices, etc.). "Uncleanness" has to do with the ceremonial laws governing holiness and who can approach God. Thus, for the Jew, defilement would also convey the idea of spiritual unfaithfulness and physical immorality. So these 144,000 were true to God in every way—undefiled—even though many of them may probably be married.

**14:4b**   The 144,000 are described here as being "purchased (redeemed) from among men and offered as firstfruits to God... ." Some Bible notes and commentaries say that this phrase indicates that they were martyred. However, if they are to be evangelists during the Tribulation period, resulting in a great harvest of souls (see chapter 7), then I would tend to hold that the above phrase indicates that they were the first of Israel to believe ("firstfruits"), guaranteeing more of the same to come.

**14:6**   There seems to be four gospels mentioned in the Scriptures:
1. The Gospel of the Torah: "Do this and you shall live." The problem was that no one could do it (Gal.3:12).
2. The Gospel of the Kingdom: "The Kingdom of God is at hand." The problem was that the Jewish nation rejected it (Matt.3:2; Jn.1:12).
3. The Gospel of Grace: "Believe, and you shall be saved." This is foolishness to the world but wisdom to the elect (Acts 16:31).
4. The Eternal Gospel (The Gospel of Judgment): "The judgment of God has come. Fear him, give him glory and worship him. He is still in charge" (Rev.14:6,7).

**Q. 14:6-9** What is the chronology and placement of these events?

**Q.** When is the mark of the Beast required?
**A.** It would seem sometime after the midpoint of the Tribulation.

**Q.** When does Babylon fall?
**A.** "Babylon," as the center of world religion (ch.17), falls at the

midpoint of the Tribulation when the Antichrist enters the Temple, announces that he is God, and destroys all forms of worship but to himself.

"Babylon," as the center of world politics and economy (ch.18), falls at the end of the Tribulation under the judgment of the Seventh Bowl (16:17-19).

**Q. 14:6-11**  Will these pronouncements be supernatural in character or done through human agencies supernaturally empowered?

**A.**

**Q. 14:6-20**  Is there any significance to the pattern of three angels, Christ, then three more angels in this chapter?

**A.**

**14:13**  If this is the midpoint of the Tribulation, it could well be said (for believers) that it would be better to die than to live through the coming terrors of the Great Tribulation.

**14:15**  "harvest is ripe" (Gk. ἐξηράνθη—exāRANthā) = "dried, withered, over-ripe."

Compare with...

**14:18**  "grapes are ripe" (Gk. ἤκμασαν—ĀKmasan = "to be fully grown or in prime condition."

**General Observation: Ch.16**  The Greek adjective, μεγάλης—meGAlās, is used many times in this chapter:

| | | |
|---|---|---|
| vs. 1 "loud" (great) voice | μεγάλης | From The Bible |
| vs. 9 "intense" heat | μέγα | Knowledge Com- |
| vs.12 "great" river Euphrates | μέγαν | mentary: "The judg- |
| vs.14 "great" day | μεγάλης | ments being poured |
| vs.17 "loud" voice | μεγάλη | out are greater, more |
| vs.18 "severe" (great) earthquake | μέγας | severe, more intense |
| vs.19 the "great" city | μεγάλη | than anything that |
| Babylon the "Great" | μεγάλη | has happened in the |
| vs.21 "huge" (great) hailstones | μεγάλη | preceding events." |
| "terrible" (great) plague | μεγάλη | |

**16:2** The foul and loathsome sores only break out upon those who have the mark of the Beast and who worship his image. Other non-believers evidently are exempt from this plague.

**Q. 16:3** What is the character or appearance of the blood of a dead man?

**A.** Dark, brownish-red in color, watery, putrid. No oxygen. No circulation. The waters congeal (cf. vs.4; 8:8; 11:6; Ex.7:17-21). Salt water: the great cleansing agent of the world's ecological system, gone. Also **(16:4-7)** Rivers and springs of water become blood. Sources of drinking water gone.

**General Comments:**

1. It seems that the waters literally turn into blood, otherwise the words of verse 6 don't make sense. And this refers back to 16:3 where it is likely also that the oceans turned into literal blood.

2. It may be that the entire ocean turning to blood is but an extension (continuation) of the 2$^{nd}$ Trumpet Judgment.

**16:9-11** "Refused to repent." Actually, they could not repent even if they wanted to (which they didn't) because those who had received the mark of the Beast (14:9-11) had by that action sealed their own doom. That seal marked "the point of no return," spiritually, from which there was no recourse.

**16:10** This was no doubt the same kind of darkness that fell upon Egypt (see comments on Ex.10:21, p.41).

**16:11** The Bowl Judgments occur in very quick succession as indicated by this verse. This is the 5th judgment, but the people are still suffering greatly from the ugly and painful sores of the first Bowl. We could be looking at a time period of merely several weeks up to two months.

**16:12** The Euphrates is dried up (predicted in Isa.11:15) to prepare the way for the kings from the east. Revelation 16:13,14,16 is parenthetical describing how the coming of these armies came about.

**16:13,14** Some commentaries say that the kings came to Palestine for the war of the great day of God Almighty. I understand this as a statement of the ultimate purpose of God for their summons, though not intended by the Antichrist. In the worldwide crises caused by the first five bowl judgments, the Antichrist's kingdom began to crumble in earnest. In a desperate move to restore it, the Antichrist, Satan and the False Prophet send evil spirit-controlled messengers to all the kings of the earth to gather them together for a major conference. The Antichrist is sure that these miracle-working messengers will assure the kings that he still had supernatural powers and the ability to rule and resolve the present world crisis.

These kings, however, had other things in mind. Fed up with their sufferings and the obvious powerlessness of the Antichrist to save the earth from destruction, they came—with their armies—to war against him and overthrow his kingdom! Those pro- and those con- met and began to fight, only to unite together against the descending Christ and be annihilated by his word in the Battle of Armageddon.

**Q. 16:15** Why is this promise of his coming included right here?

**A.** I suspect that, because of the horribleness of the Bowl Judgments, everyone despairs of life, but the Lord is encouraging his people to hang on just a bit longer, and it will soon be over.

### Similarities between the Trumpet and Bowl Judgments

| Trumpets | Bowls |
|---|---|
| 1. earth (8:7) | land (16:2) |
| 2. sea (8:8) | sea (16:3) |
| 3. rivers, springs (8:10) | rivers, springs (16:4) |
| 4. sun, moon, stars (8:12) | sun (16:8,9) |
| 5. sun, sky darkened (9:1-3) | darkness (16:10) |
| demonic agony (9:1-3) | agony from sores (16:10,11) |
| 6. River Euphrates (9:13,14) | River Euphrates dried up (16:12) |
| 7. Great Tribulation ending (11:15-19) | "It is done! (16:17) |
| earthquake, hail (11:19) | earthquake, hail (16:18,21) |

## Striking Difference between
## the Trumpet and Bowl Judgments

| Trumpets | Bowls |
|---|---|
| 1/3 of earth or heaven affected. | Entire earth affected, judgments much more severe and final in character. |

So it cannot be said that both judgments occur at the same time, or are different aspects of the same judgments.

**16:19** Babylon the Great.  Most likely Babylon rebuilt next to the Euphrates River, the capital of the final world government.  When Saddam Hussein was ruling Iraq, he was reportedly very energetically trying to rebuild Babylon on its old site, striving to outdo Nebuchadnezzar's efforts in beauty and architecture.  Nebuchadnezzar was his hero, but he wanted to eclipse him in both glory and riches.  Yet Jeremiah 51:62-64 seems to imply that Babylon will never be rebuilt. If this is so, then the war against Saddam Hussein (March-April 2003), which stopped his construction, is of prophetic significance, and the city would have to be built elsewhere – or perhaps Rome renamed.

**Q.** The context of chapters 17 and 18 seem to be describing the same
   city.  Yet chapter 17 depicts Babylon as the religious ruler over the kings of the earth which ruler they want to destroy.  However, the Antichrist will not seek to destroy his own capital city.  What is going on here?
**A.** Religious Babylon holds sway for the first 3½ years in an alliance
   with political Babylon.  It is the religious system that is destroyed in chapter 17, not the city itself, thus making way for the Antichrist to claim deity and worship.

**Q. 16:19**  How do chapters 17 & 18 figure in with this verse?
**A.** Babylon the Great — the "great city" (cf.17:18) — split into three
   parts.
   What is clear is that the woman of chapter 17 is Babylon.
   The beast in chapter 17 is evidently the empire over which the woman rules (yet 17:8 personalizes the beast as an individual.  No problem since cities and nations are frequently referred to in this

way.) This empire (beast) once was, now is not, and will come out of the Abyss.

17:5 seems to indicate a religious system, the center of which is located in the city of Babylon. So it is the system that is destroyed (17:16), not the literal city whose destruction takes place under the Seventh Bowl Judgment (16:17-21) and is detailed for us in chapter 18. So the religious Babylon is destroyed in chapter 17, and the political and economic Babylon is destroyed in chapter 18.

The parallel imagery used to describe both systems does not mean that both are identical. If they were, then the Antichrist and the ten kings would be destroying their own capital (17:16-18) which is incongruous and also conflicts with 16:17-21 where it is obvious that God is the One doing the destroying.

**16:21** List of mankind's failures to repent: 2:21; 9:21; 16:9,21.

**17:3** "Names of blasphemy" probably refer to the names of all deities that have been a substitute for God from the beginning. This would fit with the title given to the woman in verse 5 since false religions in Scripture are always denounced as spiritual adultery and abomination. (For an interesting commentary on the influence of ancient Babylonian mystery religions on Christianity, see The Bible Knowledge Commentary, p.970, col.2, par.3 to p.971, col.1, par.1.) There seems to be a natural progression from Babylon to Pergamum to Rome!

**17:3,5,16 with 18:2,19** The [Great] Harlot sits in the wilderness and becomes a wilderness. She has great wealth outwardly, but is a great wilderness inwardly.

**Q. 17:8** What does "was and is not and yet is" refer to in regard to the Beast and his kingdom?

**A.** The beast that once was, now is not, and will come up out of the Abyss and go to destruction, seems to refer to a political system. Even though 17:9-11 speaks of five kingdoms and a revived Roman Empire, this beast, which is the 8th, proceeds from the 7th but is of the character of ancient Babylon, as alluded to in chapters 17 and 18. So Babylon, which once was, now is not (Rome ruling), and will come up out of the Abyss (demonically restored in character under the Antichrist) only to be destroyed.

**17:9-11** Seven kings, or kingdoms. Five have fallen (Egypt, Assyria, Babylon, Medo-Persia and Greece); one is (Rome); and the other has not yet come (revived Roman Empire with the characteristics of Babylon which will remain for a "little while," i.e., 3½ years).

**17:15** "There will be one ecumenical world religious system, embracing all nations and languages" (Bible Knowledge Commentary, p.972).

**17:16** "Naked...eat her flesh" = plundered wealth.
  "burn her with fire" = everything not useable or salvageable is burned.

**17:18** "That great city" is not a literal city, but symbolic as the religious center for false religion (Bible Knowledge Commentary, p.972).

**18:1-24** Political/Economic Babylon in view here. Destroyed at the end of the seven year period by an earthquake (not by the 10 kings—see 16:17-21 and the Bible Knowledge Commentary, p.973).

**18:24** "slain on the earth" (Gk. ἐσφαγμένων—esphagMEnōn means "put to death by violence.")

**19:6** with **1:15** and **14:2** "voice the sound of many waters." "Many waters" indicates a mighty, encompassing roar.

**Q. 19:7,9** If the wedding of the Lamb and the wedding supper occur after the destruction of Babylon, which occurs at the end of the Tribulation, how does this figure with the imagery of John 14:1-3?
**A.** First of all, the marriage has already taken place by this time in Heaven.
  The Greek aorist tense is used here (ἦλθεν—ĀLthen meaning "came," indicating something that has happened and finished in the past. In fact, the Bride is here referred to as the Lamb's wife (γυνὴ—gunĀ), indicating that the wedding had already occurred.
  Secondly, according to the Bible Knowledge Commentary and other commentaries, the Millennium fulfills the symbolism of the Wedding Supper. Verse 9 would seem to lend credence to this view. However, unless the Supper is different from the seven day Marriage Feast, this view would seem to violate the picture Christ was using

in John 14:1-3 regarding his return for his Bride, etc. I am puzzled by the fact that the wedding guests are enjoying the wedding feast while the Bridegroom and Bride are in the wedding chamber for seven days, at the end of which the Bridegroom brings his wife out to present her to the wedding guests. If the seven days are symbolic of the seven years of tribulation, as some think, then the "presentation" would have to occur at the Second Coming, the feast being over. It would seem to me that the Millennium would rather be the "beginning of married life and service" for the Bridegroom and his Wife. I guess we'll just have to wait and see on this one.

**19:12** Many crowns—compare with 12:3 (7 diadems) and 13:1 (7 diadems).

**19:14** "The armies of heaven" include the angels (Matt.25:31) and New Testament believers (1 Thes.3:13; Rev.17:14).

**19:15** "Out of his mouth comes a sharp sword" (Gk. ῥομφαία—hromPHAIa — a Thracian broadsword usually carried on the right shoulder. (Bible Knowledge Commentary, p.977) "An unusually long sword and sometimes used as a spear, thus indicating a piercing action" (cf. Heb.4:12). See also Psalm 57:4, "I am in the midst of lions; I lie among ravenous beasts—men whose teeth are spears and arrows, whose tongues are sharp swords." And Proverbs 18:21a, "The tongue has the power of life and death."

In this imagery, we see the power of the word of Christ. Note:
1. By his word he created the world (Heb.11:3; Gen.1; 2 Pet.3:5).
2. By his word he sustains all things (Heb.1:3).
3. By his word he will destroy the nations (Rev.19:15; 2 Pet.3:7).
4. By his word he will destroy the heavens and earth (2 Pet.3:7).
5. By his word he will create new heavens and a new earth [2 Pet.3:13]. Since he created the first heaven and earth by his word, we can safely assume that he will also create the new heavens and earth by his word.

**19:15 with 20:7-9** "rod of iron" — The heart of man is bent upon independence from all law and restriction to personal liberty. No matter Jesus' very presence, no matter the Millennial blessings and prosperity, no matter the lack of disease and crime permitting people to live longer and safer; when push comes to shove, mankind will throw all that away, choosing to take their chances with the resulting disasters and grief that come from maintaining their personal independence from God and all law! They would rather die than submit, and that they will.

**19:20; 20:10** The Antichrist and the False Prophet will be in the Lake of Fire 1,000 years more than anyone else, including the Devil. Just as there are gradations of reward in Heaven (1 Cor.3:11-15), so there will be gradations of punishment in the Lake of Fire (Rev.20:12,13). Were the assignments mine, at the very bottom would be Satan, then his angels, followed by Judas Iscariot, the Antichrist and the False Prophet. Everyone else will follow from there up.

**20:1-3,7** I envision the "weakest and most insignificant" of the angels being given this assignment and Satan furious but totally incapable of resisting him. Yet even in the Abyss, Satan will not admit defeat. He schemes and strategizes for his escape—yet remains there 1,000 years. I imagine, at the end of that time, God telling that angel to "return and unlock the door to the Abyss, but leave it closed." Satan comes against the door once again—and it yields to him! "Aha! I <u>knew</u> God couldn't withstand my power! Now I am free and can conquer and rule the world with my greater strength! God is history!" Perhaps in the Lake of Fire (20:10) it will finally dawn on him that he has been beaten, but I wouldn't count on it.

[**NOTE:** Satan has to be released so that the inward rebellion that mankind cannot express (because of Christ's "rod-of-iron" rule) can finally find an outward expression. In this last rebellion there can be no doubt as to man's sinfulness and God's righteousness in judging it.]

**THOUGHT:** At the beginning of the Millennium, there will be more of us to rule than those to rule over!

**20:4** with **6:9-11** The <u>Bible Knowledge Commentary</u> puts forward the idea of "intermediate bodies" for the saints awaiting the resurrection, supported by the fact that John could see them (he could not see their souls if they were in spirit form). Compared with Luke 16, the language here implies a body that can feel pain, etc., even though the dead have not yet been resurrected.

**20:4,5** There is no resurrection of the saints ever mentioned after this one, so I assume from this that, in the Millennium, believers will not die; only unbelievers will (cf. Isa.65:20 — no believer would ever be considered "accursed").

Scripture speaks of two resurrections: the resurrection to life and the resurrection to death (Dan.12:2). But the first resurrection has several parts:

| 1st Resurrection | 2nd Resurrection |
|---|---|
| a. Christ (Matt.28:5,6) | All unbelievers (Rev.20:5,6, |
| b. Saints near Jerusalem | i.e., "The rest of the dead" |
| (Matt.27:51-53) | rise to face the Second |
| c. The Rapture (1 Thes.4:16) | Death, the Lake of Fire) |
| d. Old Testament and Tribulation | |
| saints (Dan.12:13; Rev.20:4) | |

**Q.** When are the O.T. and Tribulation saints judged/rewarded?
**A.** After their resurrection at the end of the Tribulation (cf. Dan.12: 13; Lk.14:14; Rev.20:4).

In Ezekiel 20:33-38, the Messiah judges and rewards Israel, including, I assume from the above references, the O.T. saints; and in Matthew 25: 31-46, he judges and rewards the nations, including the Tribulation saints.)

**20:12,15** Books were opened. Also the Book of life. The dead were judged according to their works recorded in the books. Anyone whose name was not found written in the Book of Life was cast into the Lake of Fire. So as each name came up and the works noted, that name was also searched for in the Book of Life. Not being found, that person was cast into the Lake of Fire.

In this context, it would seem that all human beings' names and works are recorded in Heaven's books, but only those who are saved are recorded in the Book of Life. Thus the same books used to judge the wicked are also used to judge believers, because they have to do with who has been born and what he has done. The only difference between us and the unbelievers is our faith in Christ.

**21:1** New earth (see also Isa.65:17; 66:22 and 2 Pet.3:10-13).
"No longer any sea." Perhaps for two reasons:
1. The sea serves to purify the environment. In the new earth, everything is pure; therefore no need for the sea.
2. The sea divides nations from nations. That symbol of division is no longer necessary.

**Q.** If this is so, then where will the fish be? They are a very unique part of God's creation.

**A.** The Bible doesn't say there won't be any big lakes!

**21:9,10,12,14** Just a thought. It would seem that the Wife of God in the Old Testament (Jer.31:32) is the Bride of Christ in the New Testament (Ex.3:14; Jn.8:58 with Rev.21:9,10). Both will be brought together as one in the New Jerusalem (vs.12,14).

**21:9-27** Imagine for a moment that, after a long journey, you are finally approaching the New Jerusalem. What would you see? What would it be like? How would you feel?

## JOURNEY TO THE NEW JERUSALEM

For a long time I had longed to see the New Jerusalem and to worship there before the Throne of God. At last I had leave to go to my heart's desire. The journey was long, but the immensity of the City filled the earth with an ever brighter light the closer I got to it. No map needed there! Soaring 1,500 miles into the sky, the City was easily seen from thousands of miles distant like a radiant jewel set against the deep royal blue of space.

As I drew closer, the general outlines of the City became increasingly clear. "They are <u>both</u> right!" I exclaimed in amazement. "The City <u>is</u> like a rounded pyramid but its encircling walls are a transparent cube!" At the top of the City was the most brilliant cloud that I had ever seen from which all the light seems to radiate. "The Shekinah Glory Cloud," I said to myself. "It <u>has</u> to be that!"

Pondering that sight, I recalled being puzzled about reading, "and the street of it... ." One street for such a huge city? My eyes sought the pyramid below the cloud and discovered only one main street spiraling up to the very top where the Throne of God and of Christ is. "So the River of the Water of Life, flowing down the middle of this street, courses and throbs throughout the entire City!"

I continued my journey. Soon the twelve-layered foundation of the City took on individual identity, each one bearing the indelible inscription of one of the twelve Apostles. What the Apostle John described didn't even come close to the stunning beauty of these precious stones. I still couldn't recall their exact names, but that didn't matter, their beauty was beyond name.

Immediately above the twelve foundations was the most mammoth cornerstone I had ever seen, defying imagination for its greatness. Its length measured three times as long as its width and height of 200 feet. On its face was inscribed: "Jesus Christ, Savior of the World, KING of Kings and LORD of Lords."

I moved around the southeastern corner of the City and eventually came to a gate. It was made of an immense pearl, fashioned into two halves to form a gigantic entrance. Just looking at it, I would have guessed its width to have been 200 feet and its height nearly 500. No pearl was ever more pure or lovely to behold. As I looked closer, I saw the name "ZEBULON" written above the gate.

For some reason I didn't enter the City there, but kept on my journey northwards and after some time arrived at the middle gate, an exact replica of the first except for its name, "ISSACHAR." But from this gate issued a river with roadway on either side. Most inviting it was, so I decided to enter the City there.

As I drew nearer to the gate, my wonder increased at its awesome size and beauty. So absorbed was I at the sight that I was totally unaware of the angel guard scrutinizing my face, and more particularly my forehead. Suddenly, I became aware of his gaze and stepped backwards in startled embarrassment. But he smiled reassuringly and said, "Welcome, child of the Most High! Welcome to the Holy City and all it holds for those who bear the seal of my Master. Enter and welcome!"

My heart warmed at his words, so I entered the City—and stopped as one struck dumb. The stunning splendor of the City's brilliance, its sheer, breathtaking beauty, completely overwhelmed me. Gradually I became aware of the soft, soothing murmur of running water and then remembered the River. Suddenly I had an overpowering desire to kick off my shoes and dangle my feet in the stream; but before I knew it, I was wading and splashing in the River, finding it delightfully refreshing, invigorating, and—fun! The water almost seemed to be laughing as I splashed it over myself in pure delight, and I laughed with it. After a few minutes, I noticed that the blazing brilliance of the City was not quite so intimidating as at first. So, taking courage, I moved further in, shoes in hand, walking in the cool, refreshing waters of the River.

In just a little way I came upon a gigantic Tree bridging the River, with huge, gnarled roots penetrating each bank as if they intended to stay there forever. What a scene! This huge, ancient, wise-looking mammoth made the Giant Redwoods look like toothpicks. On the ends of each branch were crystal-clear fruit which looked like giant dewdrops distilled from the River below, sucked up into the tree and deposited on its branches for the taking. An angel offered me some of the fruit. I was so intent upon looking at it that I never thought about eating it! On the first bite, a new light fired in my eyes; I could feel it. Never had I tasted anything like this before!

Then the angel took and crushed some of the leaves into a spring-green powder and told me to mix the powder with some water from the River and drink it. The finest of wines paled into insignificance with my first draught. The taste was beyond anything I had ever experienced; it was sort of like a tingling sensation from the tips of my toes to the top of my head; I felt as if I had drunk myself a new body!

With renewed strength, I continued on up the River, having set my sights on its source: the Throne of God at the apex of the City. But the closer I got, the slower I walked, my feet leaden with a growing sense of awe, fear, love and delight all mixed together in a tangle of jumbled emotions, until, unable to continue, I stopped. "Who am I to presume to approach the Living God?" was my unspoken question. Soon an angel appeared, and seemed to understand my dilemma. "Be strong, beloved of the Father," he said encouragingly. "Do not fear to enter into his presence, for he is waiting to receive you." But still I hesitated, even though my heart was filled with joy and assurance at the angel's words. "Here, take my hand," he said with a slight hint of a laugh in his voice, "and we will go in together." At the touch of his hand, I felt a surge of new strength course through my reluctant limbs and found myself walking ever stronger, ever faster toward my Goal.

The door to the Throne Room was open. The angel bid me enter. As I looked upon the Throne and saw the Lord, I cried out, "My Lord and my God!" and fell down to worship at his feet, unable to speak another word for joy and fear.

Suddenly a voice booming, yet gentle answered: "WELCOME, My child. WELCOME, my good and faithful servant. Enter into the joy of your Lord! You will not be idle here for I have much work for you to do. But welcome! WELCOME!"

And the deep, rolling laughter resounding from the Throne let me know that I was home.

Bob Leland – August 28, 1987

**21:12** "a great high wall"—just that, not 1,500 miles high.

"12 gates"—Likely correspond with the position of the 12 tribes around the Tabernacle (cf. Num.2, p.63).

```
              Naphtali  Asher  Dan
    Benjamin                Judah
    Manasseh                Issachar
    Ephraim                 Zebulon
              Gad  Simeon  Ruben
```

**Q. 21:12-14** How is it that the New Jerusalem, the Bride of Christ, includes the 12 tribes of Israel? Is not the Church different from Israel? Some would say not. Others that it is.

**A.** It is obvious from Scripture that God's dealings with Israel are different from his dealings with the Church on earth.

1. Yet the Church is made up of both Jews and Gentiles, the truths of what they believe founded upon the prophets and the apostles. Memorializing that foundation of faith by the inclusion of the names of the 12 tribes and the 12 apostles does not mean that earthly Israel, before the Church age, is also of the Church.

2. As Christians are the Bride of Christ, so Israel was the Bride of Jehovah (Isa.54:5; Ezek.16; Hos.2:16-20). If Christ is the Jehovah of the O.T., then it appears that the believers of all ages will be united as one in the New Jerusalem as the Bride of the Lamb (cf. Heb.11:10,16; 12:22-24) even though on earth they are dealt with separately.

3. Yet the husband-wife imagery demonstrates a relationship between God and man. The different conditions governing those relationships in both the O.T. and N.T. would indicate a different kind of relationship. Therefore the Church can be different in its relationship with Christ than Israel in her relationship with Jehovah.

(See Isaiah 54:4-6, p.197—God as Husband to Israel compared with Christ as Husband to the Church.)

**21:16** "12,000 stadia" equals 2,200 km. or 1,500 miles! That is the entire length of the island of New Guinea, or from Presque Isle, Maine to St. Paul, MN! The wall is 200 feet (144 cubits) thick — that's 2/3 the length of a football field!

**Q.** The width and length of the City is 1,500 miles on a side, and its height is said to be the same, but with only a "great and high" wall (vs.12). Some, then, have postulated that the City is a cube (like the Holy of Holies). Is the City actually a cube?
**A.** I don't think so. If my suspicion is correct, that the City is actually a rounded pyramid, then the base would be 1,500 miles squared with the top of the pyramid reaching a height of 1,500 miles. The "great and high" wall itself probably less than 1,000 feet high.

**21:23** The picture here is Jesus as a lamp and the glory of God the light issuing forth from that lamp, giving light to the whole city and to the world (vs.24).

**21:23-25** No sun and no moon—no night, always light—just one continual, eternal day. There are no signs (Gen.1:14,15) to indicate the passing of time. But...

**Q.** Will there be a sense of time in Heaven?
**A.** I believe there will be. We were created as creatures of time, and our work and service assignments from the Lord will have a beginning and an end. That process would indicate some sort of "time," though it may be different from "time" as we now know it. The passing of events will also give us some sense of history in Heaven, hence a time element of some kind.

Also...if (as I originally thought) the New Jerusalem is suspended over the Millennial earth, as the earth rotates, the nations will "walk by its light." "No night there"—in the New Jerusalem, the "Son" is always shining. So no more need for sun or moon.

But in the context of Revelation 20:11 and 21:1,2, it would seem that the New Jerusalem actually descends <u>after</u> the Great White Throne Judgment, before which heaven and earth flee and after which the new heavens and earth are created. So I suspect that the nations walking by its light refers to the saved from all nations of the earth living in the Eternal State.

**Q. 22:2** Is it one tree or two?
**A.** "On each side of the river stood the (singular) tree of life." One
tree straddling the river with the water flowing underneath it, like the giant sequoia tree through which one can drive a car, only a lot bigger.

**22:2** "The leaves of the tree are for the healing of the nations." "Healing" (Gk.θεραπείαν—theraPEIan meaning "health" or "health-giving"). The intent here is not for healing from illness, but for the nourishing the physical well-being of those in the eternal state.

## MATHEMATICAL PROJECTIONS REGARDING THE NEW JERUSALEM AND MILLENNIAL EARTH

**Rev.21:16** In thinking of the New Jerusalem, I began to wonder just how many people could it hold? I am not a mathematician. Even my check books never balance! So my mathematical meanderings below may be way off. But I'm still curious. So let's see where my meanderings take us.

The measurements and capacity of the New Jerusalem are staggering. Earth's surface, at present, sustains 7.5 billion people on 57,259,000 sq. mi. of land (excluding Antarctica which would add another 5.1 million sq. miles). Assuming the usability of Antarctica in the Millennium (62,359,000 sq. mi. total land), that would provide 615,969,145,600,000 sq. ft. of land, which, divided by 400 sq. ft. (comfortable living space) for each person, would give us enough space for nearly 1.5 trillion (1,539,922,864,000) people (of course, not allowing for forests, farms and other open areas which would cut the total down a bit).

If the New Jerusalem is a rounded pyramid, it would contain a surface area of approximately 4,500,000 square miles (118.5 trillion square feet). Divide that by 400 sq. feet and we come out to the possibility of 296 billion people! If the New Jerusalem has interior dwellings, it would have a potential population of a trillion or more! Minus space for parks, forests and other wide-open spaces…we still end up with a lot of people.

But when we take into account the vast, innumerable multitudes saved during the Tribulation period, then consider another 1,000 years of no curse, human fertility and little death, it would take a much greater mind than mine to project the probable human population the Millennial earth could sustain, let alone the New Jerusalem and the new earth. In the end, only the Lord knows, and we are left to wonder. So let's wonder...!

Of the 7.5 billion people on earth today, there would be perhaps 400 million left (and that may be high — see **TRIBULATION CASUALTIES**, p.366) by the end of the Tribulation. Let's say that ten percent (the "sheep" of Matthew 25) to go into the Millennium. If the population of the earth doubled every generation (40 years), then, 1,000 divided by 40 = 25 doublings, or 1.5 pentillion people by the end of the Millennium! But with people living 1,000 years in a totally healthy environment, and fertile beyond what we know now, the parents of the first generation will keep on having children into the generations to come, so while the second generation doubles the earth's population, the third could well triple it, the fourth...? So we would have an over-filled earth in a matter of a few generations. Where would they be cared for?

**Q.** Could it be that there will be space travel then, and colonization of other planets in order to keep earth's population at a manageable level?

**A.** I don't think so because Psalm 115:16 says that "the heavens are the LORD'S; but the earth he has given to the children of men." That pretty well limits our "living space." And Revelation 20:8 says that Satan "will go out to deceive the nations in the four corners of the earth—Gog and Magog—to gather them for battle." If there were space colonization, the phrase "from one end of heaven to the other," would also have to be used. So I think we can eliminate space colonization as a possibility.

But, back down to earth...I suspect that marriage and child-bearing might revert to the same pattern as before the flood. Isaiah 65:20b gives us a hint of this when it says: "He who dies at a hundred will be thought a mere youth; he who fails to reach a hundred will be considered accursed." In Genesis 5 we read of families having children after 130 years, etc. So generations of 40 years in the Millennium may not apply. We could be looking at more like 80 to 100-year generations. If so, then earth's population would be considerably less than what is projected above, obviating any need for space colonization and remaining at a reasonable level. But even then it could be an astronomical 40.9 trillion people!

Well, with all these population uncertainties, any calculations fade into the fog of possibilities and, perhaps, improbabilities. In the end, it's beyond our understanding how many people will be living then, and exactly how many the New Jerusalem and the new earth will actually accommodate. Someday we'll know!

## TRIBULATION CASUALTIES

I have often wondered just how many people will die during the Tribulation period and how many "sheep" and "goats" will be left when Jesus returns and divides them (cf. Matt.25:31,32). The simple answer is a lot will die and only a small percentage will be left! There's no way to really calculate it, but I'm going to try a very rough attempt anyway!

Consider:

The world's population now (2020) is 7.8 billion. By 2023 demographers expect it to be 8 billion. Using that figure –

8,000,000,000
-2,000,000,000 (6:8) Death and Hades given power to kill
6,000,000,000         1/4th of the earth's people.
-2,000,000,000 (9:18) Demonic hoards kill 1/3 of humankind.
4,000,000,000         Earth's population cut by half.
-    5,023,500 (Ezek.39:4,5) Combined Russian and allies'
3,994,976,500         armies (Google) decimated.
- 1,026,080,655 (16:19,20) Mountains flattened, islands gone;
2,968,895,845         wholesale death (Google on island and
                      major cities populations).
- 2,775,000,000 ??? (7:9) Martyrs and deaths from other
193,895,845         causes.
-    50,000,000 ??? (14:19,20) Combined world armies at
                      the Battle of Armageddon leaving
143,895,845 ??? alive when Jesus returns. That's about 14% of
                 China's population today! The rest of the world
                 is empty! How many of those remaining alive
                 will be "sheep"?

Now it's easier to "see" what the Lord meant in Matthew 24:22 when he said, "If those days had not been cut short, no one would survive, but for the sake of the elect those days will be shortened."

\* \* \* \*

One final thought: The Lord will have to rule the earth with a "rod of iron." That means that the majority of the people living then won't like being under his rule! So even in a "wealth, health and prosperity" environment, most people will turn against the One providing it! They would rather suffer the tragedies of sin in retaining their independence than submit to the Savior and receive his blessings. What a commentary on the human heart!

# POSTSCRIPT

I hope you've enjoyed our different kind of journey through the Scriptures as much as I have in preparing it. Obviously, there are a lot of unanswered questions yet to be answered, but they are few, compared with the volume of Scripture, and in no way take away from its Divine inspiration.

If you have come away from this attempt to answer unanswered or un-thought-of questions with a greater desire to search the Scripture for answers to yet other questions, then I have accomplished my desire to stir up greater curiosity in your heart as you read the Bible.

May the Lord grant you wisdom as you seek answers for your yet unanswered questions, and through those answers cause your faith to grow and draw you closer to himself.

**Bob Leland**
January 2023

# APPENDICES

# APPENDIX I
# GOD OF THE IMPOSSIBLE

1. He brought forth everything out of nothing (creation) just by a word (1:1-2:3 with Heb.11:3).
2. He gave life to the inanimate (2:7).
3. He created a woman from the rib of a man (2:21,22).
4. He handed down various judgments because of sin, then seeing to it that each one was fulfilled (3:14-19).
5. He brought a flood on the entire earth (7:4).
6. He altered the earth's climates and seasons (8:22).
7. He put dread and fear in the heart of every beast toward human beings (9:2).
8. He mixed up mankind's language at Babel (11:7,8).
9. He protected Sarah from Pharaoh's desires (12:10,17-19).
10. He promised descendants to Abraham (12:1-3,7; 13:15-17) in spite of Sarah's barrenness (15:1-16:1). The promise repeated (17:1-21; 18:10). The key verse: "Is anything too hard for the LORD?" (18:14). Isaac was born (21:1-3).
11. He gave Abraham victory over the armies of five kings with only 318 trained servants in a night battle to deliver Lot and the Sodomites out of their hands (14:1-17).
12. He protected Sarah from Abimelech through a dream (20:3-7).
13. He provided Hagar and Ishmael with water in the wilderness and promised Ishmael a great nation (21:13-19).
14. If Abraham had sacrificed Isaac, God would have had to raise him from the dead, something never done before (22:5 with Heb. 11:17-19).
15. He immediately answered the prayer of Abraham's servant (24:12-15).
16. He enabled Rebekah, barren, to conceive (25:21-23).
17. He opened Leah's womb, closed Rachel's (29:31), then opened it (30:22).
18. He overruled any attempts of Laban's to do harm to Jacob (31:7,9-12,24,29,42).
19. He protected Jacob and family from revenge for the Shechem slaughter (35:5).
20. He made a ruler from a jailed slave (Joseph—39:20; 45:9).
21. He gave dream interpretations to Joseph (40:8; 41:25).
22. He governed the details of Jacob's life to accomplish his purpose (45:5-8; 50:20).

# EXODUS

23. He provided households for the midwives who feared him (1:21).
24. Contrary to the laws of Pharaoh, he caused Pharaoh's daughter to have compassion on Moses, allowing his mother to nurse him, then bringing him up in Pharaoh's own household. The irony of this situation is unbelievable! (2:1-10).
25. In his presence, the burning bush was not consumed (3:2,3).
26. He caused Aaron's rod to become a serpent (4:2,3), his hand to become leprous (4:6,7), and the poured water to become blood (4:9).
27. His promised plagues on Egypt and blessings on Israel (4:6,7) were carried out to the full (chs.7-12; 12:35,36).
28. He overrules any physical weakness or inability (4:11,12).
29. He freed a whole nation from bondage (6:1-8) when neither they nor their rulers wanted them to be (5:2; 6:12; 12:51)!
30. He made Moses like God to Pharaoh (6:30; 7:1), Israel "favorably disposed" to the Egyptians, and Moses highly regarded by Pharaoh's officials and the people (11:2,3; 12:36).
31. He kept the following plagues away from Israel (8:22,23; 9:4,6,26; 10:22,23; 11:7).
32. He promised the land of Canaan as Israel's possession (13:10,11).
33. He led Israel by a pillar of cloud by day and a pillar of fire by night (13:21,22). So Israel had its "night light" for the next 40 years.
34. He "set up" Pharaoh by putting Israel in an impossible situation (14:2-18).
35. He made an impenetrable darkness lie between Pharaoh's army and Israel, yet at the same time gave light to Israel (14:19,20).
36. He divided the waters of the Red Sea, causing dry land to appear (14:21,22).
37. He un-wheeled the Egyptian chariots, stalling the whole army, then brought back the water, drowning them (14:24-28).
38. Water impossible to drink (15:23,24). God showed Moses a tree that could make the water sweet (15:25).
39. He has control over disease to cause sickness or healing (15:26).
40. He provided manna for 40 years (16:35) for all Israel to eat 16:4)... and quails at one time (16:13-16).
41. He made water come out of a rock—enough for all of Israel (perhaps over two million people!—17:6 with Num.20:11).

42. He helped Israel defeat Amalek (17:8-11).
43. He revealed his presence on Mt. Sinai with thunderings, light-nings, the sound of a trumpet blast, smoke and thick darkness (20:18,21).
44. He led Israel to the place prepared in spite of obstacles (23:20).
45. He caused greater and more numerous enemies to fear and flee (23:27-30).
46. He could have judged people with death and made of Moses a greater nation (32:9,10).
47. He promised protection when the land is defenseless (34:24).
48. He sustained Moses for 40 days & nights on the mountain without food or water (34:28).
49. He filled people with skill, wisdom, and understanding (35:30-36:1).

## LEVITICUS
50. He sent fire from heaven to consume the burnt offering (9:24).
51. He sent fire from heaven as judgment on Nadab and Abihu (10:1,2).
52. He promised to provide three years' worth of food in one year (25:21).
53. He has power to bless and power to curse (ch.26).
54. He broke the yoke of Egyptian bondage (26:13).

## NUMBERS
55. He judged the people with fire because they complained (11:1,2).
56. He provided quail for Israel for a whole month until they loathed it (11:18-20,31-33).
57. He sent a plague on those who had yielded to their cravings (11:33).
58. He struck Miriam with leprosy for speaking against Moses(12:1,10).
59. He could give Israel victory over impossible odds (13:28-30; 14:6-9).
60. He made the entire nation wander for 40 years in the wilderness (14:32-35 with 26:64,65).
61. He judged the ten spies with a deadly plague (14:37).
62. He caused the ground to split open to swallow up Korah, Dathan, Abiram and On, and fire fell and consumed the 250 men with them (16:31-35), then plagued Israel for their murmuring (16:45-50).

63. He made Aaron's rod bud, blossom and bear fruit overnight (17:7-9).
64. He brought about the defeat of the Canaanites (21:1-3).
65. He provided healing for the people from snakebites if they looked on the brazen serpent (21:9).
66. He delivered Sihon and Og into Israel's hands (21:34,35).
67. He overruled Balaam's attempts to curse Israel (chs.22-24).

## DEUTERONOMY
68. He provided completely for Israel 40 years in the wilderness so that they lacked nothing (2.5-3 million people!—2:7).
69. He took away the power of giants so that they were beaten by normal-sized men (2:20-23).
70. He hardens or softens men's hearts as he wills (2:30).
71. He kept Israel's clothing from wearing out (in 40 years—8:4)!
72. He gave Israel rest from her enemies (12:10).

## JOSHUA
73. He brought terror to the hearts of Israel's enemies (2:9-11,24).
74. He dried up the Jordan River (3:13-4:1,18).
75. He gave Jericho into Israel's hands (6:12-16,20,21).
76. He spared Rahab's house (built on the wall—so evidently that part of the wall didn't fall—6:22,23).
77. He caused the lot to fall on Achan who sinned (7:18-21).
78. He promised victory beforehand (10:8).
79. He cast down large hail stones upon the Amorite army killing more than Israel did (10:10,11).
80. He caused the sun and moon to stop—increasing daylight hours so that Israel could continue fighting the Amorites (10:12,13).
81. He promised victory and fulfilled it (11:6-8).
82. He hardened the hearts of those he intended to destroy (11:20).
83. He gave Caleb the same strength at 85 as he had at 40 (14:10,11).
84. He fulfilled his promise to Israel, giving them the land, rest (peace), and victory (when they chose to fight—see 21:43-45; 23:14).

## JUDGES
85. He alternately strengthened Israel and her enemies in the accomplishing of his purposes (3:8-10,12-15,31; 4:2,3,6,7,14,15,23,24; 6:1).
86. He uses the weak to overcome the mighty (6:14-16; 7:7,22). Gideon

was a "mighty man of valor" (6:12) not because he was one but because <u>God said he was</u> and empowered him accordingly (6:14-16, 34).

87. He sent a spirit of ill will between Abimelech and the men of Shechem (9:23,24).

88. He promised Manoah's wife, barren, a son (13:3).

89. He gave Samson great physical strength (14:6,19; 15:14; 16:3,9,12,14,28-30).

90. He provided Samson water where there was none (15:18,19).

91. He brought about the defeat of Benjamin by the other tribes after they suffered 40,000 casualties (20:28,35).

## RUTH

92. He caused Ruth to work in the field of Boaz, a close relative (2:3).

## 1 SAMUEL

93. He caused Hannah to have a child (she was barren—1:5,19, 20).

94. He caused Dagon to fall on his face before the Ark of the Covenant and finally breaking off his head and hands (5:3,4).

95. He struck the Philistines with tumors (5:6,9,11,12) and a plague of rats (6:4,5).

96. He thundered against the Philistines and threw them into confusion (7:10).

97. He empowers the weak to do great things (9:21; 10:6,7; 11:6,7).

98. He enabled David to kill the lion, the bear, and Goliath(17:36, 37,49-51).

99. He protected David by making Saul's messengers and Saul prophesy (19:20-24).

100. He protected David so that Saul could not find him no matter how hard he tried (23:14). Yet Jonathan had no trouble locating him (23:16)!

101. He caused other circumstances to arise that protected David after Saul did find him (23:26,27).

102. He kept Saul and his army in a deep sleep so that David and Abishai could enter and leave his camp unnoticed (26:12).

103. He kept David and his men from fighting against Israel (29:3-11) thus enabling them to rescue their families. Had they gone to battle, their families would have been long gone and lost to them. Even so it was 3 days or more before the rescue took place.

104. He allowed Samuel to appear to announce judgment upon Saul (28:11-19).

## 2 SAMUEL

105. He gave David victory after victory over the Philistines (5:17-25).
106. He gave David a kingdom and riches, etc. (12:7,8).
107. He raised up adversity to him from his own house because of his sin (12:11).
108. He overruled Absalom's insurrection (17:14; 18:28).
109. He delivered David form enemies much stronger than he (22:17,18).

## 1 KINGS

110. He gave 10 tribes to Jeroboam (11:11,34-37; 12:8,15,24; 2 Chr.10:15; 11:4).
111. He raised up adversaries to Solomon (11:14,23,26).
112. He restored Jeroboam's withered hand and split the altar (13:3-6).
113. He revealed Jeroboam's wife to blind Ahijah (14:5).
114. He fulfilled the prophecy of 14:10-13 (15:27-29).
115. He gave Baasha strength to become king (16:2), but Baasha misused that strength.
116. He fulfilled the prophecy of 1 Ki.16:3,4 (16:10,21).
117. He fulfilled the prophecy regarding the rebuilding of Jericho (Josh.6:26; 1 Ki.16:34).
118. He provided for Elijah through ravens (17:2-6).
119. He multiplied the contents of the flour bin and jar of oil (17:14-16).
120. He brought a child back to life (17:17-22).
121. He sent fire that consumed both the sacrifice and the altar (18:38).
122. He gave Elijah strength to run faster than Ahab's chariot (18:46).
123. He provided for Elijah's long journey (19:5-8).
124. He fulfilled prophecy (21:19 with 22:35,38).

## 2 KINGS

125. He sent fire to consume the two captains and their 50's (1:9-12).
126. He split the Jordan River so that Elijah and Elisha could cross on dry ground (2:8).
127. He took Elijah up to Heaven in a chariot of fire (2:11).

128. He split the Jordan River again for Elisha (2:14).
129. He healed the water source in Jericho (2:19-22).
130. He brought out two female bears which killed the 42 young men who cursed Elisha (2:23-26). (The majority ostensibly <u>should</u> have been able to run away, but couldn't.)
131. He provided water where there was none (3:16,17,20).
132. He delivered the Moabites into Israel's hands (3:18,19,24,25).
133. He kept the jar of oil full until all the jars were filled (4:5-7).
134. He gave the Shunammite woman a child (4:16,17).
135. He raised the Shunammite woman's son from death (4:32-37).
136. He cured the poisonous stew (4:38-41).
137. He multiplied the barley loaves (20) and grain for 100 men (4:42-44).
138. He healed Namaan from his leprosy (5:14).
139. He transferred Namaan's leprosy to Gehazi (5:27).
140. He caused the ax head to float (6:5-7).
141. He revealed to Elisha the counsels of the Syrian king (6:8-12).
142. He struck the Syrian host with blindness then restored their sight (6:18-20).
143. He caused the Syrian army to hear the noise of a great army— and flee (7:6,7).
144. He brought to pass his word re: Jehu's descendants (15:12).
145. He governs kings and their fate (19:7).
146. He governs the victories of armies (19:25-28).
147. He preserves people against impossible odds (19:29-34).
148. He slew 185,000 soldiers in one night without a weapon (19:35).
149. He added 15 years to Hezekiah's life (20:6).
150. He made the shadow on the sundial reverse its direction (20:11).

## 1,2 CHRONICLES
151. He sent fire from heaven to consume David's sacrifice (1 Chr.21:26).
152. He has the power to grant wisdom, knowledge, riches, wealth and honor (2 Chr.1:12).
153. He sent fire to consumed the burnt the burnt offering (7:1-3).
154. He caused Shishak, king of Egypt, to subdue Judah (12:1-9) but stopped him short of destroying them (vs.7).
155. He gave Abijah and Judah victory over Jeroboam's hosts (13:14-18).

156. He gave victory to Asa and Judah over the army of Ethiopia (14:11-15).
157. He caused the nations around Judah to fear coming against them in war—so there was peace (17:10; 20:29,30).
158. He saved Jehoshaphat from certain death (18:30-32).
159. He delivered Israel from the hands of Ammon, Moab and Mt. Seir without them having to shoot one arrow (20:22-24).
160. He raised up adversaries against Jehoram of Judah (21:8-10,16,17).
161. He struck Jehoram with an incurable intestinal disease (21:15,18-20).
162. He brought destruction upon Ahaziah because he also was part of the house of Ahab (22:7).
163. He intervened to save David's line when Athaliah would have destroyed it entirely (22:10-12).
164. He delivered the large Judean army into the hands of a much smaller Syrian army as punishment for forsaking him (24:24).
165. He delivered Amaziah into Joash's hands (25:20-22).
166. He struck Uzziah with leprosy when he presumed upon the office of the priests (26:16-20).
167. He brought Judah low because of the unfaithfulness of Ahaz and his wickedness (28:19).
168. He brought Manasseh to the place of repentance (33:10-16).

## EZRA
169. He worked his desire for Israel in the hearts of heathen kings (1:1-4; 6:22; 7:27,28).

## NEHEMIAH
170. He caused Nehemiah's life to be spared when he was sad in the king's presence (2:1-3).
171. He enabled the Israelites to rebuild the walls of Jerusalem in 52 days against incredible odds (6:15).

## ESTHER
172. He orchestrated the people and events which led to the Jews' deliverance from Haman's wicked plot against them.

## JOB
173. He totally limits what Satan can do (1:12; 2:6).

## PSALMS
174. He knows the number of stars and has named them all (147:4).

## ISAIAH
175. He grants or withholds protection (5:5).
176. He commands the clouds to withhold rain (5:6).
177. He governs the fate of nations (7:7,8).

178. He caused a virgin to conceive and bear a son (7:14).
179. He killed 185,000 Assyrian soldiers in one night (37:36).
180. He caused the sun's shadow to fall back 10 degrees on the sundial of Ahaz (38:8).

## JEREMIAH
181. He promised deliverance from all threats on his life (1:8).

## EZEKIEL
182. He totally annihilated the Russian and Arab allies attacking Israel (chs.38,39).

## DANIEL
183. He blessed Daniel's faithfulness by causing simple food to be more nourishing than the King's fare (1:11-16).
184. He revealed the King's dreams to Daniel (2:19; 4:19).
185. He reveals what is to come (2:29).
186. He gave Nebuchadnezzar everything he had (2:37,38). He also took it away (4:28-33) and gave it back to him again (4:34-37).
187. He rescued Shadrach, Meshach and Abednego from the fiery furnace (3:24-28).
188. He produced writing on the wall announcing Belshazzar's judgment (5:5).
189. He rescued Daniel from the lions' den (6:21,22).

## JONAH
190. He brought a terrible storm on the sea (1:4).
191. He prepared a large fish to swallow Jonah (1:17).
192. He kept Jonah alive for three days in the belly of the fish (1:17).
193. He caused the fish to spit Jonah up on the beach (2:10).
194. He convinced the Ninevehites to repent (3:5-10).
195. He caused a gourd to grow up to shade Jonah (4:6).

196. He caused a worm to destroy the gourd (4:7).
197. He prepared a vehement cast wind to blow (4:8).

## MATTHEW
198. He caused a special star to shine (2:2).
199. He enabled the wise men to leave without Herod's knowing it (2:12).

## LUKE
200. He gave Elizabeth, barren, a child (1:36).
201. He gave Mary, a virgin, a son, Jesus (1:35).

## ACTS
202. He enabled the 120 disciples to speak in languages they did not know to communicate the Gospel to pilgrims in Jerusalem (2:7,8).
203. He raised Jesus from the dead (2:24).
204. He enabled the Apostles and others to work miracles (4:30).
205. He whisked Philip away from the Ethiopian eunuch (8:39,40).
206. He released Peter from prison, saving him from execution (12:6-10).
207. He struck Herod with worms so that he died (12:22,23).
208. He got Paul to Rome in spite of Satan's six attempts to stop him (23:12; 24:27; 25:9; 27:14,42; 28:3; 28:16) .

## EPHESIANS
209. He unified Jewish and Gentile Believers by the blood of Christ (2:13-16)

## REVELATION
210. He struck the earth with three series of coordinated judgments (chs.6,8,9,15,16).
211. He preserved Israel from total destruction (12:6).
212. He created a new heaven and a new earth (21:1).

# APPENDIX II

## SATAN'S OPPOSITION
## TO EVERYTHING GOD DID (O.T.)

Throughout Scripture, Satan worked behind the scenes to hinder all that God wanted to do. Every time God did something, Satan tried to undo it or destroy it. God determined that his name would be proclaimed throughout the world through Israel and that the Messiah and Savior would come through them. Satan did everything in his power to keep that from happening. Consider:

1. **GOD** created all things good.
   *SATAN* corrupted all things through sin (Gen.1:31; Rom.8:20,21).

2. **GOD** announced man's salvation through the woman's seed (Gen.3:15).
   *SATAN* moved Cain to kill Abel (Gen.4:3-8) in an attempt to destroy that seed. **Cain did nothing to tell his children about God. Thus the need for missions was born.**

3. **GOD** gave Seth to Adam and Eve to carry on the godly line (Gen.5:3).
   *SATAN* tried to contaminate mankind through gross sin so that God would destroy them all (Gen.6:1-7), and thus eliminate the prophecy of a Savior and avoid his own defeat and condemnation at Christ's hand.

4. **GOD** destroyed mankind but saved righteous Noah (Gen.6:8; 8:20,21).
   *SATAN* led a major rebellion against God through Nimrod (Gen. 11:1-6), once again trying to thwart God's plan.

5. **GOD** scattered the rebellious ones (Gen.11:7-9), yet preserved the knowledge of himself through men such as Job and Melchizedek. **Then he called Abraham to do a special work through him** (Gen.12:1-3) **promising to bless the nations through him and his descendants** (cf. Gal.3:14).
   *SATAN* caused Sarah's barrenness to stop the line (Gen.15:2).

6. **GOD** promised Abraham a son (Gen.17:1-8).
*SATAN* tried to cause Abraham to doubt God's promise. Enter Hagar and the birth of Ishmael (Gen.16:15), whose descendants have tried over and over to eliminate the Israelites, and thus any threat to Satan's future.

7. **GOD** gave Sarah a son, Isaac (Gen.21:1-3).
*SATAN* rejoiced to see the sacrifice of Isaac, and probably gloated over God's reversal of his promise to Abraham (Gen.22:1,2).

8. **GOD** spared Isaac by substituting a ram (Gen.22:13).
*SATAN* tried again—Rebekah barren (Gen.25:20,21).

9. **GOD** gave Rebekah two sons in answer to Isaac's prayer (Gen.25:21).
*SATAN* caused enmity between the two sons so that Esau planned to kill Jacob, again bringing an end to the line of descent (Gen.27:41).

10. **GOD** protected Jacob from whom came the 12 patriarchs (Gen.28:13-15).
*SATAN* tried to destroy them again at Shechem through the cruelty of Levi and Simeon (Gen.34:25).

11. **GOD** put the fear of God on all around so that Jacob and family could flee (Gen.35:5,6).
*SATAN* sent severe famine to wipe out the family of Jacob (Gen.41:57).

12. **GOD** sent Joseph to Egypt to spare his family (Gen.45:7,8).
*SATAN* caused Pharaoh to decree to kill all Israelite baby boys (Ex.1:15,16), again so that the Seed could not be born.

13. **GOD** spared the male children (Ex.1:17), even to having Moses reared in Pharaoh's own household (Ex.2:9,10)!
*SATAN* enslaved Israel to discredit their testimony. Who will listen to a slave (Ex.1:6-10) ?

14. **GOD** raised up Moses and Aaron as his messengers to Pharaoh and Egypt (Ex.4:14-16). **He also raised up Pharaoh to make**

**his name known in all the earth** (Ex.9:16; Rom.9:17).
*SATAN* made sure there was a "fifth column" among the Israeli refugees as they left Egypt (Ex.12:38; Num.11:4), which he hoped would bring about the destruction of Israel (Num.16:44,45).

15. **GOD** had his man, Moses, in place to make atonement for Israel (Num.16:46).
*SATAN* kept Israel stirred up, murmuring and complaining; time and again God sent judgments upon them until he grew weary of them and wanted to destroy the entire lot (Ex.32:7-10).

16. **GOD** provided an intercessor, Moses, who turned away his wrath (Ex.32:11-14).
*SATAN* tried to contaminate the seed again on the plains of Moab (Num.25:1-3), but failed.

17. **GOD** cleansed Israel from the offenders (Num.25:4-9).
*SATAN* began working on the spiritual corruption of Israel (Judg.2:10-13).

18. **GOD** determined for the Levites to become teachers of the Law throughout Israel (Lev.10:10,11; Neh.8:7; 2 Chr.17:7).
*SATAN* corrupted the Levites to mislead the people and bring them to grief (Judg.17-19).

19. **GOD** raised up judges to bring them back (Judg.2:18).
*SATAN* worked to corrupt the people even worse after each judge died (Judg.2:19,20).

20. **GOD** preserved a believing remnant (from whom he chose the Judges and people like Boas and Ruth, etc.— cp.1 Ki.19:18).
*SATAN* **provoked Israel to ask for a king in order to become like the surrounding nations, compromising their testimony** (1 Sam.8:19,20).

21. **GOD raised up David and Solomon, the fame of whom spread the knowledge of God's name far and wide.** (Note Solomon's prayer with missionary vision in 2 Chr.6:32,33 and the fame of God's name indicated in 1 Kings 4:34).
*SATAN* ruined Solomon's testimony and hence the testimony of

Israel, through sexual desire. His many foreign, unbelieving wives led him and Israel into idolatry and the division of the kingdom (1 Ki.11;1-13).

22. **GOD** raised up prophets to call Israel and Judah to repentance (Zech.7:12b).
*SATAN* did all he could to keep them in idolatry and as far away from God as possible (Zech.7:11,12a).

23. **GOD sent Jonah to Nineveh to preach to them** (Jon.1:1,2).
*SATAN* used Jonah's patriotism to direct him elsewhere (Jon.1:3; 4:1,2)

24. **GOD forced Jonah to go to Nineveh and they repented** (Jon.3:1,2,5).
*SATAN* began work to undo what God had just accomplished so that Nineveh would eventually destroy Israel (2 Ki.17:3).

25. **GOD** removed and dispersed Israel from its place because of its Idolatry (2 Ki.17:7-12).
*SATAN* rejoiced and continued working on Judah. After many ups and downs in Judah, King Manasseh finally pushed beyond God's patience and Judah was removed to Babylon (2 Ki.24:2-4).

26. **GOD** promised to rebuild Judah through the remnant left in the land (Jer.42:10-12).
*SATAN* moved them to flee to Egypt where they all were destroyed (Jer.42:15,16) .

27. **GOD** promised a return of Judah from Babylon (Jer.29:10).
*SATAN* tried to cause the Jews to compromise and assimilate (Ez.1:5.
Not everyone's heart was moved to return).

28. **GOD** raised up men like Daniel, Shadrach, Meshach and Abedne-go, along with Mordecai and Esther to remind the Jews of their heritage and uniqueness before God; **also to be a witness to the Babylonian government and people.**
*SATAN* tried to make the Jews assimilate into the Babylonian culture in order to negate their testimony. Failing this, he tried to

destroy them all through Haman's efforts (Esth.3:1-11).

29. **GOD** raised up Mordecai and Esther to bring about the Jews' deliverance; then Zerubbabel, Ezra and Nehemiah to bring about their return to Judah. **Israel was cured from idolatry,** but was still turned in on itself (Esth.8:7; Ez.1:7:1,6; Neh.2:7).
*SATAN* brought Judah under bondage of Greece in order to bring about their destruction (Josephus, Antiq. xiii, vii, 2, p.277).

30. **GOD** raised up the Maccabees to deliver Judah from Greece (Josephus, Antiq. xii, vi, 1, etc., p.245).
*SATAN* raised up Rome to finish the job on Judah. It succeeded in A.D. 70; the Jews were scattered once again, BUT not before the Messiah was born, crucified and risen again, fulfilling the original promise of Genesis 3:15, and **the Gospel torch passed on to the believing Jews and Gentiles.**

**Conclusion:** Israel refused God's mission, so it was passed on to the Church and Israel was set aside. If we refuse to do what God has called us to do, he will pass on his call to someone else, and set us aside.

## SATAN'S OPPOSITION TO EVERYTHING GOD DID (N.T.)

31. **GOD** provided Mary as the vehicle for Christ's birth (Matt.1:18).
*SATAN* tried to have her accused of adultery, the punishment of which was death (Matt.1:19).

32. **GOD** convinced Joseph such was not the case (Matt.1:20,21).
*SATAN,* through Herod, tried to kill Jesus at Bethlehem.
**GOD** told Joseph to flee to Egypt where Jesus was kept safe (Matt.2:13).

33. **GOD** led Jesus into the wilderness to endure temptation from Satan and win (Matt.4:1).
*SATAN* tried the best he could to make Jesus fall, even to "quoting" Scripture (Matt.4:3,6,8,9)!

34. **GOD** demanded truth from his followers (Matt.5:37).
    ***SATAN*** filled the hearts of Ananias and Sapphira to lie to the
    Holy Spirit in order to bring disunity and division to the Church
    (Acts 5:3).

35. **JESUS** befriended sinners (Matt.11:19).
    ***SATAN*** inspired criticism of this association to discredit him.

36. **JESUS** planted God's Word in men's hearts (Matt.13:37; Jn.6:63).
    ***SATAN*** immediately tried to snatch it away (Matt.13:19).

37. **JESUS** sowed good seed (the Church, Matt.13:37,38).
    ***SATAN*** sowed counterfeit seed (unbelievers in the Church—
    Matt.13:38).

38. **GOD** sent his Son to Israel (Matt.15:24).
    ***SATAN*** moved them not to receive him (Jn.1:12).

39. **JESUS** taught his disciples by example and precept for about
    three-and-a-half years.
    ***SATAN*** kept them occupied with personal ambition (Matt.20:20-
    24; Lk.9:46).

41. **GOD** intended the truth to be proclaimed through Israel
    (Deut.4:6).
    ***SATAN*** sought to discredit the truth through the hypocrisy of
    the scribes and Pharisees (Matt.26).

42. **JESUS** treated Judas Iscariot well (Matt.26:50).
    ***SATAN*** prompted him to betray Jesus (Jn.13:2).

43. **JESUS** healed a leper and told him to keep quiet about it
    (Mk.1:43,44).
    ***SATAN*** took advantage of his disobedience to hinder Christ's
    ministry (Mk.1:45).

44. **JESUS** claimed to be Lord of the Sabbath (Mk.2:28).
    ***SATAN*** moved the Pharisees and Herodians to plot to kill him
    (Matt.12:14; 26:4; Mk.3:6). He also involved the Chief Priests and

Teachers of the Law (in envy—Mk.11:18; 14:1; 15:10), the leaders among the people (Lk.19:47) and the Sanhedrin (Jn.11:53).

45. **JESUS** cured the demon-possessed man of Gadera (Mk.5:1-13).
    *SATAN* inspired great fear in the people's hearts so that they demand that Jesus leave (Mk.5:14-17).

46. **GOD** instituted Temple worship where anyone could meet with him (Mk.11:17).
    *SATAN* turned the Temple into a "den of thieves," trying to drive people away from God (Matt.21:12,13).

47. **JESUS** had a humble background (Lk.2:22-24).
    **SATAN** tried to use this to discredit him publicly (Matt.13:53-58).

48. **JESUS** talked about God's grace being extended to the Gentiles (Lk.4:25-27)
    *SATAN* moved the Jews to fury, inciting them to kill Jesus (Lk.4:28,29)
    **JESUS** just walked away (Lk.4:30; Jn.8:59).

49. **GOD** led Jesus in choosing his 12 disciples (Lk.6:12,13).
    *SATAN* was overjoyed when Judas Iscariot is also chosen—confident of ultimate victory (Lk.26:14-16).

50. **GOD** provided money for Jesus and his disciples' use (Lk.8:2,3).
    *SATAN* motivated Judas to "help himself" from those funds, thus decreasing their use against Satan (Jn.12:6).

51. **JESUS** spoke parables against the chief priests and scribes (Lk.20:19)
    *SATAN* moved them to try to arrest him (Matt.21:45,46), and trap him in his words (Matt.22:15).

52. **GOD** raised up John the Baptist as a voice for truth to point men to Christ (Jn.1:29).
    *SATAN* had him beheaded to silence him (Matt.14:9,10).

53. **GOD** granted Jesus a fruitful teaching and healing ministry (Jn.3:2).
   *SATAN* tried to drown him in a storm (8:23-27).

54. **JESUS** performed many miracles (Jn.3:2).
   *SATAN* did his best to blind the eyes of the onlookers so that they would not believe (Matt.11:20-23; Jn.12:37).

55. **JESUS** did good works on the Sabbath and claimed God as his Father, making himself equal with God (Jn.5:18).
   *SATAN* moved the Jews to try to kill him for making himself equal with God (Jn.5:18; 10:31-33).

56. **JESUS** taught about being the true Bread from Heaven (Jn.6:51).
   *SATAN* caused the people to misunderstand, nitpick at what Jesus said (Jn.6:41,42,52,61), and leave him (Jn.6:66).

57. **JESUS** taught the truth (Jn.7:16,17).
   *SATAN* moved the Pharisees and teachers of the Law to fiercely oppose him and besiege him with questions (Lk.11:53) with the idea of discrediting him publicly by something he said (vs.54). Nothing. They sneered at him (Lk.16:14). Frontal attacks failed (Lk.20:20). A subtle approach also failed (Lk.20:26).

58. **JESUS** gained increased following (Jn.12:19).
   *SATAN* moved the Pharisees, respected leaders of Israel, to blaspheme the Holy Spirit in order to nullify Christ's influence (Matt. 9:34; 12:24).

59. **JESUS** faithfully taught his disciples (Jn.17:6,14).
   *SATAN* hardened their hearts that they might not understand (Mk.8:14-21).

60. **JESUS** stressed unity among his people (Jew and Gentile—Jn.17: 20,21; Eph.2:14-16).
   *SATAN* stressed racial differences (Acts 6:1; 10:28) and criticism against those going to the Gentiles (Acts 11:2,3).

61. **JESUS** came in God's name to declare the truth (Jn.18:37).
   *SATAN* raised up many antichrists to deceive as many people as

possible (Matt.24:5,11,24) and brought on persecution to destroy the body of believers (Matt.24:10-12). He also wanted to make sure that "no one" accepted his testimony (Jn.3:32; 6:36; 7:5).

62. **GOD** established the Church (Acts 2:17).
   *SATAN*, through the Sanhedrin, tried to squash it (Acts 4:29)

63. **GOD** raised up Jesus from the dead (Acts 2:24).
   *SATAN* moved the disciples not to believe it (Mk.16:11-13; Jn.20:25) and spread lies to discredit the resurrection (Matt.28: 11-13).

64. **GOD** worked miracles through the Apostles (Acts 5:12).
   *SATAN* empowered Simon the sorcerer to amaze people with signs and wonders from "divine power" (Acts 8:9-11), thus diluting the effects of the Apostles' ministry. He also caused the spirit of jealousy to arise in the hearts of the high priest, his associates and Sadducees (Acts 5:17) who ordered the Apostles to stop what they were doing. They didn't! (Acts 5:29-32).

65. **GOD** caused the Church to grow (Acts 6:7; 1 Cor.3:5,6).
   *SATAN* used Saul of Tarsus to try to destroy the Church (Acts 8:3; 9:1). **But** Christians witnessed as they scattered and the Church continued to grow (8:3).

66. **GOD** worked powerfully through Stephen (Acts 6:8).
   *SATAN* moved members of the Synagogue of the Freedmen to violently oppose him, falsely accuse him (Acts 6:9-13) and eventually stone him to death (Acts 7:58).

67. **JESUS** appeared personally to Saul to stop him in his tracks (9:3-6).
   *SATAN* turned on Saul and attempted to kill him (Acts 9:23,29). Not succeeding, he turned his attention to James (Acts 12:1,2) and Peter (Acts 12:3).

68. **GOD** sent Paul and Barnabas to preach the Gospel in Cyprus (Acts 13:4).
   *SATAN* opposed their preaching through Elymas, a Jewish sorcerer (Acts 13:8).

GOD struck Elymas with blindness, causing others to believe (Acts 13:11,12).

69. GOD sent Paul and Barnabas to Antioch in Pisidia to preach. Many believed (Acts 13:14).
SATAN stirred up the people to throw them out of the region (Acts 13:49,50).

70. GOD sent Paul and Barnabas to preach in Iconium (Acts 13:51).
SATAN stirred up unbelieving Jews and Gentiles, poisoning their minds against them (Acts 14:2) and plotted to kill them Acts 14:5).

71. GOD used Paul and Barnabas to heal a lame man in Lystra (Acts 14:8-10).
SATAN made the people think that their gods had come down to them, thus deflecting the significance of the miracle and the message (Acts 14:11-13). Failing with that, he influenced Jews from Antioch and Iconium to come and persuade the people to kill Paul by stoning him. But GOD raised him up (Acts 14:19,20).

72. SATAN caused strong dissension between Paul and Barnabas in order to stop their ministry (Acts 15:36-39a).
GOD used it to form **two** teams and **double** the outreach (Acts 15:39b-41)!

73. GOD sent Paul and Silas to Philippi to preach (Acts 16:11,12).
SATAN used a demon-possessed woman to mock them with the truth they were presenting (Acts 16:16-18).

74. SATAN caused a riot which ended up with Paul and Silas in prison (Acts 16:19,22,23).
GOD used an earthquake to bring the jailor and family to himself, and perhaps others as well (Acts 16:30,31).

75. GOD used Paul to preach the Gospel everywhere (Acts, chs.17-20).
SATAN followed hard after trying to quench it (Acts 17:5,13; 18:6,12; 19:9; 20:19).

76. **SATAN**, unable to quench the Church, raised up false teachers within it to corrupt it and its teachings (Acts 20:29,30).
**JESUS** promised that the gates of Hell would not be able to overcome the Church (Matt.16:18).

77. **SATAN** stirred up unbelieving Jews from Asia to turn Jerusalem against Paul, arrest and kill him (Acts 21:27,30-32).
**GOD** delivered him from their hands (Acts 21:31,32).

78. **GOD** told Paul that he must bear witness to him in Rome also (Acts 23:11).
**SATAN** tried six times to keep Paul from Rome: Acts 23:12-14; 24:17; 25:3,9-12; 27:13-15; 27:42,43; 28:3-6, but couldn't succeed.

79. **GOD** caused the Church to grow (Col.2:19).
**SATAN** brought on persecution (Lk.21:12-17) to destroy the Church (Lk.21:16). But to no avail (Lk.21:18,19).

80. **SATAN** tried to end Paul's ministry by keeping him in prison.
**GOD** used his prison times to win some from the Praetorian Guard and even from Caesar's household (Phil.1:12,13; 4:22)!—people he might not otherwise have had opportunity to reach.

81. **GOD** planned our salvation through Christ's death (1 Pet.1:18-20).
**SATAN** planned Christ's defeat in death (Rev.12:4).

82. **SATAN** tries to take over the world and rule it through the Antichrist (Rev.13:2,7).
**JESUS** returns at the end of the Tribulation to reign for a thousand years, the Antichrist and False Prophet are thrown into the Lake of Fire (19:20), Satan is cast into the Abyss.

83. **SATAN** is released from the Abyss and leads the world in one final attempt to usurp God's throne and become ruler of the universe.
**GOD** destroys Satan's "army" and casts him into the Lake of Fire (Rev.20:2,3,9,10).

\*\*\*\*

**NOTE:** It is interesting to note how many times Satan's opposition to what God was doing was to kill the messenger. So it is not surprising that that is what the world continues to do today. Satan's answer to truth is always to kill. Yet, even as Israel, the Church continues to this day and will continue because it is God's plan, and all of Satan's machinations cannot crush it nor exterminate it.

# APPENDIX III

## A GENEALOGICAL PICTURE FROM ADAM TO BENJAMIN
### (from Gen **5:3-32; 11:10-32**).

```
Adam
130 – Seth
235   105 – Enosh
325. .195 .. 90 – Kenan
395   265   160    70 – Mahalalel
460. .330 ..225 ..135 ... 65  –  Jared
622   492   387   297     227     162 – Enoch
687. .557 ..452 ..362 ...292 ...227. .  65 – Methuselah
874   744   639   549     479     414   252   187 – Lamech
930. .800 ..695 ..605 ...535 ...470. . 308  .243 ... 56
       857   752   662     592     527   365   300      113
       912 ..807 ..717 ...647 ...582. . . . . .355 ... 168
             821   731     661     596         369     182 – Noah...
             905 ..815 ...745 ...680. . . . . .453 ... 266. . . 84
                   827     757     692         465     278     96
                   910 ...840 . . . . . . . . .548 ... 361. . 179
Noah                       895         603     416     234
---   Shem. . .                        871 ... 84. . .502
595. . .93                             964    777     595
600    98   FLOOD                      969 . . . . . . . .600
602. .100 – Arphaxad. . .
637   135      35 – Shelah. . .
667. .165 ... 65 . . . . .30  – Eber. . .
701   199     99       64     34–Peleg
731. .229 .. 129 . . . . .94. . .64. . .30 – Reu. . .
763   261    161      126     96    62    32 – Serug. . .
793. .291 .. 191 ...156. .126. . 92. . .62 . . 30  – Nahor
822   320    220     185   155   121    91    59     29 – Terah. . .
892. .390 . . .290 . . .255. . 225. . 191. 161. . 129. . . .99 . . .70 – Haran..
940   438    338     303   273   239  209   177   147   118    48
941. .439 .. 339 ...304. .274. . . . . .210. .178. . 148. 119. . 49
950   448    348     313   283         219   187         128    58
       450 . .350 . . .315. .285. . . . . .221. .189. . . . . .130 – (60)
```

Shem Arphaxad  Shelah Eber  Reu  Serug>>Terah Haran
450 . . . . 350 . . . . 315. . . 285. . .221. . 189 . . . 130. .(60) Abraham
459        359        324    294   <u>239</u>   198        139    <u>??</u>      9
491 . . . . 391 . . . .356. . . 326. . . . . . .<u>230.</u> . . .171. . . . . . . . 41
525        425        390    360                          <u>205</u>          75
538 . . . <u>438</u> . . . . 403. . . 373. . . . . . . . . . . . . . . . . . . . . 88
550                   415    385                                       100
568 . . . . . . . . . . <u>433</u>. . . 403. . . . . . . . . . . . . . . . . . .118 . . .
<u>600</u>                         435                                       150
                             460. . . . . . . . . . . . . . . . . . . . .<u>175</u> . . .
                             <u>464</u>

Eber
---     >  Abraham
385. . < . . 100  –  Isaac
403   >    118       18
435. . < . . 150 . . . . 50
445   >    160       60 – Jacob (& Esau)
460. . < . . <u>175.</u> . . . .75. . . . . 15
<u>464</u>   >                79       19
                    145-158     85-98 12 children born
                    150. . . . . 90  –  Joseph
                    166       106  –  (16) – Benjamin
                    <u>180.</u> . . 120. . . . 30 . . . . 14
                             <u>147</u>       57       41
                                      <u>110</u> . . . . 94

# APPENDIX IV

## 30 LISTS OF THE TRIBES OF ISRAEL

| Gen.29:31-30:24 | Gen.35:23-26 | Gen.46:8-24 | Gen.49:3-27 |
|---|---|---|---|
| Reuben | Reuben | Reuben | Reuben |
| Simeon | Simeon | Simeon | Simeon |
| Levi | Levi | Levi | Levi |
| Judah | Judah | Judah | Judah |
| Dan | Issachar | Issachar | Zebulun |
| Naphtali | Zebulun | Zebulun | Issachar |
| Gad | Joseph | Gad | Dan |
| Asher | Benjamin | Asher | Gad |
| Issachar | Dan | Joseph | Asher |
| Zebulun | Naphtali | Benjamin | Naphtali |
| Joseph | Gad | Dan | Joseph |
| --- | Asher | Naphtali | Benjamin |
| OMITTED: | | | |
| Benjamin | Ephraim | Ephraim | Ephraim |
| Ephraim | Manasseh | Manasseh | Manasseh |
| Manasseh | --- | --- | --- |

| Ex.1:2-6 | Num.1:5-16 | Num.1:21-43 | Num.2:3-29 | Num.7:12-78 |
|---|---|---|---|---|
| Reuben | Reuben | Reuben | Judah | Judah |
| Simeon | Simeon | Simeon | Issachar | Issachar |
| Levi | Judah | Gad | Zebulun | Zebulun |
| Judah | Issachar | Judah | Reuben | Reuben |
| Issachar | Zebulun | Issachar | Simeon | Simeon |
| Zebulun | Ephraim | Zebulun | Gad | Gad |
| Benjamin | Manasseh | Ephraim | Levi | Ephraim |
| Dan | Benjamin | Manasseh | Ephraim | Manasseh |
| Naphtali | Dan | Benjamin | Manasseh | Benjamin |
| Gad | Asher | Dan | Benjamin | Dan |
| Asher | Gad | Asher | Dan | Asher |
| Joseph | Naphtali | Naphtali | Asher | Naphtali |
| --- | --- | --- | Naphtali | --- |
| OMITTED: | | | | |
| Ephraim | Levi | Levi | --- | Levi |
| Manasseh | --- | --- | --- | --- |

| Num.10:14-27 | Num.13:4-15 | Num.26:5-57 | Num.34:19-28 |
|---|---|---|---|
| Judah | Reuben | Reuben | Reuben |
| Issachar | Simeon | Simeon | Gad |
| Zebulun | Judah | Gad | Judah |
| Reuben | Issachar | Judah | Simeon |
| Simeon | Ephraim | Issachar | Benjamin |
| Gad | Benjamin | Zebulun | Dan |
| Ephraim | Zebulun | Manasseh | Manasseh |
| Manasseh | Manasseh | Ephraim | Ephraim |
| Benjamin | Dan | Benjamin | Zebulun |
| Dan | Asher | Dan | Issachar |
| Asher | Naphtali | Asher | Asher |
| Naphtali | Gad | Naphtali | Naphtali |

OMITTED:_____

| Levi | Levi | Levi | Levi |
|---|---|---|---|

=========================================

| Deut.27:12,13 | Deut.33:6-24 | Josh.13-21 | Josh.21:1-7 | Josh.21:9-38 |
|---|---|---|---|---|
| Simeon | Reuben | ½Manasseh | Judah | Judah |
| Levi | Judah | Levi | Simeon | Simeon |
| Judah | Levi | Reuben | Benjamin | Benjamin |
| Issachar | Benjamin | Gad | Ephraim | Ephraim |
| Joseph | Ephraim | Judah | Dan | Dan |
| Benjamin | Manasseh | Ephraim | ½Manasseh | ½Manasseh |
| Reuben | Zebulun | ½Manasseh | Issachar | ½Manasseh |
| Gad | Issachar | Benjamin | Asher | Issachar |
| Asher | Gad | Simeon | Naphtali | Asher |
| Zebulun | Dan | Zebulun | ½Manasseh | Naphtali |
| Dan | Naphtali | Issachar | Reuben | Zebulun |
| Naphtali | --- | Asher | Gad | Reuben |
| --- | --- | Naphtali | Zebulun | Gad |
| --- | --- | Dan | (Levi) | (Levi) |

OMITTED:_____

| Ephraim | Simeon | --- | --- | --- |
|---|---|---|---|---|
| Manasseh | Asher | --- | --- | --- |

| Judges 1 | Judges 5 | 1 Ki.4:8-19 | 1 Chr.2:1,2 | 1 Chr.4-8 |
|---|---|---|---|---|
| Judah | Ephraim | Ephraim | Reuben | Judah |
| Simeon | Benjamin | (Judah) | Simeon | Simeon |
| Benjamin | (Manasseh) | (Manasseh) | Levi | Reuben |
| Manasseh | Zebulun | (Asher) | Judah | Gad |
| Ephraim | Issachar | (Gad) | Issachar | ½Manasseh |
| Zebulun | Reuben | Naphtali | Zebulun | Levi |
| Asher | (Gad) | Issachar | Dan | Issachar |
| Naphtali | Dan | Benjamin | Joseph | Benjamin |
| Dan | Asher | --- | Benjamin | Naphtali |
| --- | Naphtali | --- | Naphtali | ½Manasseh |
| --- | --- | --- | Gad | Ephraim |
| --- | --- | --- | Asher | Asher |
| OMITTED: | | | | |
| Levi | Levi | Levi | --- | Dan |
| Gad | Judah | Dan | --- | Zebulun |
| Reuben | Simeon | Reuben | --- | --- |
| Issachar | --- | Zebulun | --- | --- |
| --- | --- | Simeon | --- | --- |

| 1 Chr.6:1,55-63 | 1 Chr.6:1,64-80 | 1 Chr.12:2-37 | 1 Chr.27:16-21 |
|---|---|---|---|
| Levi | Levi | Benjamin | Reuben |
| Judah | Judah | Gad | Simeon |
| Benjamin | Simeon | Judah | Levi |
| ½Manasseh | Benjamin | ½Manasseh | Judah |
| Issachar | Ephraim | Simeon | Issachar |
| Asher | ½Manasseh | Levi | Zebulun |
| Naphtali | ½Manasseh | Ephraim | Naphtali |
| ½Manasseh | Issachar | ½Manasseh | Ephraim |
| Reuben | Asher | Issachar | ½Manasseh |
| Gad | Naphtali | Zebulun | ½Manasseh |
| Zebulun | Zebulun | Naphtali | Benjamin |
| Simeon | Reuben | Dan | Dan |
| Dan | Gad | Asher | --- |
| --- | --- | Reuben | --- |
| OMITTED: | | | |
| Ephraim | Dan | --- | Asher |
| --- | --- | --- | Gad |

| Ezek.48:1-27 | Ezek.48:31-34 | Rev.7:5-8 | **COMMON COMBINATIONS** |
|---|---|---|---|
| Dan | Reuben | Judah | |
| Asher | Judah | Reuben | |
| Naphtali | Levi | Gad | 21x Issachar/Zebulun |
| Manasseh | Joseph | Asher | Zebulun/Issachar |
| Ephraim | Benjamin | Naphtali | 18x Asher/Naphtali |
| Reuben | Dan | Manasseh | 15x Reuben/Simeon |
| Judah | Simeon | Simeon | 13x Judah/Issachar/ |
| Benjamin | Issachar | Levi | Zebulun |
| Simeon | Zebulun | Issachar | Judah/Zebulun/ |
| Issachar | Gad | Zebulun | Issachar |
| Zebulun | Asher | Joseph | 13x Ephraim/Manasseh |
| Gad | Naphtali | Benjamin | |
| Levi | --- | --- | |
| OMITTED: | | | |
| | Ephraim | Dan | |
| | Manasseh | --- | |

==============================================

## REFERENCES LISTING THE TRIBES OF ISRAEL

| | | |
|---|---|---|
| 1. Gen.29:31-30:24 | 11. Num.13:4-15 | 21. 1 Ki.4:8-19 |
| 2. Gen.35:23-26 | 12. Num.26:5-57 | 22. 1 Chr.2:1,2 |
| 3. Gen.46:8-24 | 13. Num.34:19-28 | 23. 1 Chr.4-8 |
| 4. Gen.49:3-27 | 14. Deut.27:12,13 | 24. 1 Chr.6:1,55-63 |
| 5. Ex.1:2-6 | 15. Deut.33:6-24 | 25. 1 Chr.6:1,64-80 |
| 6. Num.1:5-16 | 16. Josh.13-21 | 26. 1 Chr.12:2-37 |
| 7. Num.1:21-43 | 17. Josh.21:1-7 | 27. 1 Chr.27:16-22 |
| 8. Num.2:3-29 | 18. Josh.21:9-38 | 28. Ezek.48:1-27 |
| 9. Num.7:12-78 | 19. Judges 1 | 29. Ezek.48:31-34 |
| 10. Num.10:14-27 | 20. Judges 5 | 30. Rev.7:5-8 |

## Percentage of Times Each Name Appears:

| | | |
|---|---|---|
| Naphtali = 100% | Zebulun = 93% | Manasseh = 73% |
| Benjamin = 97% | Gad = 87% | Ephraim = 67% |
| Judah = 97% | Simeon = 87% | Levi (Aaron) = 57% |
| Issachar = 97% | Dan = 83% | Joseph = 33% |
| Asher = 93% | Reuben = 83% | |

# APPENDIX V

## TOPICAL INDEX TO THE PSALMS

# APPENDIX VI

Activity of the Writing Prophets during the Reigns of the Kings of Israel and Judah
(As adapted from the E.S.V. p.1232)

| Year | King of Judah / Event | Prophet to Judah | Prophet to Israel | King of Israel / Event |
|---|---|---|---|---|
| | | (c.835) **Joel** | | |
| 840 B.C. | Joash | | | |
| 820 | (835-796) | | | |
| 800 | | | | |
| 780 | Amaziah | | | Jeroboam II |
| 770 | (796-767) | | | (781-753) |
| 760 | Uzziah | | (c.760) | |
| | (Azariah) | | **Amos,** | |
| | (767-740) | | **Jonah** | |
| 750 | Jotham | | | Zechariah (753-752) |
| | (750-735) | | (c.755) | Shallum (752) |
| | | | **Hosea** | Menahem (752-742) |
| | | | | Pekahiah (742-740) |
| 740 | | (c.742) **\*Mi-cah** | (c.740) **ISAI-AH** | Pekah (740-732) |
| 730 | Ahaz (735-715) | | | Hoshea (732-722) and **Fall** |
| 720 | | | | **of Samaria** (722) |
| 710 | Hezekiah (715-686) | | | |
| 700 | | | | |
| 680 | Manasseh (686-642) | | | **Key:** |
| 660 | | **Nahum** (c.660-630) | | **MAJOR** Prophets |
| 640 | Amon (642-640) | **Zephaniah** (c.640-609) | | **Minor** Prophets |
| | Josiah (640-609) | **Habakkuk** (c.640-609) | | [**Major** or **Minor** |
| 620 | | (c.627) | **B** | depending on the length |
| 600 | Jehoahaz (609) | **JERE-MIAH** | (c.605) Oba-diah **DAN-IEL** | **B** (c.597) **EZE-KIEL** of their writings] |
| | Jehoiakim (609-597) | | | |
| | Jehoiachin (597) | | | **B = In Babylon** |
| | Zedekiah (597-586) | | | |
| | **& Fall of Jerusalem** | | | |
| 580 | | | | **\***Micah's prophecy was likely directed toward |
| 560 | | | | both Judah and Israel. |
| 540 | | | | |
| 520 | **1st Exile Return** (538) | **Haggai** (c.520) | | |
| | **Temple Rebuilt** | **Zechariah** (c.520) | | |
| 500 | (516/515) | | | |
| 480 | | | | |
| 460 | **2nd Exile Return** (458) | **Malachi** (c.460) | | |
| 440 | **3rd Exile Return** (445) | | | |

# MAJOR THEMES OF THE PROPHETS

Isaiah
Redemptive work of the Messiah; God's judgment and salvation; God, the Holy One of Israel.

Jeremiah
Warnings about sin and judgment along with a message of hope and restoration. ("Don't pray for these people" — 7:16; 11:14; 14:11.)

Ezekiel
Sins which brought on God's judgment; God's future blessing for Israel. ("That they may know that I am the LORD.")

Daniel
The Seven World Kingdoms; God's sovereignty over history and empires.

Hosea
The sins of the people; the certainty of judgment; assurance of God's love. (A very dysfunctional family picturing a very disfunctional nation.)

Joel
The Day of the Lord; repentance; God dwelling among his people.

Amos
The call for repentance from social evils and pagan worship.

Obadiah
Edom stands judged; her doom is certain. (Because they killed fugitives from Judah and handed others over to their attackers—Babylon?)

Jonah
God's concern for the whole world.

Micah
A cry for social justice.

Nahum
Nineveh will be destroyed.

Habakkuk
A defense of God's goodness and power in the face of evil.

Zephaniah    Judgment and blessing in the Day of the LORD.

Haggai       A call to finish the Temple.

Zechariah    Encouragement for the people to finish the Temple.

Malachi      A call to repentance from dead orthodoxy to renewed covenant fidelity.

# APPENDIX VII

# MOUNTAINS IN SCRIPTURE

## MOUNTAINTOP EVENTS

1. (Gen.8:4)      Noah's ark on *Mt. Ararat*
2. (Gen.22:2)      Abraham and Isaac on *Mt. Moriah*
3. (Ex.19:1,2)      Moses on *Mt. Sinai*
4. (Num.20:23,24,28) Aaron died on *Mt. Hor*
5. (Deut.27:12,13)      Tribal blessings pronounced from *Mt. Gerizim* and cursings from *Mt. Ebal*
6. (Deut.32:48-50)      Moses viewed the Promised Land and died on *Mt. Nebo*
7. (Judg.4:6,7)      Barak whips Siserah's army at *Mt. Tabor*
8. (Judg.7:2,3)      Gideon's army tested and decreased at *Mt. Gilead*
9. (1 Ki.18:18,19) Elijah on *Mt. Carmel*
10. (1 Ki.19:7,8) Elijah on *Mt. Horeb (Sinai)*
11. (Isa.27:13) Place of worship [*Mt. Zion*]
12. (Matt.4:8) Christ's temptation viewing all the kingdoms of the world from *a high mountain*
13. (Jn.4:20) The Samaritans worshipped on *Mt. Gerizim*
14. (Mk.3:13) Choosing of the 12 disciples *on the mountain*
15. (Matt.5:1) Sermon on *the Mount*
16. (Jn.6:3) Jesus *on a mountain* where he fed the 5,000
17. (Matt.14:23) Jesus praying on *a mountain*
18. (Matt.17:1) *Mount of Transfiguration*
19. (Mk.11:1) The Triumphal Entry from the *Mt. of Olives*
20. (Mk.13:3-37) The Olivet Discourse (*Mt. of Olives*)
21. (Matt.28:16) The disciples receiving the Great Commission on *a mountain in Galilee.*
22. (Dan.2:35) The stone became *a great mountain*
23. (Zech.14:3,4) Jesus' return to the *Mt. of Olives*

# THE SIGNIFICANCE OF MOUNTAINS IN SCRIPTURE

<u>Place of victory</u> (control of the mountain equals control of the valley —Dan.2:35)

<u>Place of Divine revelation</u> (Sinai)

<u>Place of prayer</u> (Jesus)

<u>Place of Renewal</u> (Elijah at Horeb)

<u>Place of Worship</u> (Isa.27:13; Jn.4:20)

<u>Place of Winnowing/Testing</u> (Gideon/Jesus)

<u>Place of Decision</u> (Jesus choosing the 12)

<u>Place of Deliverance</u> (Ararat)

<u>Place of Provision</u> (the ram on Mt. Moriah; the feeding of the 5,000)

<u>Place of Sacrifice</u> (the ram, David's sacrifice, Jesus—on Mt. Moriah)

# APPENDIX VIII

## TITLES FOR BOOKS, SERMONS or DEVOTIONALS

Ex.19:9; Num.14:10 **MOSES: HERO TO ZERO**—(fr. John Hoag, NBBI)

Ex.23:27-30 **LITTLE BY LITTLE**—The process of Christian growth; we don't become mature saints overnight!

2 Chr.36:16 **UNTIL THERE WAS NO REMEDY**—People can only reject God's offer of grace to a certain point, beyond which there is no return; all that is left is God's judgment (cf. Heb.10:26).

Josh.7:10-13 **WHEN GOD SAYS, "STOP PRAYING!"**—There are some things that we should not pray for. (cf. Deut.3:26,27; 1 Sam. 3:14; Jer.7:16; 11:11,14; 14:11; Matt.12:31; Acts 5:1-10; 1 Cor.11:30; 2 Cor.12:8,9; 1 Jn.5:16.)

2 Ki.4:5 **SHE KEPT POURING**—God's faithfulness in meeting our needs in spite of appearances.

Job 26:14 **THE WHISPER OF HIS GRACE**—God's compassionate help in hard times.

Ps.20:7 **CHARIOTS OF WEAKNESS** The futility of putting our trust in anything but the Lord.

Ps.21:6 **GLAD WITH THE JOY OF YOUR PRESENCE**—Living in the awareness of God's presence as we spend time with him and become more like him.

Psalm 31:20 **IN THE SHELTER OF HIS PRESENCE**—God's protection of his own in the storms of life.

Psalm 32:10 **SURROUNDED BY HIS LOVE**—The Lord's love surrounds and comforts us like a downy blanket on a cold day. We are secure in him.

Psalm 63:8  **SINGING IN THE SHADOW OF HIS WINGS**—
Even in the direst of circumstances, there can be a song in our hearts,
knowing that God is totally in control of our circumstances and is our
Protector.

Psalm 104:3  **RIDING ON THE WINGS OF THE WIND**—
Living above the circumstances of life as we walk with the Lord.

Psalm 107:27  **AT WITS-END CORNER** — The futility of trying to
plan and run our lives in our own strength and wisdom without the
Lord.  We desperately need him who knows the beginning from the
end and has the power (vs. 29) to get us there (vs.30).

Psalm 110:3  **FROM THE WOMB OF THE DAWN**—A
consideration of God's amazing works.

Psalm 148:14  **A PEOPLE CLOSE TO HIS HEART**—The
yearning of a holy God for intimate fellowship with his people.

Isa.49:16  **INSCRIBED ON THE PALMS OF HIS HANDS**—
No matter what, God will not forget his own.

Isa.52:3  **SOLD FOR NOTHING**—Sin's promises don't deliver.
Those who sell themselves to sin come up empty-handed.

Isa.55:1  **BOUGHT WITH NOTHING**—The miracle of our
redemption (cf. Ps.49:7-9 with 1 Pet.1:18,19).

Isa.60:21  **THE DISPLAY OF HIS SPLENDOR**—Through
creation and Christians reflecting God's character (cf. Rom.1:20; 8:29).

Isa.61:3  **OAKS OF RIGHTEOUSNESS**—the role and influence of
older, mature Christians in the Church.

Isa.66:19  **PROCLAIM MY GLORY AMONG THE NATIONS**
—Missions

Jer.7:28  **TRUTH HAS PERISHED**—Lies and deception in high places
and low, in education and even in our churches have made truth the
"mortal enemy" of tolerance. [Mankind would rather follow a lie

than the truth, because truth compels them to acknowledge God and be responsible to him, both of which they are unwilling to do.  They would rather be free and miserable than bound by God's truth and be at peace.]

Jer.10:5    **SCARECROWS IN A MELLON PATCH**—The impotency of idols and anything worshipped other than God.

Jer.16:19    **INHERITED LIES**—The deception of belief in false gods.

Jer.51:58 with Hab.2:13    **FUEL FOR THE FLAMES**—The futility of useless works (cf. 1 Cor.3:12-15).

Hos.2:15    **DOOR OF HOPE**—Victory over sin through the door of escape (1 Cor.10:13).

Hos.4:16    **LAMBS IN THE MEADOW**—The daily comfort and security of the Lord's people under his care.

Hos.6:8    **FOOTPRINTS OF BLOOD**—The story of persecutors of the Church who have come to know Christ.

Hos.8:5    **INCAPABLE OF PURITY**—The uselessness of self-improvement apart from the power of God.

Hos.8:7    **SOWING THE WIND, REAPING THE WHIRL-WIND**—The futility of life without Christ (Jn.15:5).  We reap what we sow!

Hos.8:11-13a    **ALTARS FOR SINNING**—How good things in our lives can become our downfall.

Hos.9:7,8    **HOSTILITY IN THE HOUSE OF GOD**—Christians rejecting the message and messenger of God.

Hos.10:15    **YOUR WICKEDNESS IS GREAT**—Man's depravity and total inability to do anything about it (Isa.64:6; Rom.1:18-32; 3:9-18).

Hos.11:4 **TIES OF LOVE** — Stories of God's goodness in good times and bad.

Hos.11:12 **SURROUNDED WITH LIES**—On cults and idol worship.

Hos.12:1 **FEEDING ON THE WIND**—Putting our trust in man rather than the Lord. Or…putting all our eggs in man's basket rather than the Lord's.

Hos.13:5 **IN THE LAND OF BURNING HEAT**—Stories of the persecuted Church.

Hos.14:9 **WALKING IN THE WAYS OF THE LORD**—The results of pleasing the Lord through a life of obedience and worship.

Joel 3:14 **IN THE VALLEY OF DECISION**—Discerning the will of God in the press and confusion of life's circumstances.

Amos 3:8 **THE LION HAS ROARED**—God has spoken, and we'd do well to listen!

Amos 4:11 **A BURNING STICK SNATCHED FROM THE FIRE**—(with 1 Cor.3:10-15 and Jn.15:5,6,) The price of living a worldly life as a Christian.

Amos 8:11,12 **THE COMING FAMINE**—The apostasy of the last days—the Word rejected becomes the Word taken away (2 Thes.2:9-12).

Amos 9:1-4 **NO HIDING PLACE DOWN HERE!**—No possibility of escape from God's presence or judgment (cf. Ps.139:7-12).

Amos 9:9 **PEBBLES AMONG THE WHEAT**—Unbelieving "Christians" in the church (Matt.7:21-23 with Jn.6:29 and 1 Jn.3:23 re: what the Father's will is as mentioned in vs.21). A call for self-examination to be sure your salvation is based on faith in Christ, not faith in ministry results.

Jonah 1:2,3; 4:1,2 **GOD'S RELUCTANT MISSIONARY**— What happens when we say, "No" to God.

Jonah 2:8 **FORFEITED GRACE**—Misplaced faith causes us to lose out on what God wants to do (cf. Mk.6:5,6).

Nahum 1:3 **THE DUST OF HIS FEET (CLOUDS)**—The purposeful action of God in this world.

Hab.1:13; 3:16b **THE THUNDER OF GOD'S SILENCE**—What is God doing when it seems like he is doing nothing? A perspective on God's timing from the view of eternity.

Hab.2:11 **THE STONES CRY OUT** (from Moody Institute of Science)—Archaeological proof of the truthfulness and accuracy of the Scriptures.

Hab.2:13 **EXHAUSTED FOR NOTHING** — The ultimate futility of expending one's energies for material wealth, only to end up with nothing (1 Tim.6:6-10,17-19).

Hab.3:17,18 **NOTHING ELSE BUT HIM**—In the end, Christ is all we need...ever (cf. Phil.3:7,8).

Zeph.3:17 **QUIETED WITH HIS LOVE**—The comfort of the Lord in times of sorrow, strain and stress. His presence quiets the agitated spirit (cf. Phil.4:6,7 and Isa.26:3).

Hag.1:6 **A PURSE FULL OF HOLES**—Seeking our welfare ahead of God's Kingdom is living without God's blessing (see vs.2-11).

Zech.3:2 **SNATCHED FROM THE FIRE**—Stories of God's miraculous interventions in dangerous or life-threatening situations (Dan.3).

Zech.9:12 **PRISONERS OF HOPE**— or Israel in exile, it was, "Next year in Jerusalem." For the Church, wandering in the earth, it is the Rapture when we will all be changed. Christians "bound" in this world look with hope to the future (Rom.8:18-25).

Zech.10:11 **PASSING THROUGH THE SEA OF TROUBLE—** The Lord's discipline (1 Pet.4:1) and grace in times of stress (2 Cor. 12:9).

Zech.13:1 **THE FOUNTAIN OF CLEANSING—**Stories of those who have come to know Christ and the cleansing and renewal he brought into their lives.

Mal.4:2 **IN THE LAND OF THE RISING SUN—**The spiritual and physical restoration of Israel when the Lord returns.

Mk.10:43 **NOT SO WITH YOU—**Living according to Heavenly, not earthly, standards.

1 Cor. chs.1-2 **CALLED TO BE HOLY—**Defining our true position in a sinful world.

Eph.1:7 **THE RICHES OF HIS GRACE—**All that we have in Christ (cf. 2 Pet.1:3,4).

Titus 1:16 **UNFIT FOR DOING ANYTHING GOOD —** Apart from God's grace, none of us can do anything good (cf. Rom.3:12)!

Heb.1:9 **ANNOINTED WITH THE OIL OF JOY—**The deep joy that results from believing God, yielding to him, and doing what is right. Loving righteousness and hating sin.

Heb.2:9 **BUT WE SEE JESUS—**A divine perspective in the midst of trials and troubling situations.

2 Pet.3:11-14 **LIVING IN LIGHT OF ETERNITY—**How the coming judgment and eternal state should influence how we live now.

Rev.5:9,10 **REDEEMED TO SERVE—**For we who have been redeemed, the word "secular" should not be in our vocabulary. All that we do is to be done in service to our Lord.

# APPENDIX IX
## VARIOUS QUOTES AND THOUGHTS

(Not all of the following quotes are documented since I picked them up "on the fly" so to speak. But they're still worth thinking about.)

**1. John 15:1-8** A blessing from a student's chapel message. He spoke from John 15:1-8, a passage that I had wrestled with for years, trying to get a handle on what Christ was saying. Then it hit me clearly as he shared: The issue here is fruit-bearing, <u>not</u> salvation. Those who are not bearing fruit are "cut off from ministry" and set aside.

Those bearing fruit are "pruned" in order to bear more fruit. This is the same issue that we find in 1 Corinthians 3:10-15. The <u>Foundation</u> is <u>Christ</u> for both the fruitful (gold, silver, precious stones) Christian as well as the unfruitful (hay, wood, stubble) Christian. The latter will be saved because of his faith in Christ, but all his useless works will be burned up (cut out of the vine, gathered into piles and burned).

**2.** "The proliferation of evil in the States is nothing more than God's call to the Church to wake up to its ministry and take its relationship to him seriously."

**3.** "Focus on the Lord of the work, not on the work of the Lord."
   "Are you building your own house or the Lord's House?"

**4.** "God is gracious. He will not force us to go against our will. If we say, 'Thy will be done,' He replies, 'Thy will be done.' If our will is to do his will, then all will be well."

**5.** "Greed for acknowledgement led Ananias and Sapphira into deceit. We can be greedy for material things as well as spiritual blessings."
—Mr. Quek Mong Hua, Bethesda Church, Frankel Estate, Singapore—Feb.18,1996.

**6.** "Whenever the Holy Spirit prompts us, we must act promptly and prayerfully. Some use 'prayer' as an excuse <u>not</u> to do something, or to delay it."

**7.** "Nothing in Christianity is compulsory, but it is compelling."

**8.** "Satan can counterfeit nearly all the miracles of the Spirit, but he can <u>never</u> produce the fruit of the Spirit."
— Edwin Lam (BPMC, Singapore), Feb.25,1996

**9.** "When we KNOW who we are in Christ, we will not fear rejection from others. Our identity is in him: our Authority (Ex.3:13,14), Authenticity (Ex.4:24), Ability (Ex.4:10), Availability (Ex.4:13-16), and Acceptance (Ex.33:2). God loves us even though he knows the worst about us. He accepts us, and when he accepts us, our value is found in his Word, and we 'measure up.'"
— Edwin Lam (BPMC, Singapore), Mar.3,1996

**10.** "Until God pushes us out of our comfort zone, we will never enter our learning zone."

**11.** "A man with experience is never at a disadvantage with a man with an argument."

**12.** "You will never grow by just reading the Bible; you grow by reading the Bible and obeying it."

**13.** "Adam had a beautiful garden, Moses a palace, but Christ a stable, then a shameful death."
— Rev. Lawrence Khong (Faith Community
Baptist Church, Singapore), Mar.10,1996

**14.** From Challengers Sunday School class at Mission Hills Church (Denver), taught by Pastor Chuck ver Stratten.

"We are saved from the:      Adam was able not to sin.
Penalty of sin—at salvation;      After sin entered...
Power of sin—presently;      Adam was unable not to sin.
Presence of sin—when glorified.      Christ was unable to sin.
     In Christ, we are able not to sin.
     Glorified, we will be unable to sin."

**15.** "Man is only limited in sin by the knowledge he has to commit it."

**16.** "The reason the Church isn't winning the war is because it hasn't shown up for the battle."

**17.** This century began with 1.6 billion people. The year 2,000 has begun with 6 billion people, most of whom are living in China, India, the U.S., Indonesia, Brazil, Nigeria and Pakistan.

**18.** "The Lord's love is not cancelled out because of wickedness (Jn. 13:2-5). He washed Judas's feet too. God's love is a forgiving love, aware of the needs of others and willing to sacrifice anything to meet their needs. Jesus' love supersedes social hindrances, status, ethnic background and education, etc."

**19.** "You are called to be servants, not masters."

**20.** "To understand God is to stand under God."        — anonymous

**21.** "The difference between the LAW and GRACE is that …
the LAW demands the death of the offender;
GRACE provides a substitute for him."

**22.** "God's Word is powerful, personal, practical and purposeful."

**22.** "God doesn't call the qualified; he qualifies the called."

**24.** "God is responsible for the consequences of our obedience."
— Janice Robbins, Pastor Don Robbins' wife,
State Street Baptist Church, Presque Isle, ME.

**25.** "The world doesn't want broken things. The world wants perfect things. But God wants broken things so he can reshape them."
—Ismael Carmo (Portugal)

**26.** "The irony in the government's eliminating the Bible and the Ten Commandments from public life is that they have to turn around and legislate its principles back into society in an attempt to regain the order we once had under those teachings."

**27.** "Fearing is faith in Satan; Faith is fearing God."

The following are from Dr. Ed Hindson
**28.** "God always allows the enemy to come in when his people do not obey his voice."

**29.** "When the presence of God is gone, his power is gone and the building may as well be torn down."

**30.** "It doesn't matter where you are when God finds you; it's what you allow God to do after that.

_____

**31.** (Luke 8:22-25) Regarding the disciples in the storm: "What was threatening to go over their heads was already under their feet!"

**32.** "Shortly after I became a Christian, someone wrote in the flyleaf of my Bible these words: 'This book will keep you from sin, or sin will keep you from this book.' That was true then, and it's still true today. Dusty Bibles always lead to dirty lives. In fact, you are either in the Word and the Word is conforming you to the image of Jesus Christ, or you are in the world and the world is squeezing you into its mold."

— Howard Hendricks

**33.** "What I do is always the result of what I truly believe."

The following are from Dr. Ray Pritchard:
**34.** "What you chose to do yesterday determines what you are today.

"What you choose to do today will determine what you are tomorrow.

"We are not locked into our heritage, environment or social influences.

"God has given us the power to choose which way we want to take."

**35.** "Lord, do things we're not used to! Show me the truth about myself."

**36.** "Everybody wants progress; nobody wants change."

**37.** "If you want what you've never had, you have to do what you've never done."

**38.** "How much are you willing to risk to be all that God wants you to be?"

**39.** "Gentleness is my emotions under God's control."

**40.** "When it comes to solving problems, the first price you pay is the cheapest!"

**41.** "A life of integrity is:
*above reproach*, i.e. nothing hidden because there is nothing to hide!
(1 Tim.3:2);
*unblameable*, i.e. unindictable, unimpeachable (Titus 1:6)."

**42.** "Jesus died for us a substitutionary death (Rom.6:4).
Jesus arose to give us a substitutionary life (Rom.8:11).
Now we have his power to say 'No' to sin!"

**43.** "Jesus gave Judas the bag, not because he didn't know who Judas was, but because Judas didn't know who he himself was!"

**44.** "Jesus had Peter, James and John in his inner circle because they needed the most attention."

**45.** "Jesus loves me not because of who I am, but because of the sinner I am."

**46.** "Men usually learn very little from their successes, but a <u>lot</u> from their failures."

**47.** "The Christian race is not a sprint, nor a marathon, but a relay race passing the baton to the next runner."

**48.** "Safety is not the absence of danger; safety is the presence of Christ."

———————————

**49.** "We don't mind learning a few lessons from our difficulties—but we want to choose the difficulties!—and the lessons!—and then write a paper on what we have learned and be done with it."
—Roger Jardine's pastor

**50.** In reference to God—"I don't understand your ways, but I know your heart." —Anonymous

**51.** "Freedom is not doing what you want to, but being able to do what you know you should do."                    — Anonymous

**52.** When interpreting Scripture: "When common sense makes sense, seek no other sense."                    — Anonymous

**53.** "If you demand perfection from your sweetheart in order to love her, you demand more from her than God demands from you!"
—Eddy Gunawan, Erikson-Tritt
Theological College, Papua, Indonesia

**54.** From a February 2009 sermon by Dr. John Piper:

"HONORING GOD IN HARD TIMES"

Here are five possible reasons God [allows a] recession:
1. He intends for [a] recession to expose hidden sin and so bring us to repentance and cleansing.
2. He intends to wake us up to the constant and desperate conditions of much of the developing world where there is always and only recession of the worst kind.
3. He intends to relocate the roots of our joy in his grace rather than in our goods, in his mercy rather than our money, in his worth rather than our wealth.
4. He intends to advance his saving mission in the world—the spread of the gospel and the growth of his church—precisely at a time when human resources are least able to support it. This is how he guards his glory.
5. He intends for the church to care for its hurting members and to grow in the gift of love.

---

**55.** "'Remorse' — Sorrow for the consequences of sin.
'repentance' — Condemning the sin that brought the consequences."                    —Source unknown

**56.** "The Bible is the greatest of all books; to study it is the noblest of all pursuits; to understand it the highest of all goals."
—Charles C. Ryrie

The following are from my mother, Edith Leland:

**57.** "When we refuse to forgive, we burn the very bridge we need to cross over!"

On the Book of James:

**58.** "Works are Faith dressed up in overalls."

**59.** "People knowing without doing are like farmers who plow without sowing."

**60.** "Works are like a photograph of the Faith within us."

**61.** "We are never too old to learn something new about God or about ourselves."

_____

**62.** "Prophecy is not the light at the end of history's long tunnel. Prophecy is the light that illuminates our path through the tunnel."
—Jim Showers, Friends of Israel Gospel Ministry, quoting a colleague (Jan.2018 letter).

**63.** "Worldliness is what any particular culture does to make sin look normal and righteousness look strange." —David Wells

**64.** "The most beautiful sight this earth affords is a man or woman so filled with love that duty is only a name, and its performance the natural outflow and expression of the love which has become the central principle of their life." —Josiah Gilbert Holland

**65.** People often claim to hunger for truth, but seldom like the taste when it's served up.

The following are from Pastor Buck Booker, State Street Baptist Church, Presque Isle, Maine.

**66.** "Jesus is the only one who agreed to His birth!"

**67.** "Religion without Christ is like being married without a wife!"

# BIBLIOGRAPHY

Alcorn, Randy, <u>Dominion.</u>  Sisters, OR: Multnomah Books, 1996.

Bullinger, E.W., (<u>Number in Scripture</u>.  Grand Rapids: Kregel Publications, 1980.

Copan, Paul, <u>Is God a Moral Monster?</u>.  Grand Rapids: Baker  Books, 2011.

Harkavy, Alexander, <u>The Holy Scriptures</u>.  New York: Hebrew Publishing Company, 1951.

Irwin, C.H., <u>Irwin's Bible Commentary</u>.  Phildelphia: The John C. Winston Co., 1928.

(I.S.B.E.) <u>The International Standard Bible Encyclopedia</u>.  Vol III, Grand Rapids: Wm. B. Eerdmans Publishing Co., 1939.

<u>Israel My Glory</u>. Oct/Nov.1995, vol.53, No.5, Friends of Israel Gospel Ministry, Inc., Westville: New Jersey.

Jamieson, Robert, Fausset, A.R., and Brown, David, <u>A Commentary on the Old and New Testaments</u>. Vol. One, Grand Rapids: William B. Eerdmans Pub. Co. 1946.

Jeremiah, Dr. David, T.V. sermon (on "Turning Point"), "The Herald," 3/22/20.

<u>Nelson's Complete Book of Bible Maps & Charts</u>.  Nashville, TN: Thomas Nelson Publishers, 1996.

<u>Rose Book of Charts, Maps & Time Lines</u>. Peabody, MA: Hendrickson Publishers, 2005.

Schaeffer, Francis, <u>Genesis in Time and Space</u>. Downers Grove: I.V. Press, 1972.

Showers, Renald, <u>Israel My Glory</u> magazine.  Oct./Nov. 2000, Westville, NJ: Friends of Israel Gospel Ministry, Inc.

BIBLIOGRAPHY, 414

U.S. News & World Report. "Inside the Teen Brain," August 9, 1999.

Varner, William, Jacob's Dozen. Bellmawr, NJ: Friends of Israel Gospel Ministry, Inc., 2016.

Walvoord, John F. & Zuck, Roy B., The Bible Knowledge Commentary, Old Testament. Wheaton: Victor Books, 1985.

Walvoord, John F. & Zuck, Roy B., The Bible Knowledge Commentary, New Testament. Wheaton: Victor Books, 1985.

Webster's Seventh New Collegiate Dictionary. G. & C. Merriam Company, Publishers, Springfield, MA: 1969.

Whiston, William, A.M. translator, The Complete Works of Flavius Josephus. Grand Rapids: Kregel Publications, 1963.

Wood, Leon, A Survey of Israel's History. Grand Rapids: Zondervan, 1970.

# ABOUT THE AUTHOR

Dr. Robert J. Leland, the oldest of five children, was born in 1942 to Gordon and Edith Leland, and grew up in Oak Park, Illinois. He accepted the Lord as his Savior when just four years old and dedicated his life to foreign missions when he was six.

He received his B.A. degree in Secondary English Ed. from Northern Illinois University in 1966; his M.A. in Biblical Ed. from Columbia International University in 1971; and his D.Min. from Trinity International University in 1994.

He and his wife, (Ruth) Amber (married in 1966), served in Papua, Indonesia from 1971-2002 as church planters in the Citak (CHEE-tuck) tribe on the south coast, house parents at TEAM's hostel for missionary children in Sentani (Sen-TAH-nee) on the north coast near the Papua New Guinea border, office administrator (Bob) and bookkeeper (Amber) in Manokwari (MAH-no-KWAH-ri), and the last nineteen years of their service at the Erikson-Tritt Theological College near Manokwari. They also spent nine months in Singapore (1996) teaching at the Asian Cross-Cultural Training Institute while awaiting their visa renewal for Indonesia.

His Major Project for his D.Min., *Conformed to His Image*, was translated into Indonesian and published in Indonesia. Upon return from the field in 2002, he translated Mounce's *The Analytical Lexicon to the Greek New Testament* from English into Indonesian, which has since been published in Indonesia for use in Bible schools and seminaries where Greek is taught. He also has previously published *The Saga of a Bent Nail*, verbal "snapshots" of their 31 years in Papua, and *Unexpected Transformation*, a multi-use examination of the characteristics, titles and names of Christ, and how we are to reflect those in our daily lives.

He and Amber have also been teaching extension courses from the New England Bible College and Seminary (formerly Grace Evangelical College and Seminary, located in Bangor, Maine) up in Aroostook County, Maine, where they now reside.